500013295433

BR

CW01597886

CONTENTS

8

HOURS A DAY

5

DAYS A WEEK

48

WEEKS A YEAR

It better be

GOOD

WE CAN SPEND YEARS THINKING ABOUT WHAT JOB WE'D LIKE TO DO THEN, WHEN THE TIME COMES, GIVE HARDLY ANY THOUGHT ABOUT WHERE WE'D LIKE TO DO IT.

CHOOSING THE RIGHT COMPANY IS JUST AS IMPORTANT AS CHOOSING THE RIGHT CAREER. A GOOD EMPLOYER WILL HELP YOU DEVELOP BOTH PROFESSIONALLY AND PERSONALLY. AND THEY'LL MAKE SURE YOU HAVE A GOOD TIME WHILE YOU'RE DOING IT.

WORKING THROUGH THE BOOK

In the next few pages we'll show you how we score each company. Part two of the guide lists organisations by their star ranking. And at the end you'll find a list of KILLER QUESTIONS you should be asking – either your prospective employer or yourself – before taking that job.

JUDGE FOR YOURSELF

REMEMBER, THIS BOOK IS A GUIDE AND THE DECISION OF WHETHER AN EMPLOYER IS GOOD FOR YOU IS DOWN TO YOU. SO TRY AND THINK ABOUT YOUR OWN VALUES AND AMBITIONS, THEN FIND AN ORGANISATION THAT MATCHES THEM.

THIS BOOK IS BROUGHT TO YOU BY THE PEOPLE WHO REALLY KNOW WHAT A COMPANY IS LIKE TO WORK FOR...

...THE EMPLOYEES

E=mc2
GREAT WORKPLACE = HAPPY EMPLOYEES

HOW IT ALL WORKS

An organisation's success is driven by its employees. And for the partnership to work, employees need to feel part of that organisation. So to find out how fulfilled, motivated and engaged their employees really are, employers come to us – Best Companies.

Of course, the fact that an organisation is in this book means it is already listening to its employees and taking their comments on board. So they're off to a pretty good start!

ASK THE EMPLOYEES

We've developed a rigorous way in which to assess what it is like to work for a company. It's a system that's unique, but it's not rocket science: we simply ask the employees what matters to them (over 500,000 of them, in nearly 2,000 organisations).

However, the questions we ask and how we analyse the data, now that is rocket science.

BCI SCORES

The Best Companies three star accreditation system is based on **employee engagement** - a model Best Companies Ltd have developed and refined over the last six years, using data from more than 500,000 employees across thousands of UK organisations. So it's not surprising the employee engagement methodology is now recognised throughout the world, as well as being used to produce the prestigious Sunday Times list of the 100 Best Companies to Work For.

The purpose of the accreditation methodology is to produce a set of absolute standards for organisations which reflect their levels of employee engagement. Based on a single Best Companies Index (BCI) score, these standards are absolute and do not change over time. The BCI score applies equally to organisations of all sizes.

You can find the full story, the stats and the science of the employee engagement methodology at: www.bestcompanies.co.uk/methodology

Year on year statistical analysis has shown that there are eight main factors driving employee engagement:

- Leadership
- My Company
- Personal Growth
- My Manager
- My Team
- Giving Something Back
- Fair Deal
- Wellbeing

The accreditation methodology uses scores from 16 key questions, which are central to the eight workplace factors. Every organisation in the guide is ranked on all eight workplace factors and we list their top three, so you can gauge whether their values match your own.

HOW THE BEST COMPANIES INDEX AND STAR STATUS WORKS

Based on confidential employee answers to our survey, each organisation is given a Best Companies Index (BCI) score on a scale of 1 to 1000. Depending on an organisation's BCI, it may achieve one, two or three star status. Those who have not attained star status are listed as Ones To Watch.

1000

EXTRAORDINARY ★★★

OUTSTANDING ★★

FIRST CLASS ★

ONES TO WATCH

500

0

WORK

OK, so you may not want to be married to your work. But to get the most from it, you do need to be engaged.

Employees tell us that there are eight factors which engage them. Or in other words, determine how much they LOVE where they work.

92% of employees in three star organisations are 'actively engaged' compared to a national average of only 33%.

FACTORS AT WORK

LEADERSHIP

MY COMPANY

PERSONAL GROWTH

MY MANAGER

MY TEAM

GIVING SOMETHING BACK

FAIR DEAL

WELLBEING

LEADERSHIP

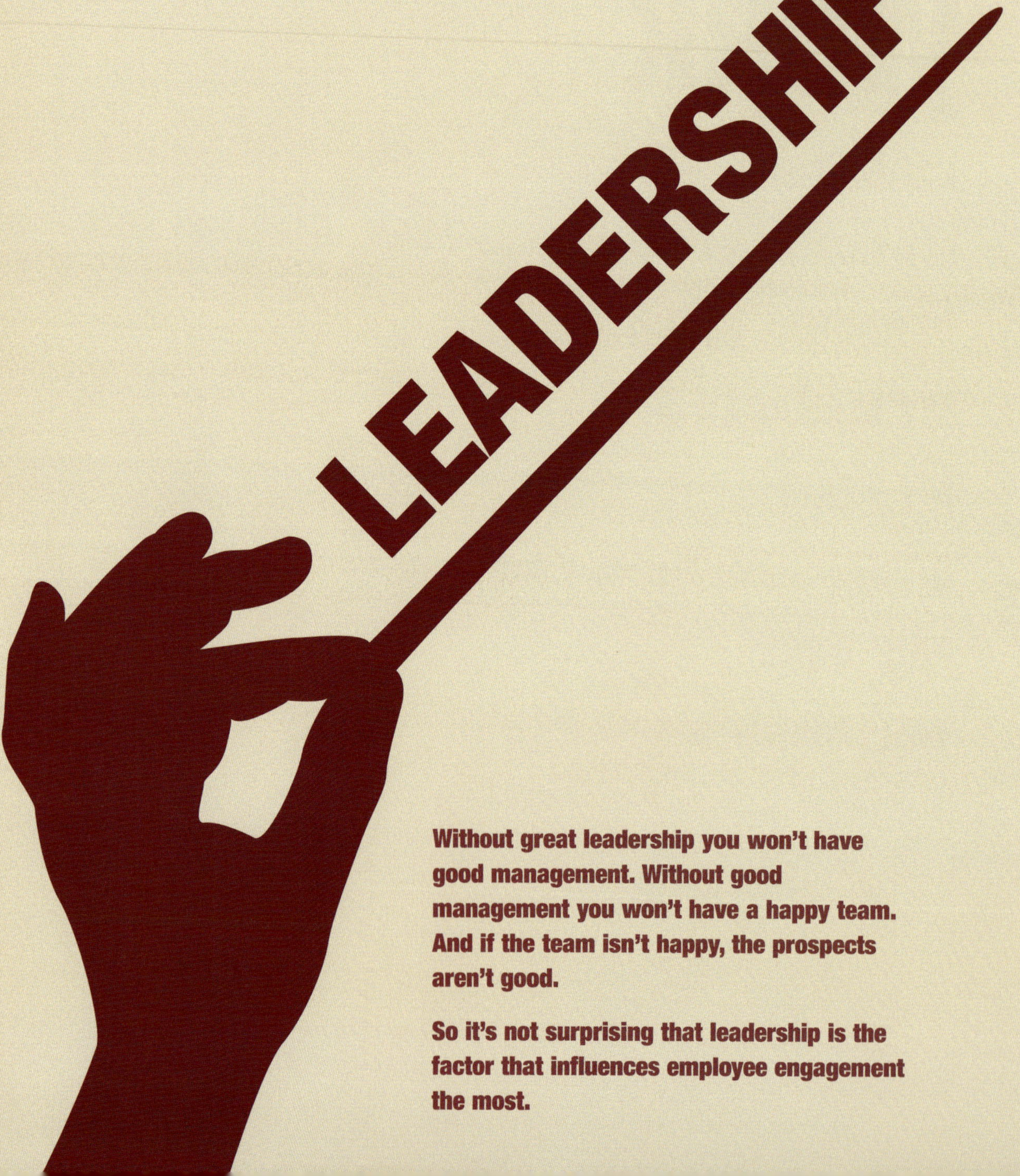

Without great leadership you won't have good management. Without good management you won't have a happy team. And if the team isn't happy, the prospects aren't good.

So it's not surprising that leadership is the factor that influences employee engagement the most.

A job well done makes you feel good. And having pride in where you work makes going there a positive experience.

This factor focuses on how much people value their company, how proud they are to work there, and whether they feel they can make a difference

PERSONAL GROWTH

If we don't grow, we stagnate. That's why we constantly need to learn new things and take up new challenges.

This factor measures whether employees feel challenged by their job, if their current skills are being used and if they have the opportunity to advance.

Training and development should mean a career isn't just work, but an education.

MY MANAGER

It is said that seven out of ten people who leave their employer are leaving their manager, not the company. So the working relationship with your manager is probably the most important of all.

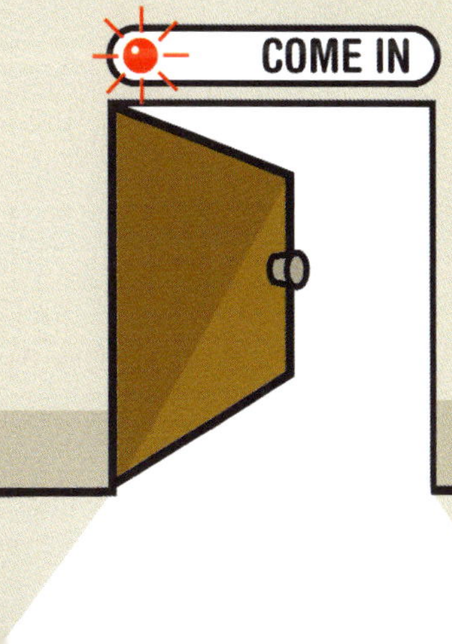

MY TEAM

It doesn't matter how great your company is, if you don't get on with your co-workers you're not going to stay there. Friendship and support from your work buddies makes a big difference to your working day. And good employers will realise that team spirit, having fun and belonging actually increase productivity.

GIVING SOMETHING BACK

More and more organisations now realise the value of investing in people, the local community and wider society. Sort of company karma.

This factor explores how much people think their employers put back into society and whether they believe this effort is driven by a desire for good publicity.

FAIR DEAL

While money should not be your only motivation, it is difficult to be engaged with your work if you feel you are not being fairly paid compared to others.

This factor measures how well employees are treated in terms of pay and benefits compared to similar organisations.

WELLBEING

All work and no play doesn't make for happy employees.

This factor measures stress, pressure, the balance between work and home life and the impact they have on personal health and performance. A good organisation will not encourage a long hours culture, in fact they will do the exact opposite.

EXTRAORDINARY

ARMSTRONG CONSULTANTS

ARMSTRONG

UK locations	N.West, London, E.England
UK sites	3
Sector	IT/Internet Services
Definition	Software Developers/Resellers
How owned	Private
Founded	1993
Turnover	£6.7m
Profit	Not disclosed
Staff	64
Average age	32
Male : Female	73 : 27
Earnings £35,000+	52%

BEST COMPANIES INDEX

EXTRAORDINARY

★ ★ ★

2007 BCI = 751.8

WORKPLACE INSIGHTS

Armstrong Consultants provide employees with team building weekends to encourage a strong group ethic and a sense of loyalty to the organisation. Financial benefits include performance and profit related pay as well as free private healthcare for all.

Every director is involved in writing and delivering each employee's review. This "hands on" approach enables an informal, but extremely "well informed" process to take place with both parties willing to engage in open discussion and creative dialogue.

Every new member of staff is welcomed to the whole company as part of an evening out. They also do a presentation to the directors and have a photo taken which is posted up on the company website in a "Meet the Team" section.

MISSION / VISION

Vision: To provide the most recommended software solutions in the industry.
Mission: To be successful by consistently providing the highest quality software solutions and support to an ever growing and more satisfied customer base.

BEST WORKPLACE FACTORS

FAIR DEAL
PERSONAL GROWTH
MY TEAM

GRADUATE VACANCIES

No specific graduate vacancies have been indicated.

EMPLOYEE COMMENTS

"They do make every effort to entice employees to stay for the long term."

"A work hard play hard environment, with great training and career advancement opportunities."

"Excellent team of people, with a strong work ethic whilst remaining fun and friendly."

CONTACT DETAILS

Armstrong Consultants Ltd, Aston Court, Marlborough Park, Harpenden, Herts AL5 1NL
Tel: 01582 465100 www.armstrong-consultants.com

KEY

- **Holidays:** Companies offering a minimum of 25 days annual leave
- **Maternity:** Companies offering over Statutory Maternity Pay
- **Childcare:** On-site nursery or vouchers
- **Women:** At least 33% of senior managers are women
- **Long Service:** 40% of employees with more than 5 years' service
- **Pensions:** Companies offering a final salary or non-contributory/contributory pension scheme
- **Charity Activities:** 10% of staff undertake charitable activities during business hours
- **Gym:** On-site gym or subsidised gym memberships
- **Shares:** Companies where employees are offered share options
- **Health Insurance:** Full family cover

AUDLEY TRAVEL

UK locations	S.East
UK sites	1
Sector	Travel
Definition	Tour Operator
How owned	Private
Founded	1996
Turnover	£26.2m
Profit	£0.8m
Staff	123
Average age	29
Male : Female	43 : 57
Earnings £35,000+	12%

BEST COMPANIES INDEX

best company 2007

EXTRAORDINARY ★ ★ ★

2007 BCI = 744.8

2006 BCI = 725.0 (★★)

WORKPLACE INSIGHTS

As the company has grown quickly, the leader, Craig Burkinshaw, has focused on keeping a small business feeling by maintaining 2 way communication and ensuring that everyone understands what is happening in the business and why decisions have been made.

Audley Travel offer employees a number of benefits including on site gym with showers and free fruit for everyone. Employees are able to travel extensively via educational trips to the areas they specialise in such as Southeast Asia, Africa and Australia.

They set up the Audley Charity Portfolio to focus efforts on a small group of charities. They try to help a wide variety of causes from wildlife, human rights issues and education through to the environment and conservation.

MISSION / VISION

To create bespoke travel arrangements for clients with service levels far exceeding the client's expectations based on first hand knowledge of the destination accommodation & activities. Our people should be paid above average & offered the maximum opportunity for personal development & internal promotion.

BEST WORKPLACE FACTORS

LEADERSHIP
FAIR DEAL
GIVING SOMETHING BACK

GRADUATE VACANCIES

Sales & Procurement.

EMPLOYEE COMMENTS

"Craig is an inspirational leader and truly wants Audley to be the best place to work."

"A fun place to work with a lot of emphasis put on reward & recognition for all staff."

"Company does lots for the environment with charities."

CONTACT DETAILS

Audley Travel, New Mill, New Mill Lane, Witney, Oxfordshire OX29 9SX
Tel: 01993 838000 www.audleytravel.com

KEY

- **Holidays:** Companies offering a minimum of 25 days annual leave
- **Maternity:** Companies offering over Statutory Maternity Pay
- **Childcare:** On-site nursery or vouchers
- **Women:** At least 33% of senior managers are women
- **Long Service:** 40% of employees with more than 5 years' service
- **Pensions:** Companies offering a final salary or non-contributory/ contributory pension scheme
- **Charity Activities:** 10% of staff undertake charitable activities during business hours
- **Gym:** On-site gym or subsidised gym memberships
- **Shares:** Companies where employees are offered share options
- **Health Insurance:** Full family cover

To find out more about this company visit www.bestcompaniesguide.co.uk

1000

<741

ones to watch

500

0

BACARDI-MARTINI

BACARDI-MARTINI LIMITED

UK locations	S.East
UK sites	1
Sector	Marketing & Sales
Definition	Premium Spirit Supplier.
How owned	Private
Founded	1862
Turnover	£250.9m
Profit	£16.1m
Staff	253
Average age	32
Male : Female	58 : 42
Earnings £35,000+	34%

BEST COMPANIES INDEX

★ ★ ★ best company 2007

EXTRAORDINARY

★ ★ ★

2007 BCI = 740.6

2006 BCI = 739.5 (★★)

WORKPLACE INSIGHTS

Bacardi Martini's overall aim is to develop a workplace that provides a balance of fun and challenge whilst developing people to their maximum potential.

Bacardi's Vital Few are supported by the company's commitment to develop people. Bacardi believe it is attitude and behaviour which drive high performance.

We have a Surprise and Delight - managers provided with nominal budget to surprise their teams with a small gift when they have been working extra hard. Fun charity sponsorship. Regular monthly competitions on our B-Line intranet and in our company magazine.

MISSION / VISION

To build an extraordinary organisation aligned to be the outstanding developer of consumer-desired premium bar-call spirits.

BEST WORKPLACE FACTORS

MY COMPANY
PERSONAL GROWTH
MY TEAM

GRADUATE VACANCIES

Sales.

EMPLOYEE COMMENTS

"The people. Passion for brands. People care about each other. Letting employees be responsible."

"The company is highly supportive in terms of my day to day role and in training opportunities."

"People work excellently in teams and support colleagues .... Working on the brands excites everybody."

CONTACT DETAILS

Bacardi-Martini, West Bay Road, Southampton, Hampshire SO15 1DT
Tel: 02380 318000 www.bacardi.com

KEY

- **Holidays:** Companies offering a minimum of 25 days annual leave
- **Maternity:** Companies offering over Statutory Maternity Pay
- **Childcare:** On-site nursery or vouchers
- **Women:** At least 33% of senior managers are women
- **Long Service:** 40% of employees with more than 5 years' service
- **Pensions:** Companies offering a final salary or non-contributory/contributory pension scheme
- **Charity Activities:** 10% of staff undertake charitable activities during business hours
- **Gym:** On-site gym or subsidised gym memberships
- **Shares:** Companies where employees are offered share options
- **Health Insurance:** Full family cover

To find out more about this company visit www.bestcompaniesguide.co.uk

BEAVERBROOKS THE JEWELLERS

BEAVERBROOKS
THE JEWELLERS

UK locations	National
UK sites	60
Sector	Retail
Definition	Jewellery Retailer
How owned	Private
Founded	1919
Turnover	Not disclosed
Profit	Not disclosed
Staff	719
Average age	32
Male : Female	15 : 85
Earnings £35,000+	4%

BEST COMPANIES INDEX

★ ★ ★ best company 2007

EXTRAORDINARY

★ ★ ★

2007 BCI = 807.9

2006 BCI = 797.7 (★★★)

1000

808>

500

0

ones to watch

WORKPLACE INSIGHTS

Managing Director Mark Adlestone holds a number of focus groups every year to ensure that he listens to ideas and issues of a cross section of people. All the executive team visit the stores on a regular basis to have face to face contact with employees.

Beaverbrooks have given a minimum of 10% of their post tax profit to charity each year and have increased this to 20% from the start of 2007. They are also allowing any employee to apply for time to carry out charitable work during their normal working hours.

They present awards for Manager of the Year and Top Store Performer of the Year both regionally and company wide to the best overall performer in every area of their role.

MISSION / VISION

Vision: "Making it Special", This is our purpose
"Success with Ethics" This is our philosophy
Mission: To deliver the best customer service and to be the best employer in the UK.

BEST WORKPLACE FACTORS

LEADERSHIP
GIVING SOMETHING BACK
MY COMPANY

GRADUATE VACANCIES

No specific graduate vacancies have been indicated.

EMPLOYEE COMMENTS

"Our leader and directors are inspirational, keen, full of ideas and will listen to suggestions."

"Contribution to the community is high on the list."

"I feel like I belong and am a valued member of staff and have been encouraged every step of the way."

CONTACT DETAILS

Beaverbrooks the Jewellers, Adele House, Park Road, St.Annes-on-Sea, Lancashire FY8 1RE
Tel: 01253 721262 www.beaverbrooks.co.uk

KEY

- **Holidays:** Companies offering a minimum of 25 days annual leave
- **Maternity:** Companies offering over Statutory Maternity Pay
- **Childcare:** On-site nursery or vouchers
- **Women:** At least 33% of senior managers are women
- **Long Service:** 40% of employees with more than 5 years' service
- **Pensions:** Companies offering a final salary or non-contributory/ contributory pension scheme
- **Charity Activities:** 10% of staff undertake charitable activities during business hours
- **Gym:** On-site gym or subsidised gym memberships
- **Shares:** Companies where employees are offered share options
- **Health Insurance:** Full family cover

To find out more about this company visit www.bestcompaniesguide.co.uk

BRAVISSIMO

UK locations	National
UK sites	15
Sector	Retail
Definition	Lingerie Retail & Mailorder
How owned	Private
Founded	1995
Turnover	£29.5m
Profit	Not disclosed
Staff	357
Average age	25
Male : Female	3 : 97
Earnings £35,000+	5%

BEST COMPANIES INDEX

★ ★ ★ best company 2007

EXTRAORDINARY

★ ★ ★

2007 BCI = 767.2

WORKPLACE INSIGHTS

Bravissimo offer discounts on their products for employees and their family and friends. There is also a contributory pension scheme available where the company double the employees' minimum required contribution.

Senior managers ensure people are not staying late & set a good example by not staying late themselves. Anyone who works longer hours due to business can take time back. During the busiest times Managers are expected to assist colleagues on the shop floor.

From providing all employees with a bottle of champagne to celebrate the company's best sales week to fully funded fun and social events Bravissimo really tries to recognise and encourage teams and team work.

MISSION / VISION

We want to be known as the company for big boobed women and to be recognised and respected by our customers for the quality of service we offer. We would like to become a household name in the UK and for the term "Bravissimo girl"™ to be widely recognised and used.

BEST WORKPLACE FACTORS

FAIR DEAL
WELL BEING
MY TEAM

GRADUATE VACANCIES

No graduate vacancies have been indicated.

EMPLOYEE COMMENTS

"They offer excellent salary, benefits & reward staff with gifts as thanks for working hard."

"When work/home balance was a problem, change in working hours was offered and implemented quickly."

"It feels like a family and all team members respect and support each other."

CONTACT DETAILS

Bravissimo, Imperial Court, Holly Walk, Leamington Spa CV32 4YB
Tel: 01926 459900 www.bravissimo.com

KEY

Holidays: Companies offering a minimum of 25 days annual leave
Maternity: Companies offering over Statutory Maternity Pay
Childcare: On-site nursery or vouchers
Women: At least 33% of senior managers are women
Long Service: 40% of employees with more than 5 years' service
Pensions: Companies offering a final salary or non-contributory/contributory pension scheme
Charity Activities: 10% of staff undertake charitable activities during business hours
Gym: On-site gym or subsidised gym memberships
Shares: Companies where employees are offered share options
Health Insurance: Full family cover

To find out more about this company visit www.bestcompaniesguide.co.uk

CAMELOT GROUP

UK locations	National
UK sites	7
Sector	Retail
Definition	National Lottery operator
How owned	Private
Founded	1993
Turnover	£5012.8m
Profit	£49.5m
Staff	974
Average age	37
Male : Female	50 : 50
Earnings £35,000+	31%

BEST COMPANIES INDEX

best company 2007

EXTRAORDINARY ★★★

2007 BCI = 769.0

2006 BCI = 714.3 (★★)

WORKPLACE INSIGHTS

In 2005/06 more than 10% of employees volunteered a total of 1,611 hours to charitable activities, which amounts to a time donation of £52,613. Staff can also apply to the Camelot Foundation for match-funding of charitable activities to a maximum of £5000 per activity.

The Chief Executive Dianne Thompson and the HR Director always attend the Staff Consultative Forum and all inductions for new staff. The directors also host informal Question and Answer sessions every month around the business.

Camelot provide BUPA health benefits, opportunities for flexible working and a Wellbeing programme to make it easier for staff to access information about the health and support systems on offer – this includes a confidential help and information line.

MISSION / VISION

Vision: 'Serving the nation's dreams through The National Lottery'.
Mission: To ensure Camelot is in the best possible position to win the third licence by building a growing popular and respected National Lottery.

BEST WORKPLACE FACTORS

GIVING SOMETHING BACK
LEADERSHIP
FAIR DEAL

GRADUATE VACANCIES

HR, Legal, Marketing, PR, Business Assurance, Finance & Regulation & Governance.

EMPLOYEE COMMENTS

"Camelot gives so much back to the community. We are encouraged to become involved."

"Dianne Thompson is a true inspiration. The management are so on the ball, motivating and inspiring."

"The benefits package makes it a very attractive company to work for."

CONTACT DETAILS

Camelot Group, Magdelan House, Tolpits Lane, Watford, Herts WD18 9RN
Tel: 01923 425000 www.camelotgroup.co.uk

KEY

- **Holidays:** Companies offering a minimum of 25 days annual leave
- **Maternity:** Companies offering over Statutory Maternity Pay
- **Childcare:** On-site nursery or vouchers
- **Women:** At least 33% of senior managers are women
- **Long Service:** 40% of employees with more than 5 years' service
- **Pensions:** Companies offering a final salary or non-contributory/ contributory pension scheme
- **Charity Activities:** 10% of staff undertake charitable activities during business hours
- **Gym:** On-site gym or subsidised gym memberships
- **Shares:** Companies where employees are offered share options
- **Health Insurance:** Full family cover

1000 769> 500 0 ones to watch

CASTLEOAK CARE PARTNERSHIPS

castleoak care partnerships

UK locations	National
UK sites	13
Sector	Construction
Definition	Design & Build Specialist
How owned	Private
Founded	1984
Turnover	£30.7m
Profit	£0.8m
Staff	71
Average age	39
Male : Female	73 : 27
Earnings £35,000+	42%

BEST COMPANIES INDEX

best company 2007

EXTRAORDINARY

★ ★ ★

2007 BCI = 760.4

WORKPLACE INSIGHTS

At Castleoak the values are lived out. Everyone knows what & how they should be doing. A practical expression of living out their values, in relation to life balance & well being, is highlighted through Castleoak's planned office move.

The company has a very non-hierarchical approach. Although line management is necessary from an operational viewpoint, the prevailing spirit within the business is one of friendliness. There is easy access to senior directors at all times.

Castleoak's Community Support Programme is embedded at the heart of the culture. This commitment is highlighted from an employee's first contact with Castleoak at interview and is a central feature of the induction programme when an employee joins Castleoak.

MISSION / VISION

To be the most respected national design and build company in the social care sector, the partner of first choice. To be consistently profitable and for this financial stability to provide the foundation for all that we do. To always be a great company to work for and with.

BEST WORKPLACE FACTORS

MY COMPANY
LEADERSHIP
GIVING SOMETHING BACK

GRADUATE VACANCIES

Construction Managers, Design Managers, Project Surveyors.

EMPLOYEE COMMENTS

"The company is founded on good principles with the owners reflecting their beliefs."

"The leader of our organisation has a very solid moral grounding."

"The company is not driven by profit and looks to give value for money. They also support charity."

CONTACT DETAILS

Castleoak Care Partnerships, Raglan House, Greenwood Close, Cardiff Gate Business Park, Cardiff CF23 8RD
Tel: 0292 0545420 www.castleoak.co.uk

KEY

Holidays: Companies offering a minimum of 25 days annual leave
Maternity: Companies offering over Statutory Maternity Pay
Childcare: On-site nursery or vouchers
Women: At least 33% of senior managers are women
Long Service: 40% of employees with more than 5 years' service
Pensions: Companies offering a final salary or non-contributory/ contributory pension scheme
Charity Activities: 10% of staff undertake charitable activities during business hours
Gym: On-site gym or subsidised gym memberships
Shares: Companies where employees are offered share options
Health Insurance: Full family cover

To find out more about this company visit www.bestcompaniesguide.co.uk

COBALT RECRUITMENT

UK locations	London, N.West
UK sites	2
Sector	Recruitment
Definition	Real Estate Recruitment
How owned	Private
Founded	2001
Turnover	Not disclosed
Profit	Not disclosed
Staff	50
Average age	27
Male : Female	44 : 56
Earnings £35,000+	48%

BEST COMPANIES INDEX

best company 2007

EXTRAORDINARY

★ ★ ★

2007 BCI = 780.1

780>

ones to watch

WORKPLACE INSIGHTS

The leaders of the company have a policy of collaborative decision making in all areas of the business, involving employees in all projects, working with everyone in the business. They also encourage employee suggestions and their onward implementation.

Cobalt hire two external training firms to provide coaching and training within the company in order to improve and develop all staff members. This has proved to be a successful tool for managers to learn how they are being perceived in the workplace.

Benefits include free private healthcare for all employees and their spouse and dependants, profit and performance related pay and an annual, all inclusive, 3 day European holiday for all staff members.

MISSION / VISION

Become the UK, and ultimately the world leading property recruitment consultancy.

BEST WORKPLACE FACTORS

LEADERSHIP
MY MANAGER
FAIR DEAL

GRADUATE VACANCIES

Trainee consultants/resourcers.

EMPLOYEE COMMENTS

"There is a good atmosphere which originates from the Directors."

"It is a friendly organisation, although it is clear who the managers are, they are not separated."

"Great rewards, both financial and team building."

CONTACT DETAILS

Cobalt Recruitment, Savannah House, Charles II Street, London SW1Y 4QU
Tel: 0207 8083300 www.cobaltrecruitment.com

KEY

Holidays: Companies offering a minimum of 25 days annual leave
Maternity: Companies offering over Statutory Maternity Pay
Childcare: On-site nursery or vouchers
Women: At least 33% of senior managers are women
Long Service: 40% of employees with more than 5 years' service
Pensions: Companies offering a final salary or non-contributory/ contributory pension scheme
Charity Activities: 10% of staff undertake charitable activities during business hours
Gym: On-site gym or subsidised gym memberships
Shares: Companies where employees are offered share options
Health Insurance: Full family cover

To find out more about this company visit www.bestcompaniesguide.co.uk

DATA CONNECTION

UK locations	N.West, London, Scotland
UK sites	3
Sector	Communications/Telecom
Definition	Communications Technology
How owned	Private
Founded	1981
Turnover	£47m
Profit	£7.4m
Staff	272
Average age	35
Male : Female	79 : 21
Earnings £35,000+	53%

BEST COMPANIES INDEX

best company 2007

EXTRAORDINARY ★ ★ ★

2007 BCI = 778.0

2006 BCI = 767.1 (★★★)

<778

WORKPLACE INSIGHTS

Data Connection's unique ownership structure (wholly owned by the Data Connection Employee Benefit Trust) means everyone has an interest in and commitment to the future success of Data Connection and everyone benefits from the financial success.

With Data Connection's increasing size they are proud of the lack of bureaucracy and politics. The flat management structure, involvement of all employees in key decisions and open lines of communication from the top level show it really can work.

Data Connection's review process involves individuals having chats with management. The upper line will ask the individual for feedback on their manager's performance. This is fed back to the manager.

MISSION / VISION

Make money (and distribute it equitably). Do difficult things well (not just software and hardware development). Develop people (and fulfill their desires and potential). Have fun ('in the Data Connection sense of the word'). Continue (and advance and evolve).

BEST WORKPLACE FACTORS

FAIR DEAL
MY TEAM
MY MANAGER

GRADUATE VACANCIES

Software & hardware development & testing. Product & Project mgt. Technical Marketing & Support.

EMPLOYEE COMMENTS

"They put a lot of effort into keeping employees in terms of remuneration, morale and training."

"There is team spirit working with like minded people. Information is shared."

"The needs and desires of individuals are considered at all stages of business planning."

CONTACT DETAILS

Data Connection, 100 Church Street, Enfield, Middlesex EN2 6BQ
Tel: 0208 3661177 www.dataconnection.com

KEY

- **Holidays:** Companies offering a minimum of 25 days annual leave
- **Maternity:** Companies offering over Statutory Maternity Pay
- **Childcare:** On-site nursery or vouchers
- **Women:** At least 33% of senior managers are women
- **Long Service:** 40% of employees with more than 5 years' service
- **Pensions:** Companies offering a final salary or non-contributory/ contributory pension scheme
- **Charity Activities:** 10% of staff undertake charitable activities during business hours
- **Gym:** On-site gym or subsidised gym memberships
- **Shares:** Companies where employees are offered share options
- **Health Insurance:** Full family cover

To find out more about this company visit www.bestcompaniesguide.co.uk

DENPLAN LIMITED

Denplan

UK locations	S.East
UK sites	1
Sector	Financial
Definition	Dental Payment Plans
How owned	Private
Founded	1986
Turnover	£34m
Profit	Not disclosed
Staff	312
Average age	37
Male : Female	42 : 58
Earnings £35,000+	16%

BEST COMPANIES INDEX

EXTRAORDINARY ★ ★ ★

2007 BCI = 776.0

2006 BCI = 754.5 (★★★)

776>

WORKPLACE INSIGHTS

Managing Director Steve Gates goes on a walkabout once a month, work-shadowing each team over the course of a year and as part of the induction process, various members of the management team attend the induction to give a presentation and a Q&A session.

Each new starter spends time in all departments which helps new starters understand how important each department is and also enables employees to get to know one another, so they feel comfortable asking for help or advice outside of their department.

Denplan's Health and Wellbeing programme includes initiatives such as fitness classes and healthy eating options within the vending machines. There is also a health questionnaire available online that analyses an employee's lifestyle.

MISSION / VISION

Providing people with confident smiles for life by making mouths matter.

BEST WORKPLACE FACTORS

LEADERSHIP
MY TEAM
WELL BEING

GRADUATE VACANCIES

No specific graduate vacancies have been indicated.

EMPLOYEE COMMENTS

"Steve Gates is an excellent role model & we are lucky to work with such a fun, enthusiastic leader."

"I enjoy coming into work, looking forward to my work as well as seeing the people in my team."

"Workloads are well managed and assessed regularly so there is never too much pressure or stress."

CONTACT DETAILS

Denplan Limited, Denplan Court, Victoria Road, Winchester, Hampshire SO23 7RG
Tel: 01962 828000 www.denplan.co.uk

KEY

- **Holidays:** Companies offering a minimum of 25 days annual leave
- **Maternity:** Companies offering over Statutory Maternity Pay
- **Childcare:** On-site nursery or vouchers
- **Women:** At least 33% of senior managers are women
- **Long Service:** 40% of employees with more than 5 years' service
- **Pensions:** Companies offering a final salary or non-contributory/ contributory pension scheme
- **Charity Activities:** 10% of staff undertake charitable activities during business hours
- **Gym:** On-site gym or subsidised gym memberships
- **Shares:** Companies where employees are offered share options
- **Health Insurance:** Full family cover

To find out more about this company visit www.bestcompaniesguide.co.uk

1000

<749

ones to watch

500

0

DRIVERS JONAS

DRIVERS JONAS

UK locations	National
UK sites	7
Sector	Property
Definition	Commercial Property Consultants
How owned	Partnership/LLP
Founded	1725
Turnover	£67.4m
Profit	£13.7m
Staff	555
Average age	34
Male : Female	64 : 36
Earnings £35,000+	56%

BEST COMPANIES INDEX

best company 2007

EXTRAORDINARY ★ ★ ★

2007 BCI = 749.1

2006 BCI = 735.4 (★★)

WORKPLACE INSIGHTS

All Partners are committed to developing every employee within the firm so that individuals can reach their full potential. All staff (full and part-time, established and those on temporary or short-term contracts) have access to training opportunities.

At Drivers Jonas employees work with the owners of the business every day, the partners. They sit in open plan offices with the rest of the firm, they hold regular team meetings and they are alive to the concerns and demands of their team.

Drivers Jonas Charitable Foundation was set up by the partnership. Its aim is to be the vehicle for supporting charitable and community activities. It is given a cash allocation by the Board of Drivers Jonas to donate to worthy causes.

MISSION / VISION

To add value for our clients by giving high quality property advice.

BEST WORKPLACE FACTORS

PERSONAL GROWTH
LEADERSHIP
GIVING SOMETHING BACK

GRADUATE VACANCIES

All areas of surveying & town planning. Possible Marketing, HR, Finance & Management Consulting.

EMPLOYEE COMMENTS

"In my first year I have been encouraged and supported by my team and Drivers Jonas."

"Strong leadership as well as a rapidly expanding firm."

"They encourage a lot of charitable activities."

CONTACT DETAILS

Drivers Jonas, 6 Grosvenor Street, London W1K 4DJ
Tel: 0207 896 8000 www.driversjonas.com

KEY

- **Holidays:** Companies offering a minimum of 25 days annual leave
- **Maternity:** Companies offering over Statutory Maternity Pay
- **Childcare:** On-site nursery or vouchers
- **Women:** At least 33% of senior managers are women
- **Long Service:** 40% of employees with more than 5 years' service
- **Pensions:** Companies offering a final salary or non-contributory/contributory pension scheme
- **Charity Activities:** 10% of staff undertake charitable activities during business hours
- **Gym:** On-site gym or subsidised gym memberships
- **Shares:** Companies where employees are offered share options
- **Health Insurance:** Full family cover

To find out more about this company visit www.bestcompaniesguide.co.uk

ECOSECURITIES

ECO SECURITIES

UK locations	S.East
UK sites	1
Sector	Financial
Definition	Environmental Finance Solutions
How owned	Public (i.e. stock market listed)
Founded	1997
Turnover	£1.6m
Profit	Not disclosed
Staff	69
Average age	32
Male : Female	62 : 38
Earnings £35,000+	42%

BEST COMPANIES INDEX

best company 2007

EXTRAORDINARY

★ ★ ★

2007 BCI = 744.7

745>

ones to watch

WORKPLACE INSIGHTS

EcoSecurities will provide full funding to employees for a training course relevant to their role or a contribution to any course of their choosing. Requirements are discussed with line managers as part of individual Personal Development Plans.

EcoSecurities are working towards being carbon neutral and as part of this all their coffee and tea is Fairtrade and all the paper and the furniture in their new office is made from sustainable resources.

Employees are made to feel their opinions & suggestions count & they are rewarded for their personal performance in a fair manner. EcoSecurities have a very flat hierarchy and an open door policy which encourages interaction & a high degree of communication.

MISSION / VISION

EcoSecurities is a leading company in the business of sourcing, developing, and trading, carbon credits throughout the world. EcoSecurities transacts with companies in the developed world to supply them with carbon credits to meet their compliance targets.

BEST WORKPLACE FACTORS

PERSONAL GROWTH
GIVING SOMETHING BACK
MY COMPANY

GRADUATE VACANCIES

Accounts, IT, Business Development, Legal.

EMPLOYEE COMMENTS

"Very dynamic and exciting workplace. People with fresh ideas and lots of opportunities."

"We work for the good of the world."

"You feel that you are working for a company that makes a difference to the world."

CONTACT DETAILS

EcoSecurities, 1st Floor Park Central, 40/41 Park End Street, Oxford, Oxfordshire OX1 1JD
Tel: 01865 202635 www.ecosecurities.com

KEY

- **Holidays:** Companies offering a minimum of 25 days annual leave
- **Maternity:** Companies offering over Statutory Maternity Pay
- **Childcare:** On-site nursery or vouchers
- **Women:** At least 33% of senior managers are women
- **Long Service:** 40% of employees with more than 5 years' service
- **Pensions:** Companies offering a final salary or non-contributory/contributory pension scheme
- **Charity Activities:** 10% of staff undertake charitable activities during business hours
- **Gym:** On-site gym or subsidised gym memberships
- **Shares:** Companies where employees are offered share options
- **Health Insurance:** Full family cover

To find out more about this company visit www.bestcompaniesguide.co.uk

1000

<787

ones to watch

500

0

FIREFLY COMMUNICATIONS

FIREFLY
trailblazing communications

UK locations	London, Scotland
UK sites	2
Sector	Media
Definition	Public Relations Agency
How owned	Private
Founded	1995
Turnover	£4.2m
Profit	£0.2m
Staff	53
Average age	29
Male : Female	34 : 66
Earnings £35,000+	34%

BEST COMPANIES INDEX

best company 2007

EXTRAORDINARY ★ ★ ★

2007 BCI = 786.8

2006 BCI = 753.6 (★★★)

WORKPLACE INSIGHTS

Firefly believe in genuine career long learning and provide training at all levels of the business. Managers and senior managers are therefore well supported and better equipped within their roles.

Claire Walker CEO of Firefly is an accredited trainer for the industry and spends a large proportion of time devising new training courses and delivering training at all levels of the business.

Every month the company present the Firefly Brilliance Awards which are nominated by all employees and are based on the company values of Ballsy, Bright, Blimey, Savvy, Stellar and Smile.

MISSION / VISION

Vision: Be desired be admired
Mission: Nothing less than the highest standards and the best results for our clients and Firefly.

BEST WORKPLACE FACTORS

MY MANAGER
PERSONAL GROWTH
MY COMPANY

GRADUATE VACANCIES

Public Relations.

EMPLOYEE COMMENTS

"CEO has the right values and ways of doing things and this is fed right the way through."

"The company is run with a strong moral and ethical compass."

"Freedom, trust, responsibility and honesty make Firefly a great place to work."

CONTACT DETAILS

Firefly Communications, The Coda Centre, 189 Munster Road, Fulham, London SW6 6AW
Tel: 0207 3861400 www.fireflycomms.com

KEY

Holidays: Companies offering a minimum of 25 days annual leave
Maternity: Companies offering over Statutory Maternity Pay
Childcare: On-site nursery or vouchers
Women: At least 33% of senior managers are women
Long Service: 40% of employees with more than 5 years' service
Pensions: Companies offering a final salary or non-contributory/contributory pension scheme
Charity Activities: 10% of staff undertake charitable activities during business hours
Gym: On-site gym or subsidised gym memberships
Shares: Companies where employees are offered share options
Health Insurance: Full family cover

To find out more about this company visit www.bestcompaniesguide.co.uk

gabem
Making temporary work more profitable

GABEM MANAGEMENT

UK locations	S.East
UK sites	2
Sector	Business Services
Definition	Company Administration & Payroll
How owned	Private
Founded	1998
Turnover	£115.5m
Profit	£14.2m
Staff	101
Average age	36
Male : Female	32 : 68
Earnings £35,000+	19%

BEST COMPANIES INDEX

best company 2007

EXTRAORDINARY ★ ★ ★

2007 BCI = 738.4

2006 BCI = 711.3 (★★)

WORKPLACE INSIGHTS

Gabem provides a number of benefits, medical insurance, life assurance & three bonus schemes. In addition, MD Trudy Gordon will provide an advance on wages or loan of the company car for people finding themselves in difficult personal situations.

Due to our countryside location, employees have the opportunity to go for a run in the woods or even take the office dogs for walks through the fields at lunchtimes! Showering facilities provided to encourage employees to take advantage of the surroundings.

To help reduce their impact on the environment, Gabem incentivise car sharing for employees. Passengers in a shared car are paid £2 per day and a driver with a passenger receives £4 per day.

MISSION / VISION

To consistently offer a friendly and professional service to all of our clients whilst providing an easy and beneficial way for them to receive their wages.

BEST WORKPLACE FACTORS

FAIR DEAL
WELL BEING
GIVING SOMETHING BACK

GRADUATE VACANCIES

None specified.

EMPLOYEE COMMENTS

"We have brilliant pay and benefits, and fantastic bonuses."

"Everyone genuinely cares about your well being."

"Gives a lot to the environment. In my department we are saving stamps to save the hedgehogs."

CONTACT DETAILS

Gabem Management, Waterside, Halfway Bridge, Lodsworth, West Sussex GU28 9BP
Tel: 0870 7510581 www.gabem.com

KEY

- **Holidays:** Companies offering a minimum of 25 days annual leave
- **Maternity:** Companies offering over Statutory Maternity Pay
- **Childcare:** On-site nursery or vouchers
- **Women:** At least 33% of senior managers are women
- **Long Service:** 40% of employees with more than 5 years' service
- **Pensions:** Companies offering a final salary or non-contributory/ contributory pension scheme
- **Charity Activities:** 10% of staff undertake charitable activities during business hours
- **Gym:** On-site gym or subsidised gym memberships
- **Shares:** Companies where employees are offered share options
- **Health Insurance:** Full family cover

1000
738>
500
0
ones to watch

1000

<758

ones to watch

500

0

HANDELSBANKEN

Handelsbanken

UK locations	National
UK sites	26
Sector	Financial - Banks/Building Societies
Definition	Universal Bank
How owned	Public (i.e. stock market listed)
Founded	1982
Turnover	£36.7m
Profit	£11.5m
Staff	305
Average age	41
Male : Female	69 : 31
Earnings £35,000+	60%

BEST COMPANIES INDEX

best company 2007

EXTRAORDINARY ★ ★ ★

2007 BCI = 758.4

WORKPLACE INSIGHTS

Handelsbanken employees are not target driven and therefore not required to work until those targets are achieved. Employees are given the responsibility to plan their own workloads in order to maintain their work life balance.

Each branch is run like an individual company without interference from H.O. This business model is virtually unchanged for 35 years creating a high degree of stability allowing employees to concentrate on doing the business & developing personal skills.

Handelsbanken encourage managers to support staff through active coaching & development. Managers are trained to demonstrate trust & respect, by delegating tasks efficiently and not interfering when employees may solve problems differently to them.

MISSION / VISION

Handelsbanken's corporate philosophy: A strongly decentralised organisation - the branch is the Bank.

BEST WORKPLACE FACTORS

WELL BEING
MY COMPANY
MY MANAGER

GRADUATE VACANCIES

Branches/IT/Accounts/Payments.

EMPLOYEE COMMENTS

"Staff are considered important to the business and are well looked after."

"Individuals empowered to make decisions, express themselves & encouraged to deliver what the customer wants."

"Branch manager and line manager are very helpful & understanding."

CONTACT DETAILS

Handelsbanken, Trinity Tower, 9 Thomas More Street, London E1W 1GE
Tel: 0207 578 8000 www.handelsbanken.co.uk

KEY

- **Holidays:** Companies offering a minimum of 25 days annual leave
- **Maternity:** Companies offering over Statutory Maternity Pay
- **Childcare:** On-site nursery or vouchers
- **Women:** At least 33% of senior managers are women
- **Long Service:** 40% of employees with more than 5 years' service
- **Pensions:** Companies offering a final salary or non-contributory/ contributory pension scheme
- **Charity Activities:** 10% of staff undertake charitable activities during business hours
- **Gym:** On-site gym or subsidised gym memberships
- **Shares:** Companies where employees are offered share options
- **Health Insurance:** Full family cover

To find out more about this company visit www.bestcompaniesguide.co.uk

HEAT

UK locations	N.Ireland, Yorks & Humber
UK sites	2
Sector	Engineering
Definition	Service/Installation Company
How owned	Private
Founded	1999
Turnover	Not disclosed
Profit	Not disclosed
Staff	259
Average age	35
Male : Female	91 : 9
Earnings £35,000+	3%

BEST COMPANIES INDEX

best company 2007

EXTRAORDINARY ★ ★ ★

2007 BCI = 763.1

2006 BCI = 713.0 (★★)

WORKPLACE INSIGHTS

Some employees have taken the role of business advisers for Young Enterprise & regularly visit schools to bring business to life for young students, providing opportunities for young people to gain vocational experience with HEAT through work placement & mentoring.

HEAT hold an annual Long Service Awards evening and include categories in this such as HEAT Heroes where staff who have made outstanding contributions get particular mention, as well as a financial reward for their efforts.

During the Annual Employee Conference, Shareholders & Directors present material & encourage employees to discuss and interact, especially at the workshops which form part of the day. The leaders actively seek recommendations on improvements for the organisation.

MISSION / VISION

To be widely recognised as the most innovative and successful heating installation and maintenance contractor within the social housing market.

BEST WORKPLACE FACTORS

GIVING SOMETHING BACK
MY COMPANY
LEADERSHIP

GRADUATE VACANCIES

IT Design & Technology.

EMPLOYEE COMMENTS

"Commitment to working with community groups and sponsorship of sporting events is second to none."

"Our core values underpin the day to day activities of all involved in growing & improving the business."

"Strong leadership is the key to our success."

CONTACT DETAILS

HEAT Ltd, Fuel House, 27-29 Sydenham Road, Belfast BT3 9DH
Tel: 02890 469000 www.heat.co.uk

KEY

- **Holidays:** Companies offering a minimum of 25 days annual leave
- **Maternity:** Companies offering over Statutory Maternity Pay
- **Childcare:** On-site nursery or vouchers
- **Women:** At least 33% of senior managers are women
- **Long Service:** 40% of employees with more than 5 years' service
- **Pensions:** Companies offering a final salary or non-contributory/ contributory pension scheme
- **Charity Activities:** 10% of staff undertake charitable activities during business hours
- **Gym:** On-site gym or subsidised gym memberships
- **Shares:** Companies where employees are offered share options
- **Health Insurance:** Full family cover

HOLY CROSS SIXTH FORM COLLEGE

UK locations	N.West
UK sites	1
Sector	Education
Definition	Sixth Form College
How owned	Government
Founded	1979
Turnover	£7.7m
Profit	Not disclosed
Staff	185
Average age	40
Male : Female	33 : 67
Earnings £35,000+	23%

BEST COMPANIES INDEX

best company 2007

EXTRAORDINARY ★★★

2007 BCI = 764.1

2006 BCI = 751.7 (★★★)

<764

WORKPLACE INSIGHTS

The college has developed a higher education programme in order to respond to the needs of adults who have missed opportunities for this level of study earlier in their lives.

The Principal takes active interest in all areas of college life & visits individual departments, meets with all subjects & cross college managers at least annually and goes on 'walkabout' frequently.

Provides innovation bursaries annually which staff can apply for. Recently these have been awarded for ILT development, Teaching & Learning, Work Shadowing (Management Development). The college have paid a number of one-off honoraria to staff who have developed initiatives on an ad hoc basis.

MISSION / VISION

To provide a coherent and enriched curriculum which meets the needs and interests of learners. To ensure the highest quality educational provision. To provide high quality support and guidance. To manage the College effectively.

BEST WORKPLACE FACTORS

GIVING SOMETHING BACK
LEADERSHIP
MY TEAM

GRADUATE VACANCIES

Teaching Management & Senior Management.

EMPLOYEE COMMENTS

"A genuinely caring place - it really does reflect Christian values."

"The Principal is a man of principle and a great leader who has time for all employees."

"The organisation feels like an extended family."

CONTACT DETAILS

Holy Cross Sixth Form College, Manchester Road, Bury, Manchester BL9 9BB
Tel: 0161 7624500 www.holycross.ac.uk

KEY

Holidays: Companies offering a minimum of 25 days annual leave
Maternity: Companies offering over Statutory Maternity Pay
Childcare: On-site nursery or vouchers
Women: At least 33% of senior managers are women
Long Service: 40% of employees with more than 5 years' service
Pensions: Companies offering a final salary or non-contributory/ contributory pension scheme
Charity Activities: 10% of staff undertake charitable activities during business hours
Gym: On-site gym or subsidised gym memberships
Shares: Companies where employees are offered share options
Health Insurance: Full family cover

HYDROCK

Hydrock

UK locations	National
UK sites	5
Sector	Construction
Definition	Consultancy & Contracting.
How owned	Private
Founded	1995
Turnover	£14.5m
Profit	£0.7m
Staff	251
Average age	38
Male : Female	92 : 8
Earnings £35,000+	17%

BEST COMPANIES INDEX

★ ★ ★ best company 2007

EXTRAORDINARY

★ ★ ★

2007 BCI = 800.8

2006 BCI = 762.7 (★★★)

WORKPLACE INSIGHTS

Annual appraisals are carried out each spring. In addition to covering personal development issues, employees have an opportunity to speak their minds on a wide range of issues within the company.

Employees can apply for a £200 healthy living bonus which can be used for anything which supports a healthy lifestyle. This might be gym membership, purchase of a bicycle or running shoes or, as in one case, as a sponsorship to lose weight.

Managing Director Dr. Brian McConnell personally carries out annual appraisals with every employee & is involved in the final interview of all new employees. In this way, everyone who works for Hydrock has had personal contact with the MD from day one.

MISSION / VISION

Hydrock is a national multidisciplinary consultancy and specialist contracting company providing services for construction, infrastructure, and the environment. We will grow profitably into a national force in our industry by creating a unique, dynamic, working environment.

BEST WORKPLACE FACTORS

MY COMPANY
WELL BEING
LEADERSHIP

GRADUATE VACANCIES

Structural Engineering, Infrastructure Engineering, Geo-Environmental, Mechanical & Electrical.

EMPLOYEE COMMENTS

"Every employee is made to feel valued."

"This company is genuinely concerned with the well being of its employees."

"Our managing director is a really great guy who knows us all and seems to really want to make this a good place to work."

CONTACT DETAILS

Hydrock, Over Court Barns, Over Land, Almondsbury, Bristol BS32 4DF
Tel: 01454 619533 www.hydrock.com

KEY

- **Holidays:** Companies offering a minimum of 25 days annual leave
- **Maternity:** Companies offering over Statutory Maternity Pay
- **Childcare:** On-site nursery or vouchers
- **Women:** At least 33% of senior managers are women
- **Long Service:** 40% of employees with more than 5 years' service
- **Pensions:** Companies offering a final salary or non-contributory/ contributory pension scheme
- **Charity Activities:** 10% of staff undertake charitable activities during business hours
- **Gym:** On-site gym or subsidised gym memberships
- **Shares:** Companies where employees are offered share options
- **Health Insurance:** Full family cover

To find out more about this company visit www.bestcompaniesguide.co.uk

1000
801>
500
0
ones to watch

hydrogen

HYDROGEN GROUP

UK locations	London
UK sites	3
Sector	Recruitment
Definition	Specialist Professional Recruitment
How owned	Public (i.e. stock market listed)
Founded	1997
Turnover	£38.9m
Profit	£2.7m
Staff	252
Average age	27
Male : Female	48 : 52
Earnings £35,000+	76%

BEST COMPANIES INDEX

best company 2007

EXTRAORDINARY ★ ★ ★

2007 BCI = 743.7

WORKPLACE INSIGHTS

The Managers at Hydrogen are fantastically supportive. They are quick to congratulate when people do well and advise a better way to go about things when they don't go quite to plan.

Employee satisfaction, motivation, development & retention are priority. Hydrogen is able to offer unparalleled opportunities through being one of the fastest growing companies in Europe & through the support structure that exists to help people make the most of their abilities.

Hydrogen CEO Ian Temple and the Directors take groups on regular lunches and events to reward specific achievements and contributions. These events are part social and part an opportunity for feedback and discussion of business issues.

MISSION / VISION

To be the fastest organically growing public recruitment company.

BEST WORKPLACE FACTORS

MY MANAGER
MY COMPANY
LEADERSHIP

GRADUATE VACANCIES

Recruitment Consultancy & Sales.

EMPLOYEE COMMENTS

"Senior Managers are always keen to give advice and help you push your career forward."

"Great place to work if you are excited about recruitment consulting."

"Everyone from the most Senior Manager to the receptionist is open and friendly."

CONTACT DETAILS

Hydrogen Group PLC, 26-28 Bedford Row, London WC1R 4HE
Tel: 0207 845 4200 www.hydrogengroup.com

KEY

- **Holidays:** Companies offering a minimum of 25 days annual leave
- **Maternity:** Companies offering over Statutory Maternity Pay
- **Childcare:** On-site nursery or vouchers
- **Women:** At least 33% of senior managers are women
- **Long Service:** 40% of employees with more than 5 years' service
- **Pensions:** Companies offering a final salary or non-contributory/ contributory pension scheme
- **Charity Activities:** 10% of staff undertake charitable activities during business hours
- **Gym:** On-site gym or subsidised gym memberships
- **Shares:** Companies where employees are offered share options
- **Health Insurance:** Full family cover

To find out more about this company visit www.bestcompaniesguide.co.uk

IRIS

UK locations	London, N.West
UK sites	2
Sector	Advertising
Definition	Integrated Marketing Agency
How owned	Private
Founded	1999
Turnover	£26m
Profit	£0.7m
Staff	231
Average age	30
Male : Female	58 : 42
Earnings £35,000+	40%

BEST COMPANIES INDEX

★ ★ ★ best company 2007

EXTRAORDINARY

★ ★ ★

2007 BCI = 748.4

2006 BCI = 726.2 (★★)

WORKPLACE INSIGHTS

Iris have developed their own training academy which offers a comprehensive programme of essential and non-essential personal development courses, from negotiation & presentation skills to German lessons and life drawing classes.

The ability of line managers to set meaningful objectives for employees development is enhanced by iris' robust induction programme, "Aloha!" which includes an intranet, a meaty induction pack and a development template.

Iris have a number of committees; Lash, Sport, Green, Smile, all responsible for enhancing a different aspect of company culture. Employees can sign up for any of these committees. There is also an initiative called This is your Space, where employees can design images for walls & meeting rooms.

MISSION / VISION

Vision: To be the best agency our clients want to work with, and the only agency talent wants to work for.
Mission: To deliver outstanding value by exposing mediocrity and releasing potential (in both our clients and ourselves).

BEST WORKPLACE FACTORS

PERSONAL GROWTH
MY MANAGER
MY TEAM

GRADUATE VACANCIES

Account Handling & Creative.

EMPLOYEE COMMENTS

"Clear path for succession & really good personal coaching and training available where required."

"Doors are always open and people will always listen. Management set a great example to staff."

"It's a fun, vibrant, funky, slightly quirky agency to work for, which is brilliant."

CONTACT DETAILS

iris, iris Towers, 185 Park Street, London SE1 9DY
Tel: 0207 6547900 www.irisnation.com

KEY

Holidays: Companies offering a minimum of 25 days annual leave
Maternity: Companies offering over Statutory Maternity Pay
Childcare: On-site nursery or vouchers
Women: At least 33% of senior managers are women
Long Service: 40% of employees with more than 5 years' service
Pensions: Companies offering a final salary or non-contributory/ contributory pension scheme
Charity Activities: 10% of staff undertake charitable activities during business hours
Gym: On-site gym or subsidised gym memberships
Shares: Companies where employees are offered share options
Health Insurance: Full family cover

1000

748>

★ ★ ★ ★ ★ ★

ones to watch

500

0

ISIS TELECOMMUNICATIONS

Isis Telecommunications

UK locations	London
UK sites	2
Sector	Communications/Telecom
Definition	Telecommunications Service Provider
How owned	Public (i.e. stock market listed)
Founded	1994
Turnover	£20.6m
Profit	£0.6m
Staff	68
Average age	29
Male : Female	69 : 31
Earnings £35,000+	28%

BEST COMPANIES INDEX

best company 2007

EXTRAORDINARY ★★★

2007 BCI = 750.0

2006 BCI = 773.3 (★★★)

WORKPLACE INSIGHTS

Peter Johnston, Management Team & Board of Directors are inspirational individuals. Passionate about the business & welfare of employees, dedicated, incredibly motivated & hardworking. Approachable, known to everyone & everyone is known to them.

Isis operate flexi hours for working parents & those who are studying. Managers & directors tell people to go home when they work too many hours! They provide a sympathetic/empathetic environment and endeavour to be as lenient as they can regarding illness & family matters.

Isis has Employee of the Month award. Employee of the month is an individual who has worked in an outstanding way, often behind the scenes & it is a wonderful opportunity to reward someone in a public way at our monthly company meeting.

MISSION / VISION

At Isis, we believe that business is about people; we believe that by maintaining Isis as a great company to work for, we can maintain it as a great company to work with.

BEST WORKPLACE FACTORS

LEADERSHIP
WELL BEING
MY TEAM

GRADUATE VACANCIES

Account Management, IT, Finance & Billing.

EMPLOYEE COMMENTS

"The management team and the board of directors are all inspirational individuals."

"I really enjoy the way Isis looks after staff and regularly treats us to good hospitality & benefits."

"We have a very strong Team ethos at Isis and everyone understands their role."

CONTACT DETAILS

Isis Telecommunications, 92-100 Warwick Road, Ealing, London W5 5PT
Tel: 0870 1635000 www.isistelecom.com

KEY

- **Holidays:** Companies offering a minimum of 25 days annual leave
- **Maternity:** Companies offering over Statutory Maternity Pay
- **Childcare:** On-site nursery or vouchers
- **Women:** At least 33% of senior managers are women
- **Long Service:** 40% of employees with more than 5 years' service
- **Pensions:** Companies offering a final salary or non-contributory/contributory pension scheme
- **Charity Activities:** 10% of staff undertake charitable activities during business hours
- **Gym:** On-site gym or subsidised gym memberships
- **Shares:** Companies where employees are offered share options
- **Health Insurance:** Full family cover

To find out more about this company visit www.bestcompaniesguide.co.uk

JUDD FARRIS PROPERTY RECRUITMENT

UK locations	National
UK sites	4
Sector	Recruitment
Definition	Specialist Recruitment Consultancy
How owned	Private
Founded	1998
Turnover	£10.2m
Profit	£0.9m
Staff	69
Average age	27
Male : Female	41 : 59
Earnings £35,000+	41%

BEST COMPANIES INDEX

EXTRAORDINARY ★★★

2007 BCI = 764.9

2006 BCI = 765.2 (★★★)

WORKPLACE INSIGHTS

At least twice every quarter one of the two Founding Directors, Dominic Judd and Mark Farris, will visit each regional office, spending time with individual consultants and taking the teams out to discuss how people think the company can be improved.

Judd Farris encourages teams to spend time together and bond through regular team dinners and social events. They also take all staff on an annual 2 day trip to France flying by private jet.

Great emphasis placed on career development and giving internal candidates the opportunity to run teams and offices. Judd Farris encourages people to take on a greater level of responsibility and provides the support of senior people within the business.

MISSION / VISION

We believe in creating long-term working relationships with clients and candidates. Our commitment to clients is to ensure that the very best candidate is found for them to fit their requirement. This commitment also extends to our candidates.

BEST WORKPLACE FACTORS

LEADERSHIP
MY TEAM
MY MANAGER

GRADUATE VACANCIES

Recruitment.

EMPLOYEE COMMENTS

"Great management led by two inspiring yet approachable individuals."

"I have never worked at a company where people get on so well with each other."

"Judd Farris empowers employees to stand on their own feet and make a difference."

CONTACT DETAILS

Judd Farris Property Recruitment, 37 Golden Square, London W1F 9LA
Tel: 0207 494 2555 www.juddfarris.co.uk

KEY

- **Holidays:** Companies offering a minimum of 25 days annual leave
- **Maternity:** Companies offering over Statutory Maternity Pay
- **Childcare:** On-site nursery or vouchers
- **Women:** At least 33% of senior managers are women
- **Long Service:** 40% of employees with more than 5 years' service
- **Pensions:** Companies offering a final salary or non-contributory/ contributory pension scheme
- **Charity Activities:** 10% of staff undertake charitable activities during business hours
- **Gym:** On-site gym or subsidised gym memberships
- **Shares:** Companies where employees are offered share options
- **Health Insurance:** Full family cover

To find out more about this company visit www.bestcompaniesguide.co.uk

1000 765> 500 0 ones to watch

KPMG

UK locations	National
UK sites	32
Sector	Professional Services
Definition	Audit Tax Advisory
How owned	Partnership/LLP
Founded	1987
Turnover	Not disclosed
Profit	Not disclosed
Staff	10,763
Average age	33
Male : Female	54 : 46
Earnings £35,000+	49%

BEST COMPANIES INDEX

best company 2007

EXTRAORDINARY ★★★

2007 BCI = 769.8

2006 BCI = 777.1 (★★★)

WORKPLACE INSIGHTS

Social events are arranged and sponsored by KPMG allowing all employees to socialise and enjoy themselves. Staff have competed in Dragon Boat racing, taken part in monthly pub quizzes organised by KPMG and ridden the dodgems at the KPMG Christmas Ball.

KPMG provide employees with extensive flexible benefits including free private healthcare for employees and families, Critical Illness, Life Assurance, concierge service and bikes for work. They spend £1 million+ annually on a wellness programme for employees.

KPMG provide all employees with a monthly time allocation of 3.5 hours to volunteer in their local communities. One in three of KPMG employees volunteered this year, contributing a record 30,000 hours.

MISSION / VISION

We aim to be recognised as leaders in terms of the services we provide and the industries we serve. This means driving ourselves to be the best in everything we do.

BEST WORKPLACE FACTORS

MY TEAM
FAIR DEAL
GIVING SOMETHING BACK

GRADUATE VACANCIES

All areas.

EMPLOYEE COMMENTS

"The people are great to work with."

"It is a true meritocracy; contribution/ effort fairly rewarded with respect to pay and recognition."

"Our CSR programme shows a great commitment to helping our communities and the environment."

CONTACT DETAILS

KPMG, 8 Salisbury Square, London EC4Y 8BB
Tel: 0207 3111000 www.kpmg.co.uk

KEY

Holidays: Companies offering a minimum of 25 days annual leave
Maternity: Companies offering over Statutory Maternity Pay
Childcare: On-site nursery or vouchers
Women: At least 33% of senior managers are women
Long Service: 40% of employees with more than 5 years' service
Pensions: Companies offering a final salary or non-contributory/ contributory pension scheme
Charity Activities: 10% of staff undertake charitable activities during business hours
Gym: On-site gym or subsidised gym memberships
Shares: Companies where employees are offered share options
Health Insurance: Full family cover

To find out more about this company visit www.bestcompaniesguide.co.uk

META-MORPHOSE INTERNATIONAL

UK locations	S.West, Wales
UK sites	2
Sector	Recruitment
Definition	Sales Recruitment/Training
How owned	Private
Founded	1994
Turnover	£2.6m
Profit	£0.3m
Staff	52
Average age	35
Male : Female	44 : 56
Earnings £35,000+	19%

BEST COMPANIES INDEX

EXTRAORDINARY

★ ★ ★

2007 BCI = 765.3

WORKPLACE INSIGHTS

Meta-morphose encourages team interaction through a number of social events including a Summer boat trip, a Christmas party and trips abroad as rewards for high performance. They also fund Friday night drinks with colleagues.

Meta-morphose present the Hamish Award, named for a retired employee and valued team member, to recognise a member of the team who has excelled over and above the call of duty. Someone who consistently through the year has over delivered, gone that extra mile.

Meta-morphose practice what they preach. Sales/ Sales support staff undertake relevant training where appropriate. Commitment to promote from within relies on understanding individual's capabilities and potential to develop in line with personal preferences.

MISSION / VISION

To be the largest operator in the field of graduate recruitment and training in the UK. At the same time to be regarded as the provider of both the highest quality in service and people.

BEST WORKPLACE FACTORS

MY TEAM
MY COMPANY
MY MANAGER

GRADUATE VACANCIES

Graduate Recruitment.

EMPLOYEE COMMENTS

"We have a passionate team of fantastic people, who have total belief in what we do."

"It is a very unique place to work with a real buzz."

"The management team are highly competent and professional."

CONTACT DETAILS

meta-morphose International, Idsall House, Prestbury, Cheltenham, Gloucestershire GL52 3AY
Tel: 0870 3306000 www.meta-morphose.com

KEY

Holidays: Companies offering a minimum of 25 days annual leave
Maternity: Companies offering over Statutory Maternity Pay
Childcare: On-site nursery or vouchers
Women: At least 33% of senior managers are women
Long Service: 40% of employees with more than 5 years' service
Pensions: Companies offering a final salary or non-contributory/ contributory pension scheme
Charity Activities: 10% of staff undertake charitable activities during business hours
Gym: On-site gym or subsidised gym memberships
Shares: Companies where employees are offered share options
Health Insurance: Full family cover

MORGAN STANLEY UK

Morgan Stanley

UK locations	London, Scotland
UK sites	2
Sector	Financial
Definition	US Investment Bank
How owned	Public (i.e. stock market listed)
Founded	1977
Turnover	Not disclosed
Profit	Not disclosed
Staff	6,155
Average age	30
Male : Female	65 : 35
Earnings £35,000+	82%

BEST COMPANIES INDEX

best company 2007

EXTRAORDINARY ★★★

2007 BCI = 739.5

2006 BCI = 720.2 (★★)

WORKPLACE INSIGHTS

Morgan Stanley has worked to foster the ownership culture so that every employee feels pride and responsibility working for the organisation. They seek to do first class business in a first class way, never losing sight of their values and principles.

Morgan Stanley want employees to take a degree of ownership for their training so rather than mandate the requirements, they provide a menu for employees to choose from, in order to meet their objectives.

Jonathan Chenevix-Trench hosts a Summer Party and also holds a quarterly presentation to provide employees with real time feedback on Morgan Stanley's performance and to enable employees to ask open and unscripted questions.

MISSION / VISION

To deliver the finest financial thinking products and execution in the world.

BEST WORKPLACE FACTORS

MY COMPANY
PERSONAL GROWTH
LEADERSHIP

GRADUATE VACANCIES

Equities, Fixed Income, Investment Banking, IT, Private Wealth Management, Finance & Operations.

EMPLOYEE COMMENTS

"I feel I work for a family run organisation. Everyone seems to have the same values and ideas."

"Ability to manage your professional development, support given as you progress."

"Openness of senior management and their accessibility create a sense of transparency and inclusion."

CONTACT DETAILS

Morgan Stanley UK, 25 Cabot Square, Canary Wharf, London E14 4QA
Tel: 0207 425 3000 www.morganstanley.com

KEY

- **Holidays:** Companies offering a minimum of 25 days annual leave
- **Maternity:** Companies offering over Statutory Maternity Pay
- **Childcare:** On-site nursery or vouchers
- **Women:** At least 33% of senior managers are women
- **Long Service:** 40% of employees with more than 5 years' service
- **Pensions:** Companies offering a final salary or non-contributory/ contributory pension scheme
- **Charity Activities:** 10% of staff undertake charitable activities during business hours
- **Gym:** On-site gym or subsidised gym memberships
- **Shares:** Companies where employees are offered share options
- **Health Insurance:** Full family cover

To find out more about this company visit www.bestcompaniesguide.co.uk

NAPP PHARMACEUTICAL HOLDINGS

UK locations	E.England
UK sites	1
Sector	Pharmaceutical
Definition	Pharma Manufacture/Sales
How owned	Private
Founded	1967
Turnover	Not disclosed
Profit	Not disclosed
Staff	774
Average age	39
Male : Female	56 : 44
Earnings £35,000+	31%

BEST COMPANIES INDEX

★ ★ ★ best company 2007

EXTRAORDINARY

★ ★ ★

2007 BCI = 777.7

WORKPLACE INSIGHTS

In addition to financing the company sports and social club, providing free drinks, private healthcare and negotiating reduced gym membership, Napp are also launching a cycle to work scheme for all employees.

Members, including new staff, experience core values workshops where company values are discussed. Values are integrated into recruitment, promotion and performance management and are prominently displayed i.e. on employee computer wallpaper.

Senior leadership recently involved in developing a leadership programme that seeks to identify attributes of great leadership. Every company member will participate in a two-day programme with at least one member of senior leadership team present.

MISSION / VISION

We aim to be a successful and enterprising UK pharmaceutical business. We aim to have a great place to work. We aim to enable our independent associate companies to have successful businesses. We want patients to benefit from what we do.

BEST WORKPLACE FACTORS

WELL BEING
MY COMPANY
LEADERSHIP

GRADUATE VACANCIES

Applications from graduates are welcome in all areas of our business and at all levels.

EMPLOYEE COMMENTS

"As a whole the company looks after its employees exceptionally well."

"Organisation runs from the bottom upwards. If you want to make changes, the mechanism is in place."

"We have very strong leadership but still everyone here feels like they have a voice."

CONTACT DETAILS

Napp Pharmaceutical Holdings, Cambridge Science Park, Milton Road, Cambridge CB4 0GW
Tel: 01223 424444 www.napp.co.uk

KEY

- **Holidays:** Companies offering a minimum of 25 days annual leave
- **Maternity:** Companies offering over Statutory Maternity Pay
- **Childcare:** On-site nursery or vouchers
- **Women:** At least 33% of senior managers are women
- **Long Service:** 40% of employees with more than 5 years' service
- **Pensions:** Companies offering a final salary or non-contributory/ contributory pension scheme
- **Charity Activities:** 10% of staff undertake charitable activities during business hours
- **Gym:** On-site gym or subsidised gym memberships
- **Shares:** Companies where employees are offered share options
- **Health Insurance:** Full family cover

To find out more about this company visit www.bestcompaniesguide.co.uk

1000
778>
ones to watch
500
0

P3 THE SOCIAL INCLUSION CHARITY

UK locations	E.Midlands
UK sites	10
Sector	Charity
Definition	Providing opportunities for disadvantaged people
How owned	Trust/Employee owned/Mutual
Founded	1972
Turnover	£4.2m
Profit	Not disclosed
Staff	118
Average age	38
Male : Female	34 : 66
Earnings £35,000+	3%

BEST COMPANIES INDEX

★ ★ ★ best company 2007

EXTRAORDINARY

★ ★ ★

2007 BCI = 850.4

2006 BCI = 757.7 (★★★)

WORKPLACE INSIGHTS

P3 deliver various levels of management development training including NVQ Level 4, First Line Management Training with Institute of Leadership and Management, and develop practical skills for the workplace, such as Conducting Investigations training.

P3 operate an Employee Suggestion Scheme where employees have the opportunity to suggest new ideas, improved ways of working. Outstanding contributions rewarded on an individual basis with gifts and employees are thanked both individually and publicly.

New employees undergo extensive four day induction programme covering essential training and key issues they will need to embark upon their career with P3, day one focusing on P3 themselves with sessions facilitated by Senior Management.

MISSION / VISION

To be the best and to seek excellence by continuously improving the services we provide so they more closely match our service users needs.

BEST WORKPLACE FACTORS

MY MANAGER
MY COMPANY
PERSONAL GROWTH

GRADUATE VACANCIES

No graduate vacancies have been indicated.

EMPLOYEE COMMENTS

"The management team are extremely supportive to all staff members."

"I have never had a job that I have enjoyed so much; the job gives me great satisfaction."

"P3 gives excellent training opportunities, support with issues, whether work related or personal."

CONTACT DETAILS

P3 the social inclusion charity, Gladstone House, Market Street, Ilkeston, Derbyshire DE7 5RB
Tel: 0115 9306661 www.p3charity.com

KEY

- **Holidays:** Companies offering a minimum of 25 days annual leave
- **Maternity:** Companies offering over Statutory Maternity Pay
- **Childcare:** On-site nursery or vouchers
- **Women:** At least 33% of senior managers are women
- **Long Service:** 40% of employees with more than 5 years' service
- **Pensions:** Companies offering a final salary or non-contributory/ contributory pension scheme
- **Charity Activities:** 10% of staff undertake charitable activities during business hours
- **Gym:** On-site gym or subsidised gym memberships
- **Shares:** Companies where employees are offered share options
- **Health Insurance:** Full family cover

To find out more about this company visit www.bestcompaniesguide.co.uk

PANNONE
THE COMPLETE LAW FIRM

PANNONE

UK locations	N.West
UK sites	1
Sector	Law
Definition	Legal Firm
How owned	Partnership/LLP
Founded	1852
Turnover	£38.5m
Profit	£11m
Staff	680
Average age	35
Male : Female	35 : 65
Earnings £35,000+	38%

BEST COMPANIES INDEX

★ ★ ★ best company 2007

EXTRAORDINARY

★ ★ ★

2007 BCI = 797.9

2006 BCI = 796.7 (★★★)

798>

500

ones to watch

WORKPLACE INSIGHTS

Pannone are all located on site. This is a deliberate tactic and is a factor that they believe plays an important part in making their communications so effective. Both from the perspective of employee relations and the service to clients.

Development available for everyone, not just professional staff. Pannone are unique because they recognise they already employ a lot of the talent that they need for the future & they work hard to retain staff & develop them whatever their role.

Subsidised law courses can be taken whether or not employees are currently doing lawyer's job. The only criteria is they have to have worked with Pannone for at least a year & be doing well in their current role.

MISSION / VISION

Pannone staff are our most important asset and we go to great lengths to ensure that we recruit lawyers and support specialists who are both technically capable, and also commercially astute and secretarial and administrative staff who are accurate, efficient and think matters through.

BEST WORKPLACE FACTORS

MY TEAM
PERSONAL GROWTH
FAIR DEAL

GRADUATE VACANCIES

Legal, trainee solicitors or paralegals.

EMPLOYEE COMMENTS

"Have an open door policy; I can speak to my manager as & when necessary should I have any concerns."

"I think all employees feel valued and are supported to grow and achieve their career ambitions."

"Plenty of benefits available to all staff ranging from social events to great training opportunities."

CONTACT DETAILS

Pannone, 123 Deansgate, Manchester M3 2BU
Tel: 0161 9093000 www.pannone.com

KEY

- **Holidays:** Companies offering a minimum of 25 days annual leave
- **Maternity:** Companies offering over Statutory Maternity Pay
- **Childcare:** On-site nursery or vouchers
- **Women:** At least 33% of senior managers are women
- **Long Service:** 40% of employees with more than 5 years' service
- **Pensions:** Companies offering a final salary or non-contributory/ contributory pension scheme
- **Charity Activities:** 10% of staff undertake charitable activities during business hours
- **Gym:** On-site gym or subsidised gym memberships
- **Shares:** Companies where employees are offered share options
- **Health Insurance:** Full family cover

To find out more about this company visit www.bestcompaniesguide.co.uk

POWER TECHNOLOGY SOLUTIONS

www.ptsol.co.uk

UK locations	Scotland, S.East, N.West
UK sites	3
Sector	Engineering
Definition	Power Systems Consultancy
How owned	Private
Founded	1999
Turnover	£4.6m
Profit	£0.2m
Staff	65
Average age	43
Male : Female	91 : 9
Earnings £35,000+	55%

BEST COMPANIES INDEX

best company 2007

EXTRAORDINARY ★ ★ ★

2007 BCI = 776.8

2006 BCI = 781.7 (★★★)

WORKPLACE INSIGHTS

Power Technology Solutions encourage health and fitness, as well as teamwork, in their employees through a number of social and sporting events including 5-a-side football, rugby and golf days.

PTS encourage staff to aim for personal targets as well as job or work related ones by funding staff for any training or experience they feel will increase their personal development, not only for the good of the company but also the individual.

Power Technology Solutions offer a number of benefits such as performance related pay, free private healthcare and bonuses. Coupled with attractive salary they believe the overall package they offer to be one of the best available in the industry.

MISSION / VISION

The vision of the business is to be the best high voltage project delivery provider in the UK.

BEST WORKPLACE FACTORS

WELL BEING
PERSONAL GROWTH
FAIR DEAL

GRADUATE VACANCIES

Electrical Engineering.

EMPLOYEE COMMENTS

"All of us feel part of a large PTS family, supporting one another when necessary."

"Training and development opportunities available to allow individuals to grow within the company."

"The salary package and benefits are extremely generous compared to other companies in this industry."

CONTACT DETAILS

Power Technology Solutions, Concepts House, 3 Watchgate, Newby Road Industrial Estate, Hazel Grove, Stockport SK7 5DB
Tel: 0845 6341133 www.ptsol.co.uk

KEY

- **Holidays:** Companies offering a minimum of 25 days annual leave
- **Maternity:** Companies offering over Statutory Maternity Pay
- **Childcare:** On-site nursery or vouchers
- **Women:** At least 33% of senior managers are women
- **Long Service:** 40% of employees with more than 5 years' service
- **Pensions:** Companies offering a final salary or non-contributory/contributory pension scheme
- **Charity Activities:** 10% of staff undertake charitable activities during business hours
- **Gym:** On-site gym or subsidised gym memberships
- **Shares:** Companies where employees are offered share options
- **Health Insurance:** Full family cover

To find out more about this company visit www.bestcompaniesguide.co.uk

PPS GROUP

UK locations	National
UK sites	5
Sector	Consulting
Definition	Public Affairs Consultancy
How owned	Private
Founded	1990
Turnover	£3.1m
Profit	£0.4m
Staff	51
Average age	28
Male : Female	51 : 49
Earnings £35,000+	43%

BEST COMPANIES INDEX

best company 2007

EXTRAORDINARY ★ ★ ★

2007 BCI = 741.1

WORKPLACE INSIGHTS

PPS actively encourages a light management style at every level. This begins at the top. The intention is to deliver the minimum of senior management intervention sufficient to support good decision-making.

Learning/Development covers whole process of staff developing skills necessary to produce high quality work.

PPS share with all staff a thorough understanding of how things are done based on best practice and experience built up over many years.

MISSION / VISION

For our clients, we aim to be expert guides who will deliver the best-possible service and results. We want to be an essential part of our clients' team and the natural choice in our field. For our staff, we want to offer a friendly and supportive workplace offering testing and fascinating work.

BEST WORKPLACE FACTORS

MY MANAGER
PERSONAL GROWTH
MY TEAM

GRADUATE VACANCIES

Public Affairs.

EMPLOYEE COMMENTS

"Good managers who care about their staff."

"I feel that the experience PPS has given me is invaluable to my career progression."

"There is a great relationship between team members and everyone seems to work well together."

CONTACT DETAILS

PPS Group, 69 Grosvenor Street, London W1K 3JW
Tel: 0207 5291700 www.ppsgroup.co.uk

KEY

- **Holidays:** Companies offering a minimum of 25 days annual leave
- **Maternity:** Companies offering over Statutory Maternity Pay
- **Childcare:** On-site nursery or vouchers
- **Women:** At least 33% of senior managers are women
- **Long Service:** 40% of employees with more than 5 years' service
- **Pensions:** Companies offering a final salary or non-contributory/ contributory pension scheme
- **Charity Activities:** 10% of staff undertake charitable activities during business hours
- **Gym:** On-site gym or subsidised gym memberships
- **Shares:** Companies where employees are offered share options
- **Health Insurance:** Full family cover

1000 741> 500 0 ones to watch

To find out more about this company visit www.bestcompaniesguide.co.uk

Project 1

PROJECT ONE CONSULTING

UK locations	National
UK sites	4
Sector	Consulting
Definition	Programme Management Consultancy
How owned	Private
Founded	1998
Turnover	£7.7m
Profit	Not disclosed
Staff	59
Average age	43
Male : Female	80 : 20
Earnings £35,000+	92%

BEST COMPANIES INDEX

EXTRAORDINARY

★ ★ ★

2007 BCI = 753.8

WORKPLACE INSIGHTS

Provides employees with benefits such as performance related pay, private healthcare for employees & their families and Life Assurance 4 times salary. In addition, sabbaticals of up to 6 weeks paid leave may be taken with one year's service.

Project One place a strong emphasis on work life balance and ensuring employees get home on time each night. They have facilitated this by splitting the business geographically allowing consultants to work in their home regions as much as possible.

Since their inception in 1998 Project One have developed and maintained a core set of values and beliefs which they communicate to all employees via their business plan which they receive as part of their induction into the company.

MISSION / VISION

To be the obvious partner to deliver change. We will achieve this by: defining, planning and implementing, major programmes, providing confidence of delivery, with the customer in control. By driving delivery to achieve business benefits.

BEST WORKPLACE FACTORS

FAIR DEAL
WELL BEING
MY COMPANY

GRADUATE VACANCIES

No graduate vacancies have been indicated.

EMPLOYEE COMMENTS

"The company provides interesting work, a great reward package and great colleagues."

"The organisation encourages employees to ensure the right work/ home balance for each individual."

"The company is founded on a fantastic set of values, putting employees at the centre of the business."

CONTACT DETAILS

Project One Consulting, Church House, Parkway, Holmes Chapel, Cheshire CW4 7BA
Tel: 01477 544462 www.projectoneconsulting.co.uk

KEY

- **Holidays:** Companies offering a minimum of 25 days annual leave
- **Maternity:** Companies offering over Statutory Maternity Pay
- **Childcare:** On-site nursery or vouchers
- **Women:** At least 33% of senior managers are women
- **Long Service:** 40% of employees with more than 5 years' service
- **Pensions:** Companies offering a final salary or non-contributory/ contributory pension scheme
- **Charity Activities:** 10% of staff undertake charitable activities during business hours
- **Gym:** On-site gym or subsidised gym memberships
- **Shares:** Companies where employees are offered share options
- **Health Insurance:** Full family cover

To find out more about this company visit www.bestcompaniesguide.co.uk

RED GATE SOFTWARE

UK locations	E.England
UK sites	1
Sector	IT/Internet Services
Definition	Software Development
How owned	Private
Founded	1999
Turnover	Not disclosed
Profit	Not disclosed
Staff	58
Average age	28
Male : Female	69.31
Earnings £35,000+	38%

BEST COMPANIES INDEX

best company 2007

EXTRAORDINARY ★ ★ ★

2007 BCI = 771.4

WORKPLACE INSIGHTS

Red Gate pays a bonus to all employees when defined company sales milestones are reached. This was paid three times in 2006. In addition every employee is entitled to company stock options when they complete their initial probation period.

Red Gate believe the work they do is challenging and encourages people to develop & learn from each other. They ensure employees have the best equipment & resources to do their jobs properly & receive training they require to advance their skills & career.

Red Gate ensures every employee can do their job in comfort by providing top quality work stations, monitors and chairs as well as several comfortable seating areas for informal meetings, and a staff room with TV and table football.

MISSION / VISION

Red Gate builds markets and sells ingeniously simple tools for Microsoft database professionals.

BEST WORKPLACE FACTORS

FAIR DEAL
PERSONAL GROWTH
WELL BEING

GRADUATE VACANCIES

Graduate-Software Developer, Software Tester & Marketing Associate.

EMPLOYEE COMMENTS

"I don't know anywhere else that offers such great benefits."

"Training to ensure all have the tools needed, management & owners work hard ensuring staff are invested in & empowered."

"The directors are genuinely concerned for us and treat us very fairly."

CONTACT DETAILS

Red Gate Software Ltd, St John's Innovation Centre, Cowley Road, Cambridge CB4 0WS
Tel: 0870 160 0037 www.red-gate.com

KEY

- **Holidays:** Companies offering a minimum of 25 days annual leave
- **Pensions:** Companies offering a final salary or non-contributory/ contributory pension scheme
- **Maternity:** Companies offering over Statutory Maternity Pay
- **Charity Activities:** 10% of staff undertake charitable activities during business hours
- **Childcare:** On-site nursery or vouchers
- **Gym:** On-site gym or subsidised gym memberships
- **Women:** At least 33% of senior managers are women
- **Shares:** Companies where employees are offered share options
- **Long Service:** 40% of employees with more than 5 years' service
- **Health Insurance:** Full family cover

To find out more about this company visit www.bestcompaniesguide.co.uk

1000

ROBERT HALF INTERNATIONAL

RHI Robert Half International
A Global Leader in Professional Services Since 1948

UK locations	National
UK sites	30
Sector	Recruitment
Definition	Financial & Administrative Recruitment
How owned	Public (i.e. stock market listed)
Founded	1948
Turnover	Not disclosed
Profit	Not disclosed
Staff	527
Average age	29
Male : Female	38 : 62
Earnings £35,000+	not disclosed

<740

BEST COMPANIES INDEX

★ ★ ★ best company 2007

EXTRAORDINARY

★ ★ ★

2007 BCI = 739.9

2006 BCI = 712.8 (★★)

ones to watch

WORKPLACE INSIGHTS

Employees at Robert Half are able to give feedback on their manager's performance in a number of ways including through their internal survey, two way appraisals and 360 degree feedback.

Robert Half runs a number of employee reward programmes, such as Reach for the Stars, which is a global programme recognising top performers. Both sales and sales support staff can be recognised through these schemes.

Both Managing Directors of Robert Half are committed to visiting each of their branches as often as possible. They sit in the middle of the office with the consultants so that they can be asked questions or can compliment good work.

500

MISSION / VISION

To be the premier provider in all the markets we serve adhering to the highest ethical standards.

BEST WORKPLACE FACTORS

MY MANAGER
PERSONAL GROWTH
LEADERSHIP

GRADUATE VACANCIES

No graduate vacancies have been indicated.

EMPLOYEE COMMENTS

"Great support from my manager."

"Good opportunities to develop within the company."

"Strong leadership, stability, fair compensation and team morale."

CONTACT DETAILS

Robert Half International, Corporate Service Centre, Washington House, International Square off Starley Way, Birmingham B37 7GN Tel: 0121 767 6100 www.roberthalf.co.uk

KEY

- **Holidays:** Companies offering a minimum of 25 days annual leave
- **Maternity:** Companies offering over Statutory Maternity Pay
- **Childcare:** On-site nursery or vouchers
- **Women:** At least 33% of senior managers are women
- **Long Service:** 40% of employees with more than 5 years' service
- **Pensions:** Companies offering a final salary or non-contributory/ contributory pension scheme
- **Charity Activities:** 10% of staff undertake charitable activities during business hours
- **Gym:** On-site gym or subsidised gym memberships
- **Shares:** Companies where employees are offered share options
- **Health Insurance:** Full family cover

0

To find out more about this company visit www.bestcompaniesguide.co.uk

RPM

UK locations	London
UK sites	2
Sector	Marketing
Definition	Experiential Marketing Agency
How owned	Private
Founded	1993
Turnover	£10.5m
Profit	Not disclosed
Staff	67
Average age	28
Male : Female	46 : 54
Earnings £35,000+	33%

BEST COMPANIES INDEX

EXTRAORDINARY ★ ★ ★

2007 BCI = 749.4

2006 BCI = 727.8 (★★)

WORKPLACE INSIGHTS

RPM encourage team bonding through funding regular Friday night drinks and providing an experience fund for each team to go out together on outings such as film viewings and sporting events.

RPM was set up to be different. They recognise that people are their best asset & have built an agency that is orientated around those that work there, ensuring they have an opportunity to grow, develop & ultimately be part of something they can be proud of.

RPM put together personal development plans for each individual employee including areas where they have said they would like to grow and learn and areas they feel need improving or where there is talent that they would like to nurture.

MISSION / VISION

To create experiences founded in the essence of the brand, connecting consumers in a creative and compelling way.

BEST WORKPLACE FACTORS

MY TEAM
MY COMPANY
PERSONAL GROWTH

GRADUATE VACANCIES

Account Handling, Production, Planning, Creative.

EMPLOYEE COMMENTS

"People at all levels approachable, complete lack of office politics and a real sense of 'team'."

"Everyone is very proud of the work we do & are willing to go the extra mile to achieve great results."

"Comprehensive training & also accommodates personal development, work related or otherwise."

CONTACT DETAILS

RPM, The Old Treacle Factory, 24-40 Goodwin Road, London W12 9JW
Tel: 0208 735 5100 www.rpmltd.com

KEY

Holidays: Companies offering a minimum of 25 days annual leave
Maternity: Companies offering over Statutory Maternity Pay
Childcare: On-site nursery or vouchers
Women: At least 33% of senior managers are women
Long Service: 40% of employees with more than 5 years' service
Pensions: Companies offering a final salary or non-contributory/contributory pension scheme
Charity Activities: 10% of staff undertake charitable activities during business hours
Gym: On-site gym or subsidised gym memberships
Shares: Companies where employees are offered share options
Health Insurance: Full family cover

To find out more about this company visit www.bestcompaniesguide.co.uk

1000 749> 500 0 ones to watch

1000

<819

ones to watch

SANDWELL COMMUNITY CARING TRUST

Community Caring Trust

UK locations	W. Midlands
UK sites	46
Sector	Health
Definition	Care Provider
How owned	Trust/Employee owned/Mutual
Founded	1997
Turnover	£6.6m
Profit	£0.1m
Staff	286
Average age	38
Male : Female	17 : 83
Earnings £35,000+	2%

BEST COMPANIES INDEX

best company 2007

EXTRAORDINARY

★ ★ ★

2007 BCI = 818.8

2006 BCI = 828.0 (★★★)

WORKPLACE INSIGHTS

Sandwell ensure all managers & senior managers are well rounded by ensuring their training includes a balance of leadership & management. At least 30% of their working week is spent on leadership tasks in addition to their day to day management.

Have a clear family friendly policy, aimed at ensuring individual employees have personal work life balance built around childcare issues, marital issues, caring for sick relatives & any other short, medium & long-term personal commitments.

Employees at Sandwell have the potential to earn a maximum of 36 day's holiday a year. They receive an extra 5 days through promotion to manager grade and another 5 days through completing 5 years service.

500

MISSION / VISION

To promote the relief of, and provide relief support and assistance to, individuals, who by reason of old age or physical or mental illness or disability, require special care and attention.

BEST WORKPLACE FACTORS

MY MANAGER
WELL BEING
FAIR DEAL

GRADUATE VACANCIES

No specific graduate vacancies have been indicated.

EMPLOYEE COMMENTS

"Management will do their best to help you if you have problems."

"Every member of the work team is very supportive."

"The wages and bonuses are exceptionally good."

CONTACT DETAILS

Sandwell Community Caring Trust, West Plaza 9th Floor, 144 High Street, West Bromwich B70 6JJ
Tel: 0121 553 2722 www.sandwellcct.org.uk

KEY

- **Holidays:** Companies offering a minimum of 25 days annual leave
- **Maternity:** Companies offering over Statutory Maternity Pay
- **Childcare:** On-site nursery or vouchers
- **Women:** At least 33% of senior managers are women
- **Long Service:** 40% of employees with more than 5 years' service
- **Pensions:** Companies offering a final salary or non-contributory/contributory pension scheme
- **Charity Activities:** 10% of staff undertake charitable activities during business hours
- **Gym:** On-site gym or subsidised gym memberships
- **Shares:** Companies where employees are offered share options
- **Health Insurance:** Full family cover

0

Slimming WORLD
discover the amazing you

SLIMMING WORLD

UK locations	E.Midlands
UK sites	1
Sector	Health
Definition	Slimming & Weight Management
How owned	Private
Founded	1969
Turnover	Not disclosed
Profit	Not disclosed
Staff	238
Average age	39
Male : Female	16 : 84
Earnings £35,000+	13%

BEST COMPANIES INDEX

best company 2007

EXTRAORDINARY ★★★

2007 BCI = 740.9

2006 BCI = 743.4 (★★★)

WORKPLACE INSIGHTS

Slimming World's own charity SMILES was created by Margaret Miles Bramwell to raise money and donate to all the children's charities (with no money taken out for admin costs) in particular, 'Full Stop' to stop the abuse of children in society.

At Slimming World, the Managing Director is passionate about people and staff development and therefore maintains a personal interest in all staff members and their progress and development in the Company.

Staff, consultants & members of Slimming World receive performance incentives such as gifts & prizes, parties for employees' children, anniversary celebrations. They always look to improve what they do & how they do it for the benefit of everyone.

MISSION / VISION

To remain the largest and most effective slimming organisation in this country. To have a significant impact on the image of slimming in this country. To establish a company culture in which mutual co-operation and mutual trust are valued.

BEST WORKPLACE FACTORS

GIVING SOMETHING BACK
LEADERSHIP
FAIR DEAL

GRADUATE VACANCIES

No graduate vacancies have been indicated.

EMPLOYEE COMMENTS

"We make a huge difference to people's lives."

"The openness and honesty of the leaders."

"I am in no doubt they treat everyone fairly & with respect - employees, suppliers and customers alike."

CONTACT DETAILS

Slimming World, P.O. Box 55, Alfreton, Derbyshire DE55 4UE
Tel: 0870 3307733 www.slimming-world.com

1000
741>
500
0
ones to watch

KEY

- **Holidays:** Companies offering a minimum of 25 days annual leave
- **Maternity:** Companies offering over Statutory Maternity Pay
- **Childcare:** On-site nursery or vouchers
- **Women:** At least 33% of senior managers are women
- **Long Service:** 40% of employees with more than 5 years' service
- **Pensions:** Companies offering a final salary or non-contributory/ contributory pension scheme
- **Charity Activities:** 10% of staff undertake charitable activities during business hours
- **Gym:** On-site gym or subsidised gym memberships
- **Shares:** Companies where employees are offered share options
- **Health Insurance:** Full family cover

1000

THE JJ GROUP

UK locations	S.East
UK sites	1
Sector	Marketing
Definition	Integrated Marketing Agency
How owned	Private
Founded	1989
Turnover	£11.2m
Profit	£0.5m
Staff	81
Average age	32
Male : Female	48 : 52
Earnings £35,000+	28%

<755

BEST COMPANIES INDEX

best company 2007

EXTRAORDINARY

★ ★ ★

2007 BCI = 755.1

2006 BCI = 696.5 (★)

ones to watch

WORKPLACE INSIGHTS

JJ strives to employ a team of motivated and talented professionals who want to add value and make a difference to their clients, to their colleagues and to their work atmosphere.

JJ's Senior Management set a great example by being truly inspirational and motivational in their approach. They demonstrate passion about the work that they do, the Clients that they work for and most importantly about the employees that they employ.

JJ are committed to developing its internal skills and talents. They aim to optimise individual, team and company performance and to give employees the opportunity to progress and develop in their roles.

500

MISSION / VISION

To be acknowledged by our clients, prospects, and industry peers, as 'the truly integrated agency'.

BEST WORKPLACE FACTORS

MY COMPANY
MY MANAGER
PERSONAL GROWTH

GRADUATE VACANCIES

Marketing including Client Services Events & PR.

EMPLOYEE COMMENTS

"Fantastic place to work! I love it."

"JJ is a great place to work as the senior management do what they say rather than just lip service."

"JJ offers me the opportunity to learn and grow within my role by supporting me in either funding, learning or providing me with the tools to do my job."

CONTACT DETAILS

The JJ Group, Little Baldon House, Little Baldon, Oxford, Oxfordshire OX44 9PU
Tel: 01865 343100 www.thejjgroup.com

KEY

Holidays: Companies offering a minimum of 25 days annual leave

Maternity: Companies offering over Statutory Maternity Pay

Childcare: On-site nursery or vouchers

Women: At least 33% of senior managers are women

Long Service: 40% of employees with more than 5 years' service

Pensions: Companies offering a final salary or non-contributory/ contributory pension scheme

Charity Activities: 10% of staff undertake charitable activities during business hours

Gym: On-site gym or subsidised gym memberships

Shares: Companies where employees are offered share options

Health Insurance: Full family cover

0

To find out more about this company visit www.bestcompaniesguide.co.uk

THE SG GROUP

UK locations	London
UK sites	2
Sector	Recruitment
Definition	Marketing & HR Recruitment
How owned	Private
Founded	1993
Turnover	£22.1m
Profit	£0.8m
Staff	104
Average age	36
Male : Female	11 : 89
Earnings £35,000+	47%

BEST COMPANIES INDEX

best company 2007

EXTRAORDINARY ★★★

2007 BCI = 773.0

2006 BCI = 754.0 (★★★)

WORKPLACE INSIGHTS

All new staff find the SG Group an incredibly caring culture in which to work in which colleagues look out for each other and being supportive is the norm.

Claire Owen, founder and MD is passionate about people & her energy/enthusiasm for making the company a great place to work fuels a culture which celebrates difference & empowers individuals to stretch themselves, take on new challenges & make the most of life both in/out of the office.

Encourage staff to make a greater contribution, practical & financial. This year SG established staff run charity team to formulate a policy & drive charitable activities, including introduction of 2 charity days/year for staff to spend on voluntary activities.

MISSION / VISION

To be judged THE BEST at placing people into work they WANT and CAN DO by both clients and candidates - the agency that changes perceptions of recruitment by daring to be different and being passionate about people.

BEST WORKPLACE FACTORS

WELL BEING
MY COMPANY
GIVE SOMETHING BACK

GRADUATE VACANCIES

No graduate vacancies have been indicated.

EMPLOYEE COMMENTS

"Great locations and offices, good facilities, great perks & genuine desire to improve people's wellbeing."

"This is a friendly, warm, honest place – it really does have a 'family' feel, fully supported by Senior Management."

"The fact that the company gives so much back, both to the employees and the wider community."

CONTACT DETAILS

The SG Group, Goodwin House, 5 Union Court, Richmond, Surrey TW9 1AA
Tel: 0208 3327656 www.the-sg-group.com

KEY

Holidays: Companies offering a minimum of 25 days annual leave
Maternity: Companies offering over Statutory Maternity Pay
Childcare: On-site nursery or vouchers
Women: At least 33% of senior managers are women
Long Service: 40% of employees with more than 5 years' service
Pensions: Companies offering a final salary or non-contributory/contributory pension scheme
Charity Activities: 10% of staff undertake charitable activities during business hours
Gym: On-site gym or subsidised gym memberships
Shares: Companies where employees are offered share options
Health Insurance: Full family cover

To find out more about this company visit www.bestcompaniesguide.co.uk

1000

<751

500

0

ones to watch

TOTEMIC

totemic

UK locations	E.Midlands
UK sites	4
Sector	Financial
Definition	Debt Solutions Company
How owned	Private
Founded	1993
Turnover	£9.6m
Profit	£0.4m
Staff	284
Average age	33
Male : Female	24 : 76
Earnings £35,000+	6%

BEST COMPANIES INDEX

★ ★ ★ best company 2007

EXTRAORDINARY

★ ★ ★

2007 BCI = 750.5

2006 BCI = 715.3 (★★)

WORKPLACE INSIGHTS

Totemic run a wellbeing scheme for their employees which encourages people to learn about and get involved with nutrition and exercise. Employees are able to take time off from work to attend the classes.

Totemic have adopted the charity Vitalise, who provide respite for disabled individuals & their carers. They gave them a lump sum of £20,000 in December 2005 and since then the organisation & individuals have organised many money raising events.

Totemic arrange a number of social events to encourage employees to spend time together out of work, often providing free food & a free bar for everyone. Events include a quiz night, a treasure hunt, a summer bbq and an Alton Towers trip.

MISSION / VISION

To inspire individuals to achieve personal greatness and make a difference. Although we are a business, it is fun, it is growth and it is extraordinary.

BEST WORKPLACE FACTORS

WELL BEING
GIVING SOMETHING BACK
MY TEAM

GRADUATE VACANCIES

No graduate vacancies have been indicated.

EMPLOYEE COMMENTS

"The company really cares for its employees."

"Our company not only sponsors a local charity but gives opportunities within the company for employees to sponsor theirs."

"Very friendly & sociable, lots of 'get togethers' so you can get to know other members of the company."

CONTACT DETAILS

Totemic Limited, Kempton House, Kempton Way, Dysart Road, Grantham, Lincolnshire NG31 7LE
Tel: 01476 539200 www.payplan.com

KEY

- **Holidays:** Companies offering a minimum of 25 days annual leave
- **Maternity:** Companies offering over Statutory Maternity Pay
- **Childcare:** On-site nursery or vouchers
- **Women:** At least 33% of senior managers are women
- **Long Service:** 40% of employees with more than 5 years' service
- **Pensions:** Companies offering a final salary or non-contributory/ contributory pension scheme
- **Charity Activities:** 10% of staff undertake charitable activities during business hours
- **Gym:** On-site gym or subsidised gym memberships
- **Shares:** Companies where employees are offered share options
- **Health Insurance:** Full family cover

To find out more about this company visit www.bestcompaniesguide.co.uk

VIRGIN RADIO

UK locations	London
UK sites	1
Sector	Media
Definition	Radio Broadcaster
How owned	Public (i.e. Stockmarket listed)
Founded	2000
Turnover	£22.4m
Profit	£4.9m
Staff	95
Average age	29
Male : Female	48 : 52
Earnings £35,000+	33%

BEST COMPANIES INDEX

best company 2007

EXTRAORDINARY

★ ★ ★

2007 BCI = 764.3

WORKPLACE INSIGHTS

Team interaction at Virgin Radio starts early, with new starter drinks sessions every month to welcome new team members. In addition, every six weeks some employees are chosen at random to go out to dinner fully funded by the company.

As part of staff meetings, Virgin Radio present "hidden hero" awards for those who have made an outstanding contribution or had great new ideas in the previous six months. The best are then picked for annual recognition at the company weekend away.

To support individual's personal development, use a blended learning approach with internal workshops, training courses & online tools. Their training forum runs a variety of business & personal development related workshops to address employee's needs.

MISSION / VISION

To become the world's most famous radio brand, by delivering the best in music based entertainment, by ensuring that we belong to the hearts and minds of our audiences, and by pioneering all future opportunities offered by a digitally advancing world.

BEST WORKPLACE FACTORS

MY TEAM
MY COMPANY
PERSONAL GROWTH

GRADUATE VACANCIES

No graduate vacancies have been indicated.

EMPLOYEE COMMENTS

"It's a vibrant and fun place to work with a great group of people who all get on with one another."

"The work culture and the people reflect the brand values perfectly in everything we do."

"Has an excellent working environment that allows me to learn & gain valued experience in my role."

CONTACT DETAILS

Virgin Radio 1 Golden Square, London W1F 9DJ
Tel: 0207 663 2000 www.virginradio.co.uk

KEY

- **Holidays:** Companies offering a minimum of 25 days annual leave
- **Maternity:** Companies offering over Statutory Maternity Pay
- **Childcare:** On-site nursery or vouchers
- **Women:** At least 33% of senior managers are women
- **Long Service:** 40% of employees with more than 5 years' service
- **Pensions:** Companies offering a final salary or non-contributory/ contributory pension scheme
- **Charity Activities:** 10% of staff undertake charitable activities during business hours
- **Gym:** On-site gym or subsidised gym memberships
- **Shares:** Companies where employees are offered share options
- **Health Insurance:** Full family cover

To find out more about this company visit www.bestcompaniesguide.co.uk

W L GORE & ASSOCIATES (UK)

Creative Technologies Worldwide

UK locations	Scotland
UK sites	3
Sector	Manufacturing
Definition	Gore-Tex Manufacturer
How owned	Private
Founded	1958
Turnover	£106.4m
Profit	Not disclosed
Staff	454
Average age	42
Male : Female	64 : 36
Earnings £35,000+	not disclosed

BEST COMPANIES INDEX

best company 2007

EXTRAORDINARY

★ ★ ★

2007 BCI = 830.7

2006 BCI = 858.5

WORKPLACE INSIGHTS

Each individual chooses a person to help them grow & develop, maximise their potential as individuals (they call it a sponsor - which can be described as a mentor & a lot more!). There is expectation on them as Associates to grow & increase their contribution.

W L Gore do what they can to share their ideas with other bodies (schools), where time permits. They have their second apprentice - following a successful first and offer work experience/placement for school children.

W L Gore employees are decision makers with responsibility & accountability for success. They gain satisfaction from having the freedom to help each other grow and develop in an environment where mistakes and risk taking are necessary for their collective advancement.

MISSION / VISION

Vision: The world leader in understanding and applying PTFE. An innovative responsive supplier of unique high quality high value products worldwide. An exciting and rewarding place to work. A legal ethical and fair Enterprise.
Mission: Make money and have fun.

BEST WORKPLACE FACTORS

PERSONAL GROWTH
GIVING SOMETHING BACK
MY COMPANY

GRADUATE VACANCIES

No graduate vacancies have been indicated.

EMPLOYEE COMMENTS

"It allows you to grow professionally as well as personally."

"This is an organisation which is sympathetic to the needs of the family."

"There is a strong emphasis on working hard and having fun."

CONTACT DETAILS

W L Gore & Associates (UK), Kirkton South Road, Kirkton Campus, Livingston, Scotland EH54 7BT
Tel: 01506 460123 www.gore.com

KEY

Holidays: Companies offering a minimum of 25 days annual leave
Maternity: Companies offering over Statutory Maternity Pay
Childcare: On-site nursery or vouchers
Women: At least 33% of senior managers are women
Long Service: 40% of employees with more than 5 years' service
Pensions: Companies offering a final salary or non-contributory/ contributory pension scheme
Charity Activities: 10% of staff undertake charitable activities during business hours
Gym: On-site gym or subsidised gym memberships
Shares: Companies where employees are offered share options
Health Insurance: Full family cover

To find out more about this company visit www.bestcompaniesguide.co.uk

XIROS

UK locations	Yorks & Humber, E.Midlands
UK sites	2
Sector	Pharmaceutical
Definition	Medical Device Manufacturer
How owned	Private
Founded	1984
Turnover	Not disclosed
Profit	Not disclosed
Staff	67
Average age	40
Male : Female	30 : 70
Earnings £35,000+	10%

BEST COMPANIES INDEX

best company 2007

EXTRAORDINARY ★ ★ ★

2007 BCI = 752.3

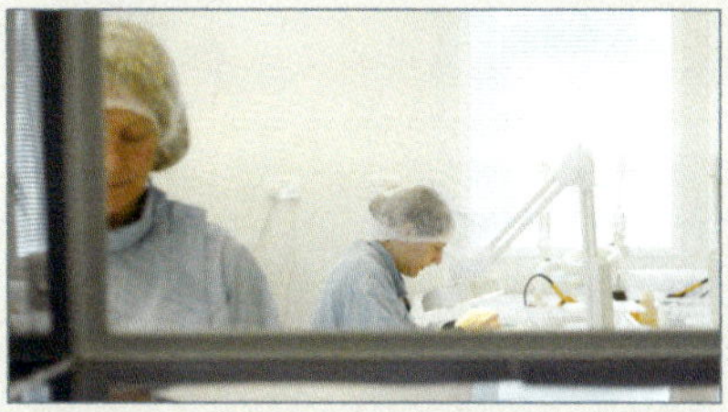

WORKPLACE INSIGHTS

Xiros has a charities committee made up of representatives from staff. The committee is responsible for allocating an annual fund to charity & for organising fundraising activities. Recently, organised a Macmillan coffee morning and on-line auction.

Xiros offers employees the choice of a working pattern to suit their lifestyle providing it fits in with the needs of the business. Employees are able to select their own flexible working policy and dependant on their role, some can work from home.

Xiros has recently implemented a flexible benefits scheme. Core benefits are complemented by a choice of flexible benefits including private healthcare, permanent health insurance, additional pension contributions and additional holiday.

MISSION / VISION

A World Class Company: Xiros plc is fully committed to achieving excellence in its business operations, including the design and manufacture of medical devices, and their continual improvement. We want to be among the very best in our industry.

BEST WORKPLACE FACTORS

GIVING SOMETHING BACK
WELL BEING
FAIR DEAL

GRADUATE VACANCIES

R&D.

EMPLOYEE COMMENTS

"Due to the strong ethical ethos the working environment is extremely pleasant to work in."

"The whole ethos of the company is involved with the genuine well being of the staff and the management team work hard to ensure this."

"Good package of rewards and benefits."

CONTACT DETAILS

Xiros plc, Springfield House, Whitehouse Lane, Leeds LS19 7UE
Tel: 0113 238 7200 www.xiros.eu.com

KEY

Holidays: Companies offering a minimum of 25 days annual leave
Maternity: Companies offering over Statutory Maternity Pay
Childcare: On-site nursery or vouchers
Women: At least 33% of senior managers are women
Long Service: 40% of employees with more than 5 years' service
Pensions: Companies offering a final salary or non-contributory/ contributory pension scheme
Charity Activities: 10% of staff undertake charitable activities during business hours
Gym: On-site gym or subsidised gym memberships
Shares: Companies where employees are offered share options
Health Insurance: Full family cover

“PLEASURE IN THE JOB PUTS

PERFECTION

IN THE WORK”

ARISTOTLE

OUTSTANDING

ALLSOP

UK locations	National
UK sites	4
Sector	Property
Definition	Property Consultants
How owned	Partnership/Limited Liability Partnership
Founded	1906
Turnover	£31.6m
Profit	£13.1m
Staff	156
Average age	34
Male : Female	59 : 41
Earnings £35,000+	54%

BEST COMPANIES INDEX

OUTSTANDING ★ ★

2007 BCI = 728.9

WORKPLACE INSIGHTS

Allsop has a committee called The Link Group. It consists of staff from all levels and provides employees with an opportunity to give feedback regarding what they would like to do in terms of social events. These range from bowling events to dinner dances.

Allsop offer a range of excellent benefits including free private health care and life insurance. Within the Allsop pension scheme the company will contribute 6.5% to the employees' 2.5%.

All members of the team work in an open plan office. The senior partner sits in the middle of the floor and is in prime position to talk to everyone. There are numerous one to one and team lunches where team members can interact with managers.

MISSION / VISION

Our vision is to remain an independent, friendly, and open partnership and operate only in those markets where the firm can excel and remain profitable.

BEST WORKPLACE FACTORS

MY TEAM
FAIR DEAL
MY MANAGER

GRADUATE VACANCIES

Across all professional areas of the business.

EMPLOYEE COMMENTS

"The people are all very nice, respectful, professional, good fun and enjoy their work."

"Keen to reward those deserving just reward."

"Positive senior management."

CONTACT DETAILS

Allsop, 27 Soho Square, London W1D 3AY
Tel: 0207 4376977 www.allsop.co.uk

KEY

- **Holidays:** Companies offering a minimum of 25 days annual leave
- **Maternity:** Companies offering over Statutory Maternity Pay
- **Childcare:** On-site nursery or vouchers
- **Women:** At least 33% of senior managers are women
- **Long Service:** 40% of employees with more than 5 years' service
- **Pensions:** Companies offering a final salary or non-contributory/contributory pension scheme
- **Charity Activities:** 10% of staff undertake charitable activities during business hours
- **Gym:** On-site gym or subsidised gym memberships
- **Shares:** Companies where employees are offered share options
- **Health Insurance:** Full family cover

AMERICAN EXPRESS SERVICES EUROPE

UK locations	National
UK sites	100
Sector	Financial
Definition	Travel & Financial Services
How owned	Public (i.e. stock market listed)
Founded	1850
Turnover	£2,098m
Profit	Not disclosed
Staff	6314
Average age	36
Male : Female	42 : 58
Earnings £35,000+	31%

BEST COMPANIES INDEX

best company 2007

OUTSTANDING

★ ★

2007 BCI = 709.2

2006 BCI = 684.8 (★)

1000

709>

ones to watch

500

0

WORKPLACE INSIGHTS

American Express functional leaders are given a departmental budget from which social events are funded.

AMEX hold skip level reviews throughout the year where leaders invite employees of all levels to an informal breakfast or lunch session to discuss business issues & workplace matters. Employees are invited & encouraged to raise any general ideas, thoughts or concerns they have.

American Express has an Employee Assistance Programme (EAP) which gives confidential advice and support to employees whenever needed, e.g. individual treatment, bullying & harassment. In addition to this they have flexible working.

MISSION / VISION

To become the worlds most respected service brand.

BEST WORKPLACE FACTORS

MY TEAM
MY MANAGER
WELL BEING

GRADUATE VACANCIES

Technologies, Customer Service, Project Management, Sales, Marketing, Finance.

EMPLOYEE COMMENTS

"Great team work, everyone's always there to help you and advise you appropriately."

"My manager takes an interest in everyone's work and personal life so you never feel like you are just a number."

"My company/leaders are caring and flexible when private/personal issues arise."

CONTACT DETAILS

American Express Services Europe, Portland House, Stag Place, London SW1E 5BZ
Tel: 0207 8345555 www.americanexpress.co.uk

KEY

- **Holidays:** Companies offering a minimum of 25 days annual leave
- **Maternity:** Companies offering over Statutory Maternity Pay
- **Childcare:** On-site nursery or vouchers
- **Women:** At least 33% of senior managers are women
- **Long Service:** 40% of employees with more than 5 years' service
- **Pensions:** Companies offering a final salary or non-contributory/ contributory pension scheme
- **Charity Activities:** 10% of staff undertake charitable activities during business hours
- **Gym:** On-site gym or subsidised gym memberships
- **Shares:** Companies where employees are offered share options
- **Health Insurance:** Full family cover

AMGEN UK AND IRELAND

UK locations	London, E.England
UK sites	2
Sector	Marketing & Sales
Definition	Sales & Marketing in Biotechnology
How owned	Public (i.e. stock market listed)
Founded	1989
Turnover	Not disclosed
Profit	Not disclosed
Staff	130
Average age	36
Male : Female	44 : 56
Earnings £35,000+	70%

BEST COMPANIES INDEX

★ ★ best company 2007

OUTSTANDING

★ ★

2007 BCI = 698.5

2006 BCI = 734.0 (★★)

WORKPLACE INSIGHTS

Amgen is a values driven company that walks its talk. The leaders are role models for the company values which are communicated to employees via the company website, through performance reviews, inductions and posters and visual aids.

Amgen run the "3 L forum" - Listen, Learn and Lunch. This is a public meeting for all staff to attend where they are able to interact with managers and leaders and raise any concerns they have.

Staff at Amgen have an Individual Development Plan. These plans are collated into an organisational training programme. Managers have access to an international development programme in Brussels. An online learning management system for e-learning is available to all employees.

MISSION / VISION

To serve patients.

BEST WORKPLACE FACTORS

MY COMPANY
MY MANAGER
PERSONAL GROWTH

GRADUATE VACANCIES

No graduate vacancies have been indicated.

EMPLOYEE COMMENTS

"We have clear values which are worked and adhered to every day."

"Managers care about their teams and everyone is made to feel equal."

"Excellent training courses for people motivated to learn."

CONTACT DETAILS

Amgen UK and Ireland, 240 The Science Park, Milton Rd, Cambridge CB4 0WD
Tel: 01223 420305 www.amgen.co.uk

KEY

Holidays: Companies offering a minimum of 25 days annual leave
Maternity: Companies offering over Statutory Maternity Pay
Childcare: On-site nursery or vouchers
Women: At least 33% of senior managers are women
Long Service: 40% of employees with more than 5 years' service
Pensions: Companies offering a final salary or non-contributory/ contributory pension scheme
Charity Activities: 10% of staff undertake charitable activities during business hours
Gym: On-site gym or subsidised gym memberships
Shares: Companies where employees are offered share options
Health Insurance: Full family cover

1000 <699 500 0 ones to watch

To find out more about this company visit www.bestcompaniesguide.co.uk

AMNESTY INTERNATIONAL

UK locations	National
UK sites	4
Sector	Not for Profit
Definition	Human Rights Movement
How owned	Trust/Employee owned/Mutual
Founded	1961
Turnover	£20.1m
Profit	Not disclosed
Staff	146
Average age	36
Male : Female	35 : 65
Earnings £35,000+	34%

BEST COMPANIES INDEX

best company 2007

OUTSTANDING

★ ★

2007 BCI = 718.4

WORKPLACE INSIGHTS

The Human Rights Action Centre which is the name of Amnesty's Head Office is also a venue for Human Rights events and exhibitions. Staff & volunteers have the opportunity to attend these events thereby enriching their understanding of Human Rights Issues.

People at Amnesty enjoy challenge and are articulate. This attribute enables Amnesty to take forward Organisational Development ideas in a robust and constructive manner.

Amnesty promotes diversity in many ways, for example staff are permitted 2 additional day's leave for religious reasons. They also have a prayer room. Amnesty have established a Diversity and Equalities group that is seeking to embed it's work into the organisational systems and ways of working.

MISSION / VISION

Our vision is of a world in which every person enjoys all the human rights enshrined in the Universal Declaration of Human Rights and other international human rights standards.

BEST WORKPLACE FACTORS

GIVING SOMETHING BACK
MY COMPANY
FAIR DEAL

GRADUATE VACANCIES

No graduate vacancies have been indicated.

EMPLOYEE COMMENTS

"The Human Rights Actions Centre is a great working environment & centre for the public to share our Human Rights work."

"Commitment of people who work here & willingness to take forward ideas in a positive and learning spirit."

"Our work is really important & the organisation treats us with respect as individuals."

CONTACT DETAILS

Amnesty International, Human Rights Action Centre, 17-25 New Inn Yard, London EC2A 3EA
Tel: 0207 0331500 www.amnesty.org.uk

KEY

- **Holidays:** Companies offering a minimum of 25 days annual leave
- **Maternity:** Companies offering over Statutory Maternity Pay
- **Childcare:** On-site nursery or vouchers
- **Women:** At least 33% of senior managers are women
- **Long Service:** 40% of employees with more than 5 years' service
- **Pensions:** Companies offering a final salary or non-contributory/ contributory pension scheme
- **Charity Activities:** 10% of staff undertake charitable activities during business hours
- **Gym:** On-site gym or subsidised gym memberships
- **Shares:** Companies where employees are offered share options
- **Health Insurance:** Full family cover

1000

718>

★ ★ ★

★ ★

★

ones to watch

500

0

To find out more about this company visit www.bestcompaniesguide.co.uk

ARUP

ARUP

UK locations	National
UK sites	18
Sector	Engineering
Definition	Design Engineering Consultants
How owned	Trust/Employee owned/Mutual
Founded	1946
Turnover	£244.2m
Profit	Not disclosed
Staff	3,356
Average age	37
Male : Female	71 : 29
Earnings £35,000+	45%

BEST COMPANIES INDEX

best company 2007

OUTSTANDING ★ ★

2007 BCI = 727.6

2006 BCI = 696.3 (★)

<728

WORKPLACE INSIGHTS

This year, Arup have chosen to raise money for WaterAid. Events held include world water day; world toilet day; a Mexican wave and they even sold a glass of water on eBay for £100! They have also printed Arup calendars & WaterAid Christmas cards.

At Arup, in-house training courses are available as face-to-face learning activities and alongside a raft of e-learning activities which are available to all staff. They also have a range of training programmes registered with professional institutions.

Arup's values and philosophy were set out by their founder, Sir Ove Arup, in his keynote speech in 1970. This 'Key Speech', contains the firm's vision statement and is still a huge part of the firm today - every employee receives a copy when they join the firm.

MISSION / VISION

We shape a better world.

BEST WORKPLACE FACTORS

GIVING SOMETHING BACK
PERSONAL GROWTH
MY COMPANY

GRADUATE VACANCIES

Engineering and relevant specialist backgrounds.

EMPLOYEE COMMENTS

"The aims and goals of the company are positive and make a difference in the world."

"Always opportunities to receive further training and Arup do invest a lot in their employees."

"An organisation driven by it's values, not dominated by profit, but by quality, innovation and 'making a difference'."

CONTACT DETAILS

Arup, 13 Fitzroy Street, London W1T 4BQ
Tel: 0207 6361531 www.arup.com

KEY

- **Holidays:** Companies offering a minimum of 25 days annual leave
- **Maternity:** Companies offering over Statutory Maternity Pay
- **Childcare:** On-site nursery or vouchers
- **Women:** At least 33% of senior managers are women
- **Long Service:** 40% of employees with more than 5 years' service
- **Pensions:** Companies offering a final salary or non-contributory/contributory pension scheme
- **Charity Activities:** 10% of staff undertake charitable activities during business hours
- **Gym:** On-site gym or subsidised gym memberships
- **Shares:** Companies where employees are offered share options
- **Health Insurance:** Full family cover

To find out more about this company visit www.bestcompaniesguide.co.uk

Assael

ASSAEL ARCHITECTURE

UK locations	London
UK sites	1
Sector	Professional Services
Definition	Architects
How owned	Private
Founded	1994
Turnover	£4.8m
Profit	£0.5m
Staff	70
Average age	33
Male : Female	56 : 44
Earnings £35,000+	49%

BEST COMPANIES INDEX

best company 2007

OUTSTANDING

★ ★

2007 BCI = 727.0

2006 BCI = 771.8 (★★★)

727>

ones to watch

WORKPLACE INSIGHTS

Assael is dedicated to looking after the wellbeing of their employees. They spend more on entertaining the staff than they do on entertaining their clients.

Assael encourage new experiences and are happy to go above and beyond the standard holiday allowance so staff can visit far away places.

Assael contributes up to 1% of turnover or 10% of profit in match funding for money raised by staff for charitable causes.

MISSION / VISION

To be a specialist practice of tenacious research led architects, renowned for exceptional quality in design, reliability in execution, & integrity in all matters.

BEST WORKPLACE FACTORS

WELL BEING
FAIR DEAL
GIVING SOMETHING BACK

GRADUATE VACANCIES

Architectural.

EMPLOYEE COMMENTS

"I think that Assael really cares about the well being of the staff."

"They genuinely seem to support me, trust me and rely on me to do my job and enjoy my job."

"Assael have a strong commitment to charitable work and dedicate time and resources to this."

CONTACT DETAILS

Assael Architecture, Studio 13 50, Carnwath Road, London SW6 3EG
Tel: 0207 7367744 www.assael.co.uk

KEY

- **Holidays:** Companies offering a minimum of 25 days annual leave
- **Maternity:** Companies offering over Statutory Maternity Pay
- **Childcare:** On-site nursery or vouchers
- **Women:** At least 33% of senior managers are women
- **Long Service:** 40% of employees with more than 5 years' service
- **Pensions:** Companies offering a final salary or non-contributory/ contributory pension scheme
- **Charity Activities:** 10% of staff undertake charitable activities during business hours
- **Gym:** On-site gym or subsidised gym memberships
- **Shares:** Companies where employees are offered share options
- **Health Insurance:** Full family cover

1000

★ ★ ★

<734 ★ ★

★

ones to watch

500

0

BADENOCH & CLARK

Badenoch & Clark
A member of MPS Group International

UK locations	National
UK sites	17
Sector	Recruitment
Definition	Professional Services Recruitment
How owned	Private
Founded	1980
Turnover	£196.2m
Profit	£54.5m
Staff	515
Average age	28
Male : Female	45 : 55
Earnings £35,000+	17%

BEST COMPANIES INDEX

best company 2007 ★ ★

OUTSTANDING
★ ★
2007 BCI = 734.2
2006 BCI = 755.7 (★★★)

WORKPLACE INSIGHTS

The company spent a phenomenal £672,016 on employee social events last year which demonstrates a commitment to the personal relationships fostered at work.

Badenoch and Clark have regular "workforce forums" where, in small groups, individuals are encouraged to raise & discuss issues relating to working life. There are weekly and monthly meetings where each manager discusses operational goals, initiatives & progress with their own teams.

Badenoch and Clark have monthly evenings out hosted by members of the senior leader team to celebrate success with top performers. They have an "open door" policy with business leaders working day to day amongst the business with constant informal contact.

MISSION / VISION

To be known for developing strong & mutually beneficial relationships through the application of expertise & knowledge.

BEST WORKPLACE FACTORS

MY TEAM
MY MANAGER
LEADERSHIP

GRADUATE VACANCIES

Graduate Recruitment Consultant.

EMPLOYEE COMMENTS

"A big emphasis is placed on the team and helping your colleagues."

"The managers are people who have worked here for a long time & truly believe in the company, what it stands for and where the future will take it."

"The desire of the senior management to really lead the way."

CONTACT DETAILS

Badenoch & Clark, Millennium Bridge House, 2 Lambeth Hill, London EC4V 4BG
Tel: 0207 5830073 www.badenochandclark.com

KEY

Holidays: Companies offering a minimum of 25 days annual leave
Maternity: Companies offering over Statutory Maternity Pay
Childcare: On-site nursery or vouchers
Women: At least 33% of senior managers are women
Long Service: 40% of employees with more than 5 years' service
Pensions: Companies offering a final salary or non-contributory/ contributory pension scheme
Charity Activities: 10% of staff undertake charitable activities during business hours
Gym: On-site gym or subsidised gym memberships
Shares: Companies where employees are offered share options
Health Insurance: Full family cover

To find out more about this company visit www.bestcompaniesguide.co.uk

BDO

BDO STOY HAYWARD

BDO Stoy Hayward

UK locations	National
UK sites	15
Sector	Professional Services
Definition	Accountants
How owned	Partnership/LLP
Founded	1903
Turnover	£288m
Profit	£70.2m
Staff	3,027
Average age	34
Male : Female	52 : 48
Earnings £35,000+	47%

BEST COMPANIES INDEX

best company 2007

OUTSTANDING ★ ★

2007 BCI = 722.5

2006 BCI = 731.9 (★★)

WORKPLACE INSIGHTS

BDO Stoy Hayward employees had the opportunity to pose questions about anything they wanted, to Managing Partner Jeremy Newman during his annual roadshow. He then selected random questions from a box & answered them. All submitted questions were placed on BDO's intranet site with answers.

BDO's goal is to develop more structured, focused & business-driven learning & development solutions. One way they have done this is by introducing a policy allowing employees additional days for volunteering during the year if a personal development opportunity is involved.

BDO Stoy Hayward recently launched an interactive, on-line flexible working toolkit which gives advice to employees & managers on aspects of flexible working, making a request & interactive salary modeler.

MISSION / VISION

Fundamental purpose: To maintain a sustainably profitable secure distinctive & independent firm. To provide a challenging environment and superior rewards to attract develop & retain the best people. To build our reputation for quality work & excellent service delivered through strong personal relationships.

BEST WORKPLACE FACTORS

LEADERSHIP
PERSONAL GROWTH
WELL BEING

GRADUATE VACANCIES

Business Assurance, Business Restructuring Forensic Services Management, Consulting, Tax.

EMPLOYEE COMMENTS

"The managing partner lives and breathes the values."

"There are good opportunities to progress, with the organisation supporting individuals wishing to study for higher or further qualifications."

"BDO positively encourages a great work/life balance."

CONTACT DETAILS

BDO STOY HAYWARD, 8 Baker Street, London W1U 3LL
Tel: 0207 4865888 www.bdo.co.uk

1000

723>

ones to watch

500

0

KEY

Holidays: Companies offering a minimum of 25 days annual leave

Maternity: Companies offering over Statutory Maternity Pay

Childcare: On-site nursery or vouchers

Women: At least 33% of senior managers are women

Long Service: 40% of employees with more than 5 years' service

Pensions: Companies offering a final salary or non-contributory/ contributory pension scheme

Charity Activities: 10% of staff undertake charitable activities during business hours

Gym: On-site gym or subsidised gym memberships

Shares: Companies where employees are offered share options

Health Insurance: Full family cover

To find out more about this company visit www.bestcompaniesguide.co.uk

BELRON

UK locations	London, S.East
UK sites	2
Sector	Business Services
Definition	Vehicle Glass Services
How owned	Private
Founded	1984
Turnover	Not disclosed
Profit	Not disclosed
Staff	66
Average age	40
Male : Female	58 : 42
Earnings £35,000+	85%

BEST COMPANIES INDEX

best company 2007

OUTSTANDING ★ ★

2007 BCI = 735.7

WORKPLACE INSIGHTS

Belron has a charismatic leader in Chief Executive Gary Lubner. Gary is a familiar face around the office and he and his executive team are ambassadors of the Belron values.

The senior manager is coached to develop a working style that produces the optimum environment for his/her team members.

Belron is a successful business that employs high achieving individuals but at the same time manages to retain its 'heart'.

MISSION / VISION

Vision: To be the international leader in providing services and solutions for the repair and replacement of automotive glass.
Mission: The world's first choice for automotive glass repair and replacement.

BEST WORKPLACE FACTORS

LEADERSHIP
MY MANAGER
MY COMPANY

GRADUATE VACANCIES

No graduate vacancies have been indicated.

EMPLOYEE COMMENTS

"A Leader that has a clear vision of where the business is going in the long term."

"Managers spend a lot of time coaching and guiding their teams, listening to them and valuing their input."

"I cannot think of a better place to work. It is a unique workplace and one of which I am hugely proud."

CONTACT DETAILS

BELRON, The King's Observatory, Old Deer Park, Richmond, Surrey TW9 2AZ
Tel: 0208 3320099 www.belron.com

KEY

- **Holidays:** Companies offering a minimum of 25 days annual leave
- **Maternity:** Companies offering over Statutory Maternity Pay
- **Childcare:** On-site nursery or vouchers
- **Women:** At least 33% of senior managers are women
- **Long Service:** 40% of employees with more than 5 years' service
- **Pensions:** Companies offering a final salary or non-contributory/contributory pension scheme
- **Charity Activities:** 10% of staff undertake charitable activities during business hours
- **Gym:** On-site gym or subsidised gym memberships
- **Shares:** Companies where employees are offered share options
- **Health Insurance:** Full family cover

To find out more about this company visit www.bestcompaniesguide.co.uk

BENFIELD

BENFIELD

UK locations	London
UK sites	1
Sector	Financial
Definition	Reinsurance & Risk Intermediary
How owned	Public (i.e. stock market listed)
Founded	1973
Turnover	£324.1m
Profit	£53.8m
Staff	802
Average age	39
Male : Female	68 : 32
Earnings £35,000+	71%

BEST COMPANIES INDEX

best company 2007

OUTSTANDING ★ ★

2007 BCI = 701.4

701>

ones to watch

WORKPLACE INSIGHTS

Benfield Group allocates all team members a 'Lifestyle Allowance' in January each year. The purpose of the allowance is for team members to use it to support a hobby, pastime, or for their wellbeing for example, belonging to a sports club or learning a language.

Benfield's Chief Executive and Members of the Board operate an 'Open Door' policy by working in glass fronted offices in the middle of the main broking floor, encouraging team members to approach them with any queries they may have.

Benfield offer many different benefits ranging from performance related pay, free private health care and life cover. They also have merit bonuses which are awarded on the recommendation of a Team Leader to recognise outstanding individual contribution or new ideas.

MISSION / VISION

Our "Business Aim" is 'To lead the market in complex risk solutions through innovation expertise and excellence'.

BEST WORKPLACE FACTORS

WELL BEING
LEADERSHIP
FAIR DEAL

GRADUATE VACANCIES

Production & Marketing, Group Services, IT & Remetrics.

EMPLOYEE COMMENTS

"Going from full time to part time the company were very understanding and helpful."

"The enthusiasm of the Chief Executive for the business can be very inspiring."

"The benefits provided by the company are second to none in the industry."

CONTACT DETAILS

Benfield, 55 Bishopsgate, London EC2N 3BD
Tel: 0207 5787000 www.benfieldgroup.com

KEY

- **Holidays:** Companies offering a minimum of 25 days annual leave
- **Maternity:** Companies offering over Statutory Maternity Pay
- **Childcare:** On-site nursery or vouchers
- **Women:** At least 33% of senior managers are women
- **Long Service:** 40% of employees with more than 5 years' service
- **Pensions:** Companies offering a final salary or non-contributory/ contributory pension scheme
- **Charity Activities:** 10% of staff undertake charitable activities during business hours
- **Gym:** On-site gym or subsidised gym memberships
- **Shares:** Companies where employees are offered share options
- **Health Insurance:** Full family cover

To find out more about this company visit www.bestcompaniesguide.co.uk

BETTYS & TAYLORS OF HARROGATE

UK locations	Yorks & Humber
UK sites	7
Sector	Manufacturing
Definition	Manufacturing bakery & retail
How owned	Private
Founded	1962
Turnover	£57.5m
Profit	£6.7m
Staff	1,076
Average age	35
Male : Female	36 : 64
Earnings £35,000+	6%

BEST COMPANIES INDEX

best company 2007

OUTSTANDING ★ ★

2007 BCI = 701.9

2006 BCI = 718.0 (★★)

WORKPLACE INSIGHTS

Bettys & Taylors are committed to being a company that shapes and builds a better world by 'giving back' 5% of their profits to local and overseas communities.

Bettys & Taylors have a whole set of policies for Family Friendly Leave to help support both planned and unplanned circumstances. Within these policies, Bettys & Taylors treat each person's situation individually and work to find a mutually agreeable solution.

Bettys & Taylors is a family business, and their Chairman, Jonathan Wild, is the great-nephew of the founder of Bettys. Jonathan has worked for the business for 30 years and the average length of service for the Trading Board is 16 years.

MISSION / VISION

We're still a family business, and continue to stay true to Frederick's founding principles, that everything should be 'fresh and dainty', and that 'if we want things just right we have to do them ourselves'.

BEST WORKPLACE FACTORS

GIVING SOMETHING BACK
WELL BEING
LEADERSHIP

GRADUATE VACANCIES

Supply Chain, Purchasing Research & Development, Human Resources, IT.

EMPLOYEE COMMENTS

"I think that it is also great that we try and do our best to help charities by having charity events."

"Caring about staff both in and out of work hours where possible."

"Jonathan Wild who leads this organisation is a good man, a good leader, and takes an interest in the people around him."

CONTACT DETAILS

Bettys & Taylors of Harrogate, 1 Parliament Street, Harrogate, North Yorkshire HG1 2QU
Tel: 01423 877300 www.bettysandtaylors.co.uk

KEY

Holidays: Companies offering a minimum of 25 days annual leave
Maternity: Companies offering over Statutory Maternity Pay
Childcare: On-site nursery or vouchers
Women: At least 33% of senior managers are women
Long Service: 40% of employees with more than 5 years' service
Pensions: Companies offering a final salary or non-contributory/ contributory pension scheme
Charity Activities: 10% of staff undertake charitable activities during business hours
Gym: On-site gym or subsidised gym memberships
Shares: Companies where employees are offered share options
Health Insurance: Full family cover

BIRKETT LONG

UK locations	E.Anglia
UK sites	2
Sector	Law
Definition	Legal Firm
How owned	Partnership/LLP
Founded	1989
Turnover	£7.7m
Profit	£1.2m
Staff	153
Average age	42
Male : Female	27 : 73
Earnings £35,000+	26%

BEST COMPANIES INDEX

OUTSTANDING

★ ★

2007 BCI = 724.5

WORKPLACE INSIGHTS

Birkett Long offer new employees an extensive induction process that ensures each member of staff has a good working knowledge of the firm & its practices and procedures before starting. It also includes follow up meetings after six weeks & three months.

Birkett Long has maintained a "family" atmosphere where the needs of the individual are of paramount importance. They offer employee health checks & those who need support or counselling receive these in a caring & sharing environment.

All Birkett Long Employees are encouraged to contribute their own ideas to ways of improving the business and ideas which are implemented are rewarded. The annual Business Plan is written "bottom up" and all members of staff have an opportunity to contribute their ideas.

MISSION / VISION

The leading full service firm in Essex: the firm of first choice for clients, colleagues, and business partners.

BEST WORKPLACE FACTORS

PERSONAL GROWTH
WELL BEING
LEADERSHIP

GRADUATE VACANCIES

Trainee Solicitors.

EMPLOYEE COMMENTS

"The management are very understanding of all individuals and will invest in further training and education to develop staff."

"Birkett Long cares about its employees and they encourage work life balance."

"We have good leadership and we know where we are headed."

CONTACT DETAILS

Birkett Long, Essex House, 42 Crouch Street, Colchester, Essex CO3 3HH
Tel: 01206 217300 www.birkettlong.co.uk

KEY

- **Holidays:** Companies offering a minimum of 25 days annual leave
- **Maternity:** Companies offering over Statutory Maternity Pay
- **Childcare:** On-site nursery or vouchers
- **Women:** At least 33% of senior managers are women
- **Long Service:** 40% of employees with more than 5 years' service
- **Pensions:** Companies offering a final salary or non-contributory/ contributory pension scheme
- **Charity Activities:** 10% of staff undertake charitable activities during business hours
- **Gym:** On-site gym or subsidised gym memberships
- **Shares:** Companies where employees are offered share options
- **Health Insurance:** Full family cover

To find out more about this company visit www.bestcompaniesguide.co.uk

1000

725>

500

0

ones to watch

BITE COMMUNICATIONS

UK locations	London
UK sites	1
Sector	Media
Definition	PR Agency
How owned	Public (i.e. stock market listed)
Founded	1981
Turnover	£4.3m
Profit	Not disclosed
Staff	61
Average age	29
Male : Female	38 : 62
Earnings £35,000+	44%

BEST COMPANIES INDEX

OUTSTANDING ★ ★

2007 BCI = 718.2

WORKPLACE INSIGHTS

Bite holds monthly company meetings where the managers update the general team on company financials and the company direction.

Bite listen to what their staff and management team would like to see incorporated into the training programme. They also provide employees with £100 a year to put towards personal development. Employees have used this to learn a new language, singing lessons, personal training sessions, wine tasting.

One of Bite's values is to be united. They focus on the team first, then the individual and think of themselves as a united force and a collection of people working towards a common goal.

MISSION / VISION

Vision: To build a strong globally positioned consultancy that is regarded as a trusted communication advisor to C-level executives within its client base.
Mission: We help build brands through fearless and boundless communications.

BEST WORKPLACE FACTORS

MY MANAGER
PERSONAL GROWTH
MY TEAM

GRADUATE VACANCIES

Consumer B2B Non-media PR.

EMPLOYEE COMMENTS

"We have a good manager who is willing to listen, work with the team whilst also motivating individuals."

"Bite is a great place to learn and they always encourage training and give you the room to grow as an individual."

"There are a lot of people with strong friendships across the organisation."

CONTACT DETAILS

Bite Communications, The Character Building, 41b Beavor Lane, London W6 9BL
Tel: 0208 7411123 www.bitepr.com

KEY

Holidays: Companies offering a minimum of 25 days annual leave
Maternity: Companies offering over Statutory Maternity Pay
Childcare: On-site nursery or vouchers
Women: At least 33% of senior managers are women
Long Service: 40% of employees with more than 5 years' service
Pensions: Companies offering a final salary or non-contributory/contributory pension scheme
Charity Activities: 10% of staff undertake charitable activities during business hours
Gym: On-site gym or subsidised gym memberships
Shares: Companies where employees are offered share options
Health Insurance: Full family cover

To find out more about this company visit www.bestcompaniesguide.co.uk

BRABNERS CHAFFE STREET

brabners chaffe street

UK locations	N.West
UK sites	3
Sector	Law
Definition	Legal Firm
How owned	Partnership/LLP
Founded	1887
Turnover	£21m
Profit	Not disclosed
Staff	348
Average age	36
Male : Female	41 : 59
Earnings £35,000+	40%

BEST COMPANIES INDEX

best company 2007

OUTSTANDING

★ ★

2007 BCI = 698.8

2006 BCI = 669.8 (★)

WORKPLACE INSIGHTS

Brabners Chaffe Street believe in sharing their success with every single employee. This is carried out annually via the staff bonus fund which means that every member of the firm shares in the success.

There are many different initiatives in place at Brabners that support employees' work life balance & general well-being. The recently appointed social committee promote a rich social events programme including regular rounders & cricket matches & a regional five kilometre race.

Brabner's Staff Development Strategy makes use of programmed learning & development activities as well as opportunities for learning which the everyday work activities of the firm provide. They are developing on-line training packages for employees to use.

MISSION / VISION

To continue to build on our high quality client base and to be the law firm of choice in the corporate and larger private client sector in the North West for owners and executives wanting a pragmatic partner led service.

BEST WORKPLACE FACTORS

FAIR DEAL
WELL BEING
PERSONAL GROWTH

GRADUATE VACANCIES

Law.

EMPLOYEE COMMENTS

"The firm invest funds and time to train staff and give back to the staff financial rewards in line with the success of the firm."

"Essentially the firm cares about its staff and their individual well being and involvement in the firm."

"Strong encouragement and support for personal growth and development, both in training and in practical experience."

CONTACT DETAILS

Brabners Chaffe Street, 1 Dale Street, Liverpool L2 2ET
Tel: 0151 6003000 www.brabnerschaffestreet.com

KEY

- **Holidays:** Companies offering a minimum of 25 days annual leave
- **Maternity:** Companies offering over Statutory Maternity Pay
- **Childcare:** On-site nursery or vouchers
- **Women:** At least 33% of senior managers are women
- **Long Service:** 40% of employees with more than 5 years' service
- **Pensions:** Companies offering a final salary or non-contributory/ contributory pension scheme
- **Charity Activities:** 10% of staff undertake charitable activities during business hours
- **Gym:** On-site gym or subsidised gym memberships
- **Shares:** Companies where employees are offered share options
- **Health Insurance:** Full family cover

1000

699>

ones to watch

500

0

To find out more about this company visit www.bestcompaniesguide.co.uk

BRAMALL CONSTRUCTION

Bramall CONSTRUCTION

<701

UK locations	N.West, Yorks & Humber
UK sites	60
Sector	Construction
Definition	Social Housing Contractor
How owned	Private
Founded	1979
Turnover	£179.9m
Profit	£8.8m
Staff	1,253
Average age	37
Male : Female	86 : 14
Earnings £35,000+	8%

BEST COMPANIES INDEX

best company 2007

OUTSTANDING ★ ★

2007 BCI = 700.9

2006 BCI = 694.2 (★)

WORKPLACE INSIGHTS

Bramall provide fresh fruit in the offices. Staff have the option to join in group or individual sessions to enable them to stop smoking.

The company believes the people are their greatest asset and their actions speak for themselves.

Bramall work with the Outward Bound Trust to engage with schools to deliver a Team Challenge Day and a residential course in Cumbria.

MISSION / VISION

Vision: To be the market leader in community regeneration throughout the north.
Mission: Leaders in community regeneration delivering partnering excellence.

BEST WORKPLACE FACTORS

WELL BEING
MY COMPANY
GIVING SOMETHING BACK

GRADUATE VACANCIES

Construction, IT, Quantity Surveying.

EMPLOYEE COMMENTS

"Benefits, pay and holidays are all good as well as BUPA health checks, bonus and car."

"Variety of people we work with, different clients, tenants and different team members from site to site."

"Willing to support charitable causes."

CONTACT DETAILS

Bramall Construction, The Lighthouse, The Quays, Salford M50 3BF
Tel: 0161 8766000 www.bramall.com

KEY

- **Holidays:** Companies offering a minimum of 25 days annual leave
- **Maternity:** Companies offering over Statutory Maternity Pay
- **Childcare:** On-site nursery or vouchers
- **Women:** At least 33% of senior managers are women
- **Long Service:** 40% of employees with more than 5 years' service
- **Pensions:** Companies offering a final salary or non-contributory/ contributory pension scheme
- **Charity Activities:** 10% of staff undertake charitable activities during business hours
- **Gym:** On-site gym or subsidised gym memberships
- **Shares:** Companies where employees are offered share options
- **Health Insurance:** Full family cover

BRISTOL-MYERS SQUIBB

Bristol-Myers Squibb

UK locations	London
UK sites	1
Sector	Pharmaceutical
Definition	Pharma Sales & Marketing
How owned	Private
Founded	1989
Turnover	Not disclosed
Profit	Not disclosed
Staff	481
Average age	38
Male : Female	44 : 56
Earnings £35,000+	70%

BEST COMPANIES INDEX

best company 2007

OUTSTANDING

★ ★

2007 BCI = 730.0

WORKPLACE INSIGHTS

As part of Leadership Training at Bristol Myers Squibb, all managers of people are trained on Feedback and Coaching Skills which encourages managers to give and receive face to face feedback from their direct reports and colleagues.

Bristol Myers Squibb offers employees a range of learning and development options including in-house and external customised classroom training programmes, bespoke assessment centres and 'Plateau' – an e-learning platform that offers a wide range of on-line modules.

All Bristol Myers Squibb employees are entitled to a wide range of benefits including profit and performance related pay, free private healthcare, subsidised on site alternative therapies and a discount shopping and vouchers scheme.

MISSION / VISION

Vision: "We pledge - to our patients and customers, to our employees & partners, to our shareholders & neighbours, & to the world we serve - to act on our belief that the priceless ingredient of every product is the honour and integrity of its maker".
Mission: To Extend and Enhance Human Life.

BEST WORKPLACE FACTORS

MY MANAGER
PERSONAL GROWTH
FAIR DEAL

GRADUATE VACANCIES

Finance, Sales, Medical, HR.

EMPLOYEE COMMENTS

"There is a strong management team in place who are fair and hard working."

"Good training allowing new recruits time to bond and get to know each other."

"The total reward package available to all employees is great and offers people many different types of support aside from just salary."

CONTACT DETAILS

Bristol-Myers Squibb Pharmaceutical, BMS House, Sanderson Road, Uxbridge Business Park, Uxbridge UB8 1DH
Tel: 01895 523000 www.b-ms.co.uk

KEY

- **Holidays:** Companies offering a minimum of 25 days annual leave
- **Maternity:** Companies offering over Statutory Maternity Pay
- **Childcare:** On-site nursery or vouchers
- **Women:** At least 33% of senior managers are women
- **Long Service:** 40% of employees with more than 5 years' service
- **Pensions:** Companies offering a final salary or non-contributory/ contributory pension scheme
- **Charity Activities:** 10% of staff undertake charitable activities during business hours
- **Gym:** On-site gym or subsidised gym memberships
- **Shares:** Companies where employees are offered share options
- **Health Insurance:** Full family cover

BROADWAY HOMELESSNESS AND SUPPORT

UK locations	London, S.East
UK sites	8
Sector	Charity
Definition	Homeless Support Services
How owned	Trust/Employee owned/Mutual
Founded	2002
Turnover	£9.3m
Profit	Not disclosed
Staff	166
Average age	36
Male : Female	37 : 63
Earnings £35,000+	13%

BEST COMPANIES INDEX

best company 2007

OUTSTANDING ★ ★

2007 BCI = 711.1

2006 BCI = 677.3 (★)

<711

WORKPLACE INSIGHTS

Broadway offers subsidised sports facilities and activities. It also has an employee assistance programme and free flu jabs.

Broadway has an active policy of running environmentally sound offices, they recycle waste paper, bottles etc. In all their offices, fair trade goods are purchased. Staff also donate clothes, to the Broadway Centre running a second hand store.

At Broadway staff can request to work in more flexible ways balancing their work/life commitments through our flexible working request policy. This has led to active participation in part time working at all levels of the organisation.

MISSION / VISION

Vision: Every single person finds and keeps a home.
Mission: We support, guide and influence whatever it takes, however long it takes.

BEST WORKPLACE FACTORS

FAIR DEAL
GIVING SOMETHING BACK
WELL BEING

GRADUATE VACANCIES

Services, supported housing and hostels.

EMPLOYEE COMMENTS

"I feel that I am supported in my role and the benefits and working conditions are excellent."

"The work the organisation does for the homeless and less privileged people, makes this a great place to work."

"The perks of flexible working hours are excellent."

CONTACT DETAILS

Broadway Homelessness and Support, Chaucer House, White Hart Yard, London SE1 1NX
Tel: 020 7089 9500 www.broadwaylondon.org

KEY

- **Holidays:** Companies offering a minimum of 25 days annual leave
- **Maternity:** Companies offering over Statutory Maternity Pay
- **Childcare:** On-site nursery or vouchers
- **Women:** At least 33% of senior managers are women
- **Long Service:** 40% of employees with more than 5 years' service
- **Pensions:** Companies offering a final salary or non-contributory/ contributory pension scheme
- **Charity Activities:** 10% of staff undertake charitable activities during business hours
- **Gym:** On-site gym or subsidised gym memberships
- **Shares:** Companies where employees are offered share options
- **Health Insurance:** Full family cover

BYBOX

ByBox distribution revolution

UK locations	National
UK sites	13
Sector	Logistics/Wholesale/Distribution
Definition	Field Based Logistics
How owned	Private
Founded	2000
Turnover	£12.3m
Profit	Not disclosed
Staff	95
Average age	35
Male : Female	68 : 32
Earnings £35,000+	22%

BEST COMPANIES INDEX

best company 2007

OUTSTANDING ★ ★

2007 BCI = 702.5

WORKPLACE INSIGHTS

ByBox make sure the executive team is accessible, in terms of availability and openness to discuss anything. They have no assigned offices and no reserved parking spaces (except for visiting customers and disabled), which breeds a culture of openness and democracy.

ByBox have an employee awards system that always results in an extra day's holiday and a weekend away for the employee and their partner. They have awards such as the Phil Collins award for outstanding achievement (against all odds).

Bybox make sure that all employees take their holidays even if it is inconvenient for the company. They also have a ban on weekend work as they believe weekends are precious and should be protected.

MISSION / VISION

At ByBox we always expect to win. Our customers expect to win by using us. Our people expect to win by working with us and our shareholders expect to win by investing in us. ByBox. Expect to win.

BEST WORKPLACE FACTORS

LEADERSHIP
MY COMPANY
FAIR DEAL

GRADUATE VACANCIES

No graduate vacancies have been indicated.

EMPLOYEE COMMENTS

"The CEOs - they are passionate, hard working, approachable and fun. Their enthusiasm and drive for success is infectious."

"The company is extremely good at rewarding success and hard work."

"Rewards and praise for success."

CONTACT DETAILS

ByBox, Merlin House, Grove Technology Park, Wantage, Oxon OX12 9FA
Tel: 01235 767706 www.bybox.com

KEY

- **Holidays:** Companies offering a minimum of 25 days annual leave
- **Maternity:** Companies offering over Statutory Maternity Pay
- **Childcare:** On-site nursery or vouchers
- **Women:** At least 33% of senior managers are women
- **Long Service:** 40% of employees with more than 5 years' service
- **Pensions:** Companies offering a final salary or non-contributory/ contributory pension scheme
- **Charity Activities:** 10% of staff undertake charitable activities during business hours
- **Gym:** On-site gym or subsidised gym memberships
- **Shares:** Companies where employees are offered share options
- **Health Insurance:** Full family cover

To find out more about this company visit www.bestcompaniesguide.co.uk

1000 — 703> — 500 — 0

ones to watch

1000

<706

ones to watch

500

0

CALL CONNECTION

CallConnection
People you can talk to... Technology you can trust

UK locations	E.Anglia
UK sites	1
Sector	Financial - Insurance
Definition	Call Transfer Agency
How owned	Private
Founded	2001
Turnover	£25.1m
Profit	£2.9m
Staff	257
Average age	30
Male : Female	49 : 51
Earnings £35,000+	11%

BEST COMPANIES INDEX

best company 2007

OUTSTANDING

★ ★

2007 BCI = 706.1

WORKPLACE INSIGHTS

In addition to substantial bonuses and rewards and a huge range of financial benefits including a share option scheme and life assurance for all employees, Call Connection provide "Minister of Fun" to organise social events sometimes spending up to £1000 per employee.

They provide reflexology and professional chair massage sessions during work time at a subsidised rate for employees. Also, Company Medical Officer (Doctor) is available free of charge to any member of staff who has work related stress issues or needs medical advice.

At Call Connection, a Director and a Senior Manager host a weekly Tea Party with a group of approximately 10 employees. Tea, coffee, scones and sandwiches are provided to spark the chatter and 'get to know each other' rapport.

MISSION / VISION

To be recognised as a unique forward thinking call transfer provider operating leading edge convergence technology. We are committed to delivering an exceptional standard of service to our business partners & maintaining flexible working practices to maximise business opportunities.

BEST WORKPLACE FACTORS

FAIR DEAL
WELL BEING
LEADERSHIP

GRADUATE VACANCIES

No graduate vacancies have been indicated.

EMPLOYEE COMMENTS

"Benefits and bonus schemes are second to none."

"A forward thinking company which has the welfare of its staff in mind as well as profit."

"I have never experienced a Managing Director who wants to give so much to his staff, right from the top to bottom."

CONTACT DETAILS

Call Connection, Saxon House, Cromwell Square, Ipswich, Suffolk IP1 1TS
Tel: 01473 212569 www.callconnection.com

KEY

Holidays: Companies offering a minimum of 25 days annual leave
Maternity: Companies offering over Statutory Maternity Pay
Childcare: On-site nursery or vouchers
Women: At least 33% of senior managers are women
Long Service: 40% of employees with more than 5 years' service
Pensions: Companies offering a final salary or non-contributory/contributory pension scheme
Charity Activities: 10% of staff undertake charitable activities during business hours
Gym: On-site gym or subsidised gym memberships
Shares: Companies where employees are offered share options
Health Insurance: Full family cover

Rewarding Learning

CCEA

UK locations	N.Ireland
UK sites	3
Sector	Education
Definition	Education Advice and Provision
How owned	Government
Founded	1994
Turnover	£27.8m
Profit	Not disclosed
Staff	336
Average age	40
Male : Female	42 : 58
Earnings £35,000+	24%

BEST COMPANIES INDEX

best company 2007

OUTSTANDING

★ ★

2007 BCI = 703.2

703>

ones to watch

WORKPLACE INSIGHTS

At CCEA they have developed a transparent Learning and Development environment that allows employees to see the benefits of undertaking development activity.

CCEA has an exceptional record for supporting charities through fundraising. Supported charities are aligned to the nature of our business and cover a local, national and international dimension for example The African Schools Trust.

CCEA are keen to provide everyone with opportunities to climb the managerial ladder and prepare those with high potential for senior positions and offer a range of structured Leadership and Management Development programmes.

MISSION / VISION

To enable the full potential of all learners to be achieved and recognised.

BEST WORKPLACE FACTORS

PERSONAL GROWTH
GIVING SOMETHING BACK
MY MANAGER

GRADUATE VACANCIES

No graduate vacancies have been indicated.

EMPLOYEE COMMENTS

"The development scheme actively assists employees to develop skills & lead to promotion."

"Belief that we are doing something of real value in improving education."

"My manager communicates policy and strategy, plans, objectives and targets to all staff."

CONTACT DETAILS

CCEA, 29 Clarendon Road, Clarendon Dock, Belfast BT1 3BG
Tel: 02890 261200 www.ccea.org.uk

KEY

- **Holidays:** Companies offering a minimum of 25 days annual leave
- **Maternity:** Companies offering over Statutory Maternity Pay
- **Childcare:** On-site nursery or vouchers
- **Women:** At least 33% of senior managers are women
- **Long Service:** 40% of employees with more than 5 years' service
- **Pensions:** Companies offering a final salary or non-contributory/ contributory pension scheme
- **Charity Activities:** 10% of staff undertake charitable activities during business hours
- **Gym:** On-site gym or subsidised gym memberships
- **Shares:** Companies where employees are offered share options
- **Health Insurance:** Full family cover

To find out more about this company visit www.bestcompaniesguide.co.uk

1000

<699

ones to watch

500

0

COBRA BEER

UK locations	London
UK sites	1
Sector	Consumer Goods
Definition	Beer and wine sales
How owned	Private
Founded	1989
Turnover	£29.7m
Profit	£0.6m
Staff	95
Average age	33
Male : Female	71 : 29
Earnings £35,000+	20%

BEST COMPANIES INDEX

best company 2007

OUTSTANDING

★ ★

2007 BCI = 698.8

2006 BCI = 716.8 (★★)

WORKPLACE INSIGHTS

Cobra Beer has various awards that it gives out to staff. In particular the GEM award: awarded to employees who demonstrate outstanding effort or achievement & really 'go the extra mile'. Each wins £100 & there is no limit to the number of GEMs won each month.

Cobra Beer have department away days in addition to their company away day. This year, the entire Marketing department enjoyed a two-day trip to Berlin where they brainstormed new ideas and worked on the marketing plan.

The Company is distributing 5,000 Safe-Flo bottle caps to young people at university student unions, pubs, clubs and bars. The device is for personal use and is placed over the top of drinks bottles, it can be reused and prevents the spiking of drinks.

MISSION / VISION

Vision: To aspire and achieve against all odds with integrity.
Mission: To brew the finest ever Indian beer and to make it a global beer brand.

BEST WORKPLACE FACTORS

MY COMPANY
MY TEAM
GIVING SOMETHING BACK

GRADUATE VACANCIES

No graduate vacancies have been indicated.

EMPLOYEE COMMENTS

"There is a huge amount of goodwill for the brand & quality & story and you feel proud to be part of it all."

"It is an innovative and welcoming environment with vibrant staff."

"Everyone loves and believes in the brand which makes for a positive place to be."

CONTACT DETAILS

Cobra Beer, Alexander House, 14-16 Peterborough Road, London SW6 3BN
Tel: 0207 7316200 www.cobrabeer.com

KEY

Holidays: Companies offering a minimum of 25 days annual leave
Maternity: Companies offering over Statutory Maternity Pay
Childcare: On-site nursery or vouchers
Women: At least 33% of senior managers are women
Long Service: 40% of employees with more than 5 years' service
Pensions: Companies offering a final salary or non-contributory/ contributory pension scheme
Charity Activities: 10% of staff undertake charitable activities during business hours
Gym: On-site gym or subsidised gym memberships
Shares: Companies where employees are offered share options
Health Insurance: Full family cover

To find out more about this company visit www.bestcompaniesguide.co.uk

CONSUMER CREDIT COUNSELLING SERVICE

CONSUMER CREDIT Counselling Service
A Registered Charity

UK locations	National
UK sites	9
Sector	Charity
Definition	Debt Advice Charity
How owned	Trust/Employee owned/Mutual
Founded	1993
Turnover	Not disclosed
Profit	Not disclosed
Staff	525
Average age	34
Male : Female	36 : 65
Earnings £35,000+	3%

BEST COMPANIES INDEX

best company 2007

OUTSTANDING ★ ★

2007 BCI = 710.5

WORKPLACE INSIGHTS

The Consumer Credit Counselling Service offer compressed week working for staff in various departments & also piloted a Banked Hours scheme which enables staff to work additional hours during busy times of the month, to be taken as time off in quieter periods.

The Consumer Credit Counselling Service has a charity fundraising committee that organises fundraising days such as Children in Need and Comic Relief. All staff get involved & participate in events throughout these days, taking time away from work.

A Reward and Recognition scheme is in place including 'Employee of the Month' awards and team lunches. This aids morale within each department as well as illustrating the organisation's appreciation for the hard work and commitment shown by employees.

MISSION / VISION

To become acknowledged as the leading provider of free debt advice in the UK; recognised for utilising technology & efficient processes to introduce innovative services, deliver effective repayment solutions & provide best advice in all cases.

BEST WORKPLACE FACTORS

WELL BEING
GIVING SOMETHING BACK
MY TEAM

GRADUATE VACANCIES

No graduate vacancies have been indicated.

EMPLOYEE COMMENTS

"I have never in my working life come to work on Monday morning with a smile on my face, but I do here."

"I feel like I'm really making a difference in my job, which benefits many members of the public."

"The office atmosphere is fantastic; staff are really friendly and eager to help you."

CONTACT DETAILS

Consumer Credit Counselling Service, Wade House, Merrion Centre, Leeds LS2 8NG
Tel: 0113 2970121 www.cccs.co.uk

KEY

Holidays: Companies offering a minimum of 25 days annual leave

Maternity: Companies offering over Statutory Maternity Pay

Childcare: On-site nursery or vouchers

Women: At least 33% of senior managers are women

Long Service: 40% of employees with more than 5 years' service

Pensions: Companies offering a final salary or non-contributory/ contributory pension scheme

Charity Activities: 10% of staff undertake charitable activities during business hours

Gym: On-site gym or subsidised gym memberships

Shares: Companies where employees are offered share options

Health Insurance: Full family cover

To find out more about this company visit www.bestcompaniesguide.co.uk

1000

711>

ones to watch

500

0

1000

ones to watch

<726

500

0

COOPER PARRY

COOPER ■ PARRY

UK locations	E.Midlands
UK sites	3
Sector	Business Services
Definition	Business Consultants
How owned	Partnership/LLP
Founded	1850
Turnover	Not disclosed
Profit	Not disclosed
Staff	252
Average age	35
Male : Female	44 : 56
Earnings £35,000+	29%

BEST COMPANIES INDEX

best company 2007

OUTSTANDING

★ ★

2007 BCI = 725.8

WORKPLACE INSIGHTS

Cooper Parry offer employees bespoke & innovative Learning & Development initiatives including CPBAT (Cooper Parry Business Adviser Training), Managers' Routeways, individual Coaching, Mentoring Programmes, Study Policy, Psychometric profiling & structured promotion process.

During Induction Day, Chief Executive Jeremy Bowler meets all the new starters and introduces them to the history of the organisation as well as the importance of the Vision and Values. He formally welcomes each employee to Cooper Parry.

At Cooper Parry, employees have regular one-to-one sessions with their managers in which feedback is seen as a two way process. In addition, people management forms an important part of the assessment of all managers in the company.

MISSION / VISION

To be the preferred business adviser to privately owned businesses in the region.

BEST WORKPLACE FACTORS

PERSONAL GROWTH
LEADERSHIP
MY MANAGER

GRADUATE VACANCIES

Corporate Relationship Group, Business Tax ,Private Clients, Marketing.

EMPLOYEE COMMENTS

"Cooper Parry are genuinely interested in you as a person & actively promote from within the firm."

"Those in leadership roles always make time for you if you need it."

"You automatically feel welcome when you start working here. Everyone is friendly, approachable & open."

CONTACT DETAILS

Cooper Parry, 3 Centro Place, Pride Park, Derby DE24 8RF
Tel: 01332 295544 www.cooperparry.com

KEY

Holidays: Companies offering a minimum of 25 days annual leave

Maternity: Companies offering over Statutory Maternity Pay

Childcare: On-site nursery or vouchers

Women: At least 33% of senior managers are women

Long Service: 40% of employees with more than 5 years' service

Pensions: Companies offering a final salary or non-contributory/ contributory pension scheme

Charity Activities: 10% of staff undertake charitable activities during business hours

Gym: On-site gym or subsidised gym memberships

Shares: Companies where employees are offered share options

Health Insurance: Full family cover

To find out more about this company visit www.bestcompaniesguide.co.uk

COUNTRYWIDE LEGAL INDEMNITIES

UK locations	E.Anglia
UK sites	1
Sector	Financial - Insurance
Definition	Legal Indemnity Intermediary
How owned	Private
Founded	1994
Turnover	£6.3m
Profit	£0.5m
Staff	74
Average age	31
Male : Female	36 : 64
Earnings £35,000+	20%

BEST COMPANIES INDEX

best company 2007

OUTSTANDING

★ ★

2007 BCI = 721.6

722>

ones to watch

WORKPLACE INSIGHTS

Countrywide are very aware that staff have a life outside of work and make an effort to make sure that they do not develop a long hours culture. They actively discourage overtime and offer flexible working where possible.

Countrywide offers a generous pension with a minimum of 8% company contributions. They also offer private health insurance for all staff as well as spouse and dependents. They have 6 monthly bonuses and have a £1000 attendance allowance.

All Countrywide's Senior Management sit in the same open plan area as staff so they are a visible & approachable presence. The Managers actively seek the views of all staff by "walking the floor" on a frequent basis to talk to staff about work.

MISSION / VISION

Countrywide Legal Indemnities is the UK's leading legal indemnity intermediary and specifically endorsed by the Law Society. Our philosophy is to put speed, professionalism and quality before everything else.

BEST WORKPLACE FACTORS

WELL BEING
FAIR DEAL
MY MANAGER

GRADUATE VACANCIES

No graduate vacancies have been indicated.

EMPLOYEE COMMENTS

"I believe that Countrywide is an organisation that genuinely cares for its employees."

"The salary package and benefits system is excellent and very fair."

"The managers and the owner of the company really care about their staff."

CONTACT DETAILS

Countrywide Legal Indemnities, St Crispins, Duke Street, Norwich, Norfolk NR3 1PD
Tel: 01603 617617 www.countrywidelegal.co.uk

KEY

- **Holidays:** Companies offering a minimum of 25 days annual leave
- **Maternity:** Companies offering over Statutory Maternity Pay
- **Childcare:** On-site nursery or vouchers
- **Women:** At least 33% of senior managers are women
- **Long Service:** 40% of employees with more than 5 years' service
- **Pensions:** Companies offering a final salary or non-contributory/contributory pension scheme
- **Charity Activities:** 10% of staff undertake charitable activities during business hours
- **Gym:** On-site gym or subsidised gym memberships
- **Shares:** Companies where employees are offered share options
- **Health Insurance:** Full family cover

1000

<716

ones to watch

500

0

DAVIS TATE
ESTATE AGENTS

DAVIS TATE ESTATE AGENTS

UK locations	S.East
UK sites	9
Sector	Property
Definition	Estate Agents
How owned	Private
Founded	1991
Turnover	Not disclosed
Profit	Not disclosed
Staff	62
Average age	36
Male : Female	34 : 66
Earnings £35,000+	24%

BEST COMPANIES INDEX

best company 2007

OUTSTANDING

★ ★

2007 BCI = 716.2

WORKPLACE INSIGHTS

The leadership team at Davis Tate seek to interact with the employees by working closely as integral members of small teams; through on going management training, both internal and external and through a variety of social and leisure activities.

Davis Tate seek to meet each employee's individual development aspirations by identifying their changing needs and providing a structured framework for them to grow into.

A range of social events are organised for employees at Davis Tate to encourage team work and help them to relax and unwind. These events include a Barn Dance, a River Cruise and 5 a side football to encourage employees to keep fit.

MISSION / VISION

To become the agent of first choice in the Reading area.

BEST WORKPLACE FACTORS

FAIR DEAL
PERSONAL GROWTH
WELL BEING

GRADUATE VACANCIES

No graduate vacancies have been indicated.

EMPLOYEE COMMENTS

"We are all genuinely committed to providing the best service that we can."

"Great opportunities for individuals like myself to progress within the company."

"I believe that I am treated well and respected by the company."

CONTACT DETAILS

Davis Tate Estate Agents, 46 Bell Street, Henley on Thames, Oxon RG9 2BG
Tel: 01491 412345 www.davistate.com

KEY

- **Holidays:** Companies offering a minimum of 25 days annual leave
- **Maternity:** Companies offering over Statutory Maternity Pay
- **Childcare:** On-site nursery or vouchers
- **Women:** At least 33% of senior managers are women
- **Long Service:** 40% of employees with more than 5 years' service
- **Pensions:** Companies offering a final salary or non-contributory/contributory pension scheme
- **Charity Activities:** 10% of staff undertake charitable activities during business hours
- **Gym:** On-site gym or subsidised gym memberships
- **Shares:** Companies where employees are offered share options
- **Health Insurance:** Full family cover

To find out more about this company visit www.bestcompaniesguide.co.uk

DELOITTE

Deloitte.

UK locations	National
UK sites	22
Sector	Professional Services
Definition	Accountants
How owned	Partnership/LLP
Founded	1899
Turnover	£1,599.40m
Profit	£460.9m
Staff	10,767
Average age	32
Male : Female	57 : 43
Earnings £35,000+	53%

BEST COMPANIES INDEX

best company 2007

OUTSTANDING ★ ★

2007 BCI = 725.4

2006 BCI = 703.0 (★★)

WORKPLACE INSIGHTS

Deloitte place significant investment in developing employees. Many partners invest time supporting & facilitating internal development programmes & purpose built development centres help identify development needs & to ensure these needs are being addressed.

As part of their flexible benefits package which includes holidays, private healthcare & dental insurance, they also offer a bike for work scheme which gives employees between 30 & 50% discount if they get a bike with the purpose of commuting to work.

CEO John Connolly engages recent & younger partners in special dialogue sessions which provides an opportunity for him to be linked into all levels & parts of the organisation. In a similar way Directors are linked with people further down the organisation.

MISSION / VISION

Vision: To become the standard of excellence.
Mission: To be recognised as the pre-eminent & most trusted professional services firm famous for the calibre of our people & respected for the exceptional quality of our work.

BEST WORKPLACE FACTORS

PERSONAL GROWTH
FAIR DEAL
LEADERSHIP

GRADUATE VACANCIES

Accounting, Tax, Consulting, Corporate Finance, IT & Actuarial.

EMPLOYEE COMMENTS

"Having a good appraisal & mentoring scheme means there is someone you can approach for advice."

"They strongly value employees & have effective systems in place to ensure achievements are rewarded."

"I find the leadership of the firm inspiring & the team spirit within the firm is something special."

CONTACT DETAILS

Deloitte, Stonecutter Court, 1 Stonecutter Street, London EC4A 3TR
Tel: 0207 9363000 www.deloitte.co.uk

KEY

- **Holidays:** Companies offering a minimum of 25 days annual leave
- **Maternity:** Companies offering over Statutory Maternity Pay
- **Childcare:** On-site nursery or vouchers
- **Women:** At least 33% of senior managers are women
- **Long Service:** 40% of employees with more than 5 years' service
- **Pensions:** Companies offering a final salary or non-contributory/ contributory pension scheme
- **Charity Activities:** 10% of staff undertake charitable activities during business hours
- **Gym:** On-site gym or subsidised gym memberships
- **Shares:** Companies where employees are offered share options
- **Health Insurance:** Full family cover

ELAND CABLES

ELAND CABLES

<738

UK locations	National
UK sites	3
Sector	Industrial
Definition	Electrical Cable Supplier
How owned	Private
Founded	1975
Turnover	£27.5m
Profit	£1.5m
Staff	65
Average age	38
Male : Female	77 : 23
Earnings £35,000+	18%

BEST COMPANIES INDEX

best company 2007

OUTSTANDING

★ ★

2007 BCI = 737.7

WORKPLACE INSIGHTS

Employees are able to work on a 1 to 1 basis with managers/project leaders on challenging tasks, which means that they are throughly supported. There is mentoring from senior management to emerging talent.

Eland offer free private health care and subsidised gym membership. On the last Friday at the end of every month everyone's hard work is rewarded with cheese and wine.

Eland Cables has masseurs who come in once a month in order to give anyone who fancies a bit of revitalisation a massage. Working hours have also been negotiated for those who have a long drive into work, providing an early start so they can miss the traffic.

MISSION / VISION

To combine global reach, with the ability to understand the specific needs of each market, each channel, and each individual customer we serve. At Eland Cables we are all unique individuals united by our common commitment to meet or exceed the customer's expectation... each time every time.

BEST WORKPLACE FACTORS

LEADERSHIP
FAIR DEAL
WELL BEING

GRADUATE VACANCIES

Purchasing, Sales, Marketing.

EMPLOYEE COMMENTS

"There is strong and very positive senior leadership, that inspires confidence."

"You really do feel like your efforts are rewarded. We have an excellent bonus scheme."

"The company spends great time and effort in providing after work activities and social enjoyment."

CONTACT DETAILS

Eland Cables, 120 Highgate Studios, 53-79 Highgate Road, London NW5 1TL
Tel: 0207 2418787 www.eland.co.uk

KEY

- **Holidays:** Companies offering a minimum of 25 days annual leave
- **Maternity:** Companies offering over Statutory Maternity Pay
- **Childcare:** On-site nursery or vouchers
- **Women:** At least 33% of senior managers are women
- **Long Service:** 40% of employees with more than 5 years' service
- **Pensions:** Companies offering a final salary or non-contributory/contributory pension scheme
- **Charity Activities:** 10% of staff undertake charitable activities during business hours
- **Gym:** On-site gym or subsidised gym memberships
- **Shares:** Companies where employees are offered share options
- **Health Insurance:** Full family cover

To find out more about this company visit www.bestcompaniesguide.co.uk

ELMWOOD BRANDING AND DESIGN CONSULTANCY

UK locations	National
UK sites	3
Sector	Business Services
Definition	Branding and Design
How owned	Private
Founded	1989
Turnover	£5.2m
Profit	£0.7m
Staff	59
Average age	32
Male : Female	51 : 49
Earnings £35,000+	36%

BEST COMPANIES INDEX

best company 2007

OUTSTANDING

★ ★

2007 BCI = 703.3

2006 BCI = 663.3 (★)

703>

ones to watch

WORKPLACE INSIGHTS

Elmwood hold a variety of social events including pool nights, a Christmas Party, a pumpkin carving competition, Friday lunchtime drinks at the pub and cinema nights.

Elmwood thank and praise employees publicly when they have delivered "over and above the call of duty". They also give personal presents to individuals when appropriate. Elmwood try to personalise all praise, rather than standardise.

Personal Growth has always been a priority at Elmwood but over the last 2 years they have created & implemented a formal appraisal system which has proved very useful for people to chart their progress against objectives both personally and professionally.

MISSION / VISION

Vision: To be famous for our Authentic Attitude.
Mission: To be the number 1 independent branding & design consultancy in the UK by 2007. To turn over £10m by 2007. To be famous for being creative & effective.

BEST WORKPLACE FACTORS

MY TEAM
MY COMPANY
PERSONAL GROWTH

GRADUATE VACANCIES

Design.

EMPLOYEE COMMENTS

"Everyone works well together and there's a sense of genuine care and team spirit."

"The people who work here really do care about the job & want to do their best for it which is great."

"They recognise the company is only as good as its people & have a programme of personal development."

CONTACT DETAILS

Elmwood Branding and Design Consultancy, Elmwood House, Ghyll Royd, Guiseley, Leeds LS20 9LT
Tel: 01943 870229 www.elmwood.co.uk

KEY

- **Holidays:** Companies offering a minimum of 25 days annual leave
- **Maternity:** Companies offering over Statutory Maternity Pay
- **Childcare:** On-site nursery or vouchers
- **Women:** At least 33% of senior managers are women
- **Long Service:** 40% of employees with more than 5 years' service
- **Pensions:** Companies offering a final salary or non-contributory/contributory pension scheme
- **Charity Activities:** 10% of staff undertake charitable activities during business hours
- **Gym:** On-site gym or subsidised gym memberships
- **Shares:** Companies where employees are offered share options
- **Health Insurance:** Full family cover

ENCAMS - ENVIRONMENTAL CAMPAIGNS

ENCAMS

UK locations	N.West
UK sites	1
Sector	Charity
Definition	National Environmental Charity
How owned	Trust/Employee owned/Mutual
Founded	1987
Turnover	£8.4m
Profit	Not disclosed
Staff	114
Average age	37
Male : Female	49 : 51
Earnings £35,000+	23%

BEST COMPANIES INDEX

best company 2007

OUTSTANDING ★ ★

2007 BCI = 712.1

2006 BCI = 700.7 (★★)

<712

WORKPLACE INSIGHTS

Even though ENCAMS are a Charity in their own right, each year the employees vote for a 'Charity of the Year'. In the past five years they have raised more than £6500 for a number of charities including Cancer Care, Project Child and the NSPCC.

The Performance Development Review process based on their 10 key Behaviours and 11 key Management Skills is unique to ENCAMS & enables frank, formal discussion & assessment. All members of Senior Management & senior regional employees undertake this process.

ENCAMS offers a massive 41 work life balance options / benefits to all employees. They are regarded as a national exemplar for work life balance and many other organisations have shared their expertise and learnt from them.

MISSION / VISION

Vision: To generate effective action by our targeted groups to achieve excellence in local environmental quality & reduce related anti-social behaviour.
Mission: Achieving excellence in local environmental quality.

BEST WORKPLACE FACTORS

GIVING SOMETHING BACK
MY MANAGER
WELL BEING

GRADUATE VACANCIES

No graduate vacancies have been indicated.

EMPLOYEE COMMENTS

"ENCAMS does some fantastic work that as an employee you feel very proud of."

"They are keen to listen to ideas from employees to improve the working environment and benefits."

"They genuinely try and ensure a positive work-life balance."

CONTACT DETAILS

ENCAMS - Environmental Campaigns, Elizabeth House, The Pier, Wigan WN3 4EX
Tel: 01942 612621 www.encams.org

KEY

- **Holidays:** Companies offering a minimum of 25 days annual leave
- **Maternity:** Companies offering over Statutory Maternity Pay
- **Childcare:** On-site nursery or vouchers
- **Women:** At least 33% of senior managers are women
- **Long Service:** 40% of employees with more than 5 years' service
- **Pensions:** Companies offering a final salary or non-contributory/ contributory pension scheme
- **Charity Activities:** 10% of staff undertake charitable activities during business hours
- **Gym:** On-site gym or subsidised gym memberships
- **Shares:** Companies where employees are offered share options
- **Health Insurance:** Full family cover

To find out more about this company visit www.bestcompaniesguide.co.uk

ERNST & YOUNG

Quality In Everything We Do

UK locations	National
UK sites	22
Sector	Professional Services
Definition	Accountants
How owned	Partnership/LLP
Founded	1989
Turnover	£1,130m
Profit	£294m
Staff	9,112
Average age	33
Male : Female	53 : 47
Earnings £35,000+	53%

BEST COMPANIES INDEX

best company 2007

OUTSTANDING ★ ★

2007 BCI = 733.8

2006 BCI = 676.0 (★)

734>

ones to watch

WORKPLACE INSIGHTS

All employees are encouraged to submit questions to the leadership team through the "Ask EY" feature of their intranet. All questions are logged & responded by a member of the leadership team, as well as being published on the site for employees to read.

Ernst and Young's people are rewarded not only through competitive salaries, special benefits like one-off extra holidays and regular social and team events, but also through their innovative recognition programme called the 'Best of the Best' rewards scheme.

Ernst and Young support and encourage their people in making a contribution to the community during working hours with paid time off, but also financially supporting the charities their people volunteer for outside of working hours.

MISSION / VISION

Our strategy is to achieve market leadership. This means leading in every market in which we choose to operate: geographies, sectors, or service lines.

BEST WORKPLACE FACTORS

LEADERSHIP
MY COMPANY
GIVING SOMETHING BACK

GRADUATE VACANCIES

Audit, Tax, Advisory, Corporate Finance, Technology & Security Risk Services, Business Risk Services, Actuarial.

EMPLOYEE COMMENTS

"Our Chairman has reinvigorated the organisation & his emphasis on living our values has struck a chord ."

"The firm is extremely supportive of its people and tries to accommodate the needs of everyone."

"We are encouraged to improve the world outside of work and are supported in doing so."

CONTACT DETAILS

Ernst & Young, 1 More London Place, London SE1 2AF
Tel: 0207 9512000 www.ey.com/uk

KEY

- **Holidays:** Companies offering a minimum of 25 days annual leave
- **Maternity:** Companies offering over Statutory Maternity Pay
- **Childcare:** On-site nursery or vouchers
- **Women:** At least 33% of senior managers are women
- **Long Service:** 40% of employees with more than 5 years' service
- **Pensions:** Companies offering a final salary or non-contributory/ contributory pension scheme
- **Charity Activities:** 10% of staff undertake charitable activities during business hours
- **Gym:** On-site gym or subsidised gym memberships
- **Shares:** Companies where employees are offered share options
- **Health Insurance:** Full family cover

1000

FABER MAUNSELL

FABER MAUNSELL | AECOM

UK locations	National
UK sites	33
Sector	Engineering
Definition	Professional Technical Consultants
How owned	Private
Founded	1944
Turnover	£159.8m
Profit	£10.5m
Staff	2,383
Average age	36
Male : Female	75 : 25
Earnings £35,000+	29%

<708

BEST COMPANIES INDEX

best company 2007

OUTSTANDING

★ ★

2007 BCI = 707.8

2006 BCI = 668.8 (★)

ones to watch

WORKPLACE INSIGHTS

The Faber Maunsell Training Academy delivers a framework of courses divided into 3 programmes, reflecting the different stages of career development, enabling employees to gain a level of competence in their current roles and to provide a foundation for their future development.

Faber Maunsell encourages employees to participate in charitable activities by giving them 2 or 3 days per year to undertake charitable activities during work hours such as painting a hostel for the homeless through the CRASH charity.

Employees at Faber Maunsell are able to buy and sell holiday and choose from a range of insurance and other benefits to suit their needs via a flexible benefits scheme – 'FlexAbility'.

500

MISSION / VISION

Vision: To consistently deliver outstanding solutions that create a better world in which to work & live.
Mission: To apply our collective expertise to make great things happen through innovation teamwork and trust.

BEST WORKPLACE FACTORS

PERSONAL GROWTH
GIVING SOMETHING BACK
FAIR DEAL

GRADUATE VACANCIES

Buildings Services & Structural Environment, Transportation, Planning & Engineering.

EMPLOYEE COMMENTS

"Good attitudes towards training and developing its employees' personal skills."

"I'm proud of the way the company cares about the local community and are actively involved with local schools."

"They strive to give you the best opportunities in life and trust your judgement 100%."

CONTACT DETAILS

Faber Maunsell, Marlborough House, Upper Marlborough Road, St Albans, Hertfordshire AL1 UT
Tel: 0208 7845784 www.fabermaunsell.com

KEY

Holidays: Companies offering a minimum of 25 days annual leave
Maternity: Companies offering over Statutory Maternity Pay
Childcare: On-site nursery or vouchers
Women: At least 33% of senior managers are women
Long Service: 40% of employees with more than 5 years' service
Pensions: Companies offering a final salary or non-contributory/contributory pension scheme
Charity Activities: 10% of staff undertake charitable activities during business hours
Gym: On-site gym or subsidised gym memberships
Shares: Companies where employees are offered share options
Health Insurance: Full family cover

0

To find out more about this company visit www.bestcompaniesguide.co.uk

FAIRBAIRN PRIVATE BANK

fairbairn PRIVATE BANK

UK locations	Jersey, Isle of Man
UK sites	2
Sector	Financial - Banks/Building Societies
Definition	Wealth Management Services
How owned	Public (i.e. stock market listed)
Founded	1987
Turnover	£13.3m
Profit	£5.6m
Staff	116
Average age	38
Male : Female	40 : 60
Earnings £35,000+	26%

BEST COMPANIES INDEX

★ ★ best company 2007

OUTSTANDING

★ ★

2007 BCI = 722.7

2006 BCI = 688.4 (★)

723>

WORKPLACE INSIGHTS

Fairbairn Private Bank employees work in modern, open plan air conditioned offices with a fully equipped staff kitchen and lounge area with TV and free drinks. There is also a roof garden where employees can enjoy their breaks.

They support the Young Enterprise Isle of Man's 'Learn to Earn' programme at a local high school. The programme helps students to explore the concepts of success, independence & employment and shows the importance of education in preparing them for the future.

Managing Director Gregory Horton participates in the formal induction training session undertaken for all new employees and has an informal coffee and chat with all new employees within 3 months of them joining.

MISSION / VISION

Vision: To service our clients better than any other financial services organisation.
Mission: To promote & secure throughout the company high standards of service integrity & competence in order to provide quality products & services to our clients & provide for employee growth & corporate development.

BEST WORKPLACE FACTORS

WELL BEING
GIVING SOMETHING BACK
LEADERSHIP

GRADUATE VACANCIES

Marketing & Private Banking.

EMPLOYEE COMMENTS

"The people I work with are fantastic and really care for each other's well being."

"I see how much they give back to society & am proud to say that all our efforts are fully supported."

"The leadership of Greg Horton is superb his appreciation of the staff is unparalleled."

CONTACT DETAILS

Fairbairn Private Bank, St Mary's Court, 20 Hill Street, Douglas, Isle of Man IM1 1EU
Tel: 01624 645000 www.fairbairnpb.com

KEY

- **Holidays:** Companies offering a minimum of 25 days annual leave
- **Maternity:** Companies offering over Statutory Maternity Pay
- **Childcare:** On-site nursery or vouchers
- **Women:** At least 33% of senior managers are women
- **Long Service:** 40% of employees with more than 5 years' service
- **Pensions:** Companies offering a final salary or non-contributory/ contributory pension scheme
- **Charity Activities:** 10% of staff undertake charitable activities during business hours
- **Gym:** On-site gym or subsidised gym memberships
- **Shares:** Companies where employees are offered share options
- **Health Insurance:** Full family cover

1000

FLIGHT CENTRE UK

UK locations	National
UK sites	105
Sector	Travel
Definition	Retail Travel Specialists
How owned	Public (i.e. stock market listed)
Founded	1995
Turnover	Not disclosed
Profit	Not disclosed
Staff	524
Average age	29
Male : Female	39 : 61
Earnings £35,000+	11%

BEST COMPANIES INDEX

best company 2007

OUTSTANDING

★ ★

2007 BCI = 703.2

2006 BCI = 687.1 (★)

<703

ones to watch

WORKPLACE INSIGHTS

Flight Centre's one on one structure allows employees to speak openly and honestly to their leader on a monthly basis. This fosters excellent communication and allows problems to be sorted quickly and encourages two way communication and feedback.

Flight Centre places a heavy importance on colleagues getting to know and understand one another, so there is always a recognition section during their monthly "buzz nights" so people can be congratulated publicly for their efforts.

All employees are entitled to a variety of benefits including "Moneywise" – which provides financial advice on mortgage, investments and put together budgets for employees, and "Healthwise" - where advice & help is provided to all employees on all aspects of health.

500

MISSION / VISION

Vision: To be the most profitable and admired long haul travel retailer in the UK.
Mission: To open the world for those who want to see it.

BEST WORKPLACE FACTORS

MY MANAGER
MY TEAM
FAIR DEAL

GRADUATE VACANCIES

No graduate vacancies have been indicated.

EMPLOYEE COMMENTS

"There is opportunity to share views with management & very little red-tape which makes it easy to get things done."

"Great teams of people working together who get on with one another and have fun at work."

"Great benefits and incentives to perform well."

CONTACT DETAILS

Flight Centre UK, Level 6 CI Tower St, George's Square, High St, New Malden, Surrey KT3 4TE
Tel: 0870 4990040 www.flightcentre.co.uk

KEY

- **Holidays:** Companies offering a minimum of 25 days annual leave
- **Maternity:** Companies offering over Statutory Maternity Pay
- **Childcare:** On-site nursery or vouchers
- **Women:** At least 33% of senior managers are women
- **Long Service:** 40% of employees with more than 5 years' service
- **Pensions:** Companies offering a final salary or non-contributory/contributory pension scheme
- **Charity Activities:** 10% of staff undertake charitable activities during business hours
- **Gym:** On-site gym or subsidised gym memberships
- **Shares:** Companies where employees are offered share options
- **Health Insurance:** Full family cover

0

To find out more about this company visit www.bestcompaniesguide.co.uk

FRANK HASLAM MILAN & CO

UK locations	National
UK sites	3
Sector	Construction
Definition	Building Contractor
How owned	Private
Founded	1928
Turnover	£170.1m
Profit	£8.9m
Staff	1,158
Average age	37
Male : Female	84 : 16
Earnings £35,000+	7%

BEST COMPANIES INDEX

best company 2007

OUTSTANDING ★ ★

2007 BCI = 730.5

WORKPLACE INSIGHTS

They offer flexible working, particularly for employees with young children who may need to accommodate the school run. To ensure that staff are fit & healthy the company offers regular eye tests, flu jabs, free fruit and have cooled mineral water on tap.

A proactive approach to improving performance and a willingness to go the extra mile for its employees, tenants and clients has elevated Frank Haslam Milan to the forefront of its sector.

All employees are entitled to either full private healthcare or a scheme providing financial assistance towards medical costs. The company contribution for the staff pension scheme ranges from 6-10% depending upon length of service.

MISSION / VISION

Vision: To be the preferred provider of community regeneration.
Mission: To exceed the business needs of our clients.

BEST WORKPLACE FACTORS

WELL BEING
MY COMPANY
FAIR DEAL

GRADUATE VACANCIES

No graduate vacancies have been indicated.

EMPLOYEE COMMENTS

"The company recognises the importance of work/life balance & always respects family commitments."

"I have never worked for such a generous company."

"You get trusted with your own judgement and support is readily available when needed."

CONTACT DETAILS

Frank Haslam Milan & Co, The Waterfront, Lakeside Boulevard, Doncaster DN4 5PL
Tel: 01302 346604 www.frankhaslammilan.co.uk

KEY

- **Holidays:** Companies offering a minimum of 25 days annual leave
- **Maternity:** Companies offering over Statutory Maternity Pay
- **Childcare:** On-site nursery or vouchers
- **Women:** At least 33% of senior managers are women
- **Long Service:** 40% of employees with more than 5 years' service
- **Pensions:** Companies offering a final salary or non-contributory/ contributory pension scheme
- **Charity Activities:** 10% of staff undertake charitable activities during business hours
- **Gym:** On-site gym or subsidised gym memberships
- **Shares:** Companies where employees are offered share options
- **Health Insurance:** Full family cover

1000
731>
500
0
ones to watch

1000

GARDINER & THEOBALD

gardiner&theobald

UK locations	National
UK sites	20
Sector	Consulting
Definition	Construction Consultancy
How owned	Partnership/LLP
Founded	1840
Turnover	£63.6m
Profit	£13.8m
Staff	760
Average age	38
Male : Female	77 : 23
Earnings £35,000+	64%

<699

ones to watch

BEST COMPANIES INDEX

best company 2007

OUTSTANDING

★ ★

2007 BCI = 699.4

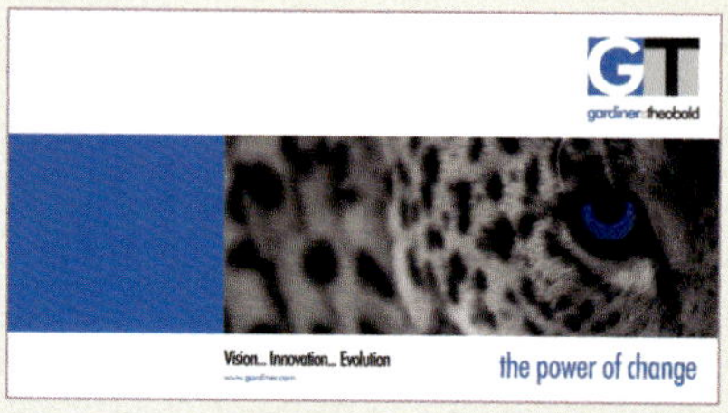

WORKPLACE INSIGHTS

Gardiner & Theobald operate as a learning organisation which allows individuals to direct their own training and development with the support and backing of their managers.

Gardiner & Theobald has and continues to make, numerous changes to ensure the requirements of employees in today's business environment are met.

Gardiner & Theobald employees all have access to career development discussions which are led by their senior partner.

500

MISSION / VISION

To be the natural first choice global services provider to all organisations whose business needs require construction or property solutions.

BEST WORKPLACE FACTORS

PERSONAL GROWTH
FAIR DEAL
MY MANAGER

GRADUATE VACANCIES

Quantity Surveying, Project Managers, Facilities Managers.

EMPLOYEE COMMENTS

"It has excellent training and personal development."

"They provide competitive packages & benefits for employees & share the profit of the business to all levels."

"My bosses are easy going and appreciate that as an employee you still need to run your life."

CONTACT DETAILS

Gardiner & Theobald, 32 Bedford Square, London WC1B 3JT
Tel: 0207 2093000 www.gardiner.com

KEY

- **Holidays:** Companies offering a minimum of 25 days annual leave
- **Pensions:** Companies offering a final salary or non-contributory/contributory pension scheme
- **Maternity:** Companies offering over Statutory Maternity Pay
- **Charity Activities:** 10% of staff undertake charitable activities during business hours
- **Childcare:** On-site nursery or vouchers
- **Gym:** On-site gym or subsidised gym memberships
- **Women:** At least 33% of senior managers are women
- **Shares:** Companies where employees are offered share options
- **Long Service:** 40% of employees with more than 5 years' service
- **Health Insurance:** Full family cover

0

To find out more about this company visit www.bestcompaniesguide.co.uk

GERALD EVE

GeraldEve

UK locations	National
UK sites	11
Sector	Property
Definition	Commercial Property Consultants
How owned	Partnership/LLP
Founded	1930
Turnover	£38.1m
Profit	£9.5m
Staff	328
Average age	37
Male : Female	65 : 35
Earnings £35,000+	58%

BEST COMPANIES INDEX

★ ★ best company 2007

OUTSTANDING

★ ★

2007 BCI = 698.4

2006 BCI = 684.0 (★)

WORKPLACE INSIGHTS

In addition to social events such as the staff away day and Christmas parties, each department head at Gerald Eve is provided with an annual social budget of £150 per person for department fun events.

The equity partners at Gerald Eve host peer group meetings with administrative staff and partners twice a year, over an informal lunch, to explain any structural changes or initiatives and to gain feedback from the groups.

At their annual away day, they present a number of awards including the Graduate of the Year for most notable business contribution; the Sports award for sporting achievement & Bad Day award which recognises various disasters that can befall any employee.

MISSION / VISION

By putting our clients first and serving them with distinction, our reputation will grow and with it all the superior profitability we need to retain and attract the very best people.

BEST WORKPLACE FACTORS

FAIR DEAL
LEADERSHIP
MY COMPANY

GRADUATE VACANCIES

Surveying (general practice), Building Surveying Planning.

EMPLOYEE COMMENTS

"I feel the company looks after its employees and rewards them well."

"Great people, great professional service to clients and a strong morally sound leader."

"The professionalism of the company is respected in the industry & I am proud to say I work for them."

CONTACT DETAILS

Gerald Eve, 7 Vere Street, London W1G 0JB
Tel: 0207 4933338 www.geraldeve.com

KEY

- **Holidays:** Companies offering a minimum of 25 days annual leave
- **Maternity:** Companies offering over Statutory Maternity Pay
- **Childcare:** On-site nursery or vouchers
- **Women:** At least 33% of senior managers are women
- **Long Service:** 40% of employees with more than 5 years' service
- **Pensions:** Companies offering a final salary or non-contributory/ contributory pension scheme
- **Charity Activities:** 10% of staff undertake charitable activities during business hours
- **Gym:** On-site gym or subsidised gym memberships
- **Shares:** Companies where employees are offered share options
- **Health Insurance:** Full family cover

1000 ★ ★ ★ ★ ★ ★ 698> ones to watch 500 0

1000

<717

ones to watch

500

0

GMAC-RFC

GMAC RFC

UK locations	National
UK sites	5
Sector	Financial - Credit/Finance/Mortgage
Definition	Mortgages
How owned	Private
Founded	1998
Turnover	£252m
Profit	£152.7m
Staff	858
Average age	31
Male : Female	42 : 58
Earnings £35,000+	24%

BEST COMPANIES INDEX

best company 2007

OUTSTANDING ★ ★

2007 BCI = 716.5

2006 BCI = 677.7 (★)

WORKPLACE INSIGHTS

GMAC RFC Executives make sure they are visible and take time to talk with Associates at all levels, this day-to-day interaction fits with their values of Care Deeply and Value Others.

All GMAC RFC employees may make a request to work flexibly. Flexible working where possible, supports balanced life and the Company can ably demonstrate this with between twenty to thirty percent of associates working on a flexible basis.

Twice a year the Executive Chairman and four Managing Directors update the business on its direction and results. This event is delivered to all Associates off-site and dialogue between Associates and the Executive team is encouraged during the event.

MISSION / VISION

We transform markets by providing innovative capital solutions to consumers and business partners world wide.

BEST WORKPLACE FACTORS

MY MANAGER
WELL BEING
LEADERSHIP

GRADUATE VACANCIES

No graduate vacancies have been indicated.

EMPLOYEE COMMENTS

"It is a place you can speak with management and discuss your views without fear of retribution."

"They have given me opportunity to balance my workload whilst living my life, which I am thankful of."

"Stephen Knight & directors recognise without associates they would not have the success it has had."

CONTACT DETAILS

GMAC-RFC Limited, Eastern Gate, Brants Bridge, Bracknell, Berks RG12 9BZ
Tel: 0844 7708100 www.gmacrfc.co.uk

KEY

Holidays: Companies offering a minimum of 25 days annual leave

Pensions: Companies offering a final salary or non-contributory/ contributory pension scheme

Maternity: Companies offering over Statutory Maternity Pay

Charity Activities: 10% of staff undertake charitable activities during business hours

Childcare: On-site nursery or vouchers

Gym: On-site gym or subsidised gym memberships

Women: At least 33% of senior managers are women

Shares: Companies where employees are offered share options

Long Service: 40% of employees with more than 5 years' service

Health Insurance: Full family cover

To find out more about this company visit www.bestcompaniesguide.co.uk

GOLDER ASSOCIATES (UK)

UK locations	National
UK sites	7
Sector	Business Services
Definition	Environmental Consultants
How owned	Trust/Employee owned/Mutual
Founded	1973
Turnover	£13.5m
Profit	Not disclosed
Staff	190
Average age	35
Male : Female	62 : 38
Earnings £35,000+	37%

BEST COMPANIES INDEX

best company 2007

OUTSTANDING

★ ★

2007 BCI = 701.6

2006 BCI = 721.3 (★★)

WORKPLACE INSIGHTS

The management system ensures staff, particularly team members & managers/supervisors, are mentored and given help & support to develop their career. Employees are supported by their manager to ensure they reach full potential through training and experience.

They established the 'Golder Trust for Orphans' to provide children who have been affected by AIDS with care and opportunities to grow and reach their full potential. In total employees have donated a total of £6000 to the trust, which the company matched.

Each office manager at Golder office holds monthly staff meetings which are used to inform all staff about office specific information such as projects, client feedback and forthcoming office events.

MISSION / VISION

To be the most respected ground engineering & environmental services company in the UK. A well managed employee owned, growth company which values its people and its clients. To be an integral part of a European & Global organisation which pursues diversity & rewards Shareholders.

BEST WORKPLACE FACTORS

PERSONAL GROWTH
GIVING SOMETHING BACK
MY MANAGER

GRADUATE VACANCIES

Land Development, Manufacturing, Mining, Power & Waste Management.

EMPLOYEE COMMENTS

"Individuals are actively encouraged to leap out of their comfort zones and grow."

"The company's values are very much aligned to my own environmentally, socially and ethically."

"Managers are very keen to keep us informed of company progress."

CONTACT DETAILS

Golder Associates (UK), Attenborough House, Browns Lane Business Park, Stanton-on-the-Wolds, Nottinghamshire NG12 5BL
Tel: 0115 937 1111 www.golder.com/uk

KEY

- **Holidays:** Companies offering a minimum of 25 days annual leave
- **Maternity:** Companies offering over Statutory Maternity Pay
- **Childcare:** On-site nursery or vouchers
- **Women:** At least 33% of senior managers are women
- **Long Service:** 40% of employees with more than 5 years' service
- **Pensions:** Companies offering a final salary or non-contributory/ contributory pension scheme
- **Charity Activities:** 10% of staff undertake charitable activities during business hours
- **Gym:** On-site gym or subsidised gym memberships
- **Shares:** Companies where employees are offered share options
- **Health Insurance:** Full family cover

1000

702>

500

0

ones to watch

To find out more about this company visit www.bestcompaniesguide.co.uk

1000

★ ★ ★ ★ ★ <710 ★

ones to watch

500

0

greene &co

GREENE & COMPANY

UK locations	London
UK sites	6
Sector	Property
Definition	Estate Agents
How owned	Private
Founded	1995
Turnover	Not disclosed
Profit	Not disclosed
Staff	61
Average age	29
Male : Female	59 : 41
Earnings £35,000+	39%

BEST COMPANIES INDEX

★ ★ best company 2007

OUTSTANDING

★ ★

2007 BCI = 709.9

WORKPLACE INSIGHTS

Greene & Co have an annual three day training meeting in Wales. This allows everyone to get away from the office and time to interact with different managers and directors to discuss performance, new practices and work procedures.

Green & Co employ the services of a Motivational Life Coach who comes in to the organisation every two weeks to speak with the employees. The coach is available to all employees for them to discuss any issue they wish.

At Green and Co, Managing Director David Pollock visits each office every quarter and takes the employees out for drinks or food. This provides an opportunity for all employees to discuss whatever issues they want with him.

MISSION / VISION

Ladies and Gentlemen. We are a MILLION times better as property agents than any of our competitors. This is because we care for our clients and we care for each other.

BEST WORKPLACE FACTORS

MY MANAGER
MY COMPANY
LEADERSHIP

GRADUATE VACANCIES

Finance, Marketing.

EMPLOYEE COMMENTS

"We have a fantastic manager that listens and gives valuable support."

"I feel proud to be associated with Greene & Co."

"The morals and principles of the leaders of the organisation are their best quality."

CONTACT DETAILS

Greene & Company, 146 West End Lane, West Hampstead, London NW6 1SD
Tel: 0207 3283232 www.greene.co.uk

KEY

Holidays: Companies offering a minimum of 25 days annual leave

Maternity: Companies offering over Statutory Maternity Pay

Childcare: On-site nursery or vouchers

Women: At least 33% of senior managers are women

Long Service: 40% of employees with more than 5 years' service

Pensions: Companies offering a final salary or non-contributory/ contributory pension scheme

Charity Activities: 10% of staff undertake charitable activities during business hours

Gym: On-site gym or subsidised gym memberships

Shares: Companies where employees are offered share options

Health Insurance: Full family cover

To find out more about this company visit www.bestcompaniesguide.co.uk

HALL AND PARTNERS EUROPE

Hall & Partners Europe

UK locations	London
UK sites	1
Sector	Business Services
Definition	Market Research Agency
How owned	Private
Founded	1991
Turnover	£12.8m
Profit	£1.4m
Staff	90
Average age	30
Male : Female	31 : 69
Earnings £35,000+	43%

BEST COMPANIES INDEX

best company 2007

OUTSTANDING ★ ★

2007 BCI = 713.6

WORKPLACE INSIGHTS

Hall & Partners have a dedicated team to set up and organise company events. Every Friday they stop work at 4pm and start the weekend, free drinks are provided. An open atmosphere means there's often people chatting and laughing in their office.

Hall & Partners have internal as well as external courses. At appraisals they make sure each individual is assigned a goal that stretches them whether it is on account work or something outside their everyday job.

Employees are able to provide feedback on their managers through their appraisal process. They hold quarterly company meetings where employees are able to talk about the good and bad and tackle any problems.

MISSION / VISION

Vision: Surpass expectations.
Mission: To be the most innovative research company in the world.

BEST WORKPLACE FACTORS

MY TEAM
PERSONAL GROWTH
MY MANAGER

GRADUATE VACANCIES

Quantitative Research Division, Qualitative Research Division.

EMPLOYEE COMMENTS

"The people are fantastic - friendly, creative, fun and intelligent."

"Excellent training programs tailored to each level."

"Top management are passionate and dedicated to making H&P a great place to work."

CONTACT DETAILS

Hall and Partners Europe, 239 Old Marylebone Road, London NW1 5QT
Tel: 0207 1734600 www.hall-and-partners.com

1000

714>

500

0

ones to watch

KEY

- **Holidays:** Companies offering a minimum of 25 days annual leave
- **Maternity:** Companies offering over Statutory Maternity Pay
- **Childcare:** On-site nursery or vouchers
- **Women:** At least 33% of senior managers are women
- **Long Service:** 40% of employees with more than 5 years' service
- **Pensions:** Companies offering a final salary or non-contributory/ contributory pension scheme
- **Charity Activities:** 10% of staff undertake charitable activities during business hours
- **Gym:** On-site gym or subsidised gym memberships
- **Shares:** Companies where employees are offered share options
- **Health Insurance:** Full family cover

1000

<717

ones to watch

500

0

haygarth

HAYGARTH

UK locations	London
UK sites	1
Sector	Marketing & Sales
Definition	Marketing Communications Agency
How owned	Private
Founded	1984
Turnover	Not disclosed
Profit	Not disclosed
Staff	137
Average age	31
Male : Female	46 : 54
Earnings £35,000+	35%

BEST COMPANIES INDEX

best company 2007

OUTSTANDING

★ ★

2007 BCI = 717.3

2006 BCI = 760.2 (★★★)

WORKPLACE INSIGHTS

Haygarth is currently running an award for the best contribution to the company in terms of driving business - with the winner receiving a holiday in France with the whole team.

Haygarth has open plan offices, no-one is tucked away in an office, instead everyone, including the leadership, sits on a cluster of desks with a mix of levels so that all can learn from each other.

They encourage everyone to pop to the local restaurant or pub every Friday lunch time. This provides opportunity for the leadership to engage & interact with staff on a non-work level, building relationships & creating a more open communication.

MISSION / VISION

Attract and win, grow & play.

BEST WORKPLACE FACTORS

MY TEAM
MY MANAGER
LEADERSHIP

GRADUATE VACANCIES

Direct, Digital & Promotional Marketing, Design, PR.

EMPLOYEE COMMENTS

"You never feel like you are alone on a job."

"There is care amongst the team & everybody receives equal treatment from senior managers to account executives."

"We have an inspirational leader, Stephen Morris, who we all love working for."

CONTACT DETAILS

Haygarth, 28-31 High Street, Wimbledon Village, London SW19 5BY
Tel: 0208 9713300 www.haygarth.co.uk

KEY

- **Holidays:** Companies offering a minimum of 25 days annual leave
- **Pensions:** Companies offering a final salary or non-contributory/contributory pension scheme
- **Maternity:** Companies offering over Statutory Maternity Pay
- **Charity Activities:** 10% of staff undertake charitable activities during business hours
- **Childcare:** On-site nursery or vouchers
- **Gym:** On-site gym or subsidised gym memberships
- **Women:** At least 33% of senior managers are women
- **Shares:** Companies where employees are offered share options
- **Long Service:** 40% of employees with more than 5 years' service
- **Health Insurance:** Full family cover

To find out more about this company visit www.bestcompaniesguide.co.uk

HEALIX GROUP OF COMPANIES

healix GROUP OF COMPANIES

UK locations	London
UK sites	3
Sector	Health
Definition	Medical Service Provision
How owned	Private
Founded	1992
Turnover	£8.7m
Profit	Not disclosed
Staff	62
Average age	39
Male : Female	26 : 74
Earnings £35,000+	34%

BEST COMPANIES INDEX

best company 2007

OUTSTANDING

★ ★

2007 BCI = 731.0

731>

ones to watch

WORKPLACE INSIGHTS

Healix encourage their employees to stay healthy by providing fitted showers at the office and storage for bicycles, encouraging them to cycle or run to work where possible.

In addition to staff getting together during social evenings, barbeques & lunches, the office itself was designed with staff social interaction in mind. There is a large lounge area adjacent to kitchen area, where all staff are able to take lunch breaks.

They are proud of their ability to recognise potential & talent in people and develop that potential, thereby giving employees incentive to stay with the company. For example, one employee left to attain a university degree, and was re-employed.

MISSION / VISION

The Healix group of companies provide healthcare solutions to clients both in the UK and around the world. We provide specialist medical services to medical assistance companies, the range of products and services offered by companies within the Group has expanded steadily over the years.

BEST WORKPLACE FACTORS

WELL BEING
MY TEAM
PERSONAL GROWTH

GRADUATE VACANCIES

IT, Insurance, Broking, Nursing and Medicine.

EMPLOYEE COMMENTS

"I feel valued, looked after and listened to and my contribution is important."

"There is a great team of people at Healix and a very relaxed but productive atmosphere."

"I have been given great opportunities for personal and professional development."

CONTACT DETAILS

Healix Group of Companies, Healix House, 15 Castle Mews High Street, Hampton, Middlesex TW12 2NP
Tel: 0208 4817777 www.healix.com

KEY

- **Holidays:** Companies offering a minimum of 25 days annual leave
- **Maternity:** Companies offering over Statutory Maternity Pay
- **Childcare:** On-site nursery or vouchers
- **Women:** At least 33% of senior managers are women
- **Long Service:** 40% of employees with more than 5 years' service
- **Pensions:** Companies offering a final salary or non-contributory/ contributory pension scheme
- **Charity Activities:** 10% of staff undertake charitable activities during business hours
- **Gym:** On-site gym or subsidised gym memberships
- **Shares:** Companies where employees are offered share options
- **Health Insurance:** Full family cover

1000

<700

ones to watch

500

0

HILTI (GT.BRITAIN)

UK locations	National
UK sites	23
Sector	Construction
Definition	Sales and Marketing
How owned	Private
Founded	1941
Turnover	£80.2m
Profit	£2.9m
Staff	478
Average age	37
Male : Female	82 : 18
Earnings £35,000+	35%

BEST COMPANIES INDEX

best company 2007

OUTSTANDING

★ ★

2007 BCI = 700.4

WORKPLACE INSIGHTS

Hilti staff take self responsibility for the development of the business, their team, and themselves. They encourage, coach and support each other to achieve outstanding results. Their culture is a journey.

When employees first join Hilti they are sent on a 4 week residential course held at their training centre in Stockport. When they return the coaching and support given by the manager is reflective of the feedback received from the training centre.

Managers have an annual conference where they discuss the companies' vision and goals for the forthcoming year, the managers then go back to their teams and discuss it further.

MISSION / VISION

We share a common purpose of passionately creating enthusiastic customers and building a better future. We encourage coach and support each other to achieve outstanding results. Our culture is a journey - Our Culture Journey.

BEST WORKPLACE FACTORS

MY COMPANY
PERSONAL GROWTH
MY MANAGER

GRADUATE VACANCIES

Field Sales, Customer Services & Technical.

EMPLOYEE COMMENTS

"What makes it a great workplace is the management team & staff all of which add their part."

"Training is good & helps you feel valued, the opportunity is always there to request further training."

"My manager is very supportive and honest."

CONTACT DETAILS

Hilti (Gt.Britain), 1 Trafford Wharf Road, Trafford Park, Manchester M17 1BY
Tel: 0161 8861000 www.hilti.co.uk

KEY

Holidays: Companies offering a minimum of 25 days annual leave
Maternity: Companies offering over Statutory Maternity Pay
Childcare: On-site nursery or vouchers
Women: At least 33% of senior managers are women
Long Service: 40% of employees with more than 5 years' service
Pensions: Companies offering a final salary or non-contributory/contributory pension scheme
Charity Activities: 10% of staff undertake charitable activities during business hours
Gym: On-site gym or subsidised gym memberships
Shares: Companies where employees are offered share options
Health Insurance: Full family cover

To find out more about this company visit www.bestcompaniesguide.co.uk

HOLIDAY EXTRAS

UK locations	S.East
UK sites	1
Sector	Travel
Definition	Holiday Extras & Short Breaks
How owned	Private
Founded	1983
Turnover	Not disclosed
Profit	Not disclosed
Staff	283
Average age	30
Male : Female	34 : 66
Earnings £35,000+	6%

BEST COMPANIES INDEX

OUTSTANDING ★ ★

2007 BCI = 701.2

2006 BCI = 715.7 (★★)

WORKPLACE INSIGHTS

The layout of the office at Holiday Extras facilitates communication as management are sat within their teams and not hidden away in offices. Managers also often provide employees with thank you's to recognise when they have worked particularly hard.

Holiday Extras have a social club who organise monthly events for employees to spend time together. These include BBQs for the whole company throughout the Summer, cooked by senior managers; an "I am a Celebrity... "gameshow event and a fireworks party.

In addition to having regular massages and reflexology available for employees and having a significant budget for counselling and welfare, Holiday Extras also run a health week providing employees with advice on nutrition, exercise and general well being.

MISSION / VISION

Exceed expectations; conducting our business ethically in an environment of trust & respect. Best choice of products best prices. Enjoy achievements & Share Rewards. Innovation kept simple. Can-do team; an environment where work can be fun. Investment in People & Technology. We will have fun!!!

BEST WORKPLACE FACTORS

MY MANAGER
MY TEAM
WELL BEING

GRADUATE VACANCIES

Web, New Business Commercial Management, Call Centre.

EMPLOYEE COMMENTS

"The support from the managers is unrelenting."

"Everyone is really friendly and help is always available if you need it."

"Good support when you have a problem personally or within workplace."

CONTACT DETAILS

Holiday Extras, Newingreen, Hythe, Kent CT21 4JF
Tel: 01303 815300 www.holidayextras.com

KEY

Holidays: Companies offering a minimum of 25 days annual leave
Maternity: Companies offering over Statutory Maternity Pay
Childcare: On-site nursery or vouchers
Women: At least 33% of senior managers are women
Long Service: 40% of employees with more than 5 years' service
Pensions: Companies offering a final salary or non-contributory/contributory pension scheme
Charity Activities: 10% of staff undertake charitable activities during business hours
Gym: On-site gym or subsidised gym memberships
Shares: Companies where employees are offered share options
Health Insurance: Full family cover

hood group

HOOD GROUP

UK locations	E.England
UK sites	1
Sector	Financial - Insurance
Definition	Home Insurance Provider
How owned	Private
Founded	1983
Turnover	£6.1m
Profit	£1.3m
Staff	145
Average age	30
Male : Female	41 : 59
Earnings £35,000+	8%

BEST COMPANIES INDEX

best company 2007

OUTSTANDING

★ ★

2007 BCI = 706.0

WORKPLACE INSIGHTS

The Hood Group ran a Well Being week focusing on smoking cessation, healthy eating, increasing walking and healthy backs. They also have a fitness room on site offering free yoga classes, body conditioning classes, free massage and weight training.

Employees at The Hood Group enjoy a variety of team social events including quiz nights, "It's a Knockout", a treasure hunt, bowling, an Hawaiian end of summer party, a golf evening, and a Casino night.

Managers and senior managers at The Hood Group regularly take part in a 'Back to the Floor' exercise, spending time working on their respective teams. This enables them to better understand the challenges facing the team members.

MISSION / VISION

To be the Employer of Choice in the local area.

BEST WORKPLACE FACTORS

WELL BEING
MY TEAM
MY MANAGER

GRADUATE VACANCIES

No graduate vacancies have been indicated.

EMPLOYEE COMMENTS

"Staff wellbeing is high on the agenda."

"I have never worked with such a great bunch of people before, they really make work great."

"The management are approachable and easy to talk to."

CONTACT DETAILS

Hood Group, 1 Maitland House, Warrior Square, Southend on Sea, Essex SS1 2ZT
Tel: 01702 443600 www.hoodgroup.co.uk

KEY

- **Holidays:** Companies offering a minimum of 25 days annual leave
- **Maternity:** Companies offering over Statutory Maternity Pay
- **Childcare:** On-site nursery or vouchers
- **Women:** At least 33% of senior managers are women
- **Long Service:** 40% of employees with more than 5 years' service
- **Pensions:** Companies offering a final salary or non-contributory/contributory pension scheme
- **Charity Activities:** 10% of staff undertake charitable activities during business hours
- **Gym:** On-site gym or subsidised gym memberships
- **Shares:** Companies where employees are offered share options
- **Health Insurance:** Full family cover

To find out more about this company visit www.bestcompaniesguide.co.uk

imex TRUCK PARTS SPECIALIST

IMEXPART

UK locations	National
UK sites	4
Sector	Logistics/Wholesale/Distribution
Definition	Truck Parts Distributors
How owned	Private
Founded	1986
Turnover	£6.3m
Profit	£0.2m
Staff	56
Average age	41
Male : Female	88 : 12
Earnings £35,000+	4%

BEST COMPANIES INDEX

best company 2007

OUTSTANDING

★ ★

2007 BCI = 717.4

WORKPLACE INSIGHTS

Imexpart's rewards and benefits package is unique and as well as encompassing a host of the usual suspects, such as: a non-contributory pension scheme; life insurance; hospital fund membership and a profit sharing scheme.

Every 60 days the employees have a 'Health and Happiness' interview with the MD. To ensure that employees are always well rested Imexpart offer 25 days paid annual leave.

All staff are encouraged to meet with the boss for open conversation in informal surroundings and definitely no agenda! It is held every 3 months, and in groups of 12, these frank exchanges give attendees a real insight into strategy at the highest level.

MISSION / VISION

To maintain profitability whilst remaining competitive. To grow the company in line with customer demand.To expand our customer base. To develop staff & look after their welfare. To project a consistent professional brand image. To develop a strong management team. To be pro-active in forward planning. To develop links between business & the community.

BEST WORKPLACE FACTORS

FAIR DEAL
WELL BEING
LEADERSHIP

GRADUATE VACANCIES

No graduate vacancies have been indicated.

EMPLOYEE COMMENTS

"Friends & family are amazed at the company when I mention the staff benefits."

"Staff well being is at the top of the owners agenda, even above customer service & profits."

"The leader of this organisation cares for his staff and is generous to them all."

CONTACT DETAILS

Imexpart, 31 Willowbridge Way, Whitwood, Castleford WF10 5NP
Tel: 01977 553936 www.imexpart.com

KEY

- **Holidays:** Companies offering a minimum of 25 days annual leave
- **Maternity:** Companies offering over Statutory Maternity Pay
- **Childcare:** On-site nursery or vouchers
- **Women:** At least 33% of senior managers are women
- **Long Service:** 40% of employees with more than 5 years' service
- **Pensions:** Companies offering a final salary or non-contributory/ contributory pension scheme
- **Charity Activities:** 10% of staff undertake charitable activities during business hours
- **Gym:** On-site gym or subsidised gym memberships
- **Shares:** Companies where employees are offered share options
- **Health Insurance:** Full family cover

To find out more about this company visit www.bestcompaniesguide.co.uk

1000

<732

ones to watch

IMPACT DEVELOPMENT TRAINING GROUP

IMPACT

UK locations	London, N.West
UK sites	3
Sector	Professional Services
Definition	Staff Development Consulting
How owned	Private
Founded	1980
Turnover	£6.8m
Profit	£0.9m
Staff	93
Average age	39
Male : Female	56 : 44
Earnings £35,000+	39%

BEST COMPANIES INDEX

★ ★ best company 2007

OUTSTANDING

★ ★

2007 BCI = 731.9

2006 BCI = 740.7

WORKPLACE INSIGHTS

They have a team dedicated to providing training, support & consultancy to agencies & organisations involved in relief projects. The team has helped various parts of the UN and a variety of organisations in places as diverse as Thailand, Pakistan and Rwanda.

500

Impact always has a full calendar of social events including a James Bond themed Christmas party, an end of financial year celebratory lunch, a barbeque cooked by the Managing Director, World Cup football nights and a 50th birthday party in a mountain hut.

Impact's management style is a very open one relying on trust and honesty and everyone holds a high level of accountability. People have managers that they can rely on and trust with regular conversations, performance reviews and catch up one to ones.

MISSION / VISION

To help people live & work together in effective organisations locally & globally. We will recruit develop & retain outstanding people, to design & deliver an expanding portfolio of powerful experiential world class learning programmes.

BEST WORKPLACE FACTORS

GIVING SOMETHING BACK
MY TEAM
MY MANAGER

GRADUATE VACANCIES

No graduate vacancies have been indicated.

EMPLOYEE COMMENTS

"We are a small company with big ambitions to make a positive difference in the world."

"Supportive and at times inspiring group of people to work with."

"Easily accessible group of managers."

CONTACT DETAILS

Impact Development Training Group, Cragwood House, Windermere, Cumbria LA23 1LQ
Tel: 01539 488333 www.impact-dtg.com

KEY

Holidays: Companies offering a minimum of 25 days annual leave

Maternity: Companies offering over Statutory Maternity Pay

Childcare: On-site nursery or vouchers

Women: At least 33% of senior managers are women

Long Service: 40% of employees with more than 5 years' service

Pensions: Companies offering a final salary or non-contributory/ contributory pension scheme

Charity Activities: 10% of staff undertake charitable activities during business hours

Gym: On-site gym or subsidised gym memberships

Shares: Companies where employees are offered share options

Health Insurance: Full family cover

0

To find out more about this company visit www.bestcompaniesguide.co.uk

INFORMATIQ CONSULTING

Informatiq CONSULTING LTD

UK locations	E.England
UK sites	1
Sector	Recruitment
Definition	Specialist Recruitment Consultancy
How owned	Private
Founded	1994
Turnover	£7.3m
Profit	£0.7m
Staff	69
Average age	31
Male : Female	45 : 55
Earnings £35,000+	23%

BEST COMPANIES INDEX

best company 2007

OUTSTANDING

★ ★

2007 BCI = 712.5

WORKPLACE INSIGHTS

All employees are entitled to a 1.5 hour lunch break a week rather than just the one hour to give them extra time to get to the gym or take part in a sporting activity.

Managers/Team leaders actively encourage everyone to follow systematic on the job learning at their own pace.

With an environment of open communication at Informatiq employees feel free to talk to managers about their opinions openly on any matter on an ongoing basis.

MISSION / VISION

Informatiq Consulting aims to deliver real competitive advantage to a diverse range of mutually exclusive best of breed organisations, through the comprehensive provision of high quality high volume recruitment services.

BEST WORKPLACE FACTORS

WELL BEING
MY MANAGER
MY TEAM

GRADUATE VACANCIES

Recruitment Consultants, Administration.

EMPLOYEE COMMENTS

"They look after us – free breakfast, lunch, ice creams, pop & legendary trips to foreign countries."

"The management are always looking to keep things fresh and stimulating."

"Everyone works together as a team."

CONTACT DETAILS

Informatiq Consulting, Gresham House, 53 Clarendon Road, Watford, Herts WD17 1FT
Tel: 01923 224481 www.informatiq.co.uk

KEY

- **Holidays:** Companies offering a minimum of 25 days annual leave
- **Maternity:** Companies offering over Statutory Maternity Pay
- **Childcare:** On-site nursery or vouchers
- **Women:** At least 33% of senior managers are women
- **Long Service:** 40% of employees with more than 5 years' service
- **Pensions:** Companies offering a final salary or non-contributory/ contributory pension scheme
- **Charity Activities:** 10% of staff undertake charitable activities during business hours
- **Gym:** On-site gym or subsidised gym memberships
- **Shares:** Companies where employees are offered share options
- **Health Insurance:** Full family cover

To find out more about this company visit www.bestcompaniesguide.co.uk

INNOCENT DRINKS

innocent
little tasty drinks

UK locations	London
UK sites	2
Sector	Manufacturing
Definition	little tasty drinks
How owned	Private
Founded	1999
Turnover	£37.9m
Profit	£4.2m
Staff	109
Average age	27
Male : Female	44 : 56
Earnings £35,000+	39%

BEST COMPANIES INDEX

★ ★ best company 2007

OUTSTANDING

★ ★

2007 BCI = 717.5

2006 BCI = 752.0 (★★★)

WORKPLACE INSIGHTS

Each year Innocent gives 10% of all their profits to their charity, the innocent foundation. The foundation is set up to give grants and work in partnership with community based projects and NGOs in the countries where they source the fruit for their drinks.

They have a monthly award called 'Lord & Lady of the sash' given for services to fruit. Nominations are picked by founders & the winners are crowned in the weekly company meeting. They have tea made for them for a month & receive £100 for a posh meal out.

Innocent's leaders run lunchtime 'chatwiches' which are an opportunity to discuss issues, present new ideas and update each other on progress over sandwiches.

MISSION / VISION

We don't have an official mission statement rather we have what we call 'the nursing home test', i.e. when we're old and sitting in our nursing homes we want to be able to look back and be proud of innocent as a company. We want to leave things a little better than we found them.

BEST WORKPLACE FACTORS

GIVING SOMETHING BACK
MY COMPANY
LEADERSHIP

GRADUATE VACANCIES

All Areas.

EMPLOYEE COMMENTS

"I've never been very aware of the environment but working for innocent has educated & converted me."

"I feel privileged to be a part of a company which makes a fantastic, healthy product."

"The directors genuinely care about the people that work here."

CONTACT DETAILS

innocent drinks, Fruit Towers, 3 The Goldhawk Estate, Brackenbury Road, London W6 0BA
Tel: 0208 6003939 www.innocentdrinks.co.uk

KEY

- **Holidays:** Companies offering a minimum of 25 days annual leave
- **Maternity:** Companies offering over Statutory Maternity Pay
- **Childcare:** On-site nursery or vouchers
- **Women:** At least 33% of senior managers are women
- **Long Service:** 40% of employees with more than 5 years' service
- **Pensions:** Companies offering a final salary or non-contributory/ contributory pension scheme
- **Charity Activities:** 10% of staff undertake charitable activities during business hours
- **Gym:** On-site gym or subsidised gym memberships
- **Shares:** Companies where employees are offered share options
- **Health Insurance:** Full family cover

To find out more about this company visit www.bestcompaniesguide.co.uk

JMC IT

UK locations	N.West
UK sites	1
Sector	IT/Internet Services
Definition	IT Reseller
How owned	Private
Founded	1981
Turnover	£8.6m
Profit	£1.2m
Staff	98
Average age	36
Male : Female	74 : 26
Earnings £35,000+	31%

BEST COMPANIES INDEX

best company 2007

OUTSTANDING ★ ★

2007 BCI = 712.0

2006 BCI = 687.8 (★)

WORKPLACE INSIGHTS

JMC IT believe that a sense of being a team & not wanting to let your colleagues down is critical & that social activities strengthen these bonds, so they emphasise having fun together during activities such as clay-pigeon shooting, climbing and skiing.

Every week, employees at JMC IT fill a large shopping basket to take to Lifeshare, a local homeless charity. Members of staff buy an additional item a week during their own shopping to add to the basket which is already part filled by the company.

JMC IT have an number of health and fitness initiatives and encourage employees to keep fit and stay healthy by providing an on site gym, weekly table tennis, circuit training and five a side football and a mountain biking club.

MISSION / VISION

To achieve ambitious growth and an impressive reputation by providing high quality computer-related solutions and services efficiently and professionally to the benefit of both the company, clients and its staff.

BEST WORKPLACE FACTORS

MY TEAM
GIVING SOMETHING BACK
WELL BEING

GRADUATE VACANCIES

Sales, support, engineering.

EMPLOYEE COMMENTS

"It's a truly caring organisation whereby each and every employee puts themselves before others."

"I feel a sense of pride in my work and my employer."

"An on-site gym, group "athletic" events, free massages & great canteen are the icing on the cake."

CONTACT DETAILS

JMC IT, Riverside, Agecroft Road, Manchester M27 8SJ
Tel: 0161 9257777 www.jmc.it

KEY

- **Holidays:** Companies offering a minimum of 25 days annual leave
- **Maternity:** Companies offering over Statutory Maternity Pay
- **Childcare:** On-site nursery or vouchers
- **Women:** At least 33% of senior managers are women
- **Long Service:** 40% of employees with more than 5 years' service
- **Pensions:** Companies offering a final salary or non-contributory/ contributory pension scheme
- **Charity Activities:** 10% of staff undertake charitable activities during business hours
- **Gym:** On-site gym or subsidised gym memberships
- **Shares:** Companies where employees are offered share options
- **Health Insurance:** Full family cover

1000 · 712> · 500 · 0 · ones to watch

1000

<723

ones to watch

500

0

Jobwise

JOBWISE

UK locations	N.West
UK sites	7
Sector	Recruitment
Definition	Commercial Recruitment Agency
How owned	Private
Founded	1979
Turnover	Not disclosed
Profit	Not disclosed
Staff	61
Average age	32
Male : Female	18 : 82
Earnings £35,000+	11%

BEST COMPANIES INDEX

★ ★ best company 2007

OUTSTANDING

★ ★

2007 BCI = 722.9

2006 BCI = 746.6 (★★★)

WORKPLACE INSIGHTS

Jobwise has menu based training programmes where staff can choose which training session they want to attend. They regularly run one to one training programmes with staff e.g. refresher training, coaching and mentoring.

Jobwise has various awards for employees. One of these is the WOW award for customer service where the winner receives a prize of £100.

This year Jobwise took some of the teams to the 'Go Ape' course in the lake district. They also treat teams to lunch when a member is leaving on maternity or when a new starter joins.

MISSION / VISION

Love your Job.

BEST WORKPLACE FACTORS

PERSONAL GROWTH
MY COMPANY
MY TEAM

GRADUATE VACANCIES

No graduate vacancies have been indicated.

EMPLOYEE COMMENTS

"Every single person has the opportunity to develop and grow to their full potential."

"Jobwise have a good reputation so I feel proud to work for them."

"I love the people I work closely with; they are caring, friendly and fun."

CONTACT DETAILS

Jobwise, 18 - 20 Bridge Street, Bolton BL1 2EA
Tel: 01204 550660 www.jobwise.co.uk

KEY

- **Holidays:** Companies offering a minimum of 25 days annual leave
- **Maternity:** Companies offering over Statutory Maternity Pay
- **Childcare:** On-site nursery or vouchers
- **Women:** At least 33% of senior managers are women
- **Long Service:** 40% of employees with more than 5 years' service
- **Pensions:** Companies offering a final salary or non-contributory/ contributory pension scheme
- **Charity Activities:** 10% of staff undertake charitable activities during business hours
- **Gym:** On-site gym or subsidised gym memberships
- **Shares:** Companies where employees are offered share options
- **Health Insurance:** Full family cover

To find out more about this company visit www.bestcompaniesguide.co.uk

John Rowan & Partners
Construction Consultants

JOHN ROWAN & PARTNERS

UK locations	London, E.England
UK sites	4
Sector	Construction
Definition	Construction Consultancy
How owned	Partnership/LLP
Founded	2002
Turnover	£3.8m
Profit	£0.6m
Staff	60
Average age	39
Male : Female	72 : 28
Earnings £35,000+	67%

BEST COMPANIES INDEX

best company 2007

OUTSTANDING

★ ★

2007 BCI = 704.1

704>

ones to watch

WORKPLACE INSIGHTS

John Rowan & Partners believe they are one of the best companies to work for because they have pride in staff and in their achievements and are one of the fastest growing companies in the industry.

Whilst John Rowan & Partners maintain a well run and profitable business, they have always recognised that they are a people based organisation and without a well motivated and dedicated workforce they will achieve nothing.

John Rowan & Partners have a collaborative leadership. All managers sit within their team in an open plan office environment fully integrating with everyone.

MISSION / VISION

To understand our clients and by doing so enable them to achieve their goals. Our proven record of achievement makes us one of the leading businesses in our industry.

BEST WORKPLACE FACTORS

MY COMPANY
FAIR DEAL
LEADERSHIP

GRADUATE VACANCIES

Quantity & Building Surveying, Project Management.

EMPLOYEE COMMENTS

"They still maintain an owner run feel whilst offering exciting opportunities, projects & a fun place to work."

"There is a good reward structure."

"There is a strong sense of "company spirit" re-enforced with various company functions."

CONTACT DETAILS

John Rowan & Partners, CP House, 97 - 107 Uxbridge Road, Ealing, London W5 5TL
Tel: 0208 5676995 www.jrp.co.uk

KEY

Holidays: Companies offering a minimum of 25 days annual leave
Maternity: Companies offering over Statutory Maternity Pay
Childcare: On-site nursery or vouchers
Women: At least 33% of senior managers are women
Long Service: 40% of employees with more than 5 years' service
Pensions: Companies offering a final salary or non-contributory/ contributory pension scheme
Charity Activities: 10% of staff undertake charitable activities during business hours
Gym: On-site gym or subsidised gym memberships
Shares: Companies where employees are offered share options
Health Insurance: Full family cover

To find out more about this company visit www.bestcompaniesguide.co.uk

1000

★
★
★
★
★
★
ones to watch

<735

500

0

LANSONS communications

LANSONS COMMUNICATIONS

UK locations	London
UK sites	1
Sector	Consulting
Definition	Public Relations Consultancy
How owned	Partnership/LLP
Founded	1989
Turnover	£8.1m
Profit	£1.2m
Staff	101
Average age	30
Male : Female	24 : 76
Earnings £35,000+	38%

BEST COMPANIES INDEX

★ ★ best company 2007

OUTSTANDING

★ ★

2007 BCI = 734.7

2006 BCI = 746.0 (★★★)

WORKPLACE INSIGHTS

Lansons' Green Committee actively encourages staff to recycle and have implemented systems to support this. They recently began using Belu water in their meeting rooms. Belu water uses its profits to fund clean water projects in the UK and overseas.

The leaders of Lansons recognise great work and achievements such as winning a pitch or passing exams by presenting employees with gifts or vouchers and they always add a personalised note or card of congratulations.

Lansons have started a team called 'Lansons Linguists' who have arranged a series of language lessons for employees as well as cultural evenings to learn more about the various countries customs and themed outings to practice their new language skills.

MISSION / VISION

To be excellent in the work we do, to be the best place to work, and to share in the rewards.

BEST WORKPLACE FACTORS

GIVING SOMETHING BACK
LEADERSHIP
PERSONAL GROWTH

GRADUATE VACANCIES

Public Relations.

EMPLOYEE COMMENTS

"Lansons is clearly committed to running a positive company based on strong moral principles."

"The senior management are approachable and are keen to help their employees progress."

"There is an excellent training programme in place for employees at all levels."

CONTACT DETAILS

Lansons Communications, 24a St John Street London EC1M 4AY
Tel: 0207 4908828 www.lansons.com

KEY

Holidays: Companies offering a minimum of 25 days annual leave

Pensions: Companies offering a final salary or non-contributory/ contributory pension scheme

Maternity: Companies offering over Statutory Maternity Pay

Charity Activities: 10% of staff undertake charitable activities during business hours

Childcare: On-site nursery or vouchers

Gym: On-site gym or subsidised gym memberships

Women: At least 33% of senior managers are women

Shares: Companies where employees are offered share options

Long Service: 40% of employees with more than 5 years' service

Health Insurance: Full family cover

To find out more about this company visit www.bestcompaniesguide.co.uk

LEXIS PUBLIC RELATIONS

LEXIS PUBLIC RELATIONS

UK locations	London
UK sites	1
Sector	Consulting
Definition	Public Relations Agency
How owned	Private
Founded	1992
Turnover	Not disclosed
Profit	Not disclosed
Staff	88
Average age	27
Male : Female	25 : 75
Earnings £35,000+	43%

BEST COMPANIES INDEX

best company 2007

OUTSTANDING ★ ★

2007 BCI = 712.9

2006 BCI = 733.5 (★★)

WORKPLACE INSIGHTS

At reviews Managers are able to pick 4 colleagues or team members to ask for feedback and the company select 4 as well. This gives managers 360 degree feedback showing areas where they can improve or are doing well already.

Lexis makes sure they live their values one of which is to bring the best out in people. This year they took the entire company away for team building and interaction to go through these values.

The CEO takes every new employee out to lunch, often with other new joiners from a different team to chat & get to know them, tell them about Lexis & find out if their previous experience, skills or knowledge can be used to improve or adapt their own methods.

MISSION / VISION

Influencing people by thinking and communicating brilliantly.

BEST WORKPLACE FACTORS

MY MANAGER
MY COMPANY
LEADERSHIP

GRADUATE VACANCIES

Public Relations.

EMPLOYEE COMMENTS

"The managers genuinely care about others' career paths and happiness in this organisation."

"We recently spent 2 days in Sussex we took part in abseiling, rock climbing & kayaking to focus on team values."

"The company has a great leader."

CONTACT DETAILS

Lexis Public Relations, 8 Bolsover Street, London W1W 6AB
Tel: 0207 9086488 www.lexispr.com

KEY

Holidays: Companies offering a minimum of 25 days annual leave

Maternity: Companies offering over Statutory Maternity Pay

Childcare: On-site nursery or vouchers

Women: At least 33% of senior managers are women

Long Service: 40% of employees with more than 5 years' service

Pensions: Companies offering a final salary or non-contributory/ contributory pension scheme

Charity Activities: 10% of staff undertake charitable activities during business hours

Gym: On-site gym or subsidised gym memberships

Shares: Companies where employees are offered share options

Health Insurance: Full family cover

1000

713>

ones to watch

500

0

LONDON & QUADRANT HOUSING GROUP

UK locations	National
UK sites	20
Sector	Housing Associations
Definition	Provide Affordable Housing
How owned	Trust/Employee owned/Mutual
Founded	1973
Turnover	£183.8m
Profit	£34.8m
Staff	830
Average age	40
Male : Female	36 : 64
Earnings £35,000+	17%

BEST COMPANIES INDEX

best company 2007

OUTSTANDING ★ ★

2007 BCI = 733.4

WORKPLACE INSIGHTS

The Group recognise the value of personally thanking staff for doing a good job or going the extra mile and seek to do this as much as possible.

As part of the Trust's employee branding they introduced a series of booklets, one entitled 'family friendly benefits for our people'. This sets out benefits that are aimed at helping to build a better work-life balance and this includes flexible working.

L & Q's work in neighbourhood regeneration over the last year has extended the range of support they provide to community and special needs groups.

MISSION / VISION

Creating places where people want to live.

BEST WORKPLACE FACTORS

FAIR DEAL
WELL BEING
GIVING SOMETHING BACK

GRADUATE VACANCIES

No specific graduate vacancies have been indicated.

EMPLOYEE COMMENTS

"They are flexible with staff in working arrangements and staff benefits are second to none."

"L&Q make me feel like a person and not just a payroll number."

"We are constantly striving to do more for our residents. Their welfare is key throughout our actions."

CONTACT DETAILS

London & Quadrant Housing Group, Osborn House, Osborn Terrace, Lee Gree, London SE3 9DR
Tel: 0208 8529181 www.lqgroup.org.

KEY

- **Holidays:** Companies offering a minimum of 25 days annual leave
- **Maternity:** Companies offering over Statutory Maternity Pay
- **Childcare:** On-site nursery or vouchers
- **Women:** At least 33% of senior managers are women
- **Long Service:** 40% of employees with more than 5 years' service
- **Pensions:** Companies offering a final salary or non-contributory/contributory pension scheme
- **Charity Activities:** 10% of staff undertake charitable activities during business hours
- **Gym:** On-site gym or subsidised gym memberships
- **Shares:** Companies where employees are offered share options
- **Health Insurance:** Full family cover

To find out more about this company visit www.bestcompaniesguide.co.uk

LUSH FRESH HANDMADE COSMETICS

UK locations	National
UK sites	94
Sector	Retail
Definition	Fresh Handmade Cosmetics
How owned	Private
Founded	1995
Turnover	£72m
Profit	£7.5m
Staff	1,448
Average age	25
Male : Female	21 : 79
Earnings £35,000+	3%

BEST COMPANIES INDEX

OUTSTANDING

★ ★

2007 BCI = 711.1

2006 BCI = 743.3 (★★★)

WORKPLACE INSIGHTS

Due to the informality and individuality of the organisation employees at Lush feel able to bring their beliefs and the causes they care about, into the workplace. In addition, Lush is against animal testing and uses minimal packaging to reduce harm to the environment.

Lush shop managers are encouraged to run their stores as though they were their own and are therefore responsible for recruiting their own teams and for building their own teams by having parties and events on an individual store and regional basis.

Lush have created a support office in London to monitor effective bonuses and to aid senior management in an effort to stop any burn out. They have also assembled a UK Retail Support Team to support managers and trainee managers in the stores.

MISSION / VISION

Wouldn't it be good if Lush were a legendary company?.

BEST WORKPLACE FACTORS

GIVING SOMETHING BACK
MY TEAM
WELL BEING

GRADUATE VACANCIES

Retail, IT, Design, Press office/PR, Publishing.

EMPLOYEE COMMENTS

"Our morals, values and principles are second to none."

"I can honestly say every person in our team is genuinely lovely and enthusiastic about Lush."

"The owners are extremely supportive of personal situations and life changes."

CONTACT DETAILS

Lush Fresh Handmade Cosmetics, 29 High Street, Poole, Dorset BH15 1AB
Tel: 01202 667830 www.lush.co.uk

KEY

Holidays: Companies offering a minimum of 25 days annual leave
Maternity: Companies offering over Statutory Maternity Pay
Childcare: On-site nursery or vouchers
Women: At least 33% of senior managers are women
Long Service: 40% of employees with more than 5 years' service
Pensions: Companies offering a final salary or non-contributory/ contributory pension scheme
Charity Activities: 10% of staff undertake charitable activities during business hours
Gym: On-site gym or subsidised gym memberships
Shares: Companies where employees are offered share options
Health Insurance: Full family cover

1000

<723

500

0

ones to watch

ManningStainton
Property Professionals

MANNING STAINTON PROPERTY PROFESSIONALS

UK locations	Yorks & Humber
UK sites	16
Sector	Property
Definition	Estate Agency
How owned	Private
Founded	2000
Turnover	£9m
Profit	Not disclosed
Staff	245
Average age	37
Male : Female	22 : 78
Earnings £35,000+	16%

BEST COMPANIES INDEX

best company 2007

OUTSTANDING ★ ★

2007 BCI = 723.1

2006 BCI = 714.7 (★★)

WORKPLACE INSIGHTS

All sales offices and sites receive visits from directors a minimum of three times a month during which they continue to personally involve themselves in the everyday work within the branches.

Manning Stainton work in small teams which brings a degree of intimacy. This has enabled them to identify staff who would like to hold less responsibility and work fewer hours thereby helping the individual to achieve a good work/life balance.

Manning Stainton's financial benefits include performance and profit related pay as well as free private healthcare. They strongly believe in rewarding those who work hard and give financial recognition to those who demonstrate this.

MISSION / VISION

To help people move by providing a service and range of associated services from a team of passionate motivated professionals who aim to consistently meet and exceed our customers expectations.

BEST WORKPLACE FACTORS

LEADERSHIP
WELL BEING
FAIR DEAL

GRADUATE VACANCIES

Residential Sales, Survey, Land & New Homes, Mortgages.

EMPLOYEE COMMENTS

"There are strong values and ethics led by passionate directors who are approachable and willing to share their knowledge."

"My position allows me the freedom to lead a fulfilling personal life as well."

"We have generous nights out in the Summer and at Christmas."

CONTACT DETAILS

Manning Stainton Property Professionals, 12 Feast Field, Horsforth, Leeds LS18 4TJ
Tel: 0113 2582657 www.manningstainton.co.uk

KEY

Holidays: Companies offering a minimum of 25 days annual leave
Maternity: Companies offering over Statutory Maternity Pay
Childcare: On-site nursery or vouchers
Women: At least 33% of senior managers are women
Long Service: 40% of employees with more than 5 years' service
Pensions: Companies offering a final salary or non-contributory/contributory pension scheme
Charity Activities: 10% of staff undertake charitable activities during business hours
Gym: On-site gym or subsidised gym memberships
Shares: Companies where employees are offered share options
Health Insurance: Full family cover

To find out more about this company visit www.bestcompaniesguide.co.uk

MARATHON

UK locations	National
UK sites	4
Sector	Utilities
Definition	Oil & Gas Operator
How owned	Partnership/LLP
Founded	1981
Turnover	Not disclosed
Profit	Not disclosed
Staff	406
Average age	42
Male : Female	78 : 22
Earnings £35,000+	78%

BEST COMPANIES INDEX

best company 2007

OUTSTANDING ★ ★

2007 BCI = 704.3

2006 BCI = 647.0 (★)

WORKPLACE INSIGHTS

Employees enjoy benefits such as a Share Incentive Plan and a 'Cycle to Work' bike hire scheme as well as a Wellness Plan that allows employees & their spouses to claim back £100 each against healthy activities such as gym membership and aerobics classes.

Marathon will finance any employee wishing to undertake further education, such as a part-time Masters Degree. The course does not have to be directly relevant to the job they do. In addition, a voluntary mentoring scheme exists to provide career development and networking assistance to employees.

The flat organisational structure at Marathon makes it an informal and trusting work environment. The management style is very informal, with an open door policy at all times.

MISSION / VISION

Grow a leading European energy business and be Marathon's international hub with each employee taking responsibility to make it happen.

BEST WORKPLACE FACTORS

FAIR DEAL
PERSONAL GROWTH
MY COMPANY

GRADUATE VACANCIES

Engineering, Supply Chain.

EMPLOYEE COMMENTS

"Marathon recognises good hard work and more than fairly rewards its staff."

"Potential is recognised and opportunities for development given."

"I could not imagine working for another company and I hope to spend the rest of my career with Marathon."

CONTACT DETAILS

Marathon, Marathon House, Hill Of Rubislaw, Anderson Drive, Aberdeen AB15 6FZ
Tel: 01224 803000 www.marathon.com

KEY

- **Holidays:** Companies offering a minimum of 25 days annual leave
- **Maternity:** Companies offering over Statutory Maternity Pay
- **Childcare:** On-site nursery or vouchers
- **Women:** At least 33% of senior managers are women
- **Long Service:** 40% of employees with more than 5 years' service
- **Pensions:** Companies offering a final salary or non-contributory/ contributory pension scheme
- **Charity Activities:** 10% of staff undertake charitable activities during business hours
- **Gym:** On-site gym or subsidised gym memberships
- **Shares:** Companies where employees are offered share options
- **Health Insurance:** Full family cover

To find out more about this company visit www.bestcompaniesguide.co.uk

1000
704>
500
0
ones to watch

MARKS SATTIN

Marks Sattin

UK locations	London
UK sites	1
Sector	Recruitment
Definition	Tailored Recruitment Consultancy
How owned	Private
Founded	1988
Turnover	Not disclosed
Profit	Not disclosed
Staff	129
Average age	25
Male : Female	63 : 37
Earnings £35,000+	52%

BEST COMPANIES INDEX

★ ★ best company 2007

OUTSTANDING

★ ★

2007 BCI = 703.1

2006 BCI = 678.4 (★)

WORKPLACE INSIGHTS

All managers are involved in training new staff across the company regardless of division.

High performing teams get an extra-long lunch paid for on Fridays. This concentrates on combined team targets and increases teamwork whilst being competitive.

Awards are voted for by all staff at Marks Sattin, not just senior management. They are not solely based on revenue like many other Recruitment Agencies. Customer Focus, relationship building and attitude within the company are considered far more important.

MISSION / VISION

To be the first choice of recruitment agency for clients and candidates in our core markets of accountancy, finance, tax and consultancy in the South East of England by offering a superior service focusing on the needs of our customers.

BEST WORKPLACE FACTORS

MY MANAGER
MY TEAM
FAIR DEAL

GRADUATE VACANCIES

Recruitment Consultants.

EMPLOYEE COMMENTS

"Relaxed team atmosphere with first rate, emotionally intelligent manager who genuinely looks out for his team."

"I have a really good relationship with my team and feel like part of a family."

"Like minded people/colleagues who are made to feel valued and rewarded for the effort they put in."

CONTACT DETAILS

Marks Sattin, 32 Haymarket, Piccadilly, London SW1Y 4TP
Tel: 0207 3215000 www.markssattin.co.uk

KEY

- **Holidays:** Companies offering a minimum of 25 days annual leave
- **Maternity:** Companies offering over Statutory Maternity Pay
- **Childcare:** On-site nursery or vouchers
- **Women:** At least 33% of senior managers are women
- **Long Service:** 40% of employees with more than 5 years' service
- **Pensions:** Companies offering a final salary or non-contributory/contributory pension scheme
- **Charity Activities:** 10% of staff undertake charitable activities during business hours
- **Gym:** On-site gym or subsidised gym memberships
- **Shares:** Companies where employees are offered share options
- **Health Insurance:** Full family cover

To find out more about this company visit www.bestcompaniesguide.co.uk

MOTABILITY OPERATIONS

Motability Operations

UK locations	London, S.West
UK sites	2
Sector	Financial
Definition	Vehicle Lease Hire
How owned	Private
Founded	1978
Turnover	£993.4m
Profit	Not disclosed
Staff	595
Average age	35
Male : Female	51 : 49
Earnings £35,000+	16%

BEST COMPANIES INDEX

best company 2007

OUTSTANDING ★ ★

2007 BCI = 722.8

WORKPLACE INSIGHTS

Motability place a key emphasis on personal contact & managers are encouraged to avoid e-mail and make face to face contact instead. Managers take the opportunity to mark & recognise personal events such as weddings by giving gifts or hosting social events.

All employees have private medical care & access to an Employee Assistance Programme. They also encourage healthy lifestyles with discounted gym memberships. On-site catering facilities offer a range of meals including healthy options & fresh deli-sandwiches.

Motability act as host and provide facilities for board meetings of various disability organisations and local associations at their London Head Office, free of charge including provision of any required parking which is valued in central London.

MISSION / VISION

To be the leading car scheme for disabled people.

BEST WORKPLACE FACTORS

MY MANAGER
WELL BEING
GIVING SOMETHING BACK

GRADUATE VACANCIES

HR, Marketing, Manufacturer Relations, Pricing and Assets, Finance, Dealer Relations, Fleet Sales, Fleet Operations, Customer Services, IT.

EMPLOYEE COMMENTS

"The management are trusting and supportive."

"I believe that the Company genuinely cares about the wellbeing of its staff."

"Opportunity to help so many other people in our daily work. It is very rewarding to work with a product of which I can be very proud."

CONTACT DETAILS

Motability Operations, City Gate House, 22 Southwark Bridge Road, London SE1 9HB
Tel: 0207 6544666 www.motability.co.uk/motabilityoperations

KEY

- **Holidays:** Companies offering a minimum of 25 days annual leave
- **Maternity:** Companies offering over Statutory Maternity Pay
- **Childcare:** On-site nursery or vouchers
- **Women:** At least 33% of senior managers are women
- **Long Service:** 40% of employees with more than 5 years' service
- **Pensions:** Companies offering a final salary or non-contributory/ contributory pension scheme
- **Charity Activities:** 10% of staff undertake charitable activities during business hours
- **Gym:** On-site gym or subsidised gym memberships
- **Shares:** Companies where employees are offered share options
- **Health Insurance:** Full family cover

MUNTERS

Munters Property Reassurance

UK locations	National
UK sites	12
Sector	Industrial
Definition	Restoration & Humidity Specialist.
How owned	Public (i.e. stock market listed)
Founded	1946
Turnover	£23.7m
Profit	£1.7m
Staff	309
Average age	39
Male : Female	77 : 23
Earnings £35,000+	8%

BEST COMPANIES INDEX

best company 2007

OUTSTANDING ★ ★

2007 BCI = 698.9

<699

ones to watch

WORKPLACE INSIGHTS

Munters are committed to improving its people and this is realised by a team of professionally accredited in-house trainers who deliver their 'Passport to Competency' programme, enabling all levels of staff to develop new skills and attain industry recognised qualifications.

Munters has various award schemes for employees such as 'The National Employee of the Year', 'Customer Service Champion' and 'Best Newcomer'. All these awards are given out at the annual conference and each winner receives various shopping/holiday vouchers.

Munters make sure that all managers are 'real world' and listen more than they tell. Managers make sure that all staff are involved in planning processes and informed about progress.

MISSION / VISION

To be recognised globally as the first choice, best value and sustainable provider of property reassurance solutions.

BEST WORKPLACE FACTORS

PERSONAL GROWTH
MY COMPANY
MY MANAGER

GRADUATE VACANCIES

No graduate vacancies have been indicated.

EMPLOYEE COMMENTS

"Excellent training & a commitment to personal development."

"Munters look after their employees. I have job satisfaction."

"Senior management offer a lot of support and communicate at all levels."

CONTACT DETAILS

Munters, Blackstone Road, Huntingdon PE29 6EE
Tel: 01480 442327 www.munters.co.uk

KEY

- **Holidays:** Companies offering a minimum of 25 days annual leave
- **Maternity:** Companies offering over Statutory Maternity Pay
- **Childcare:** On-site nursery or vouchers
- **Women:** At least 33% of senior managers are women
- **Long Service:** 40% of employees with more than 5 years' service
- **Pensions:** Companies offering a final salary or non-contributory/ contributory pension scheme
- **Charity Activities:** 10% of staff undertake charitable activities during business hours
- **Gym:** On-site gym or subsidised gym memberships
- **Shares:** Companies where employees are offered share options
- **Health Insurance:** Full family cover

To find out more about this company visit www.bestcompaniesguide.co.uk

NATIONWIDE BUILDING SOCIETY

Nationwide

UK locations	National
UK sites	759
Sector	Financial - Banks/Building Societies
Definition	Building Society
How owned	Trust/Employee owned/Mutual
Founded	1848
Turnover	£1,636m
Profit	£5.59m
Staff	16,645
Average age	36
Male : Female	29 : 71
Earnings £35,000+	13%

BEST COMPANIES INDEX

best company 2007

OUTSTANDING

★ ★

2007 BCI = 732.2

2006 BCI = 747.9 (★★★)

WORKPLACE INSIGHTS

The Nationwide Foundation was launched in 1997. Since then it has made grants totalling over £20 million, to more than 2,000 charities across the UK in its mission to encourage people to take part in building better futures in their communities.

Nationwide are keen to promote health & wellbeing and have developed an integrated approach to support their employees. This includes the proactive management of health through health screening, a complete health MOT offered to all employees, which can highlight possible concerns.

Nationwide hold monthly 'TalkBack' forums, which allow people to ask the CEO, Phillip Williamson, or another executive director a question. On-line talkback events are also held which enable people to ask questions and have an on-line debate.

MISSION / VISION

Nationwide puts members first by providing a full range of top value quality financial services that are widely available & delivered with speed, courtesy, & reliability, backed by policies of fairness, honesty, employee importance and corporate responsibility.

BEST WORKPLACE FACTORS

GIVING SOMETHING BACK
WELL BEING
LEADERSHIP

GRADUATE VACANCIES

All Areas

EMPLOYEE COMMENTS

"The organisation has very high moral & ethical standards and genuinely cares about its employees and members."

"Nationwide and its managers pay attention to the welfare of all the employees."

"The Chief Executive is inspiring, honest and does the very best for the employees."

CONTACT DETAILS

Nationwide Building Society, Nationwide House, Pipers Way, Swindon, Wiltshire SN38 1NW
Tel: 01793 655000 www.nationwide.co.uk

KEY

- **Holidays:** Companies offering a minimum of 25 days annual leave
- **Maternity:** Companies offering over Statutory Maternity Pay
- **Childcare:** On-site nursery or vouchers
- **Women:** At least 33% of senior managers are women
- **Long Service:** 40% of employees with more than 5 years' service
- **Pensions:** Companies offering a final salary or non-contributory/contributory pension scheme
- **Charity Activities:** 10% of staff undertake charitable activities during business hours
- **Gym:** On-site gym or subsidised gym memberships
- **Shares:** Companies where employees are offered share options
- **Health Insurance:** Full family cover

To find out more about this company visit www.bestcompaniesguide.co.uk

1000

732>

ones to watch

500

0

1000

<720

ones to watch

500

0

Nelson Bakewell
PROPERTY CONSULTANTS

NELSON BAKEWELL

UK locations	N.West, London, Scotland
UK sites	4
Sector	Property
Definition	Commercial property consultancy
How owned	Private
Founded	1982
Turnover	£39m
Profit	£2.5m
Staff	372
Average age	35
Male : Female	66 : 34
Earnings £35,000+	42%

BEST COMPANIES INDEX

best company 2007

OUTSTANDING

★ ★

2007 BCI = 720.3

WORKPLACE INSIGHTS

All employees at Nelson Bakewell have the opportunity to discuss their objectives and career expectations on at least an annual basis with a director. It is encouraged that these discussions take place more often - both informally and through their Managing People training.

Nelson Bakewell offices are all open plan. Their structure is flat and non-hierarchical. Teams are, typically, no larger than 7 or 8 which enables managers to work closely to staff and resolve issues/queries quickly.

Nelson Bakewell's personal growth programme is tailored to individual needs (in line with company objectives) and talents and focuses on improving personal skills. All courses contain follow up sessions with line managers.

MISSION / VISION

To provide the ultimate property solutions focused on clients' needs and sustain a working environment that attracts, retains, and develops the best employees, people who are committed to our success.

BEST WORKPLACE FACTORS

LEADERSHIP
MY MANAGER
PERSONAL GROWTH

GRADUATE VACANCIES

All areas of surveying - Landlord & Tenant, Agency Property Management, Corporate Consultancy, Valuation, Rating.

EMPLOYEE COMMENTS

"Excellent access to directors and opportunities to express your opinion to them."

"Management listen to staff ideas and will act on them."

"Careers are structured very well so there is always scope for progression."

CONTACT DETAILS

Nelson Bakewell, 25 Sackville Street, London W1S 3HQ
Tel: 0207 5442000 www.nelson-bakewell.com

KEY

- **Holidays:** Companies offering a minimum of 25 days annual leave
- **Maternity:** Companies offering over Statutory Maternity Pay
- **Childcare:** On-site nursery or vouchers
- **Women:** At least 33% of senior managers are women
- **Long Service:** 40% of employees with more than 5 years' service
- **Pensions:** Companies offering a final salary or non-contributory/ contributory pension scheme
- **Charity Activities:** 10% of staff undertake charitable activities during business hours
- **Gym:** On-site gym or subsidised gym memberships
- **Shares:** Companies where employees are offered share options
- **Health Insurance:** Full family cover

To find out more about this company visit www.bestcompaniesguide.co.uk

NORCARE

UK locations	N.East
UK sites	8
Sector	Not for Profit
Definition	Supported Housing Provider
How owned	Partnership/LLP
Founded	1984
Turnover	£3.1m
Profit	Not disclosed
Staff	82
Average age	40
Male : Female	40 : 60
Earnings £35,000+	5%

BEST COMPANIES INDEX

best company 2007

OUTSTANDING ★★

2007 BCI = 722.0

2006 BCI = 716.8 (★★)

722>

WORKPLACE INSIGHTS

Norcare have a flexible working policy that only allows employees to go 7 hours over (or under) their 37 hour working week. This is supported by a commitment at all levels that there is no expectation for employees to work over their 37 hours & a belief that they ultimately perform better with their rest time.

General wellbeing has been a key focus for Norcare for a couple of years and has seen the introduction of wellness checks, professional advice on remaining healthy in mind, body and soul.

Norcare is in its first year of laying the foundations for a number of social enterprise activities that will benefit community areas & those living within them by providing services not previously available, employment opportunities & accessibility.

MISSION / VISION

Vision: To be the first choice for clients, funders and employees.
Mission: To improve the quality of life for people who are currently socially and economically excluded.

BEST WORKPLACE FACTORS

FAIR DEAL
WELL BEING
GIVING SOMETHING BACK

GRADUATE VACANCIES

No graduate vacancies have been indicated.

EMPLOYEE COMMENTS

"Management are supportive in their flexibility and trust in my ability to perform my role."

"Norcare value the staff and are always looking to improve the quality of the staff environment."

"I feel I do make a difference in some of my clients' lives."

CONTACT DETAILS

Norcare, Third Floor Portman House, Shieldfield, Newcastle Upon Tyne NE2 1AQ
Tel: 0191 2612228 www.norcare-ltd.com

KEY

- **Holidays:** Companies offering a minimum of 25 days annual leave
- **Maternity:** Companies offering over Statutory Maternity Pay
- **Childcare:** On-site nursery or vouchers
- **Women:** At least 33% of senior managers are women
- **Long Service:** 40% of employees with more than 5 years' service
- **Pensions:** Companies offering a final salary or non-contributory/ contributory pension scheme
- **Charity Activities:** 10% of staff undertake charitable activities during business hours
- **Gym:** On-site gym or subsidised gym memberships
- **Shares:** Companies where employees are offered share options
- **Health Insurance:** Full family cover

O2 UK & AIRWAVE

UK locations	National
UK sites	519
Sector	Communications/Telecom
Definition	Mobile Network Operator
How owned	Public (i.e. stock market listed)
Founded	2001
Turnover	Not disclosed
Profit	Not disclosed
Staff	12,129
Average age	32
Male : Female	56 : 44
Earnings £35,000+	20%

BEST COMPANIES INDEX

best company 2007

OUTSTANDING

★ ★

2007 BCI = 735.4

WORKPLACE INSIGHTS

O2 believe people are special and recognise this throughout the year by giving out awards to employees who have made an outstanding contribution. One award sees 22 winners whisked away to exotic destinations such as Dubai and Las Vegas.

O2 hold a variety of events for employees to get to know each other and to just have fun. These events range from the Christmas Party to sending 11,000 staff to Alton Towers and Thorpe Park.

Board members present at all annual directorate conferences to enable their employees to more fully understand the O2 vision and future challenges. There is also a formal cascade process in Customer Services, to ensure that everyone is involved.

MISSION / VISION

To put customer experience at the heart of everything we do. To be a breath of fresh air.

BEST WORKPLACE FACTORS

FAIR DEAL
MY TEAM
MY MANAGER

GRADUATE VACANCIES

No graduate vacancies have been indicated.

EMPLOYEE COMMENTS

"Good rewards for job excellence and a good quality of benefits available for all employees."

"It's a great place because of the team spirit."

"It's very easy to find support from colleagues, managers and senior managers."

CONTACT DETAILS

O2 UK & Airwave, Wellington Street, Slough, Berkshire SL1 1YP
Tel: 0113 2722000 www.o2.com

KEY

- **Holidays:** Companies offering a minimum of 25 days annual leave
- **Maternity:** Companies offering over Statutory Maternity Pay
- **Childcare:** On-site nursery or vouchers
- **Women:** At least 33% of senior managers are women
- **Long Service:** 40% of employees with more than 5 years' service
- **Pensions:** Companies offering a final salary or non-contributory/ contributory pension scheme
- **Charity Activities:** 10% of staff undertake charitable activities during business hours
- **Gym:** On-site gym or subsidised gym memberships
- **Shares:** Companies where employees are offered share options
- **Health Insurance:** Full family cover

To find out more about this company visit www.bestcompaniesguide.co.uk

OLSWANG

OLSWANG

UK locations	London, S.East
UK sites	2
Sector	Law
Definition	Legal Firm
How owned	Partnership/LLP
Founded	1981
Turnover	£77.7m
Profit	£29.3m
Staff	549
Average age	34
Male : Female	39 : 61
Earnings £35,000+	55%

BEST COMPANIES INDEX

OUTSTANDING ★ ★

2007 BCI = 702.4

2006 BCI = 729.6 (★★)

WORKPLACE INSIGHTS

In addition to benefits such as free private healthcare, subsidised dental insurance and Life Assurance, Olswang take all staff away for a weekend every year, and provide on-site massages and emergency childcare/homecare facilities when necessary.

The Chief Executive and the Director of HR hold annual "round table" discussions with groups of up to eight members of staff, to find out what they think is positively distinctive about the firm & what they value and enjoy about their working lives.

Olswang have formed the Green Team to work on new environmental initiatives and offer practical solutions for staff to help achieve environmental goals. Their new waste recycling scheme means that as much waste as possible is recycled or disposed of in the least damaging way.

MISSION / VISION

We're quick to question accepted wisdom and we don't assume something is impossible simply because it's never been done before. We don't just look at the world from a narrow legal point of view - we see it the way our clients do.

BEST WORKPLACE FACTORS

FAIR DEAL
LEADERSHIP
GIVING SOMETHING BACK

GRADUATE VACANCIES

Legal Practice Areas, Human Resources, Marketing/ Business Development, Compliance.

EMPLOYEE COMMENTS

"The salaries and benefits are very good."

"Staff are motivated because the leadership is motivated."

"Environmental, charity, and community support provides each person the ability to make a difference outside of the office."

CONTACT DETAILS

Olswang, 90 High Holborn, London WC1V 6XX
Tel: 0207 0673000 www.olswang.com

KEY

Holidays: Companies offering a minimum of 25 days annual leave

Maternity: Companies offering over Statutory Maternity Pay

Childcare: On-site nursery or vouchers

Women: At least 33% of senior managers are women

Long Service: 40% of employees with more than 5 years' service

Pensions: Companies offering a final salary or non-contributory/ contributory pension scheme

Charity Activities: 10% of staff undertake charitable activities during business hours

Gym: On-site gym or subsidised gym memberships

Shares: Companies where employees are offered share options

Health Insurance: Full family cover

1000

702>

ones to watch

500

0

PEARCE GROUP

PEARCE

UK locations	S.West
UK sites	1
Sector	Construction
Definition	Construction/Project Management
How owned	Private
Founded	1947
Turnover	£122m
Profit	£0.5m
Staff	288
Average age	41
Male : Female	83 : 17
Earnings £35,000+	44%

BEST COMPANIES INDEX

best company 2007

OUTSTANDING ★ ★

2007 BCI = 698.2

WORKPLACE INSIGHTS

Pearce is an exciting and vibrant company to work for. Two of the four key values are to develop Pearce people and build relationships and they pride themselves in ensuring that this is evident.

Pearce Group Executive Management Team and Chief Executive are happy to talk to members of staff whenever they are approached. They also actively engage with people about how they're feeling about the Company and their jobs.

Senior Managers ensure that there are regular team meetings to share knowledge and improve communication. As well as the monthly briefing meetings, each team also have more regular meetings to discuss workload, and what's happening in the team.

MISSION / VISION

Pearce will continue to be a growing and profitable provider of construction services in the South West and to strategic customers across the UK.

BEST WORKPLACE FACTORS

MY COMPANY
LEADERSHIP
MY MANAGER

GRADUATE VACANCIES

Quantity Surveying & Construction Management.

EMPLOYEE COMMENTS

"I enjoy my job and look forward to going to work."

"Good leadership and Senior Managers with positive attitude."

"My Managers are pleasant and treat me with respect."

CONTACT DETAILS

Pearce Group, Parklands, Hambrook Lane, Stoke Gifford BS34 8QU
Tel: 0117 9236500 www.pearce.co.uk

KEY

- **Holidays:** Companies offering a minimum of 25 days annual leave
- **Maternity:** Companies offering over Statutory Maternity Pay
- **Childcare:** On-site nursery or vouchers
- **Women:** At least 33% of senior managers are women
- **Long Service:** 40% of employees with more than 5 years' service
- **Pensions:** Companies offering a final salary or non-contributory/contributory pension scheme
- **Charity Activities:** 10% of staff undertake charitable activities during business hours
- **Gym:** On-site gym or subsidised gym memberships
- **Shares:** Companies where employees are offered share options
- **Health Insurance:** Full family cover

To find out more about this company visit www.bestcompaniesguide.co.uk

PETER BRETT ASSOCIATES

peter brett associates

UK locations	National
UK sites	10
Sector	Consulting
Definition	Land Development Consultancy
How owned	Partnership/LLP
Founded	1965
Turnover	£31.6m
Profit	£3.3m
Staff	490
Average age	36
Male : Female	72 : 38
Earnings £35,000+	31%

BEST COMPANIES INDEX

best company 2007

OUTSTANDING ★ ★

2007 BCI = 696.8

2006 BCI = 735.3 (★★)

697>

WORKPLACE INSIGHTS

Founding member of Reading Initiative for Tsunami Action (RITA), registered charity committed to long term re-building of areas affected by the tsunami. RITA is targeting support in Sri Lanka, where Peter Brett are acting as technical consultant & treasurer with representation on the steering group.

Peter Brett support employee work life balance & wellbeing through various policies & initiatives. They consider all requests for flexible working. They have arranged for an occupational psychologist to be available to support staff returning to work after a period of illness.

In addition to their approved Graduate Training Schemes, they fund extensive attendance on external technical courses, run in-house project/team management training & arrange numerous lunchtime seminars, open to all.

MISSION / VISION

Vision: To become the UK's most respected independent consultancy.
Mission: PBA aims to provide the best solutions to the project related challenges faced by our Clients. Innovation, quality, and speed of service, cost effectiveness, and attention to detail, are essential factors in the PBA approach.

BEST WORKPLACE FACTORS

GIVING SOMETHING BACK
WELL BEING
PERSONAL GROWTH

GRADUATE VACANCIES

Civil Engineering and relevant specialist backgrounds.

EMPLOYEE COMMENTS

"Social responsibility, undertaken with genuine will to improve local, national and global environments."

"Flexibility - allowing people to share responsibilities between work & home life."

"Growth plans offer opportunities for everyone to develop & excellent training opportunities are provided."

CONTACT DETAILS

Peter Brett Associates, Caversham Bridge House, Waterman Place, Reading, Berks RG1 8DN
Tel: 0118 9500761 www.pba.co.uk

KEY

Holidays: Companies offering a minimum of 25 days annual leave
Maternity: Companies offering over Statutory Maternity Pay
Childcare: On-site nursery or vouchers
Women: At least 33% of senior managers are women
Long Service: 40% of employees with more than 5 years' service
Pensions: Companies offering a final salary or non-contributory/ contributory pension scheme
Charity Activities: 10% of staff undertake charitable activities during business hours
Gym: On-site gym or subsidised gym memberships
Shares: Companies where employees are offered share options
Health Insurance: Full family cover

To find out more about this company visit www.bestcompaniesguide.co.uk

PFJ

UK locations	N.West, London
UK sites	3
Sector	Recruitment
Definition	Specialist Recruitment Consultancy
How owned	Private
Founded	1992
Turnover	£6.1m
Profit	£0.4m
Staff	95
Average age	28
Male : Female	35 : 65
Earnings £35,000+	47%

BEST COMPANIES INDEX

best company 2007

OUTSTANDING ★ ★

2007 BCI = 725.3

2006 BCI = 684.9 (★)

WORKPLACE INSIGHTS

Managers play a key role in employees' development via PFJ's 'Aspire' development programme. Each employee has a personal development plan and together with their manager and the training manager they map out the plan.

PFJ encourage teams to bond and socialise together by providing a variety of social events including a beach party, trips abroad, treasure hunts and even apple bobbing on Halloween. In addition, the chairman takes the top 7 consultants out to dinner every few months.

All the Senior Management at PFJ are involved in training and development, either classroom based or at the desk or even 'live' with customers. On average they will deliver a minimum of one session a week to a group or an individual.

MISSION / VISION

By working 'More Together', PFJ aim to employ the most talented & professional people & become the 1st choice supplier of recruitment solutions to all our clients in all our markets.

BEST WORKPLACE FACTORS

MY MANAGER
MY TEAM
LEADERSHIP

GRADUATE VACANCIES

Trainee Recruitment Consultancy, IT & Marketing.

EMPLOYEE COMMENTS

"There is good communication between managers and employees."

"There is a strong team ethic where team members support or socialise with each other regularly."

"Strong leadership from our chairman and clear direction and feedback on where the company is going."

CONTACT DETAILS

PFJ, 44-44 Clipstone St, London W1W 5DW
Tel: 0870 0489100 www.pfj.co.uk

KEY

Holidays: Companies offering a minimum of 25 days annual leave
Maternity: Companies offering over Statutory Maternity Pay
Childcare: On-site nursery or vouchers
Women: At least 33% of senior managers are women
Long Service: 40% of employees with more than 5 years' service
Pensions: Companies offering a final salary or non-contributory/contributory pension scheme
Charity Activities: 10% of staff undertake charitable activities during business hours
Gym: On-site gym or subsidised gym memberships
Shares: Companies where employees are offered share options
Health Insurance: Full family cover

To find out more about this company visit www.bestcompaniesguide.co.uk

PLUS HOUSING GROUP

UK locations	National
UK sites	16
Sector	Housing Associations
Definition	Social Landlord
How owned	Trust/Employee owned/A Mutual
Founded	1977
Turnover	£27.2m
Profit	£0.2m
Staff	236
Average age	35
Male : Female	35 : 65
Earnings £35,000+	11%

BEST COMPANIES INDEX

best company 2007

OUTSTANDING ★ ★

2007 BCI = 710.2

2006 BCI = 717.5 (★★)

WORKPLACE INSIGHTS

As a social landlord, working in neighbourhoods and communities, CSR is what PLUS Housing do!!.

PLUS Housing strives to offer existing & potential staff an attractive deal to encourage people to join them and stay with them.

To improve wellbeing PLUS have introduced a non contributory Healthsure cash plan giving staff cash back on dental and other services.

MISSION / VISION

We use our strong set of founding values to achieve our vision to be a diverse Group of organisations with complementary goals.

BEST WORKPLACE FACTORS

GIVING SOMETHING BACK
FAIR DEAL
WELL BEING

GRADUATE VACANCIES

Development/Regeneration.

EMPLOYEE COMMENTS

"PLUS Housing has a great ethos on the provision of homes, the environment, recycling and enabling communities to come together to achieve their goals."

"I feel PLUS Housing is very fair and one of the best employers I have worked for as they are always looking to the future which I hope to be a part of."

"The introduction of Healthsure has been beneficial for me."

CONTACT DETAILS

PLUS Housing Group, Baltimore Buildings, 13-15 Rodney Street, Liverpool L1 9EF
Tel: 0151 7080674 www.plusgroupltd.org.uk

KEY

- **Holidays:** Companies offering a minimum of 25 days annual leave
- **Maternity:** Companies offering over Statutory Maternity Pay
- **Childcare:** On-site nursery or vouchers
- **Women:** At least 33% of senior managers are women
- **Long Service:** 40% of employees with more than 5 years' service
- **Pensions:** Companies offering a final salary or non-contributory/ contributory pension scheme
- **Charity Activities:** 10% of staff undertake charitable activities during business hours
- **Gym:** On-site gym or subsidised gym memberships
- **Shares:** Companies where employees are offered share options
- **Health Insurance:** Full family cover

1000

710>

500

0

ones to watch

PRICEWATERHOUSECOOPERS

PRICEWATERHOUSECOOPERS

<728

UK locations	National
UK sites	36
Sector	Professional Services
Definition	Accountants
How owned	Partnership/LLP
Founded	1998
Turnover	£1,980m
Profit	Not disclosed
Staff	15,347
Average age	32
Male : Female	52 : 48
Earnings £35,000+	53%

BEST COMPANIES INDEX

best company 2007

OUTSTANDING ★ ★

2007 BCI = 727.6

2006 BCI = 678.1 (★)

WORKPLACE INSIGHTS

This year PricewaterhouseCoopers invested £42million direct cash costs in learning & development activities using a variety of learning interventions and re-launched an improved online 'one stop shop' for all their learning activities and resources.

PWC provide employees with a comprehensive flexible benefits package allowing them to tailor their remuneration to individual needs. Employees choose from a range of options including dental insurance, critical illness insurance, and life assurance.

A number of recognition awards are provided to employees including 'MAD' Awards given to someone who has 'Made A Difference' and 'STAR' Recognition Awards for people who have done something exceptional or helpful. Gifts worth up to £250 are provided for both.

MISSION / VISION

We aim to be the leaders in our chosen markets by serving our clients through relationships based on quality and integrity in everything we do and being a great place to work for all our people.

BEST WORKPLACE FACTORS

PERSONAL GROWTH
FAIR DEAL
MY COMPANY

GRADUATE VACANCIES

Assurance (audit), Tax , Advisory, Actuarial, Strategy.

EMPLOYEE COMMENTS

"The graduate programme and investment made by the company is fantastic."

"Training opportunities are great & the remuneration packages very comprehensive."

"It is a very caring place to work. I feel valued, supported & protected."

CONTACT DETAILS

PricewaterhouseCoopers, 1 Embankment Place, London WC2N 6RH
Tel: 0207 5835000 www.pwc.co.uk

KEY

- **Holidays:** Companies offering a minimum of 25 days annual leave
- **Maternity:** Companies offering over Statutory Maternity Pay
- **Childcare:** On-site nursery or vouchers
- **Women:** At least 33% of senior managers are women
- **Long Service:** 40% of employees with more than 5 years' service
- **Pensions:** Companies offering a final salary or non-contributory/contributory pension scheme
- **Charity Activities:** 10% of staff undertake charitable activities during business hours
- **Gym:** On-site gym or subsidised gym memberships
- **Shares:** Companies where employees are offered share options
- **Health Insurance:** Full family cover

To find out more about this company visit www.bestcompaniesguide.co.uk

profero

PROFERO

UK locations	London
UK sites	1
Sector	Media
Definition	Digital Marketing Agency
How owned	Private
Founded	1998
Turnover	Not disclosed
Profit	Not disclosed
Staff	64
Average age	33
Male : Female	66 : 34
Earnings £35,000+	39%

BEST COMPANIES INDEX

best company 2007

OUTSTANDING ★ ★

2007 BCI = 697.0

2006 BCI = 616.8

697>

ones to watch

WORKPLACE INSIGHTS

MD Wayne Arnold has lunch with new members of the team after they've been with Profero for 3 months. This gives the team time to feed back on what they feel they like about Profero but also if there's anything they would change.

Profero have an agency day where they close the agency on a Friday during the summer to do something fun together as a team.

Teams are provided with a personal development fund which encourages them to take an activity outside of work.

MISSION / VISION

Vision: To be the most forward thinking independent communications group in the world admired and respected for our work.
Mission: To channel individual passion and creativity into the most intelligent innovative and effective solutions for our clients.

BEST WORKPLACE FACTORS

LEADERSHIP
MY COMPANY
PERSONAL GROWTH

GRADUATE VACANCIES

Client Services, Media Planning, Buying, Design & Creative.

EMPLOYEE COMMENTS

"Excellent values and morals held by Wayne. Very inspiring man who genuinely cares about the team."

"I feel places like this are quite rare and really deserves some recognition."

"Everyone is motivated & feels that we are making a positive contribution, shaping the future of digital media."

CONTACT DETAILS

Profero, Centro 3, 19 Mandela Street, London NW1 0DU
Tel: 0207 3872000 www.profero.com

KEY

- **Holidays:** Companies offering a minimum of 25 days annual leave
- **Maternity:** Companies offering over Statutory Maternity Pay
- **Childcare:** On-site nursery or vouchers
- **Women:** At least 33% of senior managers are women
- **Long Service:** 40% of employees with more than 5 years' service
- **Pensions:** Companies offering a final salary or non-contributory/ contributory pension scheme
- **Charity Activities:** 10% of staff undertake charitable activities during business hours
- **Gym:** On-site gym or subsidised gym memberships
- **Shares:** Companies where employees are offered share options
- **Health Insurance:** Full family cover

RACKSPACE MANAGED HOSTING

UK locations	London
UK sites	4
Sector	IT/Internet Services
Definition	Managed Hosting
How owned	Private
Founded	2001
Turnover	Not disclosed
Profit	Not disclosed
Staff	177
Average age	29
Male : Female	73 : 27
Earnings £35,000+	27%

BEST COMPANIES INDEX

best company 2007

OUTSTANDING ★ ★

2007 BCI = 732.4

2006 BCI = 774.5 (★★★)

WORKPLACE INSIGHTS

Rackspace has 4 'house' teams within which employees are placed on joining the company. Competitions take place between these teams such as 'The Rack Olympics' which is an all day event of games such as Connect 4, Draughts, Darts, and Mini Golf.

Rackspace have a strong, welcoming culture and ensure new starters are made to feel valuable from the start. They are sent a welcome card before they start, a range of inductions and shadowing opportunities are provided and the Managing Director takes new employees out to lunch.

From the moment they start, staff are encouraged to join a committee such as Charity, Service Excellence or Social committees, to broaden their experience and help them to develop leadership and management skills.

MISSION / VISION

To be recognised as one of the UK's great service companies along with brands like First Direct and Virgin Atlantic.

BEST WORKPLACE FACTORS

MY TEAM
MY COMPANY
MY MANAGER

GRADUATE VACANCIES

Sales Qualification Team & Datacentre Operations Technician.

EMPLOYEE COMMENTS

"I love all the people involved in this organisation, they absolutely make the place what it is."

"The atmosphere is vibrant and I cannot see myself working for any other company."

"Management involve Rackers and our opinions really do count."

CONTACT DETAILS

Rackspace Managed Hosting, 2 Long Walk Rd, Stockley Park, Uxbridge, Middlesex UB11 1BA
Tel: 0208 7342500 www.rackspace.co.uk

KEY

- **Holidays:** Companies offering a minimum of 25 days annual leave
- **Pensions:** Companies offering a final salary or non-contributory/contributory pension scheme
- **Maternity:** Companies offering over Statutory Maternity Pay
- **Charity Activities:** 10% of staff undertake charitable activities during business hours
- **Childcare:** On-site nursery or vouchers
- **Gym:** On-site gym or subsidised gym memberships
- **Women:** At least 33% of senior managers are women
- **Shares:** Companies where employees are offered share options
- **Long Service:** 40% of employees with more than 5 years' service
- **Health Insurance:** Full family cover

To find out more about this company visit www.bestcompaniesguide.co.uk

RANDSTAD WORK SOLUTIONS

randstad
work solutions

UK locations	National
UK sites	120
Sector	Recruitment
Definition	Recruitment Consultancy
How owned	Private
Founded	1960
Turnover	Not disclosed
Profit	Not disclosed
Staff	413
Average age	33
Male : Female	35 : 65
Earnings £35,000+	8%

BEST COMPANIES INDEX

best company 2007

OUTSTANDING

★ ★

2007 BCI = 716.8

2006 BCI = 708.6 (★★)

WORKPLACE INSIGHTS

Randstad organise numerous 'in-house' fun events, such as a 'world-cup table-football challenge' and a 'name the baby' competition, which provides a fun element to work and encourages team building and morale.

Randstad are unique in the way their service is delivered and also in the treatment of all stakeholders, clients, flex-workers, permanent candidates & corporate employees.

The focus on integration between management and employees at all levels is fundamental to the Randstad culture.

MISSION / VISION

Work makes the world go round. It supports individual expression and development, and shapes business society and life. We believe that the power of work as a unifying spirit rests on the quality of each individual match between employer and employee.

BEST WORKPLACE FACTORS

MY TEAM
MY COMPANY
MY MANAGER

GRADUATE VACANCIES

No graduate vacancies have been indicated.

EMPLOYEE COMMENTS

"From day one I have felt like a member of the team and my input is very valued."

"Staff, management and senior management care about people they work with more than any other company I have worked for."

"My manager is a fantastic role model in the way that she values my contribution."

CONTACT DETAILS

Randstad Work Solutions, Randstad House, London Road, Newbury, Berkshire RG14 1LA
Tel: 01635 589222 www.uk.randstad.com

KEY

- **Holidays:** Companies offering a minimum of 25 days annual leave
- **Maternity:** Companies offering over Statutory Maternity Pay
- **Childcare:** On-site nursery or vouchers
- **Women:** At least 33% of senior managers are women
- **Long Service:** 40% of employees with more than 5 years' service
- **Pensions:** Companies offering a final salary or non-contributory/contributory pension scheme
- **Charity Activities:** 10% of staff undertake charitable activities during business hours
- **Gym:** On-site gym or subsidised gym memberships
- **Shares:** Companies where employees are offered share options
- **Health Insurance:** Full family cover

1000
717>
500
0
ones to watch

To find out more about this company visit www.bestcompaniesguide.co.uk

1000

ROYAL HASKONING

ROYAL HASKONING
consultants architects engineers

UK locations	National
UK sites	18
Sector	Consulting
Definition	Professional Engineering Consultancy
How owned	Private
Founded	2000
Turnover	£26.8m
Profit	£1.8m
Staff	436
Average age	38
Male : Female	69 : 31
Earnings £35,000+	28%

BEST COMPANIES INDEX

best company 2007

OUTSTANDING ★ ★

2007 BCI = 697.0

<697

ones to watch

WORKPLACE INSIGHTS

Royal Haskoning have approved chartership programmes that allow graduates to become chartered within 3-4 years. They may follow ICE, IStructE, CIWEM or some other relevant professional path as the company have experience & knowledge to mentor & guide.

A number of Royal Haskoning staff have taken part in social projects & activities and projects at schools. A large amount of staff time is given to cater for work experience students in secondary education such as for Project Trident.

Royal Haskoning has many initiatives and policies in place to support employees' work-life balance including an Employee Assistance Helpline, flexi-time working arrangements, the buying /selling of annual holidays, free eyesight tests and subsidised sports and social activities.

MISSION / VISION

Our vision is that in the future it will become increasingly important to continually increase the value of our services for our clients and to treat their problems as our own.

500

BEST WORKPLACE FACTORS

PERSONAL GROWTH
GIVING SOMETHING BACK
WELL BEING

GRADUATE VACANCIES

Civil, Structural, Environmental Sciences, Geology, Electrical & Mechanical Engineering.

EMPLOYEE COMMENTS

"I am given guidance to help me develop and reach both my own goals and that of the company."

"Being able to make a difference - both within the organisation and to the outside world."

"Social wellbeing is of importance and the organisation is flexible to adapt to specific individual needs."

CONTACT DETAILS

Royal Haskoning, Rightwell House, Bretton, Peterborough, Cambridgeshire PE3 8DW
Tel: 01733 334455 www.royalhaskoning.com

KEY

- **Holidays:** Companies offering a minimum of 25 days annual leave
- **Maternity:** Companies offering over Statutory Maternity Pay
- **Childcare:** On-site nursery or vouchers
- **Women:** At least 33% of senior managers are women
- **Long Service:** 40% of employees with more than 5 years' service
- **Pensions:** Companies offering a final salary or non-contributory/ contributory pension scheme
- **Charity Activities:** 10% of staff undertake charitable activities during business hours
- **Gym:** On-site gym or subsidised gym memberships
- **Shares:** Companies where employees are offered share options
- **Health Insurance:** Full family cover

0

To find out more about this company visit www.bestcompaniesguide.co.uk

ROYAL SOCIETY FOR THE PROTECTION OF BIRDS

UK locations	National
UK sites	206
Sector	Charity
Definition	Biodiversity Conservation
How owned	Trust/Employee owned/Mutual
Founded	1889
Turnover	£88.3m
Profit	Not disclosed
Staff	1,670
Average age	42
Male : Female	49 : 51
Earnings £35,000+	8%

BEST COMPANIES INDEX

best company 2007 ★★

OUTSTANDING ★ ★

2007 BCI = 737.4

2006 BCI = 733.4 (★★)

737>

ones to watch

WORKPLACE INSIGHTS

Over the last five years, RSPB have increased efforts to involve people, members & public alike in their conservation activities. Participation in Big Garden Birdwatch has now reached nearly 500,000. 'Feed the Birds' day involves about 25,000 people.

The RSPB mission, to work for a better world for birds & people, has been communicated to all employees via presentations by Graham Wynne, Chief Executive. It is regularly featured in all staff training & development events & inductions.

RSPB believe personal and professional development is vital to continued success. Annually, they run over 500 courses to help people do their jobs better and develop their careers. Topics vary - from using a chainsaw, through to IT skills, project management and interpersonal skills.

MISSION / VISION

The RSPB works for a better world for birds & people. We passionately believe that: 1. Conservation of biodiversity is a moral imperative 2. The health of bird populations is indicative of the health of the planet on which the future of the human race depends 3. Birds & other wildlife enrich peoples' lives.

BEST WORKPLACE FACTORS

GIVING SOMETHING BACK
MY COMPANY
PERSONAL GROWTH

GRADUATE VACANCIES

International, IS, Conservation Science, Ecology, Marketing Personnel as well as Reserve Managers.

EMPLOYEE COMMENTS

"RSPB is involved in a very worthwhile cause that has a positive impact on the environment."

"There is a relaxed friendly feel to the workplace that brings out the best in the staff."

"There is room for me to grow & move within the organisation, supported in my personal career development."

CONTACT DETAILS

Royal Society for the Protection of Birds, The Lodge, Sandy, Bedfordshire SG19 2DL
Tel: 01767 680551 www.rspb.org.uk

KEY

- **Holidays:** Companies offering a minimum of 25 days annual leave
- **Maternity:** Companies offering over Statutory Maternity Pay
- **Childcare:** On-site nursery or vouchers
- **Women:** At least 33% of senior managers are women
- **Long Service:** 40% of employees with more than 5 years' service
- **Pensions:** Companies offering a final salary or non-contributory/ contributory pension scheme
- **Charity Activities:** 10% of staff undertake charitable activities during business hours
- **Gym:** On-site gym or subsidised gym memberships
- **Shares:** Companies where employees are offered share options
- **Health Insurance:** Full family cover

To find out more about this company visit www.bestcompaniesguide.co.uk

1000

<729

500

ones to watch

0

RUFFER

UK locations	London
UK sites	1
Sector	Financial
Definition	Clients' Investment Management
How owned	Partnership/LLP
Founded	1994
Turnover	£20.7m
Profit	Not disclosed
Staff	69
Average age	31
Male : Female	51 : 49
Earnings £35,000+	52%

BEST COMPANIES INDEX

★ ★ best company 2007

OUTSTANDING

★ ★

2007 BCI = 729.0

2006 BCI = 735.1 (★★)

WORKPLACE INSIGHTS

The CEO likes to know who everyone is so he can make conversation in the corridor with them, so before they start he wants a photo and a brief synopsis.

Ruffer have set reception hours of 8am - 6:30pm and then define the office as closed, even though some may work on - it sets a feeling that the goal is to leave on time.

Friday Lunch Clubs are an opportunity for all levels to intermingle socially & for junior staff to be able to chat to senior leaders over lunch.

MISSION / VISION

Ruffer LLP's aim is to achieve an investment performance which is 'absolutely' satisfactory. Our job can be likened to a pig hunting for truffles in the world of investment: the truffle is the investment whose rewards outweigh the risks. We try to make sure it is a sound truffle before we dig it up.

BEST WORKPLACE FACTORS

LEADERSHIP
WELL BEING
MY MANAGER

GRADUATE VACANCIES

No graduate vacancies have been indicated.

EMPLOYEE COMMENTS

"Jonathan Ruffer goes to great lengths to get to know those who contribute to the organisation."

"Ruffer seems to care about our wellbeing - free fruit & massages."

"You are not treated as a number. All management take time out to talk to staff."

CONTACT DETAILS

Ruffer, Nations House, 103 Wigmore Street, London W1U 1QS
Tel: 0207 5297900 www.ruffer.co.uk

KEY

Holidays: Companies offering a minimum of 25 days annual leave
Maternity: Companies offering over Statutory Maternity Pay
Childcare: On-site nursery or vouchers
Women: At least 33% of senior managers are women
Long Service: 40% of employees with more than 5 years' service
Pensions: Companies offering a final salary or non-contributory/ contributory pension scheme
Charity Activities: 10% of staff undertake charitable activities during business hours
Gym: On-site gym or subsidised gym memberships
Shares: Companies where employees are offered share options
Health Insurance: Full family cover

To find out more about this company visit www.bestcompaniesguide.co.uk

S J D Accountancy
Chartered Tax Advisers and Accountants

SJD ACCOUNTANCY

UK locations	National
UK sites	6
Sector	Professional Services
Definition	National Accountancy Firm
How owned	Partnership/LLP
Founded	1997
Turnover	£3.3m
Profit	£1.7m
Staff	51
Average age	30
Male : Female	45 : 55
Earnings £35,000+	31%

BEST COMPANIES INDEX

★ ★ best company 2007

OUTSTANDING

★ ★

2007 BCI = 724.3

WORKPLACE INSIGHTS

The working environment at SJD offers a perfect balance of work and home life, taking full 1 hour lunch breaks is encouraged and leaving at 5pm is a must.

Personal development is encouraged at SJD. Two employees of SJD started over seven years ago, one on the front desk as a receptionist and one as an account manager. Both are now regional directors with teams of over eight people.

The Managers at SJD are understanding and considerate. They are happy to offer advice on career prospects and provide opportunities for training.

MISSION / VISION

Our vision for the company as a whole is to double our number of clients by end of 2007 whilst retaining 99% of our existing customer base.

BEST WORKPLACE FACTORS

WELL BEING
PERSONAL GROWTH
MY MANAGER

GRADUATE VACANCIES

No graduate vacancies have been indicated.

EMPLOYEE COMMENTS

"Employees are able to have a reasonable amount of fun, resulting in people working harder and feeling happy at work."

"Opportunities available if you want to climb the ladder."

"Team members feel valued by the Managers."

CONTACT DETAILS

SJD Accountancy, High Trees, Hillfield Road, Hemel Hempstead, Herts HP2 4AY
Tel: 01442 232700 www.sjdaccountancy.com

KEY

Holidays: Companies offering a minimum of 25 days annual leave
Maternity: Companies offering over Statutory Maternity Pay
Childcare: On-site nursery or vouchers
Women: At least 33% of senior managers are women
Long Service: 40% of employees with more than 5 years' service
Pensions: Companies offering a final salary or non-contributory/contributory pension scheme
Charity Activities: 10% of staff undertake charitable activities during business hours
Gym: On-site gym or subsidised gym memberships
Shares: Companies where employees are offered share options
Health Insurance: Full family cover

1000
724>
500
0
ones to watch

SOLVAY HEALTHCARE

UK locations	S.East
UK sites	1
Sector	Pharmaceutical
Definition	Marketing pharma products
How owned	Public (i.e. stock market listed)
Founded	1962
Turnover	£35.8m
Profit	£1.4m
Staff	170
Average age	39
Male : Female	44 : 56
Earnings £35,000+	46%

BEST COMPANIES INDEX

best company 2007

OUTSTANDING ★ ★

2007 BCI = 700.8

2006 BCI = 698.8 (★)

WORKPLACE INSIGHTS

First line managers at Solvay are key to the engagement of staff & are supported/involved to ensure they fully understand the business direction. Solvay encourages people at all levels to be very open & honest, and to communicate quickly & efficiently.

Solvay provides a number of awards depending on employee roles. Office staff can be nominated for STARS awards; Sales staff have performance related Alpha and TOPPS Gold, Silver and Bronze clubs & there is also an annual Innovations Award for new initiatives put into action.

Solvay is sponsoring a trail in Itchen Valley Country Park and is getting involved in conservation in this area. Employees are helping to clear the trail which will complement the local authority's environmental education work.

MISSION / VISION

Solvay Healthcare is part of a global healthcare business that researches, develops, and provides, medicines that meet people's health needs. Respect for people who use our medicines and who work for us. The capability, creativity, and energy of our people.

BEST WORKPLACE FACTORS

MY MANAGER
MY COMPANY
GIVING SOMETHING BACK

GRADUATE VACANCIES

Sales.

EMPLOYEE COMMENTS

"My manager and national sales manager inspire and encourage me."

"Solvay is good at making everyone feel like we are one big family."

"There is a drive to meet targets and help the local community."

CONTACT DETAILS

Solvay Healthcare, Mansbridge Road, West End, Southampton, Hants SO18 3JD
Tel: 0238 0467000 www.solvayhealthcare.co.uk

KEY

- **Holidays:** Companies offering a minimum of 25 days annual leave
- **Maternity:** Companies offering over Statutory Maternity Pay
- **Childcare:** On-site nursery or vouchers
- **Women:** At least 33% of senior managers are women
- **Long Service:** 40% of employees with more than 5 years' service
- **Pensions:** Companies offering a final salary or non-contributory/contributory pension scheme
- **Charity Activities:** 10% of staff undertake charitable activities during business hours
- **Gym:** On-site gym or subsidised gym memberships
- **Shares:** Companies where employees are offered share options
- **Health Insurance:** Full family cover

1000
<701
500
0
ones to watch

To find out more about this company visit www.bestcompaniesguide.co.uk

SOUTH CHESHIRE COLLEGE

SOUTH CHESHIRE COLLEGE

UK locations	N.West
UK sites	5
Sector	Education
Definition	Tertiary College
How owned	Private
Founded	1982
Turnover	£18.6m
Profit	Not disclosed
Staff	393
Average age	43
Male : Female	42 : 58
Earnings £35,000+	18%

BEST COMPANIES INDEX

★★ best company 2007

OUTSTANDING

★ ★

2007 BCI = 718.1

2006 BCI = 703.9 (★★)

1000

718>

ones to watch

500

0

WORKPLACE INSIGHTS

The on-site ABTA travel centre offers a programme of social and cultural events for staff and their families e.g. mini cruises, shopping and theatre trips. Other on-site facilities include hair, beauty and holistic therapies (two free sessions per employee), a library and shop.

South Cheshire College is the best in the country - as judged by the FEFC in 1999 and Ofsted in 2004. No other tertiary college has achieved such high grades at inspection.

All staff, irrespective of job role or hours of work have access to a wide range of appropriate training and learning opportunities at South Cheshire College.

MISSION / VISION

To strive and achieve. South Cheshire College promotes quality teaching and learning in a supportive environment. We aim to respond flexibly to the educational and training needs of our communities, anticipating, identifying, and satisfying, these needs efficiently, and effectively.

BEST WORKPLACE FACTORS

FAIR DEAL
MY COMPANY
PERSONAL GROWTH

GRADUATE VACANCIES

Lecturing posts, Marketing, IT.

EMPLOYEE COMMENTS

"Friendly atmosphere, staff benefits such as free gym & staff sports sessions, free healthcare & 39 days paid holiday."

"There is a real sense of belonging."

"Individual staff development is encouraged and paid for."

CONTACT DETAILS

South Cheshire College, Dane Bank Avenue, Crewe CW2 8AB
Tel: 01270 654654 www.s-cheshire.ac.uk

SOUTHDALE HOMES

UK locations	National
UK sites	14
Sector	Construction
Definition	New House Build
How owned	Partnership/LLP
Founded	1992
Turnover	£39m
Profit	£2.8m
Staff	137
Average age	39
Male : Female	80 : 20
Earnings £35,000+	23%

BEST COMPANIES INDEX

best company 2007

OUTSTANDING ★ ★

2007 BCI = 710.9

WORKPLACE INSIGHTS

Southdale Homes encourage staff in choosing healthy options by providing free fruit and healthy option bars and by providing a number of active team events including bowling, go karting and racquet ball.

All trainees at Southdale are appointed a personal coach to set out a training and development plan suited to their style of learning. Southdale are able to 'fast track' trainees so that they can quickly contribute to the business and see their careers developing.

Managers host regular team briefings to ensure that people are consulted for ideas regarding the business planning process thus helping them to feel involved in decision making and informed about developments within the company.

MISSION / VISION

To be the preferred constructor of choice in delivering housing solutions.

BEST WORKPLACE FACTORS

WELL BEING
PERSONAL GROWTH
MY MANAGER

GRADUATE VACANCIES

I.T, Site Management, Quantity Surveyors, Project Managers.

EMPLOYEE COMMENTS

"A very positive and ethical company to work for who care greatly about the welfare of employees."

"Lots of opportunities for both personal and professional growth."

"All management are open, friendly and very approachable."

CONTACT DETAILS

Southdale Homes, Westholme Road, Halifax HX1 4JF
Tel: 01422 380090 www.southdale-homes.co.uk

KEY

- **Holidays:** Companies offering a minimum of 25 days annual leave
- **Maternity:** Companies offering over Statutory Maternity Pay
- **Childcare:** On-site nursery or vouchers
- **Women:** At least 33% of senior managers are women
- **Long Service:** 40% of employees with more than 5 years' service
- **Pensions:** Companies offering a final salary or non-contributory/contributory pension scheme
- **Charity Activities:** 10% of staff undertake charitable activities during business hours
- **Gym:** On-site gym or subsidised gym memberships
- **Shares:** Companies where employees are offered share options
- **Health Insurance:** Full family cover

To find out more about this company visit www.bestcompaniesguide.co.uk

ST. DAVID'S FOUNDATION HOSPICE CARE

Registered Charity No. 1010576

UK locations	Wales
UK sites	27
Sector	Charity
Definition	Hospice at Home
How owned	Trust/Employee owned/Mutual
Founded	1979
Turnover	£3.4m
Profit	£0.2m
Staff	108
Average age	47
Male : Female	23 : 77
Earnings £35,000+	3%

BEST COMPANIES INDEX

best company 2007

OUTSTANDING

★ ★

2007 BCI = 720.7

WORKPLACE INSIGHTS

St. David's offer a variety of volunteering opportunities in the community to people who are disadvantaged in some way. The volunteering opportunity may give them some useful work experience to help them into employment.

St. David's have pioneered the care of palliative care patients in the home. Their aim is to ensure patients and families have real choice on where to receive care.

Managers within St. David's have had the opportunity to attend a three day middle manager's course facilitated by "Help the Hospices".

MISSION / VISION

To provide and continue to develop a free and comprehensive specialist palliative care service of excellence throughout four unitary authorities of Gwent, for people, their families, and carers, facing a progressive life-threatening illness which is no longer curable.

BEST WORKPLACE FACTORS

GIVING SOMETHING BACK
MY COMPANY
MY MANAGER

GRADUATE VACANCIES

No graduate vacancies have been indicated.

EMPLOYEE COMMENTS

"Knowing that we make a difference to so many lives is great."

"We are a team, from the top management, to the bottom - those that make the tea and drive the bus."

"I feel able to approach my Manager."

CONTACT DETAILS

St. David's Foundation Hospice Care, Cambrian House, St. John's Road, Newport NP19 8GR
Tel: 01633 271364 www.stdavidsfoundation.co.uk

KEY

- **Holidays:** Companies offering a minimum of 25 days annual leave
- **Maternity:** Companies offering over Statutory Maternity Pay
- **Childcare:** On-site nursery or vouchers
- **Women:** At least 33% of senior managers are women
- **Long Service:** 40% of employees with more than 5 years' service
- **Pensions:** Companies offering a final salary or non-contributory/contributory pension scheme
- **Charity Activities:** 10% of staff undertake charitable activities during business hours
- **Gym:** On-site gym or subsidised gym memberships
- **Shares:** Companies where employees are offered share options
- **Health Insurance:** Full family cover

1000
721>
ones to watch
500
0

ST. LUKE'S COMMUNICATIONS

St. Luke's

UK locations	London
UK sites	1
Sector	Media
Definition	Advertising & Communications agency
How owned	Trust/Employee owned/Mutual
Founded	1995
Turnover	Not disclosed
Profit	Not disclosed
Staff	55
Average age	32
Male : Female	45 : 55
Earnings £35,000+	53%

BEST COMPANIES INDEX

★ ★ best company 2007

OUTSTANDING

★ ★

2007 BCI = 701.6

2006 BCI = 772.8 (★★★)

WORKPLACE INSIGHTS

St. Luke's is a carbon neutral company. They conduct an annual 'carbon footprint' assessment and offset their CO2 emissions through involvement in a reforestation and employment programme in Southern India as well as having a strategy to reduce their emissions such as powering their building with electricity derived from wind farms.

There are plenty of opportunities for teams to interact on St. Luke's Day. It is a celebration of the anniversary of the founding of the company which happens each October. Activities have included an army assault course, quad biking, and an espionage hunt.

St. Luke's shareholders (includes the employees) elect four individuals every year to act as the 'QUEST'. Employees are able to feedback to the QUEST any questions, concerns or praise they would like the leaders to address.

MISSION / VISION

To be the most inspiring company in the world. We seek to inspire the people who work here, other companies, our clients and their audiences through our brand communications.

BEST WORKPLACE FACTORS

GIVING SOMETHING BACK
MY TEAM
MY COMPANY

GRADUATE VACANCIES

No graduate vacancies have been indicated.

EMPLOYEE COMMENTS

"It has been founded on a good ethos which is still evident even ten years after St Luke's opened its doors."

"Each department is full of friendly, hard working people that genuinely care about each other."

"It is an employee owned company run in the best interests of the employees."

CONTACT DETAILS

St. Luke's Communications, 22 Duke's Road, London WC1H 9PN
Tel: 0207 3808888 www.stlukes.co.uk

KEY

- **Holidays:** Companies offering a minimum of 25 days annual leave
- **Maternity:** Companies offering over Statutory Maternity Pay
- **Childcare:** On-site nursery or vouchers
- **Women:** At least 33% of senior managers are women
- **Long Service:** 40% of employees with more than 5 years' service
- **Pensions:** Companies offering a final salary or non-contributory/ contributory pension scheme
- **Charity Activities:** 10% of staff undertake charitable activities during business hours
- **Gym:** On-site gym or subsidised gym memberships
- **Shares:** Companies where employees are offered share options
- **Health Insurance:** Full family cover

1000 ★★★ ★★ <702 ★ ones to watch 500 0

To find out more about this company visit www.bestcompaniesguide.co.uk

STHREE

UK locations	National
UK sites	24
Sector	Recruitment
Definition	Professional Staffing Services
How owned	Public (i.e. stock market listed)
Founded	1999
Turnover	£243.6m
Profit	£20.9m
Staff	1,041
Average age	28
Male : Female	62 : 38
Earnings £35,000+	43%

BEST COMPANIES INDEX

best company 2007

OUTSTANDING ★ ★

2007 BCI = 722.2

2006 BCI = 737.1 (★★)

722>

WORKPLACE INSIGHTS

SThree take on trainees into most roles so the development of skills and competencies is critical. They have a group training function of 15 trainers and training centre which supports the development of the individuals in the business.

There is an Annual award at the SThree Christmas party for the best idea contributed through the company intranet Business Improvement Scheme.

Although many people voluntarily work long hours SThree always aim to create an environment where people enjoy the work they do and the people they are working with.

MISSION / VISION

Vision: To be the most profitable specialist staffing business in the UK and Europe.
Mission: To maximise on client & candidate satisfaction. To achieve significant & profitable growth. To enjoy a fun and fulfilling environment & to be completely proud of what we do.

BEST WORKPLACE FACTORS

PERSONAL GROWTH
FAIR DEAL
MY TEAM

GRADUATE VACANCIES

Trainee Recruitment Consultant.

EMPLOYEE COMMENTS

"Career opportunities within the organisation are well known & everyone knows what they have to do to progress."

"Good employees and good rewards for hard work."

"Friendly banter in the office allows you to enjoy a friendly atmosphere which is nice to work in."

CONTACT DETAILS

SThree, 41 - 44 Great Windmill St., London W1D 7NB
Tel: 0207 2923838 www.sthree.com

KEY

Holidays: Companies offering a minimum of 25 days annual leave
Maternity: Companies offering over Statutory Maternity Pay
Childcare: On-site nursery or vouchers
Women: At least 33% of senior managers are women
Long Service: 40% of employees with more than 5 years' service
Pensions: Companies offering a final salary or non-contributory/ contributory pension scheme
Charity Activities: 10% of staff undertake charitable activities during business hours
Gym: On-site gym or subsidised gym memberships
Shares: Companies where employees are offered share options
Health Insurance: Full family cover

STRATEGIC TEAM GROUP

DELIVERING SERVICE EXCELLENCE | Strategic TEAM GROUP

UK locations	Yorks & Humber, Scotland
UK sites	2
Sector	Property
Definition	Property Buliding Solutions
How owned	Private
Founded	2000
Turnover	£17.1m
Profit	£1.4m
Staff	110
Average age	36
Male : Female	91 : 9
Earnings £35,000+	36%

BEST COMPANIES INDEX

best company 2007

OUTSTANDING ★ ★

2007 BCI = 698.0

WORKPLACE INSIGHTS

Strategic Team encourage an open and caring style of management by having directors sit in the middle of the team in an open plan office and having directors, managers and teams meet socially on a regular basis.

Everyone in the company receives an appraisal every quarter including directors and managers. Within this, feedback from all levels of the company is provided allowing managers to assess and make improvements to their performance.

Strategic Team Maintenance communicate their mission statement – "To deliver service excellence through our great people" – to all employees via employment handbooks, the annual report and accounts, letterheads and boards on walls in the office and on sites.

MISSION / VISION

To deliver service excellence through our great people.

BEST WORKPLACE FACTORS

LEADERSHIP
MY MANAGER
MY COMPANY

GRADUATE VACANCIES

Quantity Surveying.

EMPLOYEE COMMENTS

"The organisational skills of senior management filter down the ranks and personally inspire me."

"The management and workforce are open and honest."

"The friendly, family atmosphere within the work place makes it a wonderful place to work."

CONTACT DETAILS

Strategic Team Group, Blue Ridge Park, Thunderhead Ridge, Glasshoughton WF10 4UA
Tel: 01977 555550 www.strategicteamgroup.com

KEY

Holidays: Companies offering a minimum of 25 days annual leave
Maternity: Companies offering over Statutory Maternity Pay
Childcare: On-site nursery or vouchers
Women: At least 33% of senior managers are women
Long Service: 40% of employees with more than 5 years' service
Pensions: Companies offering a final salary or non-contributory/ contributory pension scheme
Charity Activities: 10% of staff undertake charitable activities during business hours
Gym: On-site gym or subsidised gym memberships
Shares: Companies where employees are offered share options
Health Insurance: Full family cover

To find out more about this company visit www.bestcompaniesguide.co.uk

STRYKER UK

UK locations	S.East
UK sites	1
Sector	Health
Definition	Orthopaedics Medical Devices
How owned	Private
Founded	1998
Turnover	Not disclosed
Profit	Not disclosed
Staff	286
Average age	32
Male : Female	60 : 40
Earnings £35,000+	37%

BEST COMPANIES INDEX

best company 2007

OUTSTANDING ★ ★

2007 BCI = 714.4

714>

ones to watch

WORKPLACE INSIGHTS

Stryker believe results speak louder than words. Since the Company's founding in 1941, that philosophy has made them a leader in the worldwide orthopaedic market & placed them at the forefront of medicine's most promising solutions. Today, Stryker is one of the predominant medical products & services companies in the world.

Stryker employ numerous personal development tools to maximise the strengths their employees have and set them up to succeed.

Stryker have a robust Mentorship Programme that pairs up their top potential leaders with existing leaders in their business. This programme has proved to be very successful & they currently have over 40 matches within their business.

MISSION / VISION

By 2010 Stryker will be one of the most respected & admired companies in the UK, being number 1 in each market sector in which we operate.

BEST WORKPLACE FACTORS

MY COMPANY
PERSONAL GROWTH
LEADERSHIP

GRADUATE VACANCIES

Marketing Operations, Sales.

EMPLOYEE COMMENTS

"The workplace has a good, strong, positive atmosphere."

"Talent is developed & promoted from within."

"Fantastic spirit & leadership qualities of senior directors."

CONTACT DETAILS

Stryker UK, Stryker House, Hambridge Road, Newbury, Berkshire RG14 5EG
Tel: 01635 262400 www.stryker.co.uk

KEY

- **Holidays:** Companies offering a minimum of 25 days annual leave
- **Maternity:** Companies offering over Statutory Maternity Pay
- **Childcare:** On-site nursery or vouchers
- **Women:** At least 33% of senior managers are women
- **Long Service:** 40% of employees with more than 5 years' service
- **Pensions:** Companies offering a final salary or non-contributory/ contributory pension scheme
- **Charity Activities:** 10% of staff undertake charitable activities during business hours
- **Gym:** On-site gym or subsidised gym memberships
- **Shares:** Companies where employees are offered share options
- **Health Insurance:** Full family cover

To find out more about this company visit www.bestcompaniesguide.co.uk

SWANSEA HOUSING ASSOCIATION

Swansea Housing Association
Cymdeithas Tai Abertawe

UK locations	Wales
UK sites	2
Sector	Housing Associations
Definition	Registered Social Landlord
How owned	Private
Founded	1978
Turnover	£10.5m
Profit	£0.7m
Staff	93
Average age	39
Male : Female	54 : 46
Earnings £35,000+	14%

BEST COMPANIES INDEX

best company 2007

OUTSTANDING

★ ★

2007 BCI = 706.3

WORKPLACE INSIGHTS

Promotes a scheme called BURD (Best Use, Replacement & Disposal of resources) to their tenants & within the company to make people more aware of the resources they use. They provide recycling facilities for various items at their offices & residential schemes.

SHA encourage staff to be as fit and healthy as possible by providing free annual health checks and arranging talks on various health issues. They also provide stress management training and weekly subsidised yoga and tai chi classes.

Employees receive an extra day's holiday for every year of service up to 30 days. In addition a long service award of 5 days holiday is provided at 10, 15, 20 and 25 years service which can be taken or 'sold back' to the organisation.

MISSION / VISION

Providing homes that you or your friends or children would want to live in.

BEST WORKPLACE FACTORS

GIVING SOMETHING BACK
WELL BEING
FAIR DEAL

GRADUATE VACANCIES

No graduate vacancies have been indicated.

EMPLOYEE COMMENTS

"The organisation cares about the service it provides and is always looking at ways to improve that service."

"The organisation treats its employees very well, providing a wide variety of training, development opportunities and social activities."

"The company offers excellent staff benefits, including flexi hours option."

CONTACT DETAILS

Swansea Housing Association, The Old Post Office, 11 Wind Street, Swansea SA1 1DP
Tel: 01792 479200 www.swanseaha.co.uk

KEY

- **Holidays:** Companies offering a minimum of 25 days annual leave
- **Maternity:** Companies offering over Statutory Maternity Pay
- **Childcare:** On-site nursery or vouchers
- **Women:** At least 33% of senior managers are women
- **Long Service:** 40% of employees with more than 5 years' service
- **Pensions:** Companies offering a final salary or non-contributory/contributory pension scheme
- **Charity Activities:** 10% of staff undertake charitable activities during business hours
- **Gym:** On-site gym or subsidised gym memberships
- **Shares:** Companies where employees are offered share options
- **Health Insurance:** Full family cover

1000
<706
ones to watch
500
0

To find out more about this company visit www.bestcompaniesguide.co.uk

T J CRUMP OAKWRIGHTS

OAKWRIGHTS®

UK locations	W.Midlands
UK sites	1
Sector	Construction
Definition	Oak Framed Houses
How owned	Private
Founded	1999
Turnover	£3.8m
Profit	£0.1m
Staff	53
Average age	37
Male : Female	90 : 10
Earnings £35,000+	6%

BEST COMPANIES INDEX

best company 2007

OUTSTANDING

★ ★

2007 BCI = 697.3

1000

697>

ones to watch

500

0

WORKPLACE INSIGHTS

Regular appraisals are held whereby staff have the opportunity to discuss the way forward both individually and as part of the team.

T J Crump is a company where the phrase 'bench taught, not book taught' has a real resonance. The majority of their staff come from a carpentry and oak framing background.

Regular appraisals give employees at T J Crump the opportunity to discuss all aspects of their work and general well being.

MISSION / VISION

T J Crump Oakwright's goal is to build houses to the client's exact specifications. Our philosophy is commitment to providing the highest level of service possible to help people achieve the highest quality bespoke timber framed house.

BEST WORKPLACE FACTORS

PERSONAL GROWTH
MY COMPANY
WELL BEING

GRADUATE VACANCIES

No graduate vacancies have been indicated.

EMPLOYEE COMMENTS

"Personal development is actively supported and encouraged."

"There is a sense of pride in the work people do here."

"Management are considerate & understanding when personal issues arise outside the workplace."

CONTACT DETAILS

T J Crump Oakwrights, The Lakes, Swainshill, Hereford HR4 7PU
Tel: 01432 353353 www.oakwrights.co.uk

KEY

- **Holidays:** Companies offering a minimum of 25 days annual leave
- **Maternity:** Companies offering over Statutory Maternity Pay
- **Childcare:** On-site nursery or vouchers
- **Women:** At least 33% of senior managers are women
- **Long Service:** 40% of employees with more than 5 years' service
- **Pensions:** Companies offering a final salary or non-contributory/ contributory pension scheme
- **Charity Activities:** 10% of staff undertake charitable activities during business hours
- **Gym:** On-site gym or subsidised gym memberships
- **Shares:** Companies where employees are offered share options
- **Health Insurance:** Full family cover

TANDBERG

TANDBERG

UK locations	S.East
UK sites	2
Sector	Communications/Telecom
Definition	Visual Communications Provider
How owned	Public (i.e. stock market listed)
Founded	1933
Turnover	Not disclosed
Profit	Not disclosed
Staff	53
Average age	32
Male : Female	83 : 17
Earnings £35,000+	98%

BEST COMPANIES INDEX

best company 2007

OUTSTANDING ★ ★

2007 BCI = 726.4

<726

WORKPLACE INSIGHTS

Tandberg come together every quarter for a 'Kick Off' meeting to discuss strategy and share how they are doing as an organisation. All employees are encouraged to participate & engage in the discussion.

Development for employees begins with induction & evaluation. From the output of the evaluation process, shared & agreed with the employee at all stages, a development plan is produced. Employees are allowed to explore any activity or training they feel might benefit them.

Tandberg provide video conferencing facilities and equipment to allow employees to work more from home, reducing the daily commute and the impact of travelling on the environment.

MISSION / VISION

Vision: Changing the way people communicate.
Mission: To lead the industry by making business-quality visual communication accessible to everyone.

BEST WORKPLACE FACTORS

MY COMPANY
PERSONAL GROWTH
GIVING SOMETHING BACK

GRADUATE VACANCIES

Sales.

EMPLOYEE COMMENTS

"The 5 core values we have reflect the way that we work within the organisation."

"You can work effectively with peers & learn from them."

"The values of the company are in line with my own personal values."

CONTACT DETAILS

Tandberg, Tamesis, The Glanty, Egham TW20 9AW
Tel: 01784 274600 www.tandberg.net

KEY

- **Holidays:** Companies offering a minimum of 25 days annual leave
- **Maternity:** Companies offering over Statutory Maternity Pay
- **Childcare:** On-site nursery or vouchers
- **Women:** At least 33% of senior managers are women
- **Long Service:** 40% of employees with more than 5 years' service
- **Pensions:** Companies offering a final salary or non-contributory/contributory pension scheme
- **Charity Activities:** 10% of staff undertake charitable activities during business hours
- **Gym:** On-site gym or subsidised gym memberships
- **Shares:** Companies where employees are offered share options
- **Health Insurance:** Full family cover

To find out more about this company visit www.bestcompaniesguide.co.uk

TATE

UK locations	National
UK sites	19
Sector	Recruitment
Definition	Office Recruitment Specialists
How owned	Public (i.e. stock market listed)
Founded	1985
Turnover	Not disclosed
Profit	Not disclosed
Staff	122
Average age	30
Male : Female	8 : 92
Earnings £35,000+	13%

BEST COMPANIES INDEX

best company 2007

OUTSTANDING

★ ★

2007 BCI = 708.9

WORKPLACE INSIGHTS

The senior team at Tate are completely engaged in the vision and values of the organisation and are absolutely focused on bringing them to life in all their actions.

There is a culture in the organisation of continuous feedback and staff are continually challenged to give constructive feedback to their peers and line managers.

Tate's approach to personal development mirrors their approach to business - an impeccable blend of people and process. Tate's dedicated Learning and Development Manager has recently put in place a programme of training and coaching events designed to support their people at every stage of their career with Tate.

MISSION / VISION

Tate's values are integrity and honesty, always delivering on promises, being solutions oriented, having a winning mentality, working in a collaborative manner, creating a fun environment to work in and always having respect for others.

BEST WORKPLACE FACTORS

LEADERSHIP
MY MANAGER
PERSONAL GROWTH

GRADUATE VACANCIES

No graduate vacancies have been indicated.

EMPLOYEE COMMENTS

"The senior management team are inspirational leaders who have created a vision for Tate which everybody strives for."

"I believe my success is down to my manager & her respective managers."

"I feel confident in my role & receive good training & development when needed."

CONTACT DETAILS

Tate, 5th Floor, 16 St Helen's Place, London EC3A 6DP
Tel: 0207 5621662 www.tate.co.uk

KEY

- **Holidays:** Companies offering a minimum of 25 days annual leave
- **Maternity:** Companies offering over Statutory Maternity Pay
- **Childcare:** On-site nursery or vouchers
- **Women:** At least 33% of senior managers are women
- **Long Service:** 40% of employees with more than 5 years' service
- **Pensions:** Companies offering a final salary or non-contributory/ contributory pension scheme
- **Charity Activities:** 10% of staff undertake charitable activities during business hours
- **Gym:** On-site gym or subsidised gym memberships
- **Shares:** Companies where employees are offered share options
- **Health Insurance:** Full family cover

To find out more about this company visit www.bestcompaniesguide.co.uk

1000

709>

ones to watch

500

0

1000

<717

ones to watch

500

0

THAMES REACH

UK locations	London
UK sites	1
Sector	Charity
Definition	Homeless Charity
How owned	Partnership/LLP
Founded	2001
Turnover	£15.8m
Profit	Not disclosed
Staff	332
Average age	39
Male : Female	45 : 55
Earnings £35,000+	11%

BEST COMPANIES INDEX

best company 2007

OUTSTANDING

★ ★

2007 BCI = 717.3

WORKPLACE INSIGHTS

Thames Reach believes in paying their staff well in comparison to people doing the same work elsewhere. They check their salaries periodically to ensure that they are paying, on average, at the upper quartile.

Experiments with social businesses which employ formerly homeless people to help them develop work & entrepreneurial experience, for example, Street Shine social business employs & trains people to shine shoes predominantly at City Corporate Offices.

Thames Reach run training programmes for people who have been homeless or career changers with potential but lack of experience. They are equipped with the skills through an intensive induction process, on the job training, a mentor & structured training courses.

MISSION / VISION

To help homeless and vulnerable people find decent homes, build supportive relationships and lead fulfilling lives.

BEST WORKPLACE FACTORS

FAIR DEAL
GIVING SOMETHING BACK
PERSONAL GROWTH

GRADUATE VACANCIES

No graduate vacancies have been indicated.

EMPLOYEE COMMENTS

"Good work is recognised and fairly and generously rewarded."

"The work Thames Reach does with some of the most marginalised people in the community is, in my experience, really positive and productive."

"Much time is spent in training staff, both for their own job and for development."

CONTACT DETAILS

Thames Reach, Gem House, 122-126 Backchurch Lane, London E1 1ND
Tel: 0207 7025606 www.thamesreach.org.uk

KEY

- **Holidays:** Companies offering a minimum of 25 days annual leave
- **Maternity:** Companies offering over Statutory Maternity Pay
- **Childcare:** On-site nursery or vouchers
- **Women:** At least 33% of senior managers are women
- **Long Service:** 40% of employees with more than 5 years' service
- **Pensions:** Companies offering a final salary or non-contributory/ contributory pension scheme
- **Charity Activities:** 10% of staff undertake charitable activities during business hours
- **Gym:** On-site gym or subsidised gym memberships
- **Shares:** Companies where employees are offered share options
- **Health Insurance:** Full family cover

To find out more about this company visit www.bestcompaniesguide.co.uk

THE DAVIS GROUP

THE DAVIS GROUP

UK locations	National
UK sites	4
Sector	Financial - Insurance
Definition	Corporate Insurance Brokers
How owned	Private
Founded	1975
Turnover	£5.8m
Profit	£1.7m
Staff	86
Average age	36
Male : Female	35 : 65
Earnings £35,000+	22%

BEST COMPANIES INDEX

★ ★ best company 2007

OUTSTANDING

★ ★

2007 BCI = 735.9

2006 BCI = 706.0 (★★)

1000

736>

500

0

ones to watch

WORKPLACE INSIGHTS

The Davis Group provide practical support to local causes providing mentors and funding assessors along with money raising support at weekends to The Prince's Trust. They provided financial and practical support to a local initiative raising money for local charities.

Leigh Davis Smart meets with all new staff as part of their induction programme. He takes this opportunity to find out more about them as people and to introduce them to the Group and its culture as he sees it.

Everyone is treated equally and everyone is an individual. The Davis Group have a superb HR team who strongly support their management team to ensure that people work well and that, crucially, they enjoy coming into work.

MISSION / VISION

Originally a family business, The Davis Group still retain strong family values. The family values extend beyond the office environment. The Davis Group Charitable Trust is an integral part of the organisation and reflects the emphasis we place on having positive impact on our surroundings.

BEST WORKPLACE FACTORS

GIVING SOMETHING BACK
LEADERSHIP
WELL BEING

GRADUATE VACANCIES

IT, HR & Marketing.

EMPLOYEE COMMENTS

"I think it is amazing how the company uses their reputation to benefit the local community."

"I think that all the Directors are great. They are approachable and take an interest in the staff."

"They look after their staff which is very motivating."

CONTACT DETAILS

The Davis Group, Kings Court, Newmarket, Suffolk CB8 7SG
Tel: 01638 608060 www.thedavisgroup.co.uk

KEY

Holidays: Companies offering a minimum of 25 days annual leave
Maternity: Companies offering over Statutory Maternity Pay
Childcare: On-site nursery or vouchers
Women: At least 33% of senior managers are women
Long Service: 40% of employees with more than 5 years' service
Pensions: Companies offering a final salary or non-contributory/ contributory pension scheme
Charity Activities: 10% of staff undertake charitable activities during business hours
Gym: On-site gym or subsidised gym memberships
Shares: Companies where employees are offered share options
Health Insurance: Full family cover

To find out more about this company visit www.bestcompaniesguide.co.uk

1000

<738

ones to watch

500

0

Erith

THE ERITH GROUP

UK locations	S.East
UK sites	1
Sector	Property
Definition	Construction Industry Services
How owned	Private
Founded	1967
Turnover	£29.6m
Profit	£0.8m
Staff	175
Average age	34
Male : Female	91 : 9
Earnings £35,000+	25%

BEST COMPANIES INDEX

best company 2007

OUTSTANDING

★ ★

2007 BCI = 738.0

WORKPLACE INSIGHTS

The Erith Group have no specific written policies regarding employee well being, but are very generous where specific requests are made. Each request is considered on its individual merit.

The Erith Group undertake all their operations in a safe and environmentally friendly manner and they are keen and regular sponsors of local Children's Community Activities and Charities.

The Erith Group awards prizes for new ideas implemented via company suggestion scheme. They have various social activities during the year, including Christmas, special occasion & Divisional social gatherings, company Golf Day and Race Meeting outings.

MISSION / VISION

To maintain and grow a profitable customer focused business through delivering high quality services safely & environmentally aware, within budget & timescale through our professional commitment & policy of continuous improvement.

BEST WORKPLACE FACTORS

WELL BEING
GIVING SOMETHING BACK
FAIR DEAL

GRADUATE VACANCIES

Business Development, Project/Contract Management, Health & Safety.

EMPLOYEE COMMENTS

"It's just a nice family friendly company where the company cares for us and our families."

"We do a lot of charity work."

"Everyone is treated the same and on a fair basis."

CONTACT DETAILS

The Erith Group, Riverside House, Maypole Crescent, Darent Industrial Park, Erith, Kent DA8 2JZ
Tel: 0870 9508800 www.erith.net

KEY

- **Holidays:** Companies offering a minimum of 25 days annual leave
- **Maternity:** Companies offering over Statutory Maternity Pay
- **Childcare:** On-site nursery or vouchers
- **Women:** At least 33% of senior managers are women
- **Long Service:** 40% of employees with more than 5 years' service
- **Pensions:** Companies offering a final salary or non-contributory/ contributory pension scheme
- **Charity Activities:** 10% of staff undertake charitable activities during business hours
- **Gym:** On-site gym or subsidised gym memberships
- **Shares:** Companies where employees are offered share options
- **Health Insurance:** Full family cover

To find out more about this company visit www.bestcompaniesguide.co.uk

THE ROYAL BANK OF SCOTLAND - RETAIL BANKING

RBS
The Royal Bank of Scotland

UK locations	National
UK sites	655
Sector	Financial - Banks/Building Societies
Definition	Banking/Financial Services
How owned	Public (I.e stock market listed)
Founded	1727
Turnover	Not disclosed
Profit	Not disclosed
Staff	9,256
Average age	35
Male : Female	26 : 74
Earnings £35,000+	4%

BEST COMPANIES INDEX

★ ★ best company 2007

OUTSTANDING

★ ★

2007 BCI = 711.9

2006 BCI = 703.9 (★★)

WORKPLACE INSIGHTS

A recorded message from MD Ewen Munroe goes out to all Regional/Area Managers every week, providing a high level summary of performance and areas to focus on in the following week. Managers are able to use the information in cascading the key messages to their team.

The RBS group recognises the importance of the health and wellbeing of their people in both their personal and professional lives and extend the services that are available to people in Retail.

The Bank makes every effort to recognise individual and team contributions with a varied selection of fun and social events to suit all their people.

MISSION / VISION

To be the most admired retail bank in the world.

BEST WORKPLACE FACTORS

MY MANAGER
WELL BEING
MY TEAM

GRADUATE VACANCIES

RBS Retail Network, NatWest Retail Network, Retail Marketing and Retail Risk.

EMPLOYEE COMMENTS

"I enjoy my job. My manager is supportive and wants us all to do well."

"My Branch Manager is always concerned about my well being and because of this I feel valued as an employee."

"My branch works as one team. We have a happy branch which means happy customers."

CONTACT DETAILS

The Royal Bank of Scotland - Retail Banking, PO Box 1000, Gogarburn, Edinburgh EH12 1HQ
Tel: 0131 5568555 www.rbs.co.uk

KEY

Holidays: Companies offering a minimum of 25 days annual leave

Maternity: Companies offering over Statutory Maternity Pay

Childcare: On-site nursery or vouchers

Women: At least 33% of senior managers are women

Long Service: 40% of employees with more than 5 years' service

Pensions: Companies offering a final salary or non-contributory/contributory pension scheme

Charity Activities: 10% of staff undertake charitable activities during business hours

Gym: On-site gym or subsidised gym memberships

Shares: Companies where employees are offered share options

Health Insurance: Full family cover

1000 712> 500 0 ones to watch

THECENTRE:MK

thecentre:mk

UK locations	S.East
UK sites	1
Sector	Retail
Definition	Management of Shopping Centre
How owned	Private
Founded	1979
Turnover	£5.8m
Profit	Not disclosed
Staff	138
Average age	43
Male : Female	52 : 48
Earnings £35,000+	3%

BEST COMPANIES INDEX

best company 2007

OUTSTANDING

★ ★

2007 BCI = 720.3

WORKPLACE INSIGHTS

In addition to work-focused training thecentre:mk contributes £145 annually to Personal Development. This acknowledges that some employees feel uncomfortable with structured training & allows them opportunities to develop & learn new skills not associated with the workplace.

Thecentre:mk run team building off site programmes for every team member. A typical team build involves taking part in morning and afternoon activities such as raft building and in the evening enjoying games & puzzles after dinner.

Thecentre:mk set up skillscentre:mk in partnership with a local college to ensure everyone working in retail in Milton Keynes has the opportunity to undergo training & obtain formal recognised qualifications to improve skills base of the local community.

MISSION / VISION

We are dedicated to :- Creating income and growth by delivering exceptional performance across all business areas and continuing to develop our Company Culture to provide excellence in relationships and service delivery.

BEST WORKPLACE FACTORS

WELL BEING
MY TEAM
GIVING SOMETHING BACK

GRADUATE VACANCIES

None.

EMPLOYEE COMMENTS

"Whatever the issue or problem people may face thecentre:mk can always be relied upon to help and support us."

"There is a sense of family with staff from different departments working alongside each other to help each other."

"I have never worked for such a genuine and supportive Company."

CONTACT DETAILS

thecentre:mk, 24 Silbury Arcade, Central Milton Keynes MK9 3ES
Tel: 01908 678641 www.thecentremk.com

KEY

Holidays: Companies offering a minimum of 25 days annual leave
Maternity: Companies offering over Statutory Maternity Pay
Childcare: On-site nursery or vouchers
Women: At least 33% of senior managers are women
Long Service: 40% of employees with more than 5 years' service
Pensions: Companies offering a final salary or non-contributory/ contributory pension scheme
Charity Activities: 10% of staff undertake charitable activities during business hours
Gym: On-site gym or subsidised gym memberships
Shares: Companies where employees are offered share options
Health Insurance: Full family cover

To find out more about this company visit www.bestcompaniesguide.co.uk

THINK MONEY GROUP

UK locations	N.West
UK sites	1
Sector	Financial
Definition	Financial Solutions Provider
How owned	Private
Founded	1993
Turnover	Not disclosed
Profit	Not disclosed
Staff	531
Average age	27
Male : Female	53 : 47
Earnings £35,000+	4%

BEST COMPANIES INDEX

best company 2007

OUTSTANDING

★ ★

2007 BCI = 702.6

2006 BCI = 663.8 (★)

WORKPLACE INSIGHTS

Managing Director Stephen Stylianou hosts quarterly Buzz Sessions with all employees in small groups to share what is going on in the business & the future direction of Think Money, encouraging them to put forward their own ideas on how the business can improve.

Employees can earn 'Think Miles' for things such as timekeeping, good customer service, receiving thank-you cards from customers and on their anniversary of joining the business. Miles can be spent on anything from activity days to all inclusive holidays.

Think Money volunteers as a call centre for Comic Relief. They close the business early on the day of the event & have around 200 volunteers who stay behind until the early hours of the morning taking calls from the general public pledging support.

MISSION / VISION

To take the lead in personalising Finance.

BEST WORKPLACE FACTORS

LEADERSHIP
FAIR DEAL
GIVING SOMETHING BACK

GRADUATE VACANCIES

In all areas.

EMPLOYEE COMMENTS

"I defy anyone to speak to senior management and not be inspired."

"Think Money looks after staff excellently with great bonuses and incentives."

"The level of charitable functions and effort put into such things is highly commendable."

CONTACT DETAILS

Think Money Group, Pennington House, Carolina Way, South Langworthy Road, Salford M50 2ZY
Tel: 08456 343434 www.thinkmoney.co.uk

KEY

Holidays: Companies offering a minimum of 25 days annual leave
Maternity: Companies offering over Statutory Maternity Pay
Childcare: On-site nursery or vouchers
Women: At least 33% of senior managers are women
Long Service: 40% of employees with more than 5 years' service
Pensions: Companies offering a final salary or non-contributory/contributory pension scheme
Charity Activities: 10% of staff undertake charitable activities during business hours
Gym: On-site gym or subsidised gym memberships
Shares: Companies where employees are offered share options
Health Insurance: Full family cover

To find out more about this company visit www.bestcompaniesguide.co.uk

1000 / 703> / 500 / 0 — ones to watch

1000

<734

500

0

ones to watch

THOMAS CARROLL GROUP

UK locations	Wales
UK sites	1
Sector	Financial - Insurance
Definition	Insurance Broking
How owned	Private
Founded	1972
Turnover	£3.2m
Profit	£0.6m
Staff	66
Average age	32
Male : Female	35 : 65
Earnings £35,000+	21%

BEST COMPANIES INDEX

★ ★ best company 2007

OUTSTANDING

★ ★

2007 BCI = 734.2

2006 BCI = 742.3 (★★★)

WORKPLACE INSIGHTS

Group Chairman of Thomas Carroll, John Moore, has one to one meetings with every colleague in the business. This formal meeting structure is in place to ensure a continued dialogue between senior leaders and employees.

Thomas Carroll provides fruit stations throughout the office and employees have access to nutritional and health advice and personal training. They also enroll employees in a local gym and provide flexible access to the facilities during working hours.

Thomas Carroll are involved in a number of local charity and community projects including an ongoing commitment to Ty Hafan Children's Hospice, work with local schools and a commitment to Neighbourhood Watch.

MISSION / VISION

To become the most respected provincial insurance broker in our industry. We will seek sustainable profitable growth throughout Wales based on quality not quantity.

BEST WORKPLACE FACTORS

LEADERSHIP
WELL BEING
GIVING SOMETHING BACK

GRADUATE VACANCIES

All areas.

EMPLOYEE COMMENTS

"Our chairman and board are always willing to listen and involve all members of staff."

"Management are committed to employee well being and are conscious of the welfare of staff."

"Thomas Carroll shows care for community and charity."

CONTACT DETAILS

Thomas Carroll Group, Pendragon House, Crescent Road, Caerphilly CF83 1XX
Tel: 0292 0855246 www.thomas-carroll.co.uk

KEY

- **Holidays:** Companies offering a minimum of 25 days annual leave
- **Maternity:** Companies offering over Statutory Maternity Pay
- **Childcare:** On-site nursery or vouchers
- **Women:** At least 33% of senior managers are women
- **Long Service:** 40% of employees with more than 5 years' service
- **Pensions:** Companies offering a final salary or non-contributory/ contributory pension scheme
- **Charity Activities:** 10% of staff undertake charitable activities during business hours
- **Gym:** On-site gym or subsidised gym memberships
- **Shares:** Companies where employees are offered share options
- **Health Insurance:** Full family cover

To find out more about this company visit www.bestcompaniesguide.co.uk

TOTAL MEDIA GROUP

UK locations	London, W.Midlands
UK sites	2
Sector	Media
Definition	Media Planning/Buying
How owned	Private
Founded	1982
Turnover	£5.3m
Profit	£0.4m
Staff	63
Average age	32
Male : Female	51 : 49
Earnings £35,000+	51%

BEST COMPANIES INDEX

best company 2007

OUTSTANDING ★ ★

2007 BCI = 714.6

WORKPLACE INSIGHTS

Compared to industry norms, Total Media pay staff in the top quartile of the average pay scale. They operate a holiday scheme that rewards loyalty & all staff participate in bonus schemes linked to individual company or to Group performance.

Throughout the year, members are kept informed of the trading position of their own company & Total Group. Quarterly Group all-staff meetings are held to discuss broader trading issues, share experiences across companies & ensure everyone understands Total Group's goals & objectives.

The management philosophy is to hand responsibility to staff sooner rather than later. This recently created Associate Board of middle & senior management who are currently reviewing the Group's market positioning & will carry an increasing level of decision-making power in the future.

MISSION / VISION

We constantly challenge conventions to provide innovative customer acquisition strategies which deliver disproportionate return on media investment.

BEST WORKPLACE FACTORS

FAIR DEAL
MY TEAM
MY MANAGER

GRADUATE VACANCIES

Media planning & buying.

EMPLOYEE COMMENTS

"People get treated fairly and good work is rewarded."

"Great culture. We are inspired to work together as a team."

"There is an open door and totally transparent managerial style."

CONTACT DETAILS

Total Media Group, 1st floor, 125 Kensington High Street, London W8 5SF
Tel: 0207 9373793 www.totalmedia.co.uk

KEY

- **Holidays:** Companies offering a minimum of 25 days annual leave
- **Maternity:** Companies offering over Statutory Maternity Pay
- **Childcare:** On-site nursery or vouchers
- **Women:** At least 33% of senior managers are women
- **Long Service:** 40% of employees with more than 5 years' service
- **Pensions:** Companies offering a final salary or non-contributory/contributory pension scheme
- **Charity Activities:** 10% of staff undertake charitable activities during business hours
- **Gym:** On-site gym or subsidised gym memberships
- **Shares:** Companies where employees are offered share options
- **Health Insurance:** Full family cover

1000 715> 500 0 ones to watch

1000

<704

500

0

ones to watch

TURLEY ASSOCIATES

TURLEYASSOCIATES

UK locations	National
UK sites	9
Sector	Professional Services
Definition	Planning & Urban Design
How owned	Trust/Employee owned/Mutual
Founded	1983
Turnover	£11.8m
Profit	£1.1m
Staff	165
Average age	35
Male : Female	55 : 45
Earnings £35,000+	44%

BEST COMPANIES INDEX

best company 2007

OUTSTANDING ★ ★

2007 BCI = 704.4

WORKPLACE INSIGHTS

For the past two years, around £1m per year has been distributed to the employees of Turley Associates by way of bonuses and profit share. This arrangement also enables the Board to re-invest profits back into the business to enable it to grow.

Turley Associates have adopted an Environmental policy as part of a drive to reduce their impact on the environment. Their aims include reducing their carbon footprint through careful management of resources & travel and encourage & promote more environmentally sustainable design.

Turley Associates have adopted a mentoring scheme focusing on development of the individual for new responsibilities & to aid succession within the company. It also encourages individuals to take responsibility for their learning & development.

MISSION / VISION

Sustainable Consultancy - Respecting the past - Providing for the present - Securing the future - Excelling in Planning & Urban Design across the British Isles.

BEST WORKPLACE FACTORS

FAIR DEAL
GIVING SOMETHING BACK
PERSONAL GROWTH

GRADUATE VACANCIES

Heritage, IT, Planning and Urban Design.

EMPLOYEE COMMENTS

"We have good medical & pension benefits and I am very happy with my salary and annual bonus."

"The company's policy of donating a percentage of profits to charitable causes is very worthy and makes a difference."

"Exceptional attitude towards individuals' professional development and training."

CONTACT DETAILS

Turley Associates, The Chancery, 58 Spring Gardens, Manchester M2 1EW
Tel: 0161 8311300 www.rta.co.uk

KEY

- **Holidays:** Companies offering a minimum of 25 days annual leave
- **Maternity:** Companies offering over Statutory Maternity Pay
- **Childcare:** On-site nursery or vouchers
- **Women:** At least 33% of senior managers are women
- **Long Service:** 40% of employees with more than 5 years' service
- **Pensions:** Companies offering a final salary or non-contributory/ contributory pension scheme
- **Charity Activities:** 10% of staff undertake charitable activities during business hours
- **Gym:** On-site gym or subsidised gym memberships
- **Shares:** Companies where employees are offered share options
- **Health Insurance:** Full family cover

To find out more about this company visit www.bestcompaniesguide.co.uk

URBAN SPLASH

UK locations	National
UK sites	16
Sector	Property
Definition	Regeneration & Property Development
How owned	Private
Founded	1993
Turnover	£57.3m
Profit	£8.9m
Staff	164
Average age	36
Male : Female	67 : 33
Earnings £35,000+	29%

BEST COMPANIES INDEX

best company 2007

OUTSTANDING ★ ★

2007 BCI = 708.1

2006 BCI = 743.4 (★★★)

708>

ones to watch

WORKPLACE INSIGHTS

Urban Splash doesn't have a formal internal awards process. However, at their quarterly staff meetings they highlight staff who have had a personal or work related achievement and present them with a bottle of bubbly to celebrate.

Urban Splash is about self-starters. They do not dictate the training that should be done but if employees are keen to gain further qualifications, then they can make their case to their manager and more often than not, the training is approved.

Urban Splash chairman, Tom Bloxham, meets each member of staff within three months of beginning their employment at an induction presentation. Employees have the opportunity to pick his brains and give him their feedback on their first impressions of the company.

MISSION / VISION

Urban Splash is a regeneration company whose mission is to create great buildings and neighbourhoods in which to live, work and play.

BEST WORKPLACE FACTORS

MY COMPANY
PERSONAL GROWTH
LEADERSHIP

GRADUATE VACANCIES

Development.

EMPLOYEE COMMENTS

"I'm proud to work for Urban Splash because of its achievements & what the company plans to achieve in the future."

"You can grow in your position and with the company."

"Tom Bloxham has vision, foresight and drive."

CONTACT DETAILS

Urban Splash, Timber Wharf, 16 - 22 Worsley Street, Castlefield, Manchester M15 4LD
Tel: 0161 8392999 www.urbansplash.co.uk

KEY

- **Holidays:** Companies offering a minimum of 25 days annual leave
- **Maternity:** Companies offering over Statutory Maternity Pay
- **Childcare:** On-site nursery or vouchers
- **Women:** At least 33% of senior managers are women
- **Long Service:** 40% of employees with more than 5 years' service
- **Pensions:** Companies offering a final salary or non-contributory/ contributory pension scheme
- **Charity Activities:** 10% of staff undertake charitable activities during business hours
- **Gym:** On-site gym or subsidised gym memberships
- **Shares:** Companies where employees are offered share options
- **Health Insurance:** Full family cover

1000

<719

500

0

ones to watch

WHITBYBIRD

whitbybird

UK locations	National
UK sites	7
Sector	Engineering
Definition	Engineering Consultancy
How owned	Private
Founded	2000
Turnover	Not disclosed
Profit	Not disclosed
Staff	412
Average age	32
Male : Female	74 : 26
Earnings £35,000+	27%

BEST COMPANIES INDEX

OUTSTANDING

★ ★

2007 BCI = 718.5

2006 BCI = 698.9 (★)

WORKPLACE INSIGHTS

Whitbybird believes strongly that the success of their business is because of their people. They invest a huge amount of time & money into training and personal development in order to ensure the continuous development of their team.

There is a social responsibility group at Whitbybird with the remit to look outside the company to the wider community to coordinate & facilitate the significant work undertaken by the company & staff in the charitable, voluntary & environmental sectors.

Whitbybird conduct a number of surveys within the company to ensure continuous feedback from employees including a New Starter Questionnaire, which asks a range of questions about the interview and induction process and Exit interviews when employees leave the company.

MISSION / VISION

To be one of the world's leading providers of integrated engineering services and to be widely recognised for our passion, creativity and innovative approach.

BEST WORKPLACE FACTORS

PERSONAL GROWTH
GIVING SOMETHING BACK
MY COMPANY

GRADUATE VACANCIES

Across all engineering disciplines.

EMPLOYEE COMMENTS

"Fully supportive towards all aspects of training and personal progression."

"Whitbybird push to achieve environmental targets such as sustainability, recycling and also charity events."

"The company strives to better itself with every project undertaken."

CONTACT DETAILS

Whitbybird, 60 Newman Street, London W1T 3DA
Tel: 0207 3005291 www.whitbybird.com

KEY

- **Holidays:** Companies offering a minimum of 25 days annual leave
- **Maternity:** Companies offering over Statutory Maternity Pay
- **Childcare:** On-site nursery or vouchers
- **Women:** At least 33% of senior managers are women
- **Long Service:** 40% of employees with more than 5 years' service
- **Pensions:** Companies offering a final salary or non-contributory/ contributory pension scheme
- **Charity Activities:** 10% of staff undertake charitable activities during business hours
- **Gym:** On-site gym or subsidised gym memberships
- **Shares:** Companies where employees are offered share options
- **Health Insurance:** Full family cover

To find out more about this company visit www.bestcompaniesguide.co.uk

Wieden + Kennedy

WIEDEN + KENNEDY LONDON

UK locations	London
UK sites	1
Sector	Advertising
Definition	Independent Communications Agency
How owned	Partnership/LLP
Founded	1998
Turnover	Not disclosed
Profit	Not disclosed
Staff	67
Average age	32
Male : Female	57 : 43
Earnings £35,000+	67%

BEST COMPANIES INDEX

best company 2007

OUTSTANDING

★ ★

2007 BCI = 699.2

WORKPLACE INSIGHTS

Each year a training and development plan is developed to identify key issues and areas of development. As well as training courses off-site, they also offer varied in-house training sessions by senior members of staff and 90 minute bite size workshops.

A bursary fund is available to all Wieden & Kennedy staff providing £200 towards a 'wish-fulfillment' course to develop personal creativity. Courses have included photography, short story writing and life drawing.

Big Breakfasts are weekly breakfasts held in a local cafe by the Senior Team. Four or five people from different departments are invited to come along, have breakfast and discuss the agency, make suggestions of how things could be done better and discuss concerns or initiatives.

MISSION / VISION

We aim to build the most admired creative business in the UK.

BEST WORKPLACE FACTORS

PERSONAL GROWTH
MY COMPANY
LEADERSHIP

GRADUATE VACANCIES

No graduate vacancies have been indicated.

EMPLOYEE COMMENTS

"People are encouraged to grow and develop."

"The agency mission statement: 'we're here to do the best work of our lives' is truly believed & adhered to."

"Inspirational leaders and the desire and drive to do the best work of your career."

CONTACT DETAILS

Wieden + Kennedy London, 16 Hanbury Street, London E1 6QR
Tel: 0207 1947000 www.wklondon.com

KEY

- **Holidays:** Companies offering a minimum of 25 days annual leave
- **Maternity:** Companies offering over Statutory Maternity Pay
- **Childcare:** On-site nursery or vouchers
- **Women:** At least 33% of senior managers are women
- **Long Service:** 40% of employees with more than 5 years' service
- **Pensions:** Companies offering a final salary or non-contributory/contributory pension scheme
- **Charity Activities:** 10% of staff undertake charitable activities during business hours
- **Gym:** On-site gym or subsidised gym memberships
- **Shares:** Companies where employees are offered share options
- **Health Insurance:** Full family cover

To find out more about this company visit www.bestcompaniesguide.co.uk

1000 500 0 699> ones to watch

1000

500

0

<708

ones to watch

WITAN JARDINE

Witan Jardine

UK locations	London
UK sites	1
Sector	Recruitment
Definition	Recruitment Consultancy
How owned	Private
Founded	1979
Turnover	£20.8m
Profit	£2m
Staff	114
Average age	30
Male : Female	44 : 56
Earnings £35,000+	24%

BEST COMPANIES INDEX

best company 2007

OUTSTANDING ★ ★

2007 BCI = 707.6

WORKPLACE INSIGHTS

By interacting with people and offering praise and support Witan Jardine build a cohesive and happy team who understand and support the vision.

Staff are rewarded very well. Salary is competitive but it's the extra rewards, such as – dinners & nights out, spas, hotels, flights, fresh fruit everyday that make employees feel valued for their contribution.

Each team has a budget to go out and do an activity of their choice each quarter, be that theatre, dinner or a big lunch.

MISSION / VISION

Our Mission is to continue to develop as a major quality recruitment consultancy, providing superior value, by sustaining and building on long-term relationships with high calibre clients and candidates, and continually training and developing all our people.

BEST WORKPLACE FACTORS

MY MANAGER
FAIR DEAL
MY TEAM

GRADUATE VACANCIES

No graduate vacancies have been indicated.

EMPLOYEE COMMENTS

"I have a strong motivational manager."

"Rewards are offered for those who perform, both financially and within the organisation."

"There is a good atmosphere and people work together as a team."

CONTACT DETAILS

Witan Jardine, Norfolk House, 13 Southampton Place, London WC1A 2AL
Tel: 0207 4044004 www.witanjardine.co.uk

KEY

Holidays: Companies offering a minimum of 25 days annual leave
Maternity: Companies offering over Statutory Maternity Pay
Childcare: On-site nursery or vouchers
Women: At least 33% of senior managers are women
Long Service: 40% of employees with more than 5 years' service
Pensions: Companies offering a final salary or non-contributory/contributory pension scheme
Charity Activities: 10% of staff undertake charitable activities during business hours
Gym: On-site gym or subsidised gym memberships
Shares: Companies where employees are offered share options
Health Insurance: Full family cover

To find out more about this company visit www.bestcompaniesguide.co.uk

WRIGHT VIGAR

WRIGHT VIGAR
Chartered Accountants and Business Advisers

UK locations	E.Midlands
UK sites	3
Sector	Professional Services
Definition	Chartered Accountants
How owned	Private
Founded	1977
Turnover	£1.9m
Profit	Not disclosed
Staff	54
Average age	38
Male : Female	43 : 57
Earnings £35,000+	11%

BEST COMPANIES INDEX

best company 2007

OUTSTANDING

★ ★

2007 BCI = 724.0

2006 BCI = 710.3 (★★)

724>

ones to watch

WORKPLACE INSIGHTS

Team members at Wright Vigar have the benefit of flexible start and finish times within set core hours, provided they work 40 hours a week. This allows them time for activities such as going to the gym, seeing their family or even going to the pub together.

Wright Vigar has a dedicated HR director and training manager. Any training needs identified are notified to the training manager and also, if relevant, the IT manager who runs internal training courses on Microsoft office programmes.

Each year Wright Vigar hold a team building or training day, this year held at Center Parcs, consisting of team building exercises and communications of developments in the company in the morning and free time in the afternoon.

MISSION / VISION

We will: - Enable our clients to identify achieve and surpass their business ambitions. - Provide integral support for our clients and become part of their success. - Grow our client's businesses and increase their wealth.

BEST WORKPLACE FACTORS

WELL BEING
PERSONAL GROWTH
MY COMPANY

GRADUATE VACANCIES

IT, Business Services, Tax.

EMPLOYEE COMMENTS

"Terrific support is given in times of personal difficulty."

"Training and development is second to none."

"Everyone is motivated which drives the business forward and creates an efficient and successful workplace."

CONTACT DETAILS

Wright Vigar, 15 Newland, Lincoln LN1 1XG
Tel: 01522 531341 www.wrightvigar.co.uk

KEY

Holidays: Companies offering a minimum of 25 days annual leave

Maternity: Companies offering over Statutory Maternity Pay

Childcare: On-site nursery or vouchers

Women: At least 33% of senior managers are women

Long Service: 40% of employees with more than 5 years' service

Pensions: Companies offering a final salary or non-contributory/ contributory pension scheme

Charity Activities: 10% of staff undertake charitable activities during business hours

Gym: On-site gym or subsidised gym memberships

Shares: Companies where employees are offered share options

Health Insurance: Full family cover

To find out more about this company visit www.bestcompaniesguide.co.uk

RIGHT PLACE

RIGHT TIME

You have to recognize when the right place and right time fuse and take advantage of that opportunity. There are plenty of opportunities out there. You can't sit back and wait.

Ellen Metcalf

FIRST CLASS

1000

<689

ones to watch

500

0

ADDLESHAW GODDARD

ADDLESHAW GODDARD

UK locations	London, Yorks & Humber, N.East
UK sites	3
Sector	Law
Definition	Legal Firm
How owned	Partnership/LLP
Founded	1775
Turnover	£161.0m
Profit	£61.8m
Staff	1199
Average age	35
Male : Female	40 : 60
Earnings £35,000+	54%

BEST COMPANIES INDEX

best company 2007

FIRST CLASS

★

2007 BCI = 689.2

2006 BCI = 670.0 (★)

WORKPLACE INSIGHTS

From the top leadership throughout the entire firm Addleshaw Goddard are committed to a culture where every single person gets the credit they deserve, has an opinion that is respected and an individual approach to work that it is highly valued.

Addleshaw Goddard people can enjoy working in a dynamic, business focused and supportive culture where their contribution is recognised and teamwork is the norm.

The foundation of Addleshaw Goddard's approach to personal development is to give all their people the right skills at the right times in their careers, developing them to their highest potential in terms of technical, business and personal development.

MISSION / VISION

To be recognised as one of the best 15 Law Firms in the UK.

BEST WORKPLACE FACTORS

FAIR DEAL
MY TEAM
PERSONAL GROWTH

GRADUATE VACANCIES

Trainee Solicitors.

EMPLOYEE COMMENTS

"Every member is expected to work hard but their hard work is appreciated and rewarded."

"In my team there is a strong work ethic."

"I am most impressed with the training workshop/courses they offer to employees to advance their careers."

CONTACT DETAILS

Addleshaw Goddard, 150 Aldersgate Street, London EC1A 4EJ
Tel: 0207 6068855 www.addleshawgoddard.com

KEY

- **Holidays:** Companies offering a minimum of 25 days annual leave
- **Maternity:** Companies offering over Statutory Matternity Pay
- **Childcare:** On-site nursery or vouchers
- **Women:** At least 33% of senior managers are women
- **Long Service:** 40% of employees with more than 5 years' service
- **Pensions:** Companies offering a final salary or non-contributory/ contributory pension scheme
- **Charity Activities:** 10% of staff undertake charitable activities during business hours
- **Gym:** On-site gym or subsidised gym memberships
- **Shares:** Companies where employees are offered share options
- **Health Insurance:** Full family cover

To find out more about this company visit www.bestcompaniesguide.co.uk

ALBATROSS TRAVEL GROUP

UK locations	E.Midlands
UK sites	2
Sector	Travel
Definition	UK Tour Wholesaler
How owned	Private
Founded	1985
Turnover	£12.5m
Profit	£0.6m
Staff	59
Average age	34
Male : Female	15 : 85
Earnings £35,000+	7%

BEST COMPANIES INDEX

best company 2007

FIRST CLASS

★

2007 BCI = 691.2

WORKPLACE INSIGHTS

Albatross has an effective one team spirit, which they maintain through social events, including an annual convention and the use of first name terms across the organisation.

Albatross implement a general flexibility in working hours. All requests are considered and where possible accommodated. Staff are also encouraged to leave on time where possible.

The MD and Management Team are always willing to participate and get stuck in at staff events, including the wearing of fancy dress at the annual convention gala dinner which is chosen by the staff.

MISSION / VISION

To become a leading Pan-European Wholesaler, with strong independent subsidiaries.

BEST WORKPLACE FACTORS

MY TEAM
WELL BEING
LEADERSHIP

GRADUATE VACANCIES

IT.

EMPLOYEE COMMENTS

"The team I work with are friendly and supportive making for a great atmosphere."

"The company is very flexible when it comes to working hours & is very generous with extra activities."

"The leader of the organisation is a great motivator."

CONTACT DETAILS

Albatross Travel Group, Albatross House, 14 New Hythe Lane, Larkfield, Kent ME20 6AB
Tel: 01732 879100 www.albatross-tours.com

KEY

- **Holidays:** Companies offering a minimum of 25 days annual leave
- **Maternity:** Companies offering over Statutory Mattrenity Pay
- **Childcare:** On-site nursery or vouchers
- **Women:** At least 33% of senior managers are women
- **Long Service:** 40% of employees with more than 5 years' service
- **Pensions:** Companies offering a final salary or non-contributory/ contributory pension scheme
- **Charity Activities:** 10% of staff undertake charitable activities during business hours
- **Gym:** On-site gym or subsidised gym memberships
- **Shares:** Companies where employees are offered share options
- **Health Insurance:** Full family cover

1000
691>
500
0
ones to watch

ALEXANDER MANN SOLUTIONS

UK locations	National
UK sites	38
Sector	Business Services
Definition	Recruitment Process Outsourcing
How owned	Private
Founded	1996
Turnover	£257.6m
Profit	£3.4m
Staff	368
Average age	32
Male : Female	31 : 69
Earnings £35,000+	38%

BEST COMPANIES INDEX

best company 2007

FIRST CLASS

★

2007 BCI = 664.4

2006 BCI = 663.0 (★)

WORKPLACE INSIGHTS

Alexander Mann holds induction events every six weeks for all new joiners. The CEO and Leadership Team present key highlights from the business plan together with the history of the organisation. There are also workshops based on the five company values.

The Citizen of the Year award is an opportunity for everyone within Alexander Mann to select the person who they believe embodies the values of the business and has made an unparalleled contribution during the previous year.

Alexander Mann conduct HR site visits on a regular basis in which the HR Business Partners encourage feedback from employees on their managers. This is used to gain a greater understanding of the management style and effectiveness for the team as a whole.

MISSION / VISION

Alexander Mann Solutions' vision is to be recognised as the dominant global pureplay recruitment process outsourcing (RPO) provider.

BEST WORKPLACE FACTORS

LEADERSHIP
MY COMPANY
MY MANAGER

GRADUATE VACANCIES

Recruitment.

EMPLOYEE COMMENTS

"There is very strong & visible leadership supported by clear messaging about the objectives of the organisation."

"Strong culture and values which are set and demonstrated from the leaders through managers and throughout the company."

"Excellent Team Leaders and Managers."

CONTACT DETAILS

Alexander Mann Solutions, 3 Waterhouse Square, 138-142 Holborn, London EC1N 2SW
Tel: 0207 8322700 www.alexandermannsolutions.com

KEY

- **Holidays:** Companies offering a minimum of 25 days annual leave
- **Maternity:** Companies offering over Statutory Maternity Pay
- **Childcare:** On-site nursery or vouchers
- **Women:** At least 33% of senior managers are women
- **Long Service:** 40% of employees with more than 5 years' service
- **Pensions:** Companies offering a final salary or non-contributory/ contributory pension scheme
- **Charity Activities:** 10% of staff undertake charitable activities during business hours
- **Gym:** On-site gym or subsidised gym memberships
- **Shares:** Companies where employees are offered share options
- **Health Insurance:** Full family cover

ANTISOMA

ANTISOMA

UK locations	London
UK sites	2
Sector	Pharmaceutical
Definition	Cancer Research & Development
How owned	Public (i.e. stock market listed)
Founded	1994
Turnover	Not disclosed
Profit	Not disclosed
Staff	51
Average age	30
Male : Female	55 : 45
Earnings £35,000+	61%

BEST COMPANIES INDEX

b ★ best company 2007

FIRST CLASS

★

2007 BCI = 666.6

2006 BCI = 630.2

WORKPLACE INSIGHTS

Every single member of staff at Antisoma is entitled to participate in the share option scheme. They also like to reward staff who have gone the extra mile with a spot bonus, this is usually generated by a nomination from a colleague.

Coffee mornings to raise money for the Macmillan Nurses charity are regularly held at Antisoma. They entered a team into the London triathlon last year and held a fund raising day which included on-site massage to raise money for Children in Need.

Antisoma have an employee assistance programme and they also provide all their staff with baskets of fruit every week.

MISSION / VISION

To develop novel products for the treatment of cancer.

BEST WORKPLACE FACTORS

FAIR DEAL
GIVING SOMETHING BACK
WELL BEING

GRADUATE VACANCIES

No graduate vacancies have been indicated.

EMPLOYEE COMMENTS

"The staff are motivated to make a contribution to the company's success."

"I feel proud to work for this company as I believe that they operate exactly with their values/ principles."

"I could not ask for a better team or manager to work for."

CONTACT DETAILS

Antisoma, West Africa House, Ealing Hanger Lane W53QR
Tel: 0208 7998200 www.antisoma.com

KEY

- **Holidays:** Companies offering a minimum of 25 days annual leave
- **Maternity:** Companies offering over Statutory Matternity Pay
- **Childcare:** On-site nursery or vouchers
- **Women:** At least 33% of senior managers are women
- **Long Service:** 40% of employees with more than 5 years' service
- **Pensions:** Companies offering a final salary or non-contributory/ contributory pension scheme
- **Charity Activities:** 10% of staff undertake charitable activities during business hours
- **Gym:** On-site gym or subsidised gym memberships
- **Shares:** Companies where employees are offered share options
- **Health Insurance:** Full family cover

1000 ★★★ ★★ ★ 667> ones to watch 500 0

1000

BAKER & MCKENZIE

BAKER & McKENZIE

UK locations	London
UK sites	1
Sector	Law
Definition	Global Law Firm
How owned	Partnership/LLP
Founded	1949
Turnover	£99.6m
Profit	£33.5m
Staff	689
Average age	36
Male : Female	38 : 62
Earnings £35,000+	54%

<668

BEST COMPANIES INDEX

best company 2007

FIRST CLASS

★

2007 BCI = 668.0

WORKPLACE INSIGHTS

Through ongoing consultation with staff, Baker & McKenzie determine what the business and its people consider important, then respond to what they have heard.

Baker & McKenzie has a strong tradition in professional development. They place great emphasis on training to ensure that all staff are equipped with the technical expertise and skills to deliver an excellent service to clients.

Baker & McKenzie's Flexible Working Programme proactively provides opportunities for all employees to manage their work and home lives and thereby improve its retention and increase the diversity of the workforce.

MISSION / VISION

To be "the" premier global law firm not by geographic coverage alone but more importantly by performance in key defining areas.

BEST WORKPLACE FACTORS

FAIR DEAL
PERSONAL GROWTH
WELL BEING

GRADUATE VACANCIES

Law.

500

EMPLOYEE COMMENTS

"In my opinion we are paid well for what we do."

"The training offered to all staff is exceptional."

"Sensible attitude to work/life balance."

CONTACT DETAILS

Baker & McKenzie, 100 New Bridge Street, London EC4V 6JA
Tel: 020 79191000 www.bakernet.com

KEY

Holidays: Companies offering a minimum of 25 days annual leave
Maternity: Companies offering over Statutory Matternity Pay
Childcare: On-site nursery or vouchers
Women: At least 33% of senior managers are women
Long Service: 40% of employees with more than 5 years' service
Pensions: Companies offering a final salary or non-contributory/contributory pension scheme
Charity Activities: 10% of staff undertake charitable activities during business hours
Gym: On-site gym or subsidised gym memberships
Shares: Companies where employees are offered share options
Health Insurance: Full family cover

0

ones to watch

To find out more about this company visit www.bestcompaniesguide.co.uk

BAYFORD & CO

UK locations	National
UK sites	12
Sector	Utilities
Definition	Distributor of Energy
How owned	Private
Founded	1922
Turnover	£392.0m
Profit	£3.1m
Staff	190
Average age	40
Male : Female	63 : 37
Earnings £35,000+	9%

BEST COMPANIES INDEX

best company 2007

FIRST CLASS

★

2007 BCI = 688.3

2006 BCI = 692.2 (★)

688>

ones to watch

WORKPLACE INSIGHTS

Bayford recently launched their inspirational 'Fulfill a Dream' programme. This gives employees the chance to imagine their ideal 'live the dream' experience and make it become a reality such as driving a tank or getting sports equipment for a local team.

Managing Director Jonathan Turner met with employees at his Road Show, setting out the company position and strategy. Employees got the chance to discuss ways to improve the company, resulting in new policies such as an option to buy holiday, long service awards and a buddy scheme.

Employees are assigned a 'Buddy' who acts as a personal mentor for six months, who they meet with for a weekly lunch and monthly one-to-one. In addition, job shadowing helps staff relate to other roles and identifies areas for development.

MISSION / VISION

To build a thriving, dynamic, profitable business, made up of inspired, energised, and happy people.

BEST WORKPLACE FACTORS

WELL BEING
LEADERSHIP
PERSONAL GROWTH

GRADUATE VACANCIES

No graduate vacancies have been indicated.

EMPLOYEE COMMENTS

"It is not all about work, your general well being is also considered."

"The enthusiasm of the Managing Director is boundless, a great motivator and fun to work with."

"Good opportunities for training and development."

CONTACT DETAILS

Bayford & Co, Bowcliffe Hall, Bramham, Wetherby, West Yorkshire LS23 6LP
Tel: 01937 541111 www.bayfordgroup.co.uk

KEY

- **Holidays:** Companies offering a minimum of 25 days annual leave
- **Maternity:** Companies offering over Statutory Matternity Pay
- **Childcare:** On-site nursery or vouchers
- **Women:** At least 33% of senior managers are women
- **Long Service:** 40% of employees with more than 5 years' service
- **Pensions:** Companies offering a final salary or non-contributory/ contributory pension scheme
- **Charity Activities:** 10% of staff undertake charitable activities during business hours
- **Gym:** On-site gym or subsidised gym memberships
- **Shares:** Companies where employees are offered share options
- **Health Insurance:** Full family cover

1000

<666

ones to watch

500

0

Bedell Group

BEDELL GROUP

UK locations	Jersey, Guernsey, London
UK sites	3
Sector	Financial
Definition	Legal/Fiduciary
How owned	Partnership/LLP
Founded	1939
Turnover	Not disclosed
Profit	Not disclosed
Staff	201
Average age	41
Male : Female	36 : 64
Earnings £35,000+	59%

BEST COMPANIES INDEX

best company 2007

FIRST CLASS

★

2007 BCI = 665.9

WORKPLACE INSIGHTS

Rewards vary from flowers and bottles of champagne, to a night at a hotel. Rewards are chosen to match the individual & achievement. Bedell also offer financial rewards to staff for their efforts and reward staff for introducing new recruits.

Key to their success is understanding the needs & personality not only of the Group but of individual departments. Knowing exactly where teams need strengthening and recognising the kind of person who has the appropriate skills-set & character to fit in.

Through informal and formal discussions, ideas for training are explored and proposals put forward for consideration. This is relevant to all staff regardless of their level and role.

MISSION / VISION

To ensure that Bedell Group is a leading Jersey firm which serves the local community, and supports and develops the status of Jersey as an international finance centre.

BEST WORKPLACE FACTORS

FAIR DEAL
MY COMPANY
PERSONAL GROWTH

GRADUATE VACANCIES

No graduate vacancies have been indicated.

EMPLOYEE COMMENTS

"I feel the partners do care about the staff and treat them very fairly."

"A friendly company. Plenty of social activities & the company participates in fund-raising both on a small and large scale."

"Great emphasis on training."

CONTACT DETAILS

Bedell Group, PO Box 75, 26 New Street, St Helier, Jersey Channel Islands JE4 8PP
Tel: 01534 814814 www.bedellgroup.com

KEY

- **Holidays:** Companies offering a minimum of 25 days annual leave
- **Maternity:** Companies offering over Statutory Matternity Pay
- **Childcare:** On-site nursery or vouchers
- **Women:** At least 33% of senior managers are women
- **Long Service:** 40% of employees with more than 5 years' service
- **Pensions:** Companies offering a final salary or non-contributory/ contributory pension scheme
- **Charity Activities:** 10% of staff undertake charitable activities during business hours
- **Gym:** On-site gym or subsidised gym memberships
- **Shares:** Companies where employees are offered share options
- **Health Insurance:** Full family cover

To find out more about this company visit www.bestcompaniesguide.co.uk

Benoy

BENOY

UK locations	London
UK sites	2
Sector	Architects
Definition	International Dynamic Architects
How owned	Private
Founded	1992
Turnover	Not disclosed
Profit	Not disclosed
Staff	174
Average age	35
Male : Female	67 : 33
Earnings £35,000+	41%

BEST COMPANIES INDEX

best company 2007

FIRST CLASS ★

2007 BCI = 679.3

679>

WORKPLACE INSIGHTS

Through both length of service and increasing seniority, employees are able to increase their holiday entitlement from a minimum of 21 days to a maximum of 35. They have also recently introduced a scheme whereby people can buy and sell holidays.

Individuals are able to request and pursue a specific area of training and take courses that suit their own needs and personal lives. Requests are addressed following appraisals and paid for by the company through the staff training budget.

At Benoy management and team leaders offer support to employees by means of monitoring their work loads to ensure there are no continual pressures from timescales. The balance of teams is managed and the skill base is shared fairly between all teams.

MISSION / VISION

Benoy is acknowledged for combining contemporary design with consistence & deliverability. Benoy brings together design integrity, international experience, local understanding, & real personality to create the unique. We offer a culture that is corporate and ambitious yet encouraging and conscientious imaginative yet realistic.

BEST WORKPLACE FACTORS

FAIR DEAL
PERSONAL GROWTH
WELL BEING

GRADUATE VACANCIES

Architects.

EMPLOYEE COMMENTS

"My skills are recognised by the management and I am rewarded accordingly."

"Excellent opportunities to progress within the company structure."

"The management look after their staff very well."

CONTACT DETAILS

Benoy, Handley House, Northgate, Newark, Nottinghamshire NG24 1EH
Tel: 01636 672356 www.benoy.com

KEY

- **Holidays:** Companies offering a minimum of 25 days annual leave
- **Maternity:** Companies offering over Statutory Matternity Pay
- **Childcare:** On-site nursery or vouchers
- **Women:** At least 33% of senior managers are women
- **Long Service:** 40% of employees with more than 5 years' service
- **Pensions:** Companies offering a final salary or non-contributory/ contributory pension scheme
- **Charity Activities:** 10% of staff undertake charitable activities during business hours
- **Gym:** On-site gym or subsidised gym memberships
- **Shares:** Companies where employees are offered share options
- **Health Insurance:** Full family cover

BERWIN LEIGHTON PAISNER

*berwin leighton paisner

<675

UK locations	London
UK sites	1
Sector	Law
Definition	City Law Firm
How owned	Partnership/LLP
Founded	2001
Turnover	£145.0m
Profit	£60.5m
Staff	1106
Average age	33
Male : Female	39 : 61
Earnings £35,000+	55%

BEST COMPANIES INDEX

best company 2007

FIRST CLASS

★

2007 BCI = 674.5

WORKPLACE INSIGHTS

Berwin Leighton Paisner have an in-house concierge service to ensure staff have help with time-consuming tasks like dry cleaning and buying tickets so they are free to enjoy their breaks.

Berwin Leighton Paisner have a framework which allows people to develop their careers by providing comprehensive training and development opportunities for all and a robust and transparent performance management process which includes personal development plans.

Each department has a budget for Departmental / team outings. It can be a trip to the races, go-karting, cookery class etc.

MISSION / VISION

Vision: To be the most respected law firm in London.
Mission: To always exceed client expectations. To be a more attractive place to work than our competitors.

BEST WORKPLACE FACTORS

FAIR DEAL
PERSONAL GROWTH
MY TEAM

GRADUATE VACANCIES

Trainee lawyers.

EMPLOYEE COMMENTS

"Good work is always recognised."

"I am involved in challenging work and this helps me to progress and improve my skills in every area."

"A lot of talented people making a success of the business."

CONTACT DETAILS

Berwin Leighton Paisner, Adelaide House, London Bridge, London EC4R 9HA
Tel: 0207 7601000 www.blplaw.com

KEY

- **Holidays:** Companies offering a minimum of 25 days annual leave
- **Maternity:** Companies offering over Statutory Matternity Pay
- **Childcare:** On-site nursery or vouchers
- **Women:** At least 33% of senior managers are women
- **Long Service:** 40% of employees with more than 5 years' service
- **Pensions:** Companies offering a final salary or non-contributory/ contributory pension scheme
- **Charity Activities:** 10% of staff undertake charitable activities during business hours
- **Gym:** On-site gym or subsidised gym memberships
- **Shares:** Companies where employees are offered share options
- **Health Insurance:** Full family cover

To find out more about this company visit www.bestcompaniesguide.co.uk

BI

UK locations	S.East
UK sites	1
Sector	Business Services
Definition	Communication and Motivation
How owned	Private
Founded	2002
Turnover	£15.4m
Profit	Not disclosed
Staff	117
Average age	35
Male : Female	38 : 62
Earnings £35,000+	21%

BEST COMPANIES INDEX

best company 2007

FIRST CLASS

★

2007 BCI = 678.3

1000

678>

ones to watch

500

0

WORKPLACE INSIGHTS

A member of the BI Worldwide leadership team hosts a weekly 'round-up' for all employees. Updates on wins, pitches and business in general are provided as well as beer, wine and nibbles for the team to enjoy.

BI Worldwide provide employees with Personal Development Vouchers of £100 per person to spend on anything that helps them develop new skills and knowledge, such as driving lessons, singing lessons or language courses.

Employees at BI Worldwide can achieve Award points which can be saved up and exchanged for prizes. They can receive them through generating new ideas through the 'Ideas Factory' or through the 'Be Incredible' reward and recognition scheme.

MISSION / VISION

To be the most successful global Communication and Motivation Company that everyone wants to work with because of our thought leadership, enduring commitment to quality, creativity, personality, and ultimately what we value.

BEST WORKPLACE FACTORS

LEADERSHIP
PERSONAL GROWTH
MY COMPANY

GRADUATE VACANCIES

IT, Events, Client Services.

EMPLOYEE COMMENTS

"The leadership team injects compassion, listening & enthusiasm into the company."

"There is an open and honest culture which is linked very strongly to personal development."

"There is always a buzz of challenge & achievement about the place."

CONTACT DETAILS

BI, 1 Vantage Court, Tickford Street, Newport Pagnell, Bucks MK16 9EZ
Tel: 01908 214700 www.eu.biworldwide.com

KEY

- **Holidays:** Companies offering a minimum of 25 days annual leave
- **Maternity:** Companies offering over Statutory Matternity Pay
- **Childcare:** On-site nursery or vouchers
- **Women:** At least 33% of senior managers are women
- **Long Service:** 40% of employees with more than 5 years' service
- **Pensions:** Companies offering a final salary or non-contributory/contributory pension scheme
- **Charity Activities:** 10% of staff undertake charitable activities during business hours
- **Gym:** On-site gym or subsidised gym memberships
- **Shares:** Companies where employees are offered share options
- **Health Insurance:** Full family cover

1000

BIBENDUM

www.bibendum-wine.co.uk

BIBENDUM WINE

UK locations	London
UK sites	1
Sector	Logistics/Wholesale/Distribution
Definition	Wine Distributor
How owned	Private
Founded	1988
Turnover	Not disclosed
Profit	Not disclosed
Staff	133
Average age	34
Male : Female	60 : 40
Earnings £35,000+	29%

<668

ones to watch

BEST COMPANIES INDEX

best company 2007

FIRST CLASS ★

2007 BCI = 668.1

2006 BCI = 670.6 (★)

WORKPLACE INSIGHTS

Bibendum provide employee awards known as The Lucky Seven which include categories such as The People's Champion; The Maverick & The Top Dog. The Awards carry a prize fund of £4,000 and are awarded annually to outstanding employees who have made a real difference during the year.

'The Horn' are a team of employee volunteers responsible for bringing employee ideas forward and ensuring people's voices are heard. They are also responsible for Bibendum's charity budget & organising team social events.

Managing Director Michael Saunders holds monthly discussions with employees from across the business to encourage sharing of ideas. As a result of these forums, management are introducing company wide distribution of written, quarterly updates and considering introducing sabbaticals.

500

MISSION / VISION

We'd like to be the most accessible, relevant & captivating company in the wine business. We want to be the people who make wine more approachable & we strive to present wine in a different way to other wine companies by being playful with the idea of drink.

BEST WORKPLACE FACTORS

MY COMPANY
MY TEAM
LEADERSHIP

GRADUATE VACANCIES

No graduate vacancies have been indicated.

EMPLOYEE COMMENTS

"It is a business which genuinely values its human resource & passionately believes in its mission."

"The people are all positive, dynamic and interesting. It feels like a family."

"Firm but fair leadership, led by example, integrity and with the best intent."

CONTACT DETAILS

Bibendum Wine, 113 Regents Park Road, London NW1 8UR
Tel: 0207 7225577 www.bibendum-wine.co.uk

KEY

- **Holidays:** Companies offering a minimum of 25 days annual leave
- **Maternity:** Companies offering over Statutory Maternity Pay
- **Childcare:** On-site nursery or vouchers
- **Women:** At least 33% of senior managers are women
- **Long Service:** 40% of employees with more than 5 years' service
- **Pensions:** Companies offering a final salary or non-contributory/contributory pension scheme
- **Charity Activities:** 10% of staff undertake charitable activities during business hours
- **Gym:** On-site gym or subsidised gym memberships
- **Shares:** Companies where employees are offered share options
- **Health Insurance:** Full family cover

0

To find out more about this company visit www.bestcompaniesguide.co.uk

BOYES TURNER

UK locations	S.East
UK sites	1
Sector	Law
Definition	Legal Firm
How owned	Partnership/LLP
Founded	1887
Turnover	£10.1m
Profit	Not disclosed
Staff	142
Average age	39
Male : Female	26 : 74
Earnings £35,000+	39%

BEST COMPANIES INDEX

best company 2007

FIRST CLASS ★

2007 BCI = 690.4

2006 BCI = 683.4 (★)

WORKPLACE INSIGHTS

They have a range of development tools to ensure that proactive personal development takes place. These include appraisals, frequent informal progress review meetings throughout the year, 360 degree appraisals for line managers, on the job training, in-house seminars & external training courses.

The HR department operates an 'open door' policy where employees are encouraged to raise and discuss any appropriate issues both formally and informally off the record. They also provide an employee assistance/ confidential counselling programme.

Boyes Turner recently carried out a review of the benefits package which includes regular bonuses for all staff as well as healthcare, pensions, life insurance, discounted PCs and bicycles and local restaurant discounts.

MISSION / VISION

We provide first class legal services for our clients tailored to their needs & which exceed their expectations. We ensure all of our people have rewarding stretching careers. We value & play a positive role in the communities that we are part of.

BEST WORKPLACE FACTORS

PERSONAL GROWTH
WELL BEING
FAIR DEAL

GRADUATE VACANCIES

Trainee Solicitors, Marketing, Human Resources.

EMPLOYEE COMMENTS

"Boyes Turner is very willing to support my personal development and to help me develop my career within the firm."

"We genuinely care about each other and willingly offer help and support."

"Good salary and benefits."

CONTACT DETAILS

Boyes Turner, Abbots House, Abbey Street, Reading RG1 3BD
Tel: 0118 9597711 www.boyesturner.com

KEY

Holidays: Companies offering a minimum of 25 days annual leave
Maternity: Companies offering over Statutory Matternity Pay
Childcare: On-site nursery or vouchers
Women: At least 33% of senior managers are women
Long Service: 40% of employees with more than 5 years' service
Pensions: Companies offering a final salary or non-contributory/ contributory pension scheme
Charity Activities: 10% of staff undertake charitable activities during business hours
Gym: On-site gym or subsidised gym memberships
Shares: Companies where employees are offered share options
Health Insurance: Full family cover

1000
690>
ones to watch
500
0

1000

BRAHM

brahm

UK locations	Yorks & Humber
UK sites	1
Sector	Advertising
Definition	Marketing Communications Agency
How owned	Private
Founded	1983
Turnover	£6.9m
Profit	£0.6m
Staff	133
Average age	34
Male : Female	43 : 57
Earnings £35,000+	24%

BEST COMPANIES INDEX

best company 2007

FIRST CLASS

★

2007 BCI = 662.8

2006 BCI = 653.6

<663

ones to watch

WORKPLACE INSIGHTS

Brahm is set in beautiful grounds, with a lovely garden which people are encouraged to use for work, meetings, and social activities. In addition, employees take part in events such as making pancakes on Pancake Day and chocolate making at Easter.

Brahm have constructed a purpose-built art gallery space within the reception area. Once a year, normally around Christmas time they hold a charity function, with proceeds of all artwork sold on that night going to a nominated charity.

Brahm operate a confidential helpline for employees, which is paid for by the company. Any employee or family member can contact this number at any time for confidential advice from a trained counsellor.

500

MISSION / VISION

Vision: The Agency that the best clients work with and the best people work for.
Mission: Great Insights, Great Outcomes.

BEST WORKPLACE FACTORS

MY TEAM
GIVING SOMETHING BACK
WELL BEING

GRADUATE VACANCIES

No graduate vacancies have been indicated.

EMPLOYEE COMMENTS

"We have a fantastic team who work really well together."

"Brahm offers personal as well as professional development in the form of volunteering initiatives and charitable support."

"Brahm understands that happy employees need a healthy work life balance."

CONTACT DETAILS

Brahm Limited, The Brahm Building, Alma Road, Leeds LS6 2AH
Tel: 0113 2304000 www.brahm.com

KEY

- **Holidays:** Companies offering a minimum of 25 days annual leave
- **Maternity:** Companies offering over Statutory Matternity Pay
- **Childcare:** On-site nursery or vouchers
- **Women:** At least 33% of senior managers are women
- **Long Service:** 40% of employees with more than 5 years' service
- **Pensions:** Companies offering a final salary or non-contributory/ contributory pension scheme
- **Charity Activities:** 10% of staff undertake charitable activities during business hours
- **Gym:** On-site gym or subsidised gym memberships
- **Shares:** Companies where employees are offered share options
- **Health Insurance:** Full family cover

0

Brit Insurance

BRIT INSURANCE HOLDINGS

UK locations	National
UK sites	9
Sector	Financial - Insurance
Definition	General Re/Insurance Company
How owned	Public (i.e. stock market listed)
Founded	1999
Turnover	£1,202.5m
Profit	£62.4m
Staff	651
Average age	Not available
Male : Female	58 : 42
Earnings £35,000+	56%

BEST COMPANIES INDEX

best company 2007

FIRST CLASS ★

2007 BCI = 686.0

WORKPLACE INSIGHTS

The benefits, health & pensions policies provided by Brit reflect their aim of offering a professional and caring work environment. They also aim to promote a healthy work/life balance and fun by encouraging employees to get involved with a variety of sports teams & social events.

The Executive Management Committee, Senior Managers and Non-Executive Directors hold lunches with employees on a regular basis to update them on what is happening in the company and to allow them to give feedback.

All permanent Brit Insurance employees are eligible for the 'Get a Life' scheme which entitles them to £500 towards an opportunity or activity that they feel would enhance their lives such as swimming with dolphins or driving a steam train.

MISSION / VISION

To be a leading and profitable UK-domiciled international general insurance and reinsurance group in a manner that improves the economic well-being and the quality of life of all our stakeholders.

BEST WORKPLACE FACTORS

WELL BEING
LEADERSHIP
MY COMPANY

GRADUATE VACANCIES

Underwriting Group Services & Audit.

EMPLOYEE COMMENTS

"There is a genuine concern for the welfare of staff."

"The leadership is fair, consistent and communicates regularly."

"You really do get the feeling that Brit values its employees greatly & takes pride in them."

CONTACT DETAILS

Brit Insurance Holdings, 55 Bishopsgate, London EC2N 3AS
Tel: 0207 9848800 www.britinsurance.com

1000 686> ones to watch 500 0

KEY

- **Holidays:** Companies offering a minimum of 25 days annual leave
- **Maternity:** Companies offering over Statutory Matternity Pay
- **Childcare:** On-site nursery or vouchers
- **Women:** At least 33% of senior managers are women
- **Long Service:** 40% of employees with more than 5 years' service
- **Pensions:** Companies offering a final salary or non-contributory/ contributory pension scheme
- **Charity Activities:** 10% of staff undertake charitable activities during business hours
- **Gym:** On-site gym or subsidised gym memberships
- **Shares:** Companies where employees are offered share options
- **Health Insurance:** Full family cover

1000

BRITA WATER FILTER SYSTEMS

UK locations	S.East
UK sites	1
Sector	Consumer Goods
Definition	Water Filtration
How owned	Private
Founded	1992
Turnover	Not disclosed
Profit	Not disclosed
Staff	84
Average age	33
Male : Female	39 : 61
Earnings £35,000+	29%

BEST COMPANIES INDEX

best company 2007

FIRST CLASS

★

2007 BCI = 671.1

2006 BCI = 700.1

<671

WORKPLACE INSIGHTS

BRITA's Social Responsibility Panel are a group of volunteers who develop ways to support the local community & become more environmentally friendly such as improvement of the cycle racks at BRITA; increased recycling initiatives & sponsorship of local activities.

At each Half Year Conference, BRITA awards members of staff 'Above and Beyond' awards for those who have been seen to live the Values of the Company. Employees vote for a member of their department whom they feel deserving of an award.

Managing Director David Banfield has a published commitment to meet all new people within one month of them joining BRITA. In this meeting he gets a chance to find out a bit about them and talks to them about the values and where the company is going.

500

MISSION / VISION

A challenging and passionate organisation that delivers exceptional performance by investing in our brands, our partners, and our team.

BEST WORKPLACE FACTORS

GIVING SOMETHING BACK
MY COMPANY
LEADERSHIP

GRADUATE VACANCIES

No graduate vacancies have been indicated.

EMPLOYEE COMMENTS

"Their commitment to the local community is refreshing and encouraging."

"The atmosphere in the office is always upbeat and everyone truly embraces the BRITA values."

"Our Managing Director cares for the business and the people within it."

CONTACT DETAILS

Brita Water Filter Systems, Brita House, 9 Granville Way, Bicester, Oxon OX26 4JT
Tel: 0870 4870900 www.brita.co.uk

KEY

Holidays: Companies offering a minimum of 25 days annual leave

Maternity: Companies offering over Statutory Matternity Pay

Childcare: On-site nursery or vouchers

Women: At least 33% of senior managers are women

Long Service: 40% of employees with more than 5 years' service

Pensions: Companies offering a final salary or non-contributory/ contributory pension scheme

Charity Activities: 10% of staff undertake charitable activities during business hours

Gym: On-site gym or subsidised gym memberships

Shares: Companies where employees are offered share options

Health Insurance: Full family cover

0

To find out more about this company visit www.bestcompaniesguide.co.uk

Bromford
Housing Group

BROMFORD HOUSING GROUP

UK locations	National
UK sites	52
Sector	Housing Associations
Definition	Registered Social Landlord
How owned	Government
Founded	1963
Turnover	Not disclosed
Profit	Not disclosed
Staff	754
Average age	43
Male : Female	31 : 69
Earnings £35,000+	9%

BEST COMPANIES INDEX

best company 2007

FIRST CLASS

★

2007 BCI = 696.4

WORKPLACE INSIGHTS

The Colleague Sounding Board is a team of employee volunteers, who maintain communication between employees and senior managers. Their role is to keep employees informed about the business and issues that affect them and to ensure that their views are heard.

Bromford Housing have extended access to over 80 workshops and seminars with skilled trainers to their customers which will lead to further education and employment opportunities that they may never have had before.

All managers at Bromford are part of a leadership programme that includes liberating leadership profiling which gives colleagues in their team and who work closely with them, an opportunity to give feedback on how they perform as a role model and leader.

MISSION / VISION

Creating homes & supporting communities where people really want to stay.

BEST WORKPLACE FACTORS

MY COMPANY
GIVING SOMETHING BACK
MY MANAGER

GRADUATE VACANCIES

No graduate vacancies have been indicated.

EMPLOYEE COMMENTS

"I feel part of a family that lives and breathes it's values."

"Inspirational people wanting to make a difference to the lives of those in great housing & support need."

"I love the friendliness of the management and their approachability."

CONTACT DETAILS

Bromford Housing Group, 9 Shaw Park Business Village, Shaw Road, Bushbury, Wolverhampton, West Midlands WV10 9LE
Tel: 01902 773618 www.bromford.co.uk

KEY

Holidays: Companies offering a minimum of 25 days annual leave
Maternity: Companies offering over Statutory Matternity Pay
Childcare: On-site nursery or vouchers
Women: At least 33% of senior managers are women
Long Service: 40% of employees with more than 5 years' service
Pensions: Companies offering a final salary or non-contributory/ contributory pension scheme
Charity Activities: 10% of staff undertake charitable activities during business hours
Gym: On-site gym or subsidised gym memberships
Shares: Companies where employees are offered share options
Health Insurance: Full family cover

To find out more about this company visit www.bestcompaniesguide.co.uk

1000
696>
500
0
ones to watch

BUSINESS DESIGN CENTRE

UK locations	London
UK sites	1
Sector	Hospitality
Definition	Exhibition Conference Venue
How owned	Private
Founded	1986
Turnover	Not disclosed
Profit	Not disclosed
Staff	70
Average age	33
Male : Female	54 : 46
Earnings £35,000+	37%

BEST COMPANIES INDEX

best company 2007

FIRST CLASS

★

2007 BCI = 694.6

WORKPLACE INSIGHTS

Business Design Centre treats employees individually and tailor work life balance as required depending on their circumstances. They have "wellbeing" weeks with free massages, trial gym membership and wellbeing food offered within the restaurant.

Line managers carry out Personal Development Reviews, reviewing employees' strengths and weaknesses, career strategy and appropriate training and development needs. It also includes a section on how the line manager can help them develop further.

Managing Director, Dominic Jones and the Board award 'The Starburst' to employees who have shown great initiative, achieved something special & consistently been amazing, which adds value to the business in a recognisable way. Award consists of a certificate and cheque for £250.

MISSION / VISION

A "can do" culture of teamwork and achievement, which nurtures creative, imaginative and inspiring people, who are visionary, proactive and look at things in fresh and original ways. We act today not tomorrow. We team intelligent people and a creative environment.

BEST WORKPLACE FACTORS

WELL BEING
MY MANAGER
LEADERSHIP

GRADUATE VACANCIES

No graduate vacancies have been indicated.

EMPLOYEE COMMENTS

"It is a family run business with strong moral values."

"Management who have come from junior positions understand our needs."

"Dominic Jones is a fantastic leader and a true role model for the company."

CONTACT DETAILS

Business Design Centre, 52 Upper Street, London N1 0QH
Tel: 0207 3593535 www.businessdesigncentre.co.uk

KEY

- **Holidays:** Companies offering a minimum of 25 days annual leave
- **Maternity:** Companies offering over Statutory Matternity Pay
- **Childcare:** On-site nursery or vouchers
- **Women:** At least 33% of senior managers are women
- **Long Service:** 40% of employees with more than 5 years' service
- **Pensions:** Companies offering a final salary or non-contributory/ contributory pension scheme
- **Charity Activities:** 10% of staff undertake charitable activities during business hours
- **Gym:** On-site gym or subsidised gym memberships
- **Shares:** Companies where employees are offered share options
- **Health Insurance:** Full family cover

To find out more about this company visit www.bestcompaniesguide.co.uk

BUYINGTEAM

buyingTeam

UK locations	London, Yorks & Humber
UK sites	2
Sector	Consulting
Definition	Procurement Services
How owned	Private
Founded	1994
Turnover	Not disclosed
Profit	Not disclosed
Staff	77
Average age	32
Male : Female	77 : 23
Earnings £35,000+	64%

BEST COMPANIES INDEX

best company 2007

FIRST CLASS

★

2007 BCI = 677.1

1000

★ ★ ★

★ ★

677> ★

ones to watch

500

0

WORKPLACE INSIGHTS

buyingTeam offer employees a variety of courses run both in-house and by experts, ranging from two-hour sessions to full days on topics such as negotiation skills, advanced Excel and Access, personal impact and effectiveness and coaching and development skills.

The Managing Director has given all staff three days extra holiday and effectively closed the business over the festive season, ensuring everybody has a good break. The management board felt that the staff needed a good rest in recognition of their hard work.

A member of the board or management team at buyingTeam is involved extensively in new joiner induction training. Managing Director Matthew Eatough also has one-on-one meetings with all new staff within the first 3 months of joining.

MISSION / VISION

We will be the market leader provider of purchasing services. We make our clients more profitable by applying our expertise acumen and technology.

BEST WORKPLACE FACTORS

PERSONAL GROWTH
WELL BEING
LEADERSHIP

GRADUATE VACANCIES

Solutions development team.

EMPLOYEE COMMENTS

"The company is structured to allow its team members the ability to create and innovate."

"There is a real sense of everyone working together to make something happen."

"Managing Director takes time to meet people & ask for their viewpoint on how the company is growing."

CONTACT DETAILS

buyingTeam, Eagle House, 16 Procter Street, London WC1V 6NX
Tel: 0207 6114999 www.buyingteam.com

KEY

Holidays: Companies offering a minimum of 25 days annual leave

Maternity: Companies offering over Statutory Matternity Pay

Childcare: On-site nursery or vouchers

Women: At least 33% of senior managers are women

Long Service: 40% of employees with more than 5 years' service

Pensions: Companies offering a final salary or non-contributory/ contributory pension scheme

Charity Activities: 10% of staff undertake charitable activities during business hours

Gym: On-site gym or subsidised gym memberships

Shares: Companies where employees are offered share options

Health Insurance: Full family cover

1000

at home with calico

CALICO HOUSING

UK locations	N.West
UK sites	1
Sector	Housing Associations
Definition	Social Housing Landlord
How owned	Partnership/LLP
Founded	2000
Turnover	£14.0m
Profit	Not disclosed
Staff	189
Average age	41
Male : Female	48 : 52
Earnings £35,000+	5%

BEST COMPANIES INDEX

best company 2007

FIRST CLASS

★

2007 BCI = 668.8

<669

ones to watch

WORKPLACE INSIGHTS

Calico provide Modern Apprenticeships, a PATH traineeship and work experience opportunities and as part of the Youth Inclusion Programme, editorial opportunities for young people to get their message to their customers via their in-house publication.

There are many well being benefits available to employees at Calico including corporate gym membership, Yoga classes on site and an Employee Assistance Programme (confidential counselling helpline).

In addition to providing time and funding for qualification training, Calico also encourage job shadowing and secondments which help employees try out new roles and gain new skills both within the company and with partnership agencies.

500

MISSION / VISION

To Be The Leading Choice Across East Lancashire.

BEST WORKPLACE FACTORS

GIVING SOMETHING BACK
WELL BEING
PERSONAL GROWTH

GRADUATE VACANCIES

No graduate vacancies have been indicated.

EMPLOYEE COMMENTS

"You gain plenty of job satisfaction and recognition working at Calico."

"The company really looks after the employees & provides a wonderful environment to work in."

"Calico has a successful reward & recognition scheme which values and encourages employees."

CONTACT DETAILS

Calico Housing, Centenary Court, Croft Street, Burnley, Lancashire BB11 2ED
Tel: 0800 1692407 www.calicohousing.co.uk

KEY

- **Holidays:** Companies offering a minimum of 25 days annual leave
- **Maternity:** Companies offering over Statutory Matternity Pay
- **Childcare:** On-site nursery or vouchers
- **Women:** At least 33% of senior managers are women
- **Long Service:** 40% of employees with more than 5 years' service
- **Pensions:** Companies offering a final salary or non-contributory/contributory pension scheme
- **Charity Activities:** 10% of staff undertake charitable activities during business hours
- **Gym:** On-site gym or subsidised gym memberships
- **Shares:** Companies where employees are offered share options
- **Health Insurance:** Full family cover

0

To find out more about this company visit www.bestcompaniesguide.co.uk

Transforming Communications™ Carat

CARAT

UK locations	London
UK sites	1
Sector	Media
Definition	Transforming Clients Communication
How owned	Private
Founded	1978
Turnover	Not disclosed
Profit	Not disclosed
Staff	308
Average age	28
Male : Female	53 : 47
Earnings £35,000+	31%

BEST COMPANIES INDEX

best company 2007

FIRST CLASS

★

2007 BCI = 665.6

2006 BCI = 663.2 (★)

WORKPLACE INSIGHTS

Carat is fortunate that their MD and the leadership team have all risen within Carat and have embedded a culture of openness, inclusiveness and success.

One of the themes of Carat's culture is fun which helps generate a sense of team spirit, edge and more importantly energy.

Carat has been rolling out a Performance Coaching Workshop to all people managers within the business, to ensure that they have the necessary soft skills such as receiving and giving feedback to really develop and nurture individuals in their teams.

MISSION / VISION

Vision: Champions of communication as a force for business transformation.
Mission: To continually find new and better ways to connect our clients with their customers.

BEST WORKPLACE FACTORS

LEADERSHIP
MY TEAM
MY MANAGER

GRADUATE VACANCIES

Planning, Buying, Digital Insight, Direct, Data Planning, Sponsorship.

EMPLOYEE COMMENTS

"Good visionary leadership."

"Everyone gets on with each other in my team. We have a really good laugh and get the work done."

"My Manager is excellent with supporting me and also training."

CONTACT DETAILS

Carat, Parker Tower, 43-49 Parker Street, London WC2B 5PS
Tel: 0207 4306000 www.carat.co.uk

KEY

Holidays: Companies offering a minimum of 25 days annual leave
Maternity: Companies offering over Statutory Maternity Pay
Childcare: On-site nursery or vouchers
Women: At least 33% of senior managers are women
Long Service: 40% of employees with more than 5 years' service
Pensions: Companies offering a final salary or non-contributory/contributory pension scheme
Charity Activities: 10% of staff undertake charitable activities during business hours
Gym: On-site gym or subsidised gym memberships
Shares: Companies where employees are offered share options
Health Insurance: Full family cover

CASS BUSINESS SCHOOL

Cass Business School City of London

UK locations	London
UK sites	2
Sector	Education
Definition	Business Education
How owned	Government
Founded	2002
Turnover	£36.4m
Profit	Not disclosed
Staff	298
Average age	39
Male : Female	49 : 51
Earnings £35,000+	49%

BEST COMPANIES INDEX

best company 2007

FIRST CLASS

★

2007 BCI = 663.3

2006 BCI = 676.7 (★)

WORKPLACE INSIGHTS

With regard to training, Cass Business School offers access to around 100 different off-the-job courses and development opportunities which are free of charge. Employees also have access to a mentoring scheme and robust corporate and departmental inductions.

Cass offers employees flexi time working schemes where possible and a comprehensive occupational health service offering free eye tests and ergonomic working checks, counselling services and an on-site GP.

School Meetings are held once or twice a term. These are led by the management team, but presentations are given by employees from across the organisation. Staff prizes and promotions are also recognised at this time.

MISSION / VISION

To be the business school of the City of London and its intellectual hub, serving the needs of professionals and companies through management education and by stimulating research and debate on key issues facing international business and finance.

BEST WORKPLACE FACTORS

PERSONAL GROWTH
WELL BEING
MY MANAGER

GRADUATE VACANCIES

No graduate vacancies have been indicated.

EMPLOYEE COMMENTS

"There are always opportunities to train and develop new skills."

"Great team spirit, people have fun, support each other & enjoy working with each other."

"My line manager always takes on board my thoughts."

CONTACT DETAILS

Cass Business School, 106 Bunhill Row, London EC1Y 8TZ
Tel: 0207 0408600 www.cass.city.ac.uk

KEY

- **Holidays:** Companies offering a minimum of 25 days annual leave
- **Maternity:** Companies offering over Statutory Maternity Pay
- **Childcare:** On-site nursery or vouchers
- **Women:** At least 33% of senior managers are women
- **Long Service:** 40% of employees with more than 5 years' service
- **Pensions:** Companies offering a final salary or non-contributory/ contributory pension scheme
- **Charity Activities:** 10% of staff undertake charitable activities during business hours
- **Gym:** On-site gym or subsidised gym memberships
- **Shares:** Companies where employees are offered share options
- **Health Insurance:** Full family cover

To find out more about this company visit www.bestcompaniesguide.co.uk

Cedar

CEDAR COMMUNICATIONS

UK locations	London
UK sites	1
Sector	Media
Definition	Customer Publishing Agency
How owned	Private
Founded	1992
Turnover	£20.7m
Profit	£1.7m
Staff	89
Average age	34.7
Male : Female	36 : 64
Earnings £35,000+	30%

BEST COMPANIES INDEX

best company 2007

FIRST CLASS

★

2007 BCI = 675.5

WORKPLACE INSIGHTS

100% Cedar Wellbeing offers alternative therapies and ways of promoting personal growth in the workplace through seminars, mini courses, treatments & classes on a variety of alternative therapies and self development techniques.

Each quarter, a department or team within Cedar organises a social evening. The aim of the evening is to 'educate' the rest of the business about their title or the work they do. The leadership team attend as guests along with the rest of the business.

As they do not have a large training budget, Cedar use key contacts to run lunchtime master classes and seminars and staff create and run their own training programmes. In this way, they ensure all staff have an opportunity to learn something new every month.

MISSION / VISION

We are Cedar. We publish magazines. We build websites. We work for clients.

BEST WORKPLACE FACTORS

WELL BEING
MY TEAM
FAIR DEAL

GRADUATE VACANCIES

No graduate vacancies have been indicated.

EMPLOYEE COMMENTS

"Cedar cares and nurtures their employees so that they can achieve their potential."

"It feels like a very friendly place."

"We are treated fairly and personally given praise when praise is due."

CONTACT DETAILS

Cedar Communications Ltd, Pegasus House, 37-43 Sackville Street, London W1S 3EH
Tel: 0207 5342400 www.cedarcom.co.uk

KEY

Holidays: Companies offering a minimum of 25 days annual leave
Maternity: Companies offering over Statutory Matternity Pay
Childcare: On-site nursery or vouchers
Women: At least 33% of senior managers are women
Long Service: 40% of employees with more than 5 years' service
Pensions: Companies offering a final salary or non-contributory/ contributory pension scheme
Charity Activities: 10% of staff undertake charitable activities during business hours
Gym: On-site gym or subsidised gym memberships
Shares: Companies where employees are offered share options
Health Insurance: Full family cover

To find out more about this company visit www.bestcompaniesguide.co.uk

1000 ★★★ ★★ ★ 676> ones to watch 500 0

1000

Inspirational print management
= Charterhouse

CHARTERHOUSE

UK locations	National
UK sites	10
Sector	Business Services
Definition	Inspirational Print Management
How owned	Private
Founded	1969
Turnover	£50.4m
Profit	Not disclosed
Staff	113
Average age	34
Male : Female	56 : 44
Earnings £35,000+	47%

<681

BEST COMPANIES INDEX

best company 2007

FIRST CLASS

★

2007 BCI = 681.3

ones to watch

WORKPLACE INSIGHTS

The range of benefits offered in Charterhouse's 'Staff care' package including free gym membership, annual health check, discounted medical and dental insurance and a free healthy lunch option, indicates the importance of people.

Charterhouse pay for departments to have a night out which could be a meal and comedy club or nightclub.

Charterhouse are a knowledge based company with a flat structure allowing direct access to Board members at all times. The Board encourage staff participation in all areas of the business.

500

MISSION / VISION

Innovative technology; proven processes; measurable service; award winning; print and technical expertise; print strategy; responsible business practice; independence.

BEST WORKPLACE FACTORS

MY COMPANY
MY TEAM
LEADERSHIP

GRADUATE VACANCIES

Account Management.

EMPLOYEE COMMENTS

"I get energy from the buzz in the workplace. There is a great work ethic."

"Good knowledgeable team of experienced colleagues."

"All the upper management are approachable and you can talk to any of them about anything."

CONTACT DETAILS

Charterhouse, Colonial House, 87 Great North Road, Hatfield, Hertfordshire AL9 5DA
Tel: 01707 262222 www.charterhouse.tv

KEY

- **Holidays:** Companies offering a minimum of 25 days annual leave
- **Maternity:** Companies offering over Statutory Matternity Pay
- **Childcare:** On-site nursery or vouchers
- **Women:** At least 33% of senior managers are women
- **Long Service:** 40% of employees with more than 5 years' service
- **Pensions:** Companies offering a final salary or non-contributory/ contributory pension scheme
- **Charity Activities:** 10% of staff undertake charitable activities during business hours
- **Gym:** On-site gym or subsidised gym memberships
- **Shares:** Companies where employees are offered share options
- **Health Insurance:** Full family cover

0

To find out more about this company visit www.bestcompaniesguide.co.uk

CHP CONSULTING

CHP Consulting

UK locations	London
UK sites	1
Sector	IT/Internet Services
Definition	IT Consultancy
How owned	Private
Founded	1990
Turnover	£16.9m
Profit	£5.0m
Staff	153
Average age	30
Male : Female	80 : 20
Earnings £35,000+	85%

BEST COMPANIES INDEX

best company 2007

FIRST CLASS

★

2007 BCI = 690.2

2006 BCI = 685.4 (★)

690>

WORKPLACE INSIGHTS

Employees work hard during the day, but enjoy rewards that are second to none such as go-karting & drinks after company meetings, project celebrations in Barcelona, black-tie dinners, fresh fruit, ice skating at Christmas or conferences in Dubai.

CHP give employees a good grounding in the technical aspects of the job at the same time as becoming industry experts and true consultants. Once consultants have attended the essential training courses, they develop a training plan suited to their own passions or strengths.

CHP host company meetings every two months which serve as a training & catch-up opportunity in the morning, followed by a chance for members to have some fun together which may involve speeding down the Thames in speedboats or drinks at a bar.

MISSION / VISION

We provide software solutions and consultancy services to the asset, consumer and vehicle finance industries. ALFA Systems, our flagship software solution, provides integrated lifecycle support for the sale, administration and accounting of a wide variety of finance products.

BEST WORKPLACE FACTORS

FAIR DEAL
PERSONAL GROWTH
MY TEAM

GRADUATE VACANCIES

IT Consultancy.

EMPLOYEE COMMENTS

"The pay & conditions are excellent; we are regularly treated to social events at the company's expense."

"There are excellent prospects for career development."

"There is a very strong and positive team spirit."

CONTACT DETAILS

CHP Consulting, Augustine House, 6a Austin Friars, London EC2N 2HA
Tel: 0207 5881800 www.chp.co.uk

KEY

- **Holidays:** Companies offering a minimum of 25 days annual leave
- **Maternity:** Companies offering over Statutory Matternity Pay
- **Childcare:** On-site nursery or vouchers
- **Women:** At least 33% of senior managers are women
- **Long Service:** 40% of employees with more than 5 years' service
- **Pensions:** Companies offering a final salary or non-contributory/ contributory pension scheme
- **Charity Activities:** 10% of staff undertake charitable activities during business hours
- **Gym:** On-site gym or subsidised gym memberships
- **Shares:** Companies where employees are offered share options
- **Health Insurance:** Full family cover

To find out more about this company visit www.bestcompaniesguide.co.uk

1000

<682

ones to watch

500

0

CHURCHILL RETIREMENT LIVING

Churchill retirement living
Independence • Safety • Security

UK locations	National
UK sites	6
Sector	Property
Definition	Retirement Developments
How owned	Private
Founded	1994
Turnover	£47.4m
Profit	£12.9m
Staff	192
Average age	46
Male : Female	59 : 41
Earnings £35,000+	32%

BEST COMPANIES INDEX

best company 2007

FIRST CLASS

★

2007 BCI = 681.5

2006 BCI = 693.5 (★)

WORKPLACE INSIGHTS

The employees' well being is a priority to Churchill Retirement Living and a welfare policy exists. If problems arise then Churchill provides support using external providers if necessary.

There are opportunities for everyone to progress at Churchill and workloads are well organised and managed well by the Managers.

Staff benefits at Churchill are continually reviewed to make it a very fair place to work. Also, the minimum number of day's holiday has been increased from 21 to 24.

MISSION / VISION

To create a dynamic working environment in which all colleagues feel valued and are able to benefit from the company's success.

BEST WORKPLACE FACTORS

WELL BEING
MY MANAGER
FAIR DEAL

GRADUATE VACANCIES

Design & planning.

EMPLOYEE COMMENTS

"There is a concern and regard for people's general welfare from colleagues."

"My Manager in particular is very supportive and always offers training where I need it."

"There is financial reward across the board when budgets and profits are met."

CONTACT DETAILS

Churchill Retirement Living, Millstream House, Parkside Ringwood, Hampshire BH24 3SG
Tel: 01425 462100 www.churchillretirement.co.uk

KEY

- **Holidays:** Companies offering a minimum of 25 days annual leave
- **Maternity:** Companies offering over Statutory Matternity Pay
- **Childcare:** On-site nursery or vouchers
- **Women:** At least 33% of senior managers are women
- **Long Service:** 40% of employees with more than 5 years' service
- **Pensions:** Companies offering a final salary or non-contributory/contributory pension scheme
- **Charity Activities:** 10% of staff undertake charitable activities during business hours
- **Gym:** On-site gym or subsidised gym memberships
- **Shares:** Companies where employees are offered share options
- **Health Insurance:** Full family cover

To find out more about this company visit www.bestcompaniesguide.co.uk

CliniMed®

CLINIMED

UK locations	S.East
UK sites	1
Sector	Pharmaceutical
Definition	Medical Device Supplier
How owned	Private
Founded	1982
Turnover	Not disclosed
Profit	Not disclosed
Staff	83
Average age	46
Male : Female	30 : 70
Earnings £35,000+	13%

BEST COMPANIES INDEX

best company 2007

FIRST CLASS

★

2007 BCI = 693.9

WORKPLACE INSIGHTS

The management team are respected role models and are visible at all levels of company life being closely involved in induction, setting and communicating objectives and providing recognition where appropriate.

CliniMed provide an educational grant of £130k per year to the Ostomy Lifestyle Centre. This advice centre is operated by volunteers and is recognised as a leading provider of help and support to patients in the UK.

Development objectives are regularly discussed and agreed with each employee. Once training needs are identified, they are incorporated into individual training & development plans. Training & development successes are celebrated amongst all staff where possible.

MISSION / VISION

'Developing skills and core competencies to deliver innovative healthcare solutions through strategic global alliances ventures and partnerships'.

BEST WORKPLACE FACTORS

WELL BEING
GIVING SOMETHING BACK
MY COMPANY

GRADUATE VACANCIES

Marketing.

EMPLOYEE COMMENTS

"They are a caring company and do all they can to help you."

"CliniMed is a very adaptable company, constantly striving to improve."

"The company has an ethos of listening & valuing input from the employees."

CONTACT DETAILS

CliniMed, Cavell House, Knaves Beech Way, Loudwater, Buckinghamshire HP10 9QY
Tel: 01628 850100 www.clinimed.co.uk

KEY

Holidays: Companies offering a minimum of 25 days annual leave
Maternity: Companies offering over Statutory Matternity Pay
Childcare: On-site nursery or vouchers
Women: At least 33% of senior managers are women
Long Service: 40% of employees with more than 5 years' service
Pensions: Companies offering a final salary or non-contributory/ contributory pension scheme
Charity Activities: 10% of staff undertake charitable activities during business hours
Gym: On-site gym or subsidised gym memberships
Shares: Companies where employees are offered share options
Health Insurance: Full family cover

1000
694>
500
0
ones to watch

COLEG LLANDRILLO CYMRU

ColegLlandrilloCymru

<687

UK locations	Wales
UK sites	5
Sector	Education
Definition	Further Education College
How owned	Not available
Founded	1962
Turnover	£28.0m
Profit	Not disclosed
Staff	615
Average age	47
Male : Female	38 : 62
Earnings £35,000+	6%

BEST COMPANIES INDEX

best company 2007

FIRST CLASS

★

2007 BCI = 686.6

WORKPLACE INSIGHTS

Environmental issues are delivered within the curriculum. The college feel that it is really important for learners to learn about environmental issues, sustainability and globalisation so that they can adapt their knowledge into their working environment.

There is a dedicated staff development team who provide all staff in the college with a point of contact on any areas of professional development.

Special events are organised, for example, to celebrate outstanding achievement after inspections.

MISSION / VISION

To provide learning opportunities which contribute to individual development and the social and economic advancement of the community.

BEST WORKPLACE FACTORS

GIVING SOMETHING BACK
PERSONAL GROWTH
MY TEAM

GRADUATE VACANCIES

No specific graduate vacancies have been indicated.

EMPLOYEE COMMENTS

"The college likes to give students a realistic chance to better their lives."

"There are always opportunities for staff to improve skills by attending staff development."

"I feel that my colleagues and managers are like part of a big extended family."

CONTACT DETAILS

Coleg Llandrillo Cymru, Llandudno Road, Rhos on Sea, Conwy LL28 4HZ
Tel: 01492 546666 www.llandrillo.ac.uk

KEY

- **Holidays:** Companies offering a minimum of 25 days annual leave
- **Maternity:** Companies offering over Statutory Matternity Pay
- **Childcare:** On-site nursery or vouchers
- **Women:** At least 33% of senior managers are women
- **Long Service:** 40% of employees with more than 5 years' service
- **Pensions:** Companies offering a final salary or non-contributory/contributory pension scheme
- **Charity Activities:** 10% of staff undertake charitable activities during business hours
- **Gym:** On-site gym or subsidised gym memberships
- **Shares:** Companies where employees are offered share options
- **Health Insurance:** Full family cover

To find out more about this company visit www.bestcompaniesguide.co.uk

conchango

CONCHANGO (UK)

UK locations	London, S.East
UK sites	2
Sector	IT/Internet Services
Definition	Business Technology Consultancy
How owned	Private
Founded	1991
Turnover	Not disclosed
Profit	Not disclosed
Staff	237
Average age	Not available
Male : Female	Not available
Earnings £35,000+	Not available

BEST COMPANIES INDEX

best company 2007

FIRST CLASS

★

2007 BCI = 682.3

WORKPLACE INSIGHTS

Conchango conduct annual surveys to give employees an opportunity to say how they feel and give ideas. The results are fed back via employee workshops to stimulate debate on how to improve practices within the company.

Social events for Conchango employees include a Family Day with a BBQ and entertainment for all the family and an Annual Fun Day where the office is closed for the day and do team building events such as 'it's a knock out' followed by food and drinks.

Every six weeks all Conchango employees get together for a 'Community Day' which involves forums and discussions about what is happening in the company and how it can be improved followed by a social gathering.

MISSION / VISION

Conchango is a business consultancy and systems integrator with cutting-edge digital design capabilities. Our distinctive combination of technical expertise and business acumen means we make IT innovation happen.

BEST WORKPLACE FACTORS

PERSONAL GROWTH
FAIR DEAL
MY COMPANY

GRADUATE VACANCIES

No graduate vacancies have been indicated.

EMPLOYEE COMMENTS

"People are given the opportunity to step up, take responsibility and make a difference."

"There is a genuine respect for the value of each individual."

"There is an excellent mix of people and everyone is bright, committed and able to perform."

CONTACT DETAILS

Conchango (UK), Heritage House, Church Road, Egham, Surrey TW20 9QD
Tel: 01784 222222 www.conchango.com

KEY

Holidays: Companies offering a minimum of 25 days annual leave
Maternity: Companies offering over Statutory Matternity Pay
Childcare: On-site nursery or vouchers
Women: At least 33% of senior managers are women
Long Service: 40% of employees with more than 5 years' service
Pensions: Companies offering a final salary or non-contributory/contributory pension scheme
Charity Activities: 10% of staff undertake charitable activities during business hours
Gym: On-site gym or subsidised gym memberships
Shares: Companies where employees are offered share options
Health Insurance: Full family cover

To find out more about this company visit www.bestcompaniesguide.co.uk

1000 682> 500 0 ones to watch

CUSHMAN & WAKEFIELD

UK locations	National
UK sites	6
Sector	Property
Definition	Global Real-Estate Consultancy
How owned	Partnership/LLP
Founded	1917
Turnover	£73.6m
Profit	Not disclosed
Staff	674
Average age	34
Male : Female	61 : 39
Earnings £35,000+	45%

BEST COMPANIES INDEX

best company 2007

FIRST CLASS

★

2007 BCI = 688.8

2006 BCI = 675.9 (★)

<689

WORKPLACE INSIGHTS

Cushman & Wakefield utilise an innovative online training tool to allow greater access to training and a blended approach to development. In this way, development also encompasses voluntary work, secondments, job shadowing and the sharing of best practice.

Generous provisions for maternity and paternity leave at Cushman & Wakefield. They also offer flexible working through good information technology and provide a confidential assistance programme that is open to all employees and those they live with.

Cushman & Wakefield try to keep strong ties with their local community through their Reading in Schools Programme and a school leavers initiative that promotes property as a career amongst ethnic minorities and economically disadvantaged school leavers.

MISSION / VISION

We are a global real estate services firm dedicated first and foremost to our clients. We employ the most talented professionals and invest in superior resources and technologies to provide our clients with innovative advice and bottom line results.

BEST WORKPLACE FACTORS

PERSONAL GROWTH
WELL BEING
MY COMPANY

GRADUATE VACANCIES

General Practice Surveying, Building Surveying, Planning, Research.

EMPLOYEE COMMENTS

"There is scope for everybody to improve themselves."

"I enjoy coming to work every day & feel lucky to have found a fantastic team to work with."

"An absolutely fabulous culture amongst everyone from top to bottom."

CONTACT DETAILS

Cushman & Wakefield, 43 - 45 Portman Square, London W1A 3BG
Tel: 0207 1525000 www.cushmanwakefield.com

KEY

- **Holidays:** Companies offering a minimum of 25 days annual leave
- **Maternity:** Companies offering over Statutory Maternity Pay
- **Childcare:** On-site nursery or vouchers
- **Women:** At least 33% of senior managers are women
- **Long Service:** 40% of employees with more than 5 years' service
- **Pensions:** Companies offering a final salary or non-contributory/ contributory pension scheme
- **Charity Activities:** 10% of staff undertake charitable activities during business hours
- **Gym:** On-site gym or subsidised gym memberships
- **Shares:** Companies where employees are offered share options
- **Health Insurance:** Full family cover

To find out more about this company visit www.bestcompaniesguide.co.uk

CYRIL SWEETT

cyril sweett
global knowhow

UK locations	National
UK sites	14
Sector	Construction
Definition	Construction & Property Consultancy
How owned	Trust/Employee owned/Mutual
Founded	1928
Turnover	£44.8m
Profit	£5.2m
Staff	584
Average age	38
Male : Female	73 : 27
Earnings £35,000+	56%

BEST COMPANIES INDEX

best company 2007

FIRST CLASS

★

2007 BCI = 667.4

WORKPLACE INSIGHTS

Staff at Cyril Sweett are invited to submit new ideas to the Business Improvement Group via the company intranet. Each idea or suggestion is considered by the Group at a monthly meeting and £100 is awarded for any original ideas which are implemented.

Cyril Sweett have introduced new training courses as a result of feedback from their staff survey, including; Effective Interviewing Skills, Developing the Strategic Manager, Business Writing Skills and Developing the Essential Skills of Management & Senior Management.

Cyril Sweett is wholly employee owned. They place a lot of importance in this scheme and the idea of ownership has recently been incorporated into their brand values "We are creators of our destinies because we all own our business and share in its successes."

MISSION / VISION

Vision: To be top five international construction consultancy that others want to benchmark themselves against.
Mission: To be the natural choice for construction consultancy services by being the best at everything we do.

BEST WORKPLACE FACTORS

WELL BEING
PERSONAL GROWTH
FAIR DEAL

GRADUATE VACANCIES

Cost Consultancy, Project Management, Building Surveying, Consulting, Finance and Legal services

EMPLOYEE COMMENTS

"It cares for the people throughout the organisation."

"An excellent company growing rapidly & providing real opportunities for the employees."

"Being employee owned gives the company a different working ethos & a more positive atmosphere."

CONTACT DETAILS

Cyril Sweett, 60 Grays Inn Road, London WC1X 8AQ
Tel: 0207 0619000 www.cyrilsweett.com

KEY

- **Holidays:** Companies offering a minimum of 25 days annual leave
- **Maternity:** Companies offering over Statutory Matternity Pay
- **Childcare:** On-site nursery or vouchers
- **Women:** At least 33% of senior managers are women
- **Long Service:** 40% of employees with more than 5 years' service
- **Pensions:** Companies offering a final salary or non-contributory/ contributory pension scheme
- **Charity Activities:** 10% of staff undertake charitable activities during business hours
- **Gym:** On-site gym or subsidised gym memberships
- **Shares:** Companies where employees are offered share options
- **Health Insurance:** Full family cover

1000
667>
ones to watch
500
0

To find out more about this company visit www.bestcompaniesguide.co.uk

DANONE

UK locations	London
UK sites	1
Sector	Manufacturing
Definition	Fresh Dairy Products
How owned	Public (i.e. stock market listed)
Founded	1993
Turnover	£0.1m
Profit	Not disclosed
Staff	86
Average age	30
Male : Female	47 : 53
Earnings £35,000+	55%

BEST COMPANIES INDEX

best company 2007

FIRST CLASS ★

2007 BCI = 662.2

2006 BCI = 696.8 (★)

WORKPLACE INSIGHTS

All company voluntary activities are run during the working day and employees are given time off to enable them to participate. For example reading and numbers partners with local schools, garden projects with a school, working on Young Enterprise scheme.

Management work in open plan offices and sit in the midst of their teams. Danone have a strong sense of not having a hierarchy in place and do not want managers to be seen to be different or ask to be treated differently.

Danone invest a huge amount of time in ensuring that they can say that they put the people first element of their business up front and on equal terms with the commercial requirements and business challenges of a corporate company.

MISSION / VISION

Vision: To be the number one brand in the fresh dairy market by 2012
Mission: To be the consumers first choice (partner) for life enhancing foods.

BEST WORKPLACE FACTORS

GIVING SOMETHING BACK
MY MANAGER
MY COMPANY

GRADUATE VACANCIES

Marketing, Commercial.

EMPLOYEE COMMENTS

"Their commitment to helping local charities is fantastic."

"The trust given to me by my manager to make my own decisions & manage my time."

"Danone have an open, honest culture and flexibility."

CONTACT DETAILS

Danone, 3rd Floor International House, 7 High Street, Ealing, West London W5 5DW
Tel: 0208 7995800 www.danone.com

KEY

- **Holidays:** Companies offering a minimum of 25 days annual leave
- **Maternity:** Companies offering over Statutory Matternity Pay
- **Childcare:** On-site nursery or vouchers
- **Women:** At least 33% of senior managers are women
- **Long Service:** 40% of employees with more than 5 years' service
- **Pensions:** Companies offering a final salary or non-contributory/ contributory pension scheme
- **Charity Activities:** 10% of staff undertake charitable activities during business hours
- **Gym:** On-site gym or subsidised gym memberships
- **Shares:** Companies where employees are offered share options
- **Health Insurance:** Full family cover

DENNIS PUBLISHING

UK locations	London
UK sites	1
Sector	Media
Definition	Consumer Magazine publisher
How owned	Private
Founded	1974
Turnover	£61.7m
Profit	£0.4m
Staff	361
Average age	31
Male : Female	64 : 36
Earnings £35,000+	27%

BEST COMPANIES INDEX

best company 2007

FIRST CLASS ★

2007 BCI = 682.7

683>

ones to watch

WORKPLACE INSIGHTS

Senior Managers' Q&A sessions every two months are open to all Dennis employees. During the sessions staff are updated about happenings in their department and any questions are answered. A different Senior Manager will take a session each time.

Dennis Publishing actively source their material from well-managed forests and under a chain of custody certification scheme. All of their products are chlorine free and they are actively sourcing materials from carbon offsetting schemes.

Dennis offers a huge range of courses such as editorial skills, languages, leadership skills, and sales. They have built strong relationships with expert training companies so the in-house they deliver is always tailored to the needs of the employees and the business.

MISSION / VISION

Dennis Publishing must become a leading publisher for the 21st century.

BEST WORKPLACE FACTORS

MY TEAM
MY COMPANY
PERSONAL GROWTH

GRADUATE VACANCIES

Advertising, Finance.

EMPLOYEE COMMENTS

"The team knows that they can rely on each other both in the workplace and on a personal level too."

"Hard work is recognised, fantastic rewards in place which are available for every level of staff."

"Friendly environment with excellent training and development opportunities."

CONTACT DETAILS

Dennis Publishing, 30 Cleveland Street, London W1T 4JD
Tel: 0207 9076000 www.dennis.co.uk

KEY

- **Holidays:** Companies offering a minimum of 25 days annual leave
- **Maternity:** Companies offering over Statutory Matternity Pay
- **Childcare:** On-site nursery or vouchers
- **Women:** At least 33% of senior managers are women
- **Long Service:** 40% of employees with more than 5 years' service
- **Pensions:** Companies offering a final salary or non-contributory/ contributory pension scheme
- **Charity Activities:** 10% of staff undertake charitable activities during business hours
- **Gym:** On-site gym or subsidised gym memberships
- **Shares:** Companies where employees are offered share options
- **Health Insurance:** Full family cover

To find out more about this company visit www.bestcompaniesguide.co.uk

1000

500

0

ones to watch

<660

DOUGLAS & GORDON

UK locations	London
UK sites	14
Sector	Property
Definition	Property Sales/Estate agency
How owned	Private
Founded	2002
Turnover	£15.5m
Profit	£3.5m
Staff	161
Average age	34
Male : Female	25 : 75
Earnings £35,000+	18%

BEST COMPANIES INDEX

best company 2007

FIRST CLASS

★

2007 BCI = 660.4

WORKPLACE INSIGHTS

The Chief Executive and Managing Director meet and review almost all staff members twice a year. They are available to all staff at all times and regularly visit the company's offices.

Douglas & Gordon operate flexible working, particularly for staff with children. Compassionate leave for funerals and weddings is given to allow help with family members and strong encouragement is given for staff to take holidays.

There is a strong emphasis on creating a fun and social environment at Douglas & Gordon as they want their employees to enjoy their jobs because they believe that happy employees will be successful and will remain with the company longer.

MISSION / VISION

Our goal is to reach and retain the position of market leader in every sector of of our business by combining uncompromising personal service with expert knowledge.

BEST WORKPLACE FACTORS

LEADERSHIP
WELL BEING
FAIR DEAL

GRADUATE VACANCIES

No restrictions.

EMPLOYEE COMMENTS

"The passion to achieve company goals."

"Problems, either work, health or domestic are treated sympathetically."

"You are always treated with the utmost respect and made to feel that your efforts are appreciated."

CONTACT DETAILS

Douglas & Gordon, 67/68 Warwick Square, London SW1V 2AR
Tel: 0207 9634600 www.douglasandgordon.com

KEY

- **Holidays:** Companies offering a minimum of 25 days annual leave
- **Maternity:** Companies offering over Statutory Matternity Pay
- **Childcare:** On-site nursery or vouchers
- **Women:** At least 33% of senior managers are women
- **Long Service:** 40% of employees with more than 5 years' service
- **Pensions:** Companies offering a final salary or non-contributory/ contributory pension scheme
- **Charity Activities:** 10% of staff undertake charitable activities during business hours
- **Gym:** On-site gym or subsidised gym memberships
- **Shares:** Companies where employees are offered share options
- **Health Insurance:** Full family cover

To find out more about this company visit www.bestcompaniesguide.co.uk

DYSLEXIA ACTION

Dyslexia Action
Assessment • Education • Training

UK locations	National
UK sites	27
Sector	Charity
Definition	Education Charity
How owned	Charity
Founded	1972
Turnover	£8.4m
Profit	£0.9m
Staff	347
Average age	48
Male : Female	4 : 96
Earnings £35,000+	5%

BEST COMPANIES INDEX

best company 2007

FIRST CLASS

★

2007 BCI = 683.8

2006 BCI = 685.1 (★)

1000

684>

500

0

ones to watch

WORKPLACE INSIGHTS

Specialist teachers, Senior Teachers and principals at Dyslexia Action are often involved in presenting to teachers on new projects which are piloted locally, helping to share best practice and cascading new services across the country.

Dyslexia Action has evolved a culture that supports its employees in achieving and sustaining a positive work life balance. It is continually looking at the issues surrounding this and does all that it can to make work enjoyable and flexible.

Dyslexia Action has regular open meetings for staff at their Centres and Head Office. These meetings are opportunities to share news and views and to keep staff abreast of developments within the organisation as well as trends and developments in the sector.

MISSION / VISION

Dyslexia Action believes that all individuals with dyslexia should have the opportunity to reach their full potential in order to make the maximum contribution to society.

BEST WORKPLACE FACTORS

GIVING SOMETHING BACK
MY TEAM
MY MANAGER

GRADUATE VACANCIES

Teaching Psychology.

EMPLOYEE COMMENTS

"I feel genuinely valued in this organisation and really know I can make a difference."

"A great team who work well together and care about each other."

"We have excellent team leadership and a positive working environment."

CONTACT DETAILS

Dyslexia Action, Park House, Wick Road, Egham, Surrey TW20 0HH
Tel: 01784 222300 www.dyslexiaaction.org.uk

KEY

- **Holidays:** Companies offering a minimum of 25 days annual leave
- **Maternity:** Companies offering over Statutory Maternity Pay
- **Childcare:** On-site nursery or vouchers
- **Women:** At least 33% of senior managers are women
- **Long Service:** 40% of employees with more than 5 years' service
- **Pensions:** Companies offering a final salary or non-contributory/contributory pension scheme
- **Charity Activities:** 10% of staff undertake charitable activities during business hours
- **Gym:** On-site gym or subsidised gym memberships
- **Shares:** Companies where employees are offered share options
- **Health Insurance:** Full family cover

EDP DRUG & ALCOHOL SERVICES

UK locations	S.West
UK sites	12
Sector	Charity
Definition	Addressing substance misuse
How owned	Trust/Employee owned/Mutual
Founded	1986
Turnover	£2.3m
Profit	Not disclosed
Staff	85
Average age	38
Male : Female	33 : 67
Earnings £35,000+	5%

BEST COMPANIES INDEX

best company 2007

FIRST CLASS

★

2007 BCI = 684.7

WORKPLACE INSIGHTS

EDP hold one off fundraising events in the workplace for other charities e.g. Macmillan Coffee Mornings.

EDP is acutely aware of their impact as leaders and select and coach their management team on the basis of being great professional role models for their staff.

EDP particularly acknowledge that the work they do can be stressful and actively work with staff they identify as needing support in this area to make adjustments to their roles.

MISSION / VISION

To prevent, reduce and address, the harms caused by substance misuse through work with individuals, families and local communities.

BEST WORKPLACE FACTORS

GIVING SOMETHING BACK
MY MANAGER
FAIR DEAL

GRADUATE VACANCIES

No graduate vacancies have been indicated.

EMPLOYEE COMMENTS

"Every day we are helping those that need our help and assistance."

"Trusted to get on with my job, my manager has confidence in my abilities that I can complete my work without much supervision."

"Making a real difference to other people's lives, being fairly treated as workers."

CONTACT DETAILS

EDP Drug & Alcohol Services, Dean Clarke House, Southernhay, East Exeter, Devon EX1 1PQ
Tel: 01392 666710 www.edpservices.org.uk

KEY

- **Holidays:** Companies offering a minimum of 25 days annual leave
- **Maternity:** Companies offering over Statutory Matternity Pay
- **Childcare:** On-site nursery or vouchers
- **Women:** At least 33% of senior managers are women
- **Long Service:** 40% of employees with more than 5 years' service
- **Pensions:** Companies offering a final salary or non-contributory/ contributory pension scheme
- **Charity Activities:** 10% of staff undertake charitable activities during business hours
- **Gym:** On-site gym or subsidised gym memberships
- **Shares:** Companies where employees are offered share options
- **Health Insurance:** Full family cover

To find out more about this company visit www.bestcompaniesguide.co.uk

EQUIP

UK locations	Scotland
UK sites	5
Sector	Not for Profit
Definition	Local Economic Development
How owned	Private
Founded	2001
Turnover	£2.4m
Profit	Not disclosed
Staff	66
Average age	38
Male : Female	36 : 64
Earnings £35,000+	8%

BEST COMPANIES INDEX

FIRST CLASS

★

2007 BCI = 685.1

WORKPLACE INSIGHTS

EQUIP are delivering free frontline staff awareness training that equips staff from various community and social organisations with the skills to be able to help customers with barriers such as addictions, mental health, disability etc.

EQUIP prides itself on its commitment to the development of its staff. Staff are actively encouraged to take up training opportunities to not only improve their skills at work but also to help them develop as individuals.

EQUIP puts people first. This isn't just aimed at their customers; it's also aimed at their staff. For EQUIP to effectively engage with their customers they invest heavily in the development of their workforce.

MISSION / VISION

Putting People First.

BEST WORKPLACE FACTORS

GIVING SOMETHING BACK
PERSONAL GROWTH
MY COMPANY

GRADUATE VACANCIES

Finance.

EMPLOYEE COMMENTS

"This company does some fantastic work with the people in the local community."

"Opportunities for employee self-development are always encouraged to be taken."

"The company is very customer focused and has real mission to improve the area that we work in."

CONTACT DETAILS

EQUIP, 1066 Barrhead Rd, Glasgow G53 5AB
Tel: 0141 2701880 www.equipyourself.co.uk

KEY

Holidays: Companies offering a minimum of 25 days annual leave
Maternity: Companies offering over Statutory Matternity Pay
Childcare: On-site nursery or vouchers
Women: At least 33% of senior managers are women
Long Service: 40% of employees with more than 5 years' service
Pensions: Companies offering a final salary or non-contributory/ contributory pension scheme
Charity Activities: 10% of staff undertake charitable activities during business hours
Gym: On-site gym or subsidised gym memberships
Shares: Companies where employees are offered share options
Health Insurance: Full family cover

To find out more about this company visit www.bestcompaniesguide.co.uk

E-SKILLS UK

UK locations	London
UK sites	1
Sector	Public
Definition	Sector Skills Council
How owned	Private
Founded	2003
Turnover	£8.0m
Profit	£0.2m
Staff	60
Average age	37
Male : Female	43 : 57
Earnings £35,000+	52%

BEST COMPANIES INDEX

FIRST CLASS

★

2007 BCI = 681.3

WORKPLACE INSIGHTS

e-skills award-winning Computer Clubs for Girls programme is free for schools to use and aims to change the way girls think about technology and IT careers. This initiative is already benefiting more than 60,000 girls in over 1,500 schools.

Every month a team from a cross section of the organisation organises a meeting for all employees called a Speakeasy. The CEO and managers are present to answer questions and listen to ideas and drinks and snacks are provided to encourage informal socialising.

e-skills have a flexible benefits package comprising a contributory pension, allowing for additional contributions or a 'pensions holiday', private medical insurance, interest-free season ticket loans and a range of options that can be tailored for individual needs.

MISSION / VISION

To ensure the UK has the technology-related skills it needs to compete in the global economy.

BEST WORKPLACE FACTORS

GIVING SOMETHING BACK
MY MANAGER
FAIR DEAL

GRADUATE VACANCIES

Project Management.

EMPLOYEE COMMENTS

"We care about getting it right, keeping it honest and making a difference."

"People are really prepared to go that extra mile to help a colleague."

"Achievement is rewarded regularly and publicly."

CONTACT DETAILS

e-skills UK, 1 Castle Lane, London SW1E 6DR
Tel: 0207 9638920 www.e-skills.com

KEY

- **Holidays:** Companies offering a minimum of 25 days annual leave
- **Maternity:** Companies offering over Statutory Maternity Pay
- **Childcare:** On-site nursery or vouchers
- **Women:** At least 33% of senior managers are women
- **Long Service:** 40% of employees with more than 5 years' service
- **Pensions:** Companies offering a final salary or non-contributory/contributory pension scheme
- **Charity Activities:** 10% of staff undertake charitable activities during business hours
- **Gym:** On-site gym or subsidised gym memberships
- **Shares:** Companies where employees are offered share options
- **Health Insurance:** Full family cover

To find out more about this company visit www.bestcompaniesguide.co.uk

FEATHER BROOKSBANK

UK locations	National
UK sites	4
Sector	Advertising
Definition	Advertising/Marketing communications
How owned	Private
Founded	1991
Turnover	Not disclosed
Profit	Not disclosed
Staff	87
Average age	33
Male : Female	36 : 64
Earnings £35,000+	25%

BEST COMPANIES INDEX

best company 2007

FIRST CLASS ★

2007 BCI = 690.9

2006 BCI = 745.0 (★★★)

WORKPLACE INSIGHTS

All new employees receive a "welcome gift", usually a bottle of champagne and are allocated a "buddy" who looks after them for the first few weeks, helps them integrate with the team and takes them out for lunch.

Feather Brooksbank fund and facilitate private study for people who want to consolidate experience with formal qualifications such as the IPA Foundation Certificate and the Certificate in Marketing Diploma.

Feather Brooksbank award spot bonuses to people who have done something special for the company beyond the requirements of their job. Sums range from £100 to £250 and fourteen spot bonuses have been awarded this year.

MISSION / VISION

Expect the best media buying & the best media thinking
Expect an opinion an open mind & a fresh approach
Expect specialists working as a team to create cohesive solutions that work
Expect us to look ahead to understand the future of media & its implications
Expanding ways of communicating with consumers & media

BEST WORKPLACE FACTORS

MY TEAM
MY MANAGER
MY COMPANY

GRADUATE VACANCIES

Communications planning & media buying. Digital media planning & buying.

EMPLOYEE COMMENTS

"There is a great working atmosphere with the different offices and teams integrating well together."

"Fantastic and friendly people who all strive to be the best they can be in their job."

"People are valued for who they are; give your best and you are valued for it."

CONTACT DETAILS

Feather Brooksbank, Raeburn House, 32 York Place, Edinburgh EH1 3HU
Tel: 0131 5552554 www.featherbrooksbank.co.uk

KEY

- **Holidays:** Companies offering a minimum of 25 days annual leave
- **Maternity:** Companies offering over Statutory Matternity Pay
- **Childcare:** On-site nursery or vouchers
- **Women:** At least 33% of senior managers are women
- **Long Service:** 40% of employees with more than 5 years' service
- **Pensions:** Companies offering a final salary or non-contributory/contributory pension scheme
- **Charity Activities:** 10% of staff undertake charitable activities during business hours
- **Gym:** On-site gym or subsidised gym memberships
- **Shares:** Companies where employees are offered share options
- **Health Insurance:** Full family cover

1000
691>
ones to watch
500
0

To find out more about this company visit www.bestcompaniesguide.co.uk

1000

FIRST DIRECT

first direct
Member HSBC Group

UK locations	Yorks & Humber, Scotland
UK sites	2
Sector	Financial - Banks/Building Societies
Definition	Customer Service Business
How owned	Public (i.e. stock market listed)
Founded	1989
Turnover	Not disclosed
Profit	Not disclosed
Staff	3574
Average age	35
Male : Female	29 : 71
Earnings £35,000+	4%

<671

BEST COMPANIES INDEX

b ★ best company 2007

FIRST CLASS

★

2007 BCI = 670.9

2006 BCI = 664.0 (★)

ones to watch

WORKPLACE INSIGHTS

The Equilibrium Group raises awareness of health issues and the importance of a healthy lifestyle. They arrange events on topics such as healthy eating and exercise and provide free on-site health checks twice a year and on-site smoking cessation clinics.

Full time sports and social co-ordinator at First Direct organises a wide range of social activities for employees including a week skiing in Italy, ladies day at Ascot and many sell out concerts. More than 80 events have been organised this year alone.

first direct offer on-site services to employees including a hairdresser, an ironing service, car servicing & MOT testing, chiropodist & masseuse, complimentary on-site concierge to carry out all those jobs that people just don't find time to do.

500

MISSION / VISION

The 3 elements that we are focusing on to achieve our mission to pioneer the future of money are: inspiring people, exceptional solutions, rewarding relationships.

BEST WORKPLACE FACTORS

WELL BEING
MY TEAM
FAIR DEAL

GRADUATE VACANCIES

No graduate vacancies have been indicated.

EMPLOYEE COMMENTS

"Concierge and on site facilities really help to maintain healthy work/home life balance."

"There is a sense of team work across all areas that we are all aiming for the same goal."

"The 'flexible plus' package allows me to adjust my benefit package as my life and needs change."

CONTACT DETAILS

first direct, 40 Wakefield Road, Leeds LS98 1FD
Tel: 0113 2766100 www.firstdirect.com

KEY

- **Holidays:** Companies offering a minimum of 25 days annual leave
- **Maternity:** Companies offering over Statutory Matternity Pay
- **Childcare:** On-site nursery or vouchers
- **Women:** At least 33% of senior managers are women
- **Long Service:** 40% of employees with more than 5 years' service
- **Pensions:** Companies offering a final salary or non-contributory/ contributory pension scheme
- **Charity Activities:** 10% of staff undertake charitable activities during business hours
- **Gym:** On-site gym or subsidised gym memberships
- **Shares:** Companies where employees are offered share options
- **Health Insurance:** Full family cover

0

FOUNDATION HOUSING

UK locations	Yorks & Humber
UK sites	16
Sector	Charity
Definition	Supported Housing Charity
How owned	Trust/Employee owned/Mutual
Founded	1984
Turnover	£9.5m
Profit	Not disclosed
Staff	223
Average age	41
Male : Female	40 : 60
Earnings £35,000+	2%

BEST COMPANIES INDEX

best company 2007

FIRST CLASS

★

2007 BCI = 690.7

2006 BCI = 695.8 (★)

691>

WORKPLACE INSIGHTS

Short Notice Annual Leave has recently been introduced whereby colleagues can book up to 5 of their annual leave days at short notice (usually the same day), similar to "Duvet days".

Foundation works hard to celebrate customers' achievements. A group of their residents in Scarborough have formed the "Beached Academy" expressing themselves through music and rap. They put on a performance at the charity's Annual Meeting.

Foundation Housing has flexible working practices enabling employees to start and finish at times best for them.

MISSION / VISION

Supporting people towards independence and inclusion.

BEST WORKPLACE FACTORS

FAIR DEAL
GIVING SOMETHING BACK
WELL BEING

GRADUATE VACANCIES

No graduate vacancies have been indicated.

EMPLOYEE COMMENTS

"We are kept well informed of what is happening within the organisation."

"The feeling that we are doing something worthwhile seeing the results in the empowerment of others."

"Responsive to particular circumstances enabling a much better work/life balance when circumstances have changed."

CONTACT DETAILS

Foundation Housing, Tennant Hall, Blenheim Grove, Leeds LS2 9ET
Tel: 0113 3688800 www.foundationhousing.org.uk

KEY

- **Holidays:** Companies offering a minimum of 25 days annual leave
- **Maternity:** Companies offering over Statutory Matternity Pay
- **Childcare:** On-site nursery or vouchers
- **Women:** At least 33% of senior managers are women
- **Long Service:** 40% of employees with more than 5 years' service
- **Pensions:** Companies offering a final salary or non-contributory/ contributory pension scheme
- **Charity Activities:** 10% of staff undertake charitable activities during business hours
- **Gym:** On-site gym or subsidised gym memberships
- **Shares:** Companies where employees are offered share options
- **Health Insurance:** Full family cover

To find out more about this company visit www.bestcompaniesguide.co.uk

FOX WILLIAMS

foxwilliams

UK locations	London
UK sites	1
Sector	Law
Definition	Business Law Firm
How owned	Partnership/LLP
Founded	1989
Turnover	Not disclosed
Profit	Not disclosed
Staff	93
Average age	37
Male : Female	38 : 62
Earnings £35,000+	59%

BEST COMPANIES INDEX

best company 2007

FIRST CLASS ★

2007 BCI = 674.7

2006 BCI = 678.6 (★)

WORKPLACE INSIGHTS

The Social and Charity Committee at Fox Williams organises social and fund raising events for employees every quarter. The entire firm is encouraged to attend and as much money as possible is raised for the chosen charity.

Seminars are given for all Fox Williams employees on work life balance issues such as nutrition, exercise, relaxation and wellbeing. They also allow flexible working so employees can work from home or work flexible hours.

Fox Williams provide an individually tailored career training induction programme for all new starters. In addition, there is a wide range of training run in-house including IT Workshops and Monday evening seminars. Sponsored training is also available.

MISSION / VISION

Fox Williams is an independent business law firm, based in the City of London. We aim to provide legal services to the high professional standards for which solicitors in the City of London are known.

BEST WORKPLACE FACTORS

FAIR DEAL
WELL BEING
PERSONAL GROWTH

GRADUATE VACANCIES

Legal training contracts.

EMPLOYEE COMMENTS

"Social events are run well & are very enjoyable which brings people closer together."

"Everyone respects and puts themselves out to support everyone else."

"It's a place where everyone can make a difference and good ideas count."

CONTACT DETAILS

Fox Williams, Ten Dominion Street, London EC2M 2EE
Tel: 0207 6282000 www.foxwilliams.com

KEY

- **Holidays:** Companies offering a minimum of 25 days annual leave
- **Maternity:** Companies offering over Statutory Matternity Pay
- **Childcare:** On-site nursery or vouchers
- **Women:** At least 33% of senior managers are women
- **Long Service:** 40% of employees with more than 5 years' service
- **Pensions:** Companies offering a final salary or non-contributory/ contributory pension scheme
- **Charity Activities:** 10% of staff undertake charitable activities during business hours
- **Gym:** On-site gym or subsidised gym memberships
- **Shares:** Companies where employees are offered share options
- **Health Insurance:** Full family cover

To find out more about this company visit www.bestcompaniesguide.co.uk

FSNBF

FSNBF — Fire Services National Benevolent Fund

UK locations	National
UK sites	4
Sector	Charity
Definition	Injured Firefighter Charity
How owned	Trust/Employee owned/Mutual
Founded	1942
Turnover	£9.1m
Profit	£0.3m
Staff	174
Average age	39
Male : Female	33 : 67
Earnings £35,000+	6%

BEST COMPANIES INDEX

best company 2007

FIRST CLASS ★

2007 BCI = 691.0

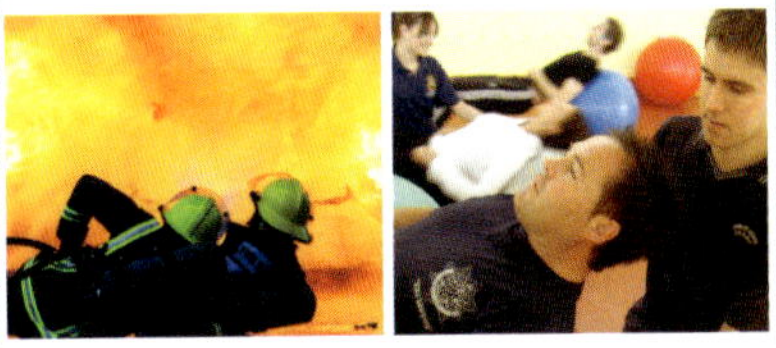

WORKPLACE INSIGHTS

The Fire Services National Benevolent Fund actively works with the Fire Safety Unit to produce messages to highlight awareness of community safety.

The Fire Services National Benevolent Fund makes use of the highly qualified physical and psychological therapists to deliver talks and therapy to all employees when required. This has manifested itself in many ways including talks on how to "cope with stress."

There is a relaxed, yet professional working ambience and this ensures staff are able to be sociable and enjoy their roles more fully.

MISSION / VISION

We want to develop our services for people of the fire service community in order to help them enhance the quality of their lives and by doing so the Fund will develop into one of the top 100 charities in the next three years.

BEST WORKPLACE FACTORS

GIVING SOMETHING BACK
WELL BEING
FAIR DEAL

GRADUATE VACANCIES

No graduate vacancies have been indicated.

EMPLOYEE COMMENTS

"It's nice/satisfying to know we can give something back to those who are willing to risk everything every day."

"There is an ethos of care and support from all levels."

"We as employees are treated fairly and equally with emphasis on empowerment and can do attitude."

CONTACT DETAILS

FSNBF, 2nd Floor Copenhagen Court, 32 New Street, Basingstoke, Hampshire RG21 7DT
Tel: 01256 366566 www.fsnbf.org.uk

KEY

- **Holidays:** Companies offering a minimum of 25 days annual leave
- **Maternity:** Companies offering over Statutory Matternity Pay
- **Childcare:** On-site nursery or vouchers
- **Women:** At least 33% of senior managers are women
- **Long Service:** 40% of employees with more than 5 years' service
- **Pensions:** Companies offering a final salary or non-contributory/ contributory pension scheme
- **Charity Activities:** 10% of staff undertake charitable activities during business hours
- **Gym:** On-site gym or subsidised gym memberships
- **Shares:** Companies where employees are offered share options
- **Health Insurance:** Full family cover

To find out more about this company visit www.bestcompaniesguide.co.uk

1000 · 691> · 500 · 0 · ones to watch

GENERAL MILLS UK

GENERAL MILLS

UK locations	London
UK sites	1
Sector	Manufacturing
Definition	Food Manufacturer
How owned	UK Limited
Founded	1860
Turnover	Not disclosed
Profit	Not disclosed
Staff	149
Average age	28
Male : Female	51 : 49
Earnings £35,000+	53%

BEST COMPANIES INDEX

best company 2007

FIRST CLASS

★

2007 BCI = 682.5

2006 BCI = 675.5 (★)

WORKPLACE INSIGHTS

General Mills are actively involved in a long term commitment within the local community alongside the Borough Youth Services with "the POINT", a mobile Youth centre. More than 17,500 young people have benefited from this scheme.

Each member of the General Mills Executive Team holds a surgery in the cafe allowing individuals who are less confident in asking questions in public to have a one to one with them and ask any questions they would like.

Employees are encouraged to get involved in General Mills community projects, enabling them to develop their coaching and communication skills, benefiting both the individual and the organisation through teambuilding and interpersonal skills.

MISSION / VISION

To grow - by bringing food to life.

BEST WORKPLACE FACTORS

GIVING SOMETHING BACK
LEADERSHIP
PERSONAL GROWTH

GRADUATE VACANCIES

Sales & Marketing.

EMPLOYEE COMMENTS

"It has a compelling vision, mission and values which drives its behaviours and actions."

"Strong leadership which is open and encourages ideas from all levels."

"Personal development is an important function and support is provided."

CONTACT DETAILS

General Mills UK, Harman House, 1 George Street, Uxbridge, Middlesex UB8 1QQ
Tel: 01895 201100 www.GeneralMills.com

KEY

Holidays: Companies offering a minimum of 25 days annual leave
Maternity: Companies offering over Statutory Matternity Pay
Childcare: On-site nursery or vouchers
Women: At least 33% of senior managers are women
Long Service: 40% of employees with more than 5 years' service
Pensions: Companies offering a final salary or non-contributory/ contributory pension scheme
Charity Activities: 10% of staff undertake charitable activities during business hours
Gym: On-site gym or subsidised gym memberships
Shares: Companies where employees are offered share options
Health Insurance: Full family cover

To find out more about this company visit www.bestcompaniesguide.co.uk

GRASS ROOTS

GRASS ROOTS
inspiring people

UK locations	S.East, E.England
UK sites	3
Sector	Business Services
Definition	Performance Improvement Business
How owned	Private
Founded	1980
Turnover	Not disclosed
Profit	Not disclosed
Staff	266
Average age	32
Male : Female	47 : 53
Earnings £35,000+	30%

BEST COMPANIES INDEX

best company 2007

FIRST CLASS

★

2007 BCI = 684.8

2006 BCI = 670.9 (★)

WORKPLACE INSIGHTS

Grass Roots commit both money and marketing expertise to a project to increase the number of nurses for Iain Rennie Hospice at Home through a nurse sponsorship scheme for local businesses.

One of the reasons why people enjoy working for Grass Roots is that David Evans, the Chairman is as visibly energetic and ambitious as he was when he started the business 25 years ago.

Head of HR regularly reviews working hours and tackles issues. There is an Occupational Health Adviser freely accessible. Individual initiatives are in place to fit a need such as temporary adjustment to hours, working from home, compassionate leave.

MISSION / VISION

To take Grass Roots' services to the widest geographical audiences possible.

BEST WORKPLACE FACTORS

GIVING SOMETHING BACK
LEADERSHIP
WELL BEING

GRADUATE VACANCIES

A intern scheme across all areas.

EMPLOYEE COMMENTS

"In a small way the work we do makes the world a better place."

"Most people have huge admiration for the CEO and MD."

"I find this company ready to listen to employees and do their best to help make staff happy."

CONTACT DETAILS

Grass Roots, Pennyroyal Court, Station Road, Tring, Herts HP23 5QY
Tel: 01442 829400 www.grg.com

KEY

- **Holidays:** Companies offering a minimum of 25 days annual leave
- **Maternity:** Companies offering over Statutory Matternity Pay
- **Childcare:** On-site nursery or vouchers
- **Women:** At least 33% of senior managers are women
- **Long Service:** 40% of employees with more than 5 years' service
- **Pensions:** Companies offering a final salary or non-contributory/ contributory pension scheme
- **Charity Activities:** 10% of staff undertake charitable activities during business hours
- **Gym:** On-site gym or subsidised gym memberships
- **Shares:** Companies where employees are offered share options
- **Health Insurance:** Full family cover

To find out more about this company visit www.bestcompaniesguide.co.uk

1000

<669

ones to watch

500

0

GREAT PLACES HOUSING GROUP

great places HOUSING GROUP

UK locations	N.West
UK sites	30
Sector	Housing Associations
Definition	Registered Social Landlord
How owned	Trust/Employee owned/Mutual
Founded	1971
Turnover	£33.8m
Profit	Not disclosed
Staff	421
Average age	40
Male : Female	30 : 70
Earnings £35,000+	5%

BEST COMPANIES INDEX

best company 2007

FIRST CLASS

★

2007 BCI = 669.0

2006 BCI = 699.0 (★)

WORKPLACE INSIGHTS

Great Places has a dedicated group – Green Places – and a Green Champion to drive forward their Environmental Strategy. They have developed a number of special eco-friendly homes using solar panels, wind turbines and other energy saving ideas.

Great Places has embraced the principles of the Fish! Philosophy – Play, Be There, Make Their Day, Choose Your Attitude. They have begun a programme of targeted events to empower teams to adapt the philosophy to suit their own individual cultures and work.

Senior managers at Great Places engage in a number of back to the floor days as well as informal visits to offices and schemes and getting involved in special projects that staff are undertaking such as the winter warmth campaign, visiting tenants in their homes.

MISSION / VISION

Exceptional Services. Great Places. Inspiring People.

BEST WORKPLACE FACTORS

GIVING SOMETHING BACK
FAIR DEAL
LEADERSHIP

GRADUATE VACANCIES

Housing Management, Development, IT.

EMPLOYEE COMMENTS

"Great places is a company that walks the talk and practices its values."

"Great benefits in addition to salary."

"Senior managers are passionate about what they do and it rubs off on the staff team."

CONTACT DETAILS

Great Places Housing Group, Southern Gate, 729 Princess Road, Manchester M20 2LT
Tel: 0161 4475000 www.greatplaces.org.uk

KEY

- **Holidays:** Companies offering a minimum of 25 days annual leave
- **Maternity:** Companies offering over Statutory Matternity Pay
- **Childcare:** On-site nursery or vouchers
- **Women:** At least 33% of senior managers are women
- **Long Service:** 40% of employees with more than 5 years' service
- **Pensions:** Companies offering a final salary or non-contributory/contributory pension scheme
- **Charity Activities:** 10% of staff undertake charitable activities during business hours
- **Gym:** On-site gym or subsidised gym memberships
- **Shares:** Companies where employees are offered share options
- **Health Insurance:** Full family cover

HALLMARK HEALTHCARE

UK locations	National
UK sites	22
Sector	Health
Definition	Nursing/Residential Homes
How owned	Private
Founded	1997
Turnover	£18.9m
Profit	Not disclosed
Staff	1116
Average age	34
Male : Female	15 : 85
Earnings £35,000+	1%

BEST COMPANIES INDEX

best company 2007

FIRST CLASS ★

2007 BCI = 668.3

2006 BCI = 712.0 (★★)

668>

WORKPLACE INSIGHTS

A pilot wellbeing programme has been launched for their employees with a leading nutritionist who has coached sports personalities. This pilot was set up in the form of weekly seminars giving people hints & tips on food, drink, fitness and wellbeing generally.

Hallmark has invested in its own motivational master class annually, including a barefoot walk over hot coals which the managers and team do together as an exercise in self belief.

Hallmark has developed an ideas board where people are encouraged to make suggestions on how the business is run. Creative suggestions from employees have resulted in the environmental drive 'Hallmark Goes Green' and an Annual Hug Day.

MISSION / VISION

Our purpose is to create communities that enhance the quality of life and give rise to new beginnings new futures.

BEST WORKPLACE FACTORS

WELL BEING
MY MANAGER
PERSONAL GROWTH

GRADUATE VACANCIES

Nursing, Marketing & Finance.

EMPLOYEE COMMENTS

"We are a family that cares for each other as well as the residents."

"The directors are committed, motivated and dedicated to all staff."

"Hallmark invests in their employees."

CONTACT DETAILS

Hallmark Healthcare, 2 Kingfisher Close, Radford Way, Billericay, Essex CM12 0EQ
Tel: 01277 655655 www.hallmarkhealthcare.co.uk

KEY

- **Holidays:** Companies offering a minimum of 25 days annual leave
- **Pensions:** Companies offering a final salary or non-contributory/ contributory pension scheme
- **Maternity:** Companies offering over Statutory Matternity Pay
- **Charity Activities:** 10% of staff undertake charitable activities during business hours
- **Childcare:** On-site nursery or vouchers
- **Gym:** On-site gym or subsidised gym memberships
- **Women:** At least 33% of senior managers are women
- **Shares:** Companies where employees are offered share options
- **Long Service:** 40% of employees with more than 5 years' service
- **Health Insurance:** Full family cover

To find out more about this company visit www.bestcompaniesguide.co.uk

HAYS TRAVEL

UK locations	N.East, Yorks & Humber
UK sites	34
Sector	Retail
Definition	Travel Agent
How owned	Private
Founded	1980
Turnover	£237.7m
Profit	£2.9m
Staff	431
Average age	29
Male : Female	11 : 89
Earnings £35,000+	2%

BEST COMPANIES INDEX

FIRST CLASS ★

2007 BCI = 665.0

2006 BCI = 670.6 (★)

WORKPLACE INSIGHTS

Work life balance is achieved within the company because they listen to the employees and make sure that emotional wellbeing and happiness is addressed. There is an ethos of understanding and flexibility when it comes to work life balance and general wellbeing.

Everyone who works for Hays Travel has a voice, everyone is listened to, all opinions are considered and everyone is treated fairly.

There is a very 'hands on' approach to leadership at Hays Travel, which starts with the managing director and leads through all senior management down to shop and branch managers.

MISSION / VISION

Hays Travel is committed to the growth and development of its business by excellent customer service which generates repeat business.

BEST WORKPLACE FACTORS

WELL BEING
MY TEAM
MY MANAGER

GRADUATE VACANCIES

No graduate vacancies have been indicated.

EMPLOYEE COMMENTS

"Always there to listen to you and help you when you need it."

"Team work within the branch is great."

"My Manager makes this a great workplace."

CONTACT DETAILS

Hays Travel, 9 - 10 Vine Place, Sunderland SR1 3NE
Tel: 0191 5661900 www.hays-travel.co.uk

KEY

- **Holidays:** Companies offering a minimum of 25 days annual leave
- **Pensions:** Companies offering a final salary or non-contributory/contributory pension scheme
- **Maternity:** Companies offering over Statutory Mattenity Pay
- **Charity Activities:** 10% of staff undertake charitable activities during business hours
- **Childcare:** On-site nursery or vouchers
- **Gym:** On-site gym or subsidised gym memberships
- **Women:** At least 33% of senior managers are women
- **Shares:** Companies where employees are offered share options
- **Long Service:** 40% of employees with more than 5 years' service
- **Health Insurance:** Full family cover

To find out more about this company visit www.bestcompaniesguide.co.uk

HCS

UK locations	E.England
UK sites	2
Sector	Not for Profit
Definition	Information Advice & Guidance
How owned	Partnership/LLP
Founded	1995
Turnover	Not disclosed
Profit	Not disclosed
Staff	202
Average age	42
Male : Female	17 : 83
Earnings £35,000+	8%

BEST COMPANIES INDEX

best company 2007

FIRST CLASS

★

2007 BCI = 691.8

WORKPLACE INSIGHTS

For the past three years, with the assistance of external sponsorship, HCS have sent a team of volunteers to East Africa to help train teachers in careers education, to enable young people to reach their potential and get out of poverty.

All staff at HCS can access therapeutic massage on-site, including back and neck, at reduced rates to help staff, who spend much of their day working at computers. In addition, fitness testing and resources on issues such as back care and stress are available.

HCS ensure that staff are rewarded and recognised for their achievements. The CEO will give public recognition at Staff Briefings, personal letters of thanks are provided and a financial Company Performance Award is awarded to all staff.

MISSION / VISION

By 2010 HCS will be an independent and thriving business with a regional and national reputation for delivering excellent services that enable our customers to develop the skills needed to shape their own futures and transform their working lives.

BEST WORKPLACE FACTORS

GIVING SOMETHING BACK
WELL BEING
FAIR DEAL

GRADUATE VACANCIES

No graduate vacancies have been indicated.

EMPLOYEE COMMENTS

"You feel good working here because our work is very worthwhile."

"Work life balance and wellbeing of staff is very strong in the company."

"Company is very supportive of staff and recognise that they are their best resource."

CONTACT DETAILS

HCS, Delta House, Avenue One, Letchworth Garden City, Herts SG6 2HU
Tel: 01462 705000 www.herts-careers.co.uk

KEY

- **Holidays:** Companies offering a minimum of 25 days annual leave
- **Maternity:** Companies offering over Statutory Matternity Pay
- **Childcare:** On-site nursery or vouchers
- **Women:** At least 33% of senior managers are women
- **Long Service:** 40% of employees with more than 5 years' service
- **Pensions:** Companies offering a final salary or non-contributory/ contributory pension scheme
- **Charity Activities:** 10% of staff undertake charitable activities during business hours
- **Gym:** On-site gym or subsidised gym memberships
- **Shares:** Companies where employees are offered share options
- **Health Insurance:** Full family cover

HEATHCOTES RESTAURANTS GROUP

UK locations	N.West
UK sites	11
Sector	Hospitality
Definition	Quality Dining Experience
How owned	Private
Founded	1990
Turnover	£7.8m
Profit	£1.4m
Staff	301
Average age	22
Male : Female	62 : 38
Earnings £35,000+	1%

BEST COMPANIES INDEX

best company 2007

FIRST CLASS

★

2007 BCI = 672.2

2006 BCI = 638.5

<672

ones to watch

WORKPLACE INSIGHTS

Many of the people from the early days now form the core managerial team that will see numbers 12, 13 & 14 restaurants open within the next four months and the principles on which the company started are still very much core to the business.

Investment in technology to make communication a lot easier – bi-weekly executive meetings and monthly restaurant board meetings enables information from board level to be communicated right down to all levels of Team Heathcotes.

Paul Heathcote integrates with all his staff. He arranges regular trips to other restaurants for his staff encouraging them to achieve their goals.

MISSION / VISION

Vision: To be the best restaurant group in the North West.
Mission: Every customer leaves wanting to recommend us.

BEST WORKPLACE FACTORS

MY TEAM
MY MANAGER
LEADERSHIP

GRADUATE VACANCIES

Sales & Marketing Manager.

EMPLOYEE COMMENTS

"The whole team including managers are great, friendly, caring, helpful and enthusiastic."

"The restaurant is well led (managed) and all are treated the same."

"Executive team inspire to create a common goal and dream."

CONTACT DETAILS

Heathcotes Restaurants Group, 23 Winckley Square, Preston PR1 3JJ
Tel: 01772 887441 www.heathcotes.co.uk

KEY

Holidays: Companies offering a minimum of 25 days annual leave
Maternity: Companies offering over Statutory Matternity Pay
Childcare: On-site nursery or vouchers
Women: At least 33% of senior managers are women
Long Service: 40% of employees with more than 5 years' service
Pensions: Companies offering a final salary or non-contributory/contributory pension scheme
Charity Activities: 10% of staff undertake charitable activities during business hours
Gym: On-site gym or subsidised gym memberships
Shares: Companies where employees are offered share options
Health Insurance: Full family cover

To find out more about this company visit www.bestcompaniesguide.co.uk

HFL

UK locations	E.England
UK sites	1
Sector	Pharmaceutical
Definition	Analytical Chemistry Laboratory
How owned	Private
Founded	1963
Turnover	£8.3m
Profit	£0.2m
Staff	136
Average age	35
Male : Female	39 : 61
Earnings £35,000+	11%

BEST COMPANIES INDEX

best company 2007

FIRST CLASS

★

2007 BCI = 692.7

2006 BCI = 648.4

693>

WORKPLACE INSIGHTS

Recently, HFL have undergone a major exercise to address Corporate Social Responsibility, identifying a "signature programme" to engage with local people. Staff volunteer to promote science & the environment to primary & secondary schools, and the wider community.

The leadership team are personally involved in Lunchtime Learning Sessions. These are open learning sessions held over lunchtimes, where a buffet lunch is provided. CEO David Hall also facilitates Creativity and Innovation Clubs, which are open to all staff.

HFL recognise employees' achievements through awards such as The Positive Thinking Award, the Touchstone awards for the individual and team of the year and the Best Improvement Award, the winner of which receives two Red Letter Day prizes.

MISSION / VISION

HFL aspires to be a unique provider of laboratory services, internationally-recognised as an example of best practice in operations research and corporate culture.

BEST WORKPLACE FACTORS

GIVING SOMETHING BACK
LEADERSHIP
MY TEAM

GRADUATE VACANCIES

Contract Research: Bioanalysis Drug Research & Immunochemistry & Biotech. Drug Surveillance. R&D.

EMPLOYEE COMMENTS

"Everyone at the company believes in what we do and how we do it."

"Fantastic leadership from a truly inspirational CEO which is fully embraced by both senior management and staff alike."

"Absolutely everyone seems to be working as part of one big team."

CONTACT DETAILS

HFL, Newmarket Road, Fordham, Cambridgeshire CB7 5WW
Tel: 01638 720500 www.hfl.co.uk

KEY

- **Holidays:** Companies offering a minimum of 25 days annual leave
- **Maternity:** Companies offering over Statutory Matternity Pay
- **Childcare:** On-site nursery or vouchers
- **Women:** At least 33% of senior managers are women
- **Long Service:** 40% of employees with more than 5 years' service
- **Pensions:** Companies offering a final salary or non-contributory/ contributory pension scheme
- **Charity Activities:** 10% of staff undertake charitable activities during business hours
- **Gym:** On-site gym or subsidised gym memberships
- **Shares:** Companies where employees are offered share options
- **Health Insurance:** Full family cover

To find out more about this company visit www.bestcompaniesguide.co.uk

HiFX
INTELLIGENT FINANCIAL SERVICES

HIFX

UK locations	S.East
UK sites	1
Sector	Financial
Definition	Foreign Exchange Services
How owned	Private
Founded	1998
Turnover	Not disclosed
Profit	Not disclosed
Staff	170
Average age	26
Male : Female	63 : 37
Earnings £35,000+	48%

BEST COMPANIES INDEX

best company 2007

FIRST CLASS

★

2007 BCI = 666.6

2006 BCI = 670.8 (★)

<667

WORKPLACE INSIGHTS

HiFX conduct an annual confidential staff survey on management to assess competency of management and areas for improvement. They actively support personal development and invest in developing employees into senior and managerial level individuals.

Employees at HiFX can benefit from an employee assistance programme which offers 24 hour support all year round. In addition, a range of social events are organised including a Golfing Day, a Spa Day and a Summer Ball.

ITN or "Interesting to note" awards are given to HiFX employees who do something above and beyond their normal remit. Prizes given include a weekend away, a cash bonus or a gift such as wine or champagne.

MISSION / VISION

To be the premier provider of commercial foreign exchange services with focus on:- Customer Service Excellence, Ensuring Staff Capability & Care, Procedural Excellence Marketing Innovation.

BEST WORKPLACE FACTORS

MY MANAGER
FAIR DEAL
MY TEAM

GRADUATE VACANCIES

Sales(Corporate FX Advisory & Dealing, Private Client) Private Client Admin, Finance/Accts, IT, Marketing.

EMPLOYEE COMMENTS

"As an employee, no matter how junior, you are listened to and your opinions are taken on board."

"We are recognised for our hard work."

"Staff are great, fantastic atmosphere in the office and everyone gets on with each other really well."

CONTACT DETAILS

HiFX, Morgan House, Madeira Walk, Windsor SL4 1EP
Tel: 01753 859170 www.hifx.co.uk

KEY

- **Holidays:** Companies offering a minimum of 25 days annual leave
- **Pensions:** Companies offering a final salary or non-contributory/ contributory pension scheme
- **Maternity:** Companies offering over Statutory Matternity Pay
- **Charity Activities:** 10% of staff undertake charitable activities during business hours
- **Childcare:** On-site nursery or vouchers
- **Gym:** On-site gym or subsidised gym memberships
- **Women:** At least 33% of senior managers are women
- **Shares:** Companies where employees are offered share options
- **Long Service:** 40% of employees with more than 5 years' service
- **Health Insurance:** Full family cover

HILL & KNOWLTON

HILL & KNOWLTON

UK locations	London
UK sites	2
Sector	Business Services
Definition	Public Relations Consultancy
How owned	Public (i.e. stock market listed)
Founded	1969
Turnover	Not disclosed
Profit	Not disclosed
Staff	277
Average age	32
Male : Female	37 : 63
Earnings £35,000+	39%

BEST COMPANIES INDEX

best company 2007

FIRST CLASS

★

2007 BCI = 676.7

WORKPLACE INSIGHTS

Hill & Knowlton has a bar in the building to encourage socialising amongst teams and all levels of staff (both senior and junior). Events are frequently held in the bar which involve all staff.

Every year there is an all staff Christmas Event to reward all teams for their hard work and encourage socialising amongst different teams.

The company operates a "career map". This outlines competencies by job title and division together with the company's training plan. Training is organised on three levels - for the individual, for a small group or a whole team.

MISSION / VISION

Vision: We will be at the centre of dealing with the world's toughest communications challenges.
Mission: To achieve real brand and business outcomes for our clients.

BEST WORKPLACE FACTORS

MY TEAM
MY MANAGER
PERSONAL GROWTH

GRADUATE VACANCIES

Marketing Comm's, Sports Marketing & Sponsorship, Corporate Comm's, Healthcare Consumer Tech & Entertainment.

EMPLOYEE COMMENTS

"Treats the team and team members in a positive constructive manner allowing individual personalities to thrive."

"The leadership of the organisation is very high performing management team."

"An atmosphere that promotes independent thoughts and ideas while supporting individual growth."

CONTACT DETAILS

Hill & Knowlton, 20 Soho Square, London W1A 1PR
Tel: 020 74133000 www.hillandknowlton.co.uk

KEY

Holidays: Companies offering a minimum of 25 days annual leave
Maternity: Companies offering over Statutory Matternity Pay
Childcare: On-site nursery or vouchers
Women: At least 33% of senior managers are women
Long Service: 40% of employees with more than 5 years' service
Pensions: Companies offering a final salary or non-contributory/ contributory pension scheme
Charity Activities: 10% of staff undertake charitable activities during business hours
Gym: On-site gym or subsidised gym memberships
Shares: Companies where employees are offered share options
Health Insurance: Full family cover

1000

HISCOX

HISCOX

UK locations	National
UK sites	8
Sector	Financial - Insurance
Definition	Leading Specialist Insurer
How owned	Public (i.e. stock market listed)
Founded	1901
Turnover	£1,006.2m
Profit	£61.1m
Staff	490
Average age	33
Male : Female	54 : 46
Earnings £35,000+	52%

<661

ones to watch

BEST COMPANIES INDEX

best company 2007

FIRST CLASS

★

2007 BCI = 661.4

2006 BCI = 704.3 (★★)

WORKPLACE INSIGHTS

At each corporate induction event the Chairman and CEO deliver a session on the company values to new arrivals. They believe it is important for new staff to hear where the values have come from and what they mean – direct from the 'horses mouth'.

For all people managers, Hiscox have created development programmes aimed at managers at differing organisational levels. In addition to workshops, managers have access to e-learning programmes, phone coaches, Books247 and Ashridge Virtual Learning Centre.

Hiscox have invested in the development of two in-house courses "Time Management" & "Managing the Pace" in an effort to equip employees with the practical skills to manage their work, maintain a healthy work life balance and look at nutrition, sleep and exercise.

500

MISSION / VISION

To be a focused global insurance business - successful in the UK Europe and USA with a great business reputation.

BEST WORKPLACE FACTORS

LEADERSHIP
PERSONAL GROWTH
MY COMPANY

GRADUATE VACANCIES

No graduate vacancies have been indicated.

EMPLOYEE COMMENTS

"The senior management team are strong leaders and role models."

"Investment in people through training programmes is excellent."

"The company believes in its principles and follows them."

CONTACT DETAILS

Hiscox, 1 Great St Helen's, London EC3A 6HX
Tel: 0207 4486000 www.hiscox.com

KEY

- **Holidays:** Companies offering a minimum of 25 days annual leave
- **Maternity:** Companies offering over Statutory Matternity Pay
- **Childcare:** On-site nursery or vouchers
- **Women:** At least 33% of senior managers are women
- **Long Service:** 40% of employees with more than 5 years' service
- **Pensions:** Companies offering a final salary or non-contributory/ contributory pension scheme
- **Charity Activities:** 10% of staff undertake charitable activities during business hours
- **Gym:** On-site gym or subsidised gym memberships
- **Shares:** Companies where employees are offered share options
- **Health Insurance:** Full family cover

0

To find out more about this company visit www.bestcompaniesguide.co.uk

HLM ARCHITECTS

HLM ARCHITECTS

UK locations	National
UK sites	6
Sector	Architects
Definition	Architects Interiors Landscape
How owned	Private
Founded	1964
Turnover	£10.2m
Profit	£0.3m
Staff	144
Average age	38
Male : Female	60 : 40
Earnings £35,000+	28%

BEST COMPANIES INDEX

best company 2007

FIRST CLASS

★

2007 BCI = 686.4

2006 BCI = 690.5 (★)

WORKPLACE INSIGHTS

By defining professional & personal development objectives and continually investing in a programme of on / off the job training, ensures each member of the team meets identified goals, improving current performance and nurturing future potential.

HLM are concerned about those less fortunate in the community and to help with this they organise a number of fundraising events for local charities.

As an organisation, HLM aim to be at the forefront of developing & implementing policies that are often over & above statutory requirements and recognise the increasingly complex lifestyles of their staff and the importance of providing a supportive working.

MISSION / VISION

To listen, analyse, offer and deliver the most innovative sustainable design solutions to meet our Clients needs, whilst maintaining the best working atmosphere for our team, creating the most stimulating environment for our Directors and Staff to profitably deliver their best work.

BEST WORKPLACE FACTORS

PERSONAL GROWTH
GIVING SOMETHING BACK
WELL BEING

GRADUATE VACANCIES

Architecture, architectural technologists, landscape architecture, interior design, IT.

EMPLOYEE COMMENTS

"Continued training and opportunity to progress in career."

"The company has a great sense of community and concern for social and environmental issues."

"I can honestly say they have always been there for me."

CONTACT DETAILS

HLM Architects, 2nd Floor The Ruskin Building, Tudor Square, Sheffield S1 2LA
Tel: 0114 2639600 www.hlmarchitects.com

KEY

- **Holidays:** Companies offering a minimum of 25 days annual leave
- **Maternity:** Companies offering over Statutory Matternity Pay
- **Childcare:** On-site nursery or vouchers
- **Women:** At least 33% of senior managers are women
- **Long Service:** 40% of employees with more than 5 years' service
- **Pensions:** Companies offering a final salary or non-contributory/ contributory pension scheme
- **Charity Activities:** 10% of staff undertake charitable activities during business hours
- **Gym:** On-site gym or subsidised gym memberships
- **Shares:** Companies where employees are offered share options
- **Health Insurance:** Full family cover

HOMESERVE GB

Homeserve

UK locations	W.Midlands
UK sites	1
Sector	Financial - Insurance
Definition	Insurer
How owned	Public (i.e. stock market listed)
Founded	1994
Turnover	£0.1m
Profit	£0.1m
Staff	1097
Average age	30
Male : Female	37 : 63
Earnings £35,000+	8%

BEST COMPANIES INDEX

best company 2007

FIRST CLASS

★

2007 BCI = 669.5

2006 BCI = 676.6 (★)

WORKPLACE INSIGHTS

In Homeserve, managers are encouraged to coach their employees on performance improvement issues. This approach means that the employees are actively encouraged to determine their own solutions and this includes suggestions for their own development.

Homeserve recently held a Wellbeing Campaign where local health professionals were invited on site to provide treatments. One of their meeting rooms became a relaxation room, filled with comfortable sofas, books on relaxation and chill out music.

A monthly award is presented by the Managing Director of Homeserve to an employee nominated by the senior management team based on the contribution they have made to the business. The winning employee receives £1000 as recognition for this award.

MISSION / VISION

To become the global worldwide Home Emergency Service for anything that goes wrong to, or in, the home.

BEST WORKPLACE FACTORS

MY MANAGER
WELL BEING
FAIR DEAL

GRADUATE VACANCIES

Marketing, Finance, HR, Call Centre.

EMPLOYEE COMMENTS

"The management team are highly motivational."

"Homeserve is a great organisation and they value employees more than any organisation I have worked for."

"Rewarded for good work and supported when things go wrong."

CONTACT DETAILS

Homeserve GB, Cable Drive, Walsall, West Midlands WS2 7BN
Tel: 01922 659700 www.homeserve.com

KEY

Holidays: Companies offering a minimum of 25 days annual leave

Maternity: Companies offering over Statutory Matternity Pay

Childcare: On-site nursery or vouchers

Women: At least 33% of senior managers are women

Long Service: 40% of employees with more than 5 years' service

Pensions: Companies offering a final salary or non-contributory/ contributory pension scheme

Charity Activities: 10% of staff undertake charitable activities during business hours

Gym: On-site gym or subsidised gym memberships

Shares: Companies where employees are offered share options

Health Insurance: Full family cover

To find out more about this company visit www.bestcompaniesguide.co.uk

HUNTRESS

UK locations	National
UK sites	15
Sector	Recruitment
Definition	Recruitment Specialists
How owned	Partnership/Limited Liability Partnership
Founded	2000
Turnover	£52.8m
Profit	Not disclosed
Staff	301
Average age	26
Male : Female	42 : 58
Earnings £35,000+	32%

BEST COMPANIES INDEX

best company 2007

FIRST CLASS ★

2007 BCI = 684.7

WORKPLACE INSIGHTS

Huntress holds an Annual Awards Dinner for all employees which includes dinner, an awards evening and fantastic entertainment. Group and team days are also planned throughout the year and team nights out or lunches may be provided as rewards for achievements.

Huntress has invested in building up an internal training department, including full time, in-house trainers, to focus on the "Huntress method". They offer induction, graduate, sales, advanced sales, best practice and management training to employees.

Leap Awards are given every quarter at Huntress, rewarding sales staff for growth and enable even newcomers to be recognised. Prizes include champagne, spa days, dinner for two at a top restaurant or a luxury weekend away.

MISSION / VISION

To provide an innovative and professional recruitment consultancy service that not only delivers but exceeds client and candidate expectations enabling Huntress to build relationships of longevity.

BEST WORKPLACE FACTORS

MY TEAM
MY MANAGER
MY COMPANY

GRADUATE VACANCIES

IT Recruitment, Office Recruitment, Finance Recruitment & Marketing.

EMPLOYEE COMMENTS

"There is a fantastic sense of team work here."

"The support I receive from my line manager is second to none."

"Recognition for good work which is motivating and gives you a sense of achievement."

CONTACT DETAILS

Huntress, Imperial House, 15-19 Kinsgway, London WC2B 6UN
Tel: 0207 7441300 www.huntress.co.uk

KEY

- **Holidays:** Companies offering a minimum of 25 days annual leave
- **Maternity:** Companies offering over Statutory Matternity Pay
- **Childcare:** On-site nursery or vouchers
- **Women:** At least 33% of senior managers are women
- **Long Service:** 40% of employees with more than 5 years' service
- **Pensions:** Companies offering a final salary or non-contributory/ contributory pension scheme
- **Charity Activities:** 10% of staff undertake charitable activities during business hours
- **Gym:** On-site gym or subsidised gym memberships
- **Shares:** Companies where employees are offered share options
- **Health Insurance:** Full family cover

1000 — 685> — 500 — 0 — ones to watch

1000

500

<686

ones to watch

0

IDIS

UK locations	S.East
UK sites	2
Sector	Pharmaceutical
Definition	Specialist Pharmaceutical Supplier
How owned	Partnership/LLP
Founded	1987
Turnover	Not disclosed
Profit	Not disclosed
Staff	94
Average age	34
Male : Female	40 : 60
Earnings £35,000+	17%

BEST COMPANIES INDEX

best company 2007

FIRST CLASS

★

2007 BCI = 685.6

WORKPLACE INSIGHTS

IDIS take part in team building events which serve a dual purpose of team building & giving to charity, such as the British Heart Foundation Sailing challenge. The IDIS Fun Committee provides a monthly charitable donation for staff and company-wide activities.

The Bright Star Awards are a company-wide initiative whereby individuals and teams are recognised and rewarded for outstanding achievements. They are presented to those who display the" IDIS X Factor".

IDIS has created their own bespoke learning environment, with their own dedicated Learning and Development Manager. As part of this, there is a Management Development programme focusing on personality preference, situational leadership & enhancing motivation.

MISSION / VISION

Managing World Medicines.

BEST WORKPLACE FACTORS

GIVING SOMETHING BACK
MY TEAM
LEADERSHIP

GRADUATE VACANCIES

No graduate vacancies have been indicated.

EMPLOYEE COMMENTS

"Everyone believes in what we are doing."

"Fantastic team spirit that enables a can do attitude."

"The leader of this company has a very strong vision for its growth."

CONTACT DETAILS

IDIS, Idis House, Churchfield Rd, Weybridge, Surrey KT13 8DB
Tel: 01932 824000 www.idispharma.com

KEY

Holidays: Companies offering a minimum of 25 days annual leave
Maternity: Companies offering over Statutory Matternity Pay
Childcare: On-site nursery or vouchers
Women: At least 33% of senior managers are women
Long Service: 40% of employees with more than 5 years' service
Pensions: Companies offering a final salary or non-contributory/ contributory pension scheme
Charity Activities: 10% of staff undertake charitable activities during business hours
Gym: On-site gym or subsidised gym memberships
Shares: Companies where employees are offered share options
Health Insurance: Full family cover

To find out more about this company visit www.bestcompaniesguide.co.uk

i-level

I-LEVEL

UK locations	London
UK sites	1
Sector	Advertising
Definition	Digital Media Communications
How owned	Private
Founded	1999
Turnover	Not disclosed
Profit	Not disclosed
Staff	97
Average age	28.7
Male : Female	55 : 45
Earnings £35,000+	36%

BEST COMPANIES INDEX

best company 2007

FIRST CLASS

★

2007 BCI = 670.2

2006 BCI = 709.7 (★★)

WORKPLACE INSIGHTS

i-level have run a series of Freshness sessions, which involved inviting speakers from a variety of backgrounds such as Virgin Radio DJ, Christian O'Connell, to come in to share their experiences with employees to stimulate innovative thinking.

i-level has a regular monthly all-staff get together which provides an opportunity for staff to present anything close to their hearts to the rest of the company, from professional to social initiatives. It is an open forum that anyone can be involved in.

Gijutkakushin (Japanese for Innovation) is i-level's monthly initiative to showcase innovative work and practices within the company. The 'Innovator of the Year' is sent to Japan to report back on the digital world there.

MISSION / VISION

The decade defining agency of the 00's.

BEST WORKPLACE FACTORS

PERSONAL GROWTH
MY TEAM
MY COMPANY

GRADUATE VACANCIES

Advertising and Search Marketing.

EMPLOYEE COMMENTS

"Great training and knowledge share among the employees."

"The people and team spirit make i-level a fantastic place to work."

"From the moment I walked in the door I have been made to feel welcome and valued."

CONTACT DETAILS

i-level, 26-30 Strutton Ground, London SW1P 2HR
Tel: 0207 3402700 www.i-level.com

KEY

- **Holidays:** Companies offering a minimum of 25 days annual leave
- **Maternity:** Companies offering over Statutory Matternity Pay
- **Childcare:** On-site nursery or vouchers
- **Women:** At least 33% of senior managers are women
- **Long Service:** 40% of employees with more than 5 years' service
- **Pensions:** Companies offering a final salary or non-contributory/ contributory pension scheme
- **Charity Activities:** 10% of staff undertake charitable activities during business hours
- **Gym:** On-site gym or subsidised gym memberships
- **Shares:** Companies where employees are offered share options
- **Health Insurance:** Full family cover

1000
670>
ones to watch
500
0

To find out more about this company visit www.bestcompaniesguide.co.uk

1000

IMPRINT PLC

IMPRINT PLC

UK locations	National
UK sites	8
Sector	Recruitment
Definition	Recruitment Executive Search
How owned	Public (i.e. stock market listed)
Founded	2001
Turnover	£51.5m
Profit	£4.1m
Staff	363
Average age	29.8
Male : Female	51 : 49
Earnings £35,000+	35%

<674

ones to watch

BEST COMPANIES INDEX

best company 2007

FIRST CLASS

★

2007 BCI = 673.5

WORKPLACE INSIGHTS

Management at Imprint act as an example to the rest of the employees by being as hands-on as possible. Members of senior management are regularly seen to 'walk the floor' in a number of the offices to maintain a visible presence.

Imprint hold an annual group conference attended by all employees across all locations. The CEO presents the conferences and updates all employees on business success and communicates the mission and values of the business and future goals.

Employees at Imprint have received both formal training and individual coaching. All employees have a bespoke training and development plan designed to equip them with the right skills and knowledge and assist them in achieving their career aspirations.

500

MISSION / VISION

To be the recognised leader in each market sector in which Imprint Plc operates by delivering service excellence, expert market knowledge and innovative recruitment solutions.

BEST WORKPLACE FACTORS

MY MANAGER
MY TEAM
FAIR DEAL

GRADUATE VACANCIES

All areas predominantly sales.

EMPLOYEE COMMENTS

"Managers take the time to listen to your opinion and respond in kind."

"There is an excellent atmosphere in the office and individuality is encouraged."

"Rewards and benefits are excellent."

CONTACT DETAILS

Imprint Plc, 2 Sheraton Street, London W1F 8BH
Tel: 0207 2878585 www.imprintplc.com

KEY

Holidays: Companies offering a minimum of 25 days annual leave

Maternity: Companies offering over Statutory Matternity Pay

Childcare: On-site nursery or vouchers

Women: At least 33% of senior managers are women

Long Service: 40% of employees with more than 5 years' service

Pensions: Companies offering a final salary or non-contributory/ contributory pension scheme

Charity Activities: 10% of staff undertake charitable activities during business hours

Gym: On-site gym or subsidised gym memberships

Shares: Companies where employees are offered share options

Health Insurance: Full family cover

0

To find out more about this company visit www.bestcompaniesguide.co.uk

ING REAL ESTATE INVESTMENT MANAGEMENT (UK)

ING REAL ESTATE

UK locations	London
UK sites	1
Sector	Financial
Definition	Property Investment Management
How owned	Private
Founded	2003
Turnover	Not disclosed
Profit	Not disclosed
Staff	135
Average age	30
Male : Female	60 : 40
Earnings £35,000+	64%

BEST COMPANIES INDEX

best company 2007

FIRST CLASS

★

2007 BCI = 691.6

WORKPLACE INSIGHTS

Leader Robert Houston meets all new starters. At these sessions, usually held over lunch, he gives a history of the company and an insight into our vision and mission. Takes time to meet everyone and walks around the office to talk to individuals within each team.

As they recognise that personal development is key to their success, training is integral to their personal development plans. ING support and encourage their employees to enrol on training schemes and financially support employees through a variety of qualifications.

ING's business policies promote involvement within the communities in which they work. They demonstrate their commitment through making donations, sponsoring and supporting numerous social activities.

MISSION / VISION

To be the UK's leading property investment manager.

BEST WORKPLACE FACTORS

LEADERSHIP
PERSONAL GROWTH
GIVING SOMETHING BACK

GRADUATE VACANCIES

Fund Accounting Investments Teams Finance.

EMPLOYEE COMMENTS

"Strong leadership, nice people, good atmosphere, supportive managers."

"Encouragement to remain well trained and provision of the tools to ensure this happens."

"I am happy to work somewhere that takes such an active role in supporting charities & local communities' projects."

CONTACT DETAILS

ING Real Estate Investment Management (UK), 6th Floor, 60 London Wall, London EC2M 5TQ
Tel: 0207 7675600 www.ingrealestate.com

KEY

Holidays: Companies offering a minimum of 25 days annual leave
Maternity: Companies offering over Statutory Matternity Pay
Childcare: On-site nursery or vouchers
Women: At least 33% of senior managers are women
Long Service: 40% of employees with more than 5 years' service
Pensions: Companies offering a final salary or non-contributory/ contributory pension scheme
Charity Activities: 10% of staff undertake charitable activities during business hours
Gym: On-site gym or subsidised gym memberships
Shares: Companies where employees are offered share options
Health Insurance: Full family cover

To find out more about this company visit www.bestcompaniesguide.co.uk

1000

INSTANT OFFICES GROUP

instant offices

UK locations	London, S.East
UK sites	2
Sector	Property
Definition	Estate Agency/Space Advisors
How owned	Private
Founded	1999
Turnover	£4.5m
Profit	Not disclosed
Staff	52
Average age	32
Male : Female	60 : 40
Earnings £35,000+	23%

BEST COMPANIES INDEX

best company 2007

FIRST CLASS

★

2007 BCI = 678.7

<679

ones to watch

WORKPLACE INSIGHTS

The leaders at Instant Offices openly present the company vision and where they are at present in quarterly meetings. All successes and failures are aired openly and they ensure the whole company is pulling together towards the same aims.

All employees are encouraged to provide their own ideas via the Instant Offices ideas box. Employees are openly congratulated for good work and ideas by email, through weekly company forums and periodically at quarterly presentations.

Instant Offices try to foster a fun, yet hard working environment so that all team members get on well together. They elect a 'Minister of Fun' to arrange monthly activities and there are annual events such as a Ski trip and Sports Day.

500

MISSION / VISION

Instant Offices was established in May 1999. It has grown since then and now consists of three different businesses operating globally through offices in the UK, France, Germany, Australia and the US. The group is a young, dynamic, entrepreneurial company that is constantly growing into new sectors.

BEST WORKPLACE FACTORS

LEADERSHIP
MY MANAGER
WELL BEING

GRADUATE VACANCIES

Sales, Corporate Sales, Marketing, IT.

EMPLOYEE COMMENTS

"The Senior management are very visible and always have time for every member of staff."

"The management are easy to approach and treat employees with respect."

"It is very entrepreneurial and people genuinely like one other."

CONTACT DETAILS

Instant Offices Group, 11/13 Knightsbridge, London SW1X 7LY
Tel: 0207 8230620 www.instantofficesgroup.com

KEY

Holidays: Companies offering a minimum of 25 days annual leave

Pensions: Companies offering a final salary or non-contributory/ contributory pension scheme

Maternity: Companies offering over Statutory Matternity Pay

Charity Activities: 10% of staff undertake charitable activities during business hours

Childcare: On-site nursery or vouchers

Gym: On-site gym or subsidised gym memberships

Women: At least 33% of senior managers are women

Shares: Companies where employees are offered share options

Long Service: 40% of employees with more than 5 years' service

Health Insurance: Full family cover

0

To find out more about this company visit www.bestcompaniesguide.co.uk

INSTARMAC GROUP

INSTARMAC

UK locations	W.Midlands
UK sites	1
Sector	Manufacturing
Definition	Highway Material Manufacturer
How owned	Private
Founded	1977
Turnover	Not disclosed
Profit	Not disclosed
Staff	98
Average age	36
Male : Female	76 : 24
Earnings £35,000+	9%

BEST COMPANIES INDEX

best company 2007

FIRST CLASS

★

2007 BCI = 660.0

WORKPLACE INSIGHTS

The Employee Benefit Trust was created by Instarmac to support employees in any eventuality allowing for the trustees to consider any employee in need. The trust has provided paid leave for long term sick, to care for a relative and to support families through bereavement.

Instarmac are committed to reducing all waste and carbon emissions and have reduced their waste by 20% in the past year. All paper is used on both sides and recycled. They have reduced carbon emissions by sourcing more efficient goods and vehicles.

Instarmac recognises and rewards each individual's contribution. All new starters meet the entire management team, including the Chairman and Managing Director. They want everyone to feel that they are contributing to the company's success.

MISSION / VISION

To be Europe's No 1 producer of innovative cement, resin and bitumen based products. Supplying the road maintenance, concrete repair, and tile adhesive & grout markets. Manufacturing to world-class standards.

BEST WORKPLACE FACTORS

WELL BEING
GIVING SOMETHING BACK
MY MANAGER

GRADUATE VACANCIES

Research and Development, Sales & Marketing.

EMPLOYEE COMMENTS

"The company shows a genuine concern for its employees."

"You are treated as a valued member of staff."

"Managers are very approachable so if there ever is a problem it gets solved quickly."

CONTACT DETAILS

Instarmac Group, Kingsbury Link, Trinity Road, Tamworth, Staffs B78 2EX
Tel: 01827 872244 www.instarmac.co.uk

KEY

- **Holidays:** Companies offering a minimum of 25 days annual leave
- **Pensions:** Companies offering a final salary or non-contributory/ contributory pension scheme
- **Maternity:** Companies offering over Statutory Matternity Pay
- **Charity Activities:** 10% of staff undertake charitable activities during business hours
- **Childcare:** On-site nursery or vouchers
- **Gym:** On-site gym or subsidised gym memberships
- **Women:** At least 33% of senior managers are women
- **Shares:** Companies where employees are offered share options
- **Long Service:** 40% of employees with more than 5 years' service
- **Health Insurance:** Full family cover

1000

660>

ones to watch

500

0

INSTITUTE OF PRACTITIONERS IN ADVERTISING

IPA
Institute of Practitioners in Advertising

UK locations	National
UK sites	3
Sector	Not for Profit
Definition	Industry Trade Body
How owned	Trust/Employee owned/Mutual
Founded	1917
Turnover	£10.0m
Profit	£0.1m
Staff	54
Average age	35
Male : Female	31 : 69
Earnings £35,000+	26%

BEST COMPANIES INDEX

best company 2007

FIRST CLASS ★

2007 BCI = 664.7

WORKPLACE INSIGHTS

IPA's position in the industry gives them the opportunity to influence their members & the way they operate. All are encouraged to be proactive & take personal responsibility for their own areas of operation. The most inexperienced are quickly able to develop to their potential.

Protection of the environment is part of the IPA's values and principles and they consider it to be sound business practice. Care for the environment is one of the IPA's key responsibilities and an important part of the way in which they do business.

The IPA is a flexible, proactive company which recognises that its greatest asset is its people. They concentrate on maximising the potential of all.

MISSION / VISION

To be seen as personal trainers, mental sparring partners, negotiators and the spokespeople for the world's best advertising media and marketing communications business.

BEST WORKPLACE FACTORS

MY MANAGER
GIVING SOMETHING BACK
MY TEAM

GRADUATE VACANCIES

No graduate vacancies have been indicated.

EMPLOYEE COMMENTS

"People set their own targets in discussion with their manager and then are enabled to achieve them."

"Everybody likes the business we're in, feels it makes an important contribution to the economy and society."

"I have a great team that works with me."

CONTACT DETAILS

Institute of Practitioners in Advertising, 44 Belgrave Square, London SW1X 8QS
Tel: 020 72357020 www.ipa.co.uk

KEY

Holidays: Companies offering a minimum of 25 days annual leave
Maternity: Companies offering over Statutory Matternity Pay
Childcare: On-site nursery or vouchers
Women: At least 33% of senior managers are women
Long Service: 40% of employees with more than 5 years' service
Pensions: Companies offering a final salary or non-contributory/contributory pension scheme
Charity Activities: 10% of staff undertake charitable activities during business hours
Gym: On-site gym or subsidised gym memberships
Shares: Companies where employees are offered share options
Health Insurance: Full family cover

To find out more about this company visit www.bestcompaniesguide.co.uk

INVENTIVE LEISURE

REVOLUTION®

UK locations	National
UK sites	52
Sector	Hospitality
Definition	City Centre Bars
How owned	Private
Founded	2000
Turnover	£50.4m
Profit	£4.1m
Staff	1611
Average age	23
Male : Female	55 : 45
Earnings £35,000+	2%

BEST COMPANIES INDEX

best company 2007

FIRST CLASS

★

2007 BCI = 671.0

WORKPLACE INSIGHTS

Each unit has a specific budget allocated to arrange two formal events each year. These range from outward bound activities to team building games.

Inventive Leisure sees the company as committed to developing and promoting people. 70% of management job holders have been promoted internally and many decide to stay and pursue their careers with Inventive Leisure.

Inventive Leisure develop employee skills and make them more confident people, rewarding performance with incentives that vary from cash, holidays and gifts such as i-pods.

MISSION / VISION

Best bars to work in, be in, and invest in.

BEST WORKPLACE FACTORS

MY TEAM
MY MANAGER
FAIR DEAL

GRADUATE VACANCIES

No graduate vacancies have been indicated.

EMPLOYEE COMMENTS

"All the people work as a team. We all get on and hang out after work and on days off."

"There is a good sense of family and friendship between staff and managers alike."

"The incentives provided by the company to me seem unparalleled to anyone else in the industry."

CONTACT DETAILS

Inventive Leisure, 21 Old Street, Ashton-under-Lyne, Lancashire OL6 6LA
Tel: 0161 3303876 www.revolution-bars.co.uk

KEY

- **Holidays:** Companies offering a minimum of 25 days annual leave
- **Maternity:** Companies offering over Statutory Maternity Pay
- **Childcare:** On-site nursery or vouchers
- **Women:** At least 33% of senior managers are women
- **Long Service:** 40% of employees with more than 5 years' service
- **Pensions:** Companies offering a final salary or non-contributory/ contributory pension scheme
- **Charity Activities:** 10% of staff undertake charitable activities during business hours
- **Gym:** On-site gym or subsidised gym memberships
- **Shares:** Companies where employees are offered share options
- **Health Insurance:** Full family cover

To find out more about this company visit www.bestcompaniesguide.co.uk

1000

<681

500

0

ones to watch

IT LAB

itlab

UK locations	London, W.Midlands
UK sites	2
Sector	IT/Internet Services
Definition	Outsource IT solutions
How owned	Private
Founded	2000
Turnover	£3.9m
Profit	£0.1m
Staff	71
Average age	31.5
Male : Female	80 : 20
Earnings £35,000+	15%

BEST COMPANIES INDEX

best company 2007

FIRST CLASS

★

2007 BCI = 680.7

WORKPLACE INSIGHTS

Managing Director Gary Thompson is very hands on and approachable and is physically located in the thick of things. Decisions are very participative with everyone's opinion valued and considered. They want employees to feel that they are part of the company's success.

IT Lab has been involved in a 'Computers to Somalia' programme looking at ways of recycling technical equipment and shipping it to Somalia for use in schools & universities. All data is safely removed and equipment is refurbished before sending.

IT Lab strongly believes in developing non-work related interests and skills. For example, everyone has the opportunity to participate in IT Lab funded courses such as languages, dance and art.

MISSION / VISION

We are committed to providing fast, efficient, professional and courteous service of the highest level. Our goal is to be recognised, by our customers, as providing a level of service that is head and shoulders better than that delivered by any of our competitors in the same market.

BEST WORKPLACE FACTORS

MY TEAM
MY COMPANY
PERSONAL GROWTH

GRADUATE VACANCIES

IT - Support, IT - Application development, IT - Web design.

EMPLOYEE COMMENTS

"The staff at this company are just all ridiculously nice."

"The leisure facilities and benefits offered are better than any other company I have worked for."

"Great opportunity for personal growth."

CONTACT DETAILS

IT Lab, The Place, 175 High Holborn, London WC1V 7AA
Tel: 0845 3590033 www.itlab.com

KEY

Holidays: Companies offering a minimum of 25 days annual leave
Maternity: Companies offering over Statutory Matternity Pay
Childcare: On-site nursery or vouchers
Women: At least 33% of senior managers are women
Long Service: 40% of employees with more than 5 years' service
Pensions: Companies offering a final salary or non-contributory/ contributory pension scheme
Charity Activities: 10% of staff undertake charitable activities during business hours
Gym: On-site gym or subsidised gym memberships
Shares: Companies where employees are offered share options
Health Insurance: Full family cover

To find out more about this company visit www.bestcompaniesguide.co.uk

JAGEX

UK locations	London, E.England
UK sites	3
Sector	IT/Internet Services
Definition	Online Games Company
How owned	Private
Founded	2001
Turnover	Not disclosed
Profit	Not disclosed
Staff	295
Average age	26
Male : Female	88 : 12
Earnings £35,000+	3%

BEST COMPANIES INDEX

best company 2007

FIRST CLASS

★

2007 BCI = 690.0

WORKPLACE INSIGHTS

Team building events often take place to welcome new starters or build motivation. These have included paint balling, waterskiing, banquets at Warwick Castle and punting down the River Cam with champagne and strawberries.

As an incentive to encourage employees to cycle to work Jagex offer a free bicycle servicing/repair programme. On a regular basis a trained bicycle mechanic visits the offices to service and undertake any repairs that are necessary.

Aims to be carbon neutral through offsetting the carbon emissions from their corporate travel and office energy usage by contributing to environmental charities to fund projects that absorb, reduce or avoid the release of equivalent amounts of CO^2 elsewhere.

MISSION / VISION

Build a world class online games business. Create exciting and challenging careers for all our team members. Develop the game engine and supporting technologies. Strive to continually improve the ways we look after our players.

BEST WORKPLACE FACTORS

MY TEAM
FAIR DEAL
GIVING SOMETHING BACK

GRADUATE VACANCIES

Software engineering, Mini games, Tech developers, Content development, Graphics.

EMPLOYEE COMMENTS

"The people who work here are fantastic and I consider them friends rather than colleagues."

"A good positive environment to work in, with excellent rewards for hard work."

"There is a sense of loyalty and family because the company values and rewards those who stick with it."

CONTACT DETAILS

Jagex, St Andrews House, St Andrews Road, Cambridge CB4 1DL
Tel: 01223 532660 www.jagex.com/corporate

KEY

- **Holidays:** Companies offering a minimum of 25 days annual leave
- **Maternity:** Companies offering over Statutory Maternity Pay
- **Childcare:** On-site nursery or vouchers
- **Women:** At least 33% of senior managers are women
- **Long Service:** 40% of employees with more than 5 years' service
- **Pensions:** Companies offering a final salary or non-contributory/ contributory pension scheme
- **Charity Activities:** 10% of staff undertake charitable activities during business hours
- **Gym:** On-site gym or subsidised gym memberships
- **Shares:** Companies where employees are offered share options
- **Health Insurance:** Full family cover

JMP CONSULTING

UK locations	National
UK sites	12
Sector	Consulting
Definition	Transport Consultancy
How owned	Private
Founded	1985
Turnover	£15.0m
Profit	£0.8m
Staff	264
Average age	33
Male : Female	69 : 31
Earnings £35,000+	34%

BEST COMPANIES INDEX

best company 2007

FIRST CLASS

★

2007 BCI = 662.7

2006 BCI = 659.7

<663

WORKPLACE INSIGHTS

JMP are Corporate Members with Transaid, a charity that supports development of some of the neediest parts of the world through the provision and support of local transport.

JMP's newest offices have been equipped with showers and changing facilities to encourage employees to cycle or walk to work in the interests of physical wellbeing and environmental sustainability.

JMP have overcome major obstacles to retain final salary pension scheme in the face of new regulations & a substantial funding deficit. They have carried out a formal consultation with all employees and are making a major contribution from profit to sustain the scheme.

MISSION / VISION

Vision: To be recognised by our clients and competitors as the best transport planning and engineering consultancy in the UK.
Mission: To deliver projects to our clients on time, in budget and to the highest professional quality.

BEST WORKPLACE FACTORS

GIVING SOMETHING BACK
WELL BEING
FAIR DEAL

GRADUATE VACANCIES

Professional & technical services in transport planning & engineering. Support services in IT & admin.

EMPLOYEE COMMENTS

"Working for a company who is trying to make a difference to climate change."

"Always someone who can assist with any problems which may crop up."

"Good benefits such as the JMP Challenge, Summer and Christmas meals out."

CONTACT DETAILS

JMP CONSULTING, Blackfriars House, Parsonage, Manchester M3 2JA
Tel: 0161 8315600 www.jmp.co.uk

KEY

Holidays: Companies offering a minimum of 25 days annual leave
Maternity: Companies offering over Statutory Matternity Pay
Childcare: On-site nursery or vouchers
Women: At least 33% of senior managers are women
Long Service: 40% of employees with more than 5 years' service
Pensions: Companies offering a final salary or non-contributory/contributory pension scheme
Charity Activities: 10% of staff undertake charitable activities during business hours
Gym: On-site gym or subsidised gym memberships
Shares: Companies where employees are offered share options
Health Insurance: Full family cover

To find out more about this company visit www.bestcompaniesguide.co.uk

JOBS@PERTEMPS

UK locations	National
UK sites	137
Sector	Recruitment
Definition	Complete Recruitment Solutions
How owned	Private
Founded	1982
Turnover	Not disclosed
Profit	Not disclosed
Staff	533
Average age	30
Male : Female	24 : 76
Earnings £35,000+	11%

BEST COMPANIES INDEX

FIRST CLASS

★

2007 BCI = 690.2

WORKPLACE INSIGHTS

Family business, operating to family values which can be seen in the way that staff at all levels can interact with both management and the strategic board who strive to develop strong personal relationships with both staff and their families.

Staff at Pertemps are actively encouraged to make suggestions to both managers and the board on new products and how to improve the efficiency of our processes and service. They want all employees to feel that their opinions count.

All employees have the opportunity to own shares in the business. Through the Employee Benefits Trust and Share Incentive Plan 90+% of the workforce have received company shares which have benefited the company through increased staff loyalty, retention and motivation.

MISSION / VISION

To create a fully inclusive company, owned and driven by its people, pioneering the future of the recruitment industry.

BEST WORKPLACE FACTORS

MY COMPANY
MY MANAGER
MY TEAM

GRADUATE VACANCIES

Contract Client.

EMPLOYEE COMMENTS

"We have strong company values which sets us apart from our competitors."

"The company believes in their staff and allows decisions to be made by all levels."

"The people are extremely friendly and work well together."

CONTACT DETAILS

Jobs@pertemps, Meriden Hall, Main Road, Meriden, Warwickshire CV7 7PT
Tel: 01676 525250 www.pertemps.co.uk

KEY

Holidays: Companies offering a minimum of 25 days annual leave
Maternity: Companies offering over Statutory Matternity Pay
Childcare: On-site nursery or vouchers
Women: At least 33% of senior managers are women
Long Service: 40% of employees with more than 5 years' service
Pensions: Companies offering a final salary or non-contributory/contributory pension scheme
Charity Activities: 10% of staff undertake charitable activities during business hours
Gym: On-site gym or subsidised gym memberships
Shares: Companies where employees are offered share options
Health Insurance: Full family cover

1000

<663

ones to watch

500

0

JOBSITE

jobsite

UK locations	S.East
UK sites	1
Sector	Recruitment
Definition	Internet Recruitment Solutions
How owned	Public (i.e. stock market listed)
Founded	1995
Turnover	£17.7m
Profit	£7.9m
Staff	125
Average age	32
Male : Female	63 : 37
Earnings £35,000+	39%

BEST COMPANIES INDEX

best company 2007

FIRST CLASS

★

2007 BCI = 663.4

2006 BCI = 696.2 (★)

WORKPLACE INSIGHTS

Jobsite staff receive an annual Christmas Bonus in the form of an internal company share scheme. Shares are awarded on performance and attendance and going that extra mile and this encourages staff to make their individual contributions to grow the business.

Jobsite are involved in a youth development scheme with local sports clubs. They have sponsored the teams, provided kit, coaching during the summer and also workshops in local schools, as well as special funds for exceptional talent progression.

Jobsite employ the services of an Occupational Health Company to look after employees for work and non-work related matters, using a Health Care Scheme which caters for many potential health threats and providing back up care.

MISSION / VISION

To continue on our path to be the U.K.'s number 1 Online Recruitment player. We will invest in people, technology and infrastructure, to provide the UK's best recruitment solution used by the most people.

BEST WORKPLACE FACTORS

FAIR DEAL
GIVING SOMETHING BACK
WELL BEING

GRADUATE VACANCIES

No graduate vacancies have been indicated.

EMPLOYEE COMMENTS

"The benefits of working for Jobsite are far greater than any other company I have worked for."

"Jobsite really make you feel as if you are making a difference."

"There is a sense that people care about you as an individual."

CONTACT DETAILS

Jobsite, Langstone Technology Park, Langstone Road, Havant PO9 1SA
Tel: 0870 7748500 www.jobsite.co.uk

KEY

- **Holidays:** Companies offering a minimum of 25 days annual leave
- **Maternity:** Companies offering over Statutory Matternity Pay
- **Childcare:** On-site nursery or vouchers
- **Women:** At least 33% of senior managers are women
- **Long Service:** 40% of employees with more than 5 years' service
- **Pensions:** Companies offering a final salary or non-contributory/ contributory pension scheme
- **Charity Activities:** 10% of staff undertake charitable activities during business hours
- **Gym:** On-site gym or subsidised gym memberships
- **Shares:** Companies where employees are offered share options
- **Health Insurance:** Full family cover

To find out more about this company visit www.bestcompaniesguide.co.uk

JONES LANG LASALLE

UK locations	National
UK sites	10
Sector	Property
Definition	Real Estate Services
How owned	Public (i.e. stock market listed)
Founded	1999
Turnover	Not disclosed
Profit	Not disclosed
Staff	1087
Average age	35
Male : Female	53 : 47
Earnings £35,000+	46%

BEST COMPANIES INDEX

best company 2007

FIRST CLASS

★

2007 BCI = 693.1

WORKPLACE INSIGHTS

Each manager and business is required to formulate an action plan in response to survey feedback, clearly communicating this to teams.

Personal development is a key priority for Jones Lang LaSalle because they recognise that people are truly their greatest asset.

All staff are invited to a central London venue (last one was held at the London Palladium) to meet and hear from the European CEO and senior management in the English business. This is followed by an informal social event.

MISSION / VISION

To be the chosen real estate expert and strategic advisor to the leading owners, occupiers and investors around the world.

BEST WORKPLACE FACTORS

MY MANAGER
PERSONAL GROWTH
LEADERSHIP

GRADUATE VACANCIES

Trainee surveyors & trainee planning consultants.

EMPLOYEE COMMENTS

"Approachable managers who take on board any queries and assist in solving them."

"Global brand but ensures employees' contribution at local level, for benefit of the business & personal development."

"Great leadership & motivation, support & training inspires you to be dedicated and empowered."

CONTACT DETAILS

Jones Lang LaSalle, 22 Hanover Square, London W1A 2BN
Tel: 020 74936040 www.joneslanglasalle.co.uk

KEY

- **Holidays:** Companies offering a minimum of 25 days annual leave
- **Maternity:** Companies offering over Statutory Matternity Pay
- **Childcare:** On-site nursery or vouchers
- **Women:** At least 33% of senior managers are women
- **Long Service:** 40% of employees with more than 5 years' service
- **Pensions:** Companies offering a final salary or non-contributory/ contributory pension scheme
- **Charity Activities:** 10% of staff undertake charitable activities during business hours
- **Gym:** On-site gym or subsidised gym memberships
- **Shares:** Companies where employees are offered share options
- **Health Insurance:** Full family cover

To find out more about this company visit www.bestcompaniesguide.co.uk

1000
693>
500
0
ones to watch

1000

LEWIS PR

UK locations	London, N.West
UK sites	2
Sector	Media
Definition	Media Relations Consultancy
How owned	Private
Founded	1995
Turnover	£4.3m
Profit	£0.04m
Staff	60
Average age	29
Male : Female	35 : 65
Earnings £35,000+	47%

BEST COMPANIES INDEX

best company 2007

FIRST CLASS ★

2007 BCI = 664.1

2006 BCI = 667.5 (★)

<664

WORKPLACE INSIGHTS

A mentoring scheme offering team members a source of advice aside from their immediate team is available at LEWIS. It is a voluntary scheme which is driven by the mentor and mentee to ensure that the process is a benefit to both participants.

LEWIS opened their company bar in 2004 called Spin Bar, on the ground floor of its Millbank Tower office suite. The bar is company subsidised and is open every Friday for staff and on various occasions throughout the year.

Managers nominate individuals each year whom they feel have made an outstanding contribution. There is one winner for each of the four regions the company operates in: UK, Europe, US and APAC. They each win a holiday for two up to the value of £2,000.

MISSION / VISION

Why is LEWIS different? In short: culture, reach and approach. The agency combines a strong media culture with a dedicated service ethic to deliver exactly what journalists and clients want. LEWIS delivers predictable results, tied tightly to client goals, at a predictable cost.

BEST WORKPLACE FACTORS

PERSONAL GROWTH
MY TEAM
FAIR DEAL

GRADUATE VACANCIES

Primarily PR.

500

EMPLOYEE COMMENTS

"All staff are encouraged to develop and progress right from the start."

"The entire team understands and works to the same core set of principles."

"The organisation is extremely ambitious and has plans for the future that excite me."

CONTACT DETAILS

LEWIS PR, 22nd Floor, Millbank Tower, Millbank, London SW1P 4RS
Tel: 0207 8022626 www.lewispr.com

KEY

- **Holidays:** Companies offering a minimum of 25 days annual leave
- **Pensions:** Companies offering a final salary or non-contributory/contributory pension scheme
- **Maternity:** Companies offering over Statutory Matternity Pay
- **Charity Activities:** 10% of staff undertake charitable activities during business hours
- **Childcare:** On-site nursery or vouchers
- **Gym:** On-site gym or subsidised gym memberships
- **Women:** At least 33% of senior managers are women
- **Shares:** Companies where employees are offered share options
- **Long Service:** 40% of employees with more than 5 years' service
- **Health Insurance:** Full family cover

0

To find out more about this company visit www.bestcompaniesguide.co.uk

lewissilkin

LEWIS SILKIN

UK locations	London, S.East
UK sites	2
Sector	Law
Definition	Commercial Law Firm
How owned	Partnership/LLP
Founded	1951
Turnover	£23.1m
Profit	£7.3m
Staff	227
Average age	37
Male : Female	40 : 60
Earnings £35,000+	56%

BEST COMPANIES INDEX

best company 2007

FIRST CLASS

★

2007 BCI = 673.6

2006 BCI = 655.8

WORKPLACE INSIGHTS

Lewis Silkin place significant emphasis on the personal development of their people since they are responsible for delivering outstanding service to the clients. They have a number of mechanisms and policies to encourage personal development.

The Partners provide funds and support for the Social Committee who organise a number of activities, including a Christmas dinner dance, Christmas party, drinks evenings and quiz nights.

Lewis Silkin has joined Business in the Community and are active in both Prohelp and London Cares which provide opportunities for staff to work in the local community. They provide pro-bono advice to selected organisations.

MISSION / VISION

For us, business revolves around relationships more than numbers. We believe that the fastest route to success is investing in relationships with our clients, our people and the markets we serve.

BEST WORKPLACE FACTORS

PERSONAL GROWTH
FAIR DEAL
GIVING SOMETHING BACK

GRADUATE VACANCIES

Law.

EMPLOYEE COMMENTS

"Their willingness to take time to assist you and help you learn."

"Good social activities and benefits."

"Our corporate social responsibility position has also vastly improved over the past year."

CONTACT DETAILS

Lewis Silkin, 5 Chancery Lane, Clifford's Inn, London EC4A 1BL
Tel: 020 70748000 www.lewissilkin.com

KEY

Holidays: Companies offering a minimum of 25 days annual leave

Maternity: Companies offering over Statutory Matternity Pay

Childcare: On-site nursery or vouchers

Women: At least 33% of senior managers are women

Long Service: 40% of employees with more than 5 years' service

Pensions: Companies offering a final salary or non-contributory/ contributory pension scheme

Charity Activities: 10% of staff undertake charitable activities during business hours

Gym: On-site gym or subsidised gym memberships

Shares: Companies where employees are offered share options

Health Insurance: Full family cover

To find out more about this company visit www.bestcompaniesguide.co.uk

1000

LIFESEARCH

Life SEARCH
More advice. Lower price

UK locations	National
UK sites	3
Sector	Financial - Insurance
Definition	Best Protection Advice
How owned	Private
Founded	1997
Turnover	Not disclosed
Profit	Not disclosed
Staff	123
Average age	28
Male : Female	50 : 50
Earnings £35,000+	28%

BEST COMPANIES INDEX

best company 2007

FIRST CLASS

★

2007 BCI = 693.2

<693

WORKPLACE INSIGHTS

Life search run a Leadership School once every 6 months to teach new skills to their future leaders. All the lessons are interactive and conducted by the company's existing leadership team. All of LifeSearch's senior management have been promoted internally.

There is a quarterly session at LifeSearch known as 'a Pint of Ideas', where three members of the leadership team and three members of staff from different parts of the business go off site, have a drink and debate new business ideas via relaxed conversation.

Each year LifeSearch hold an Adviser convention and a Support Staff Convention where a number of awards including Best New Recruit, Best Team Player, Best Development and Best Adviser. All of these awards are voted for by the staff and the management team.

MISSION / VISION

Do unto others as you would have them do unto you.

BEST WORKPLACE FACTORS

LEADERSHIP
WELL BEING
MY COMPANY

GRADUATE VACANCIES

No graduate vacancies have been indicated.

500

EMPLOYEE COMMENTS

"We are led by a great guy who has bags of energy, inspiration and passion for what we do."

"LifeSearch is a caring company that tries to treat people as fairly as possible."

"Feedback is encouraged and new ideas are taken on board if they are practical."

CONTACT DETAILS

LifeSearch, Epworth House, 25 City Road, London EC1Y 1AA
Tel: 020 70651000 www.lifesearch.co.uk

KEY

- **Holidays:** Companies offering a minimum of 25 days annual leave
- **Maternity:** Companies offering over Statutory Matternity Pay
- **Childcare:** On-site nursery or vouchers
- **Women:** At least 33% of senior managers are women
- **Long Service:** 40% of employees with more than 5 years' service
- **Pensions:** Companies offering a final salary or non-contributory/ contributory pension scheme
- **Charity Activities:** 10% of staff undertake charitable activities during business hours
- **Gym:** On-site gym or subsidised gym memberships
- **Shares:** Companies where employees are offered share options
- **Health Insurance:** Full family cover

0

To find out more about this company visit www.bestcompaniesguide.co.uk

LIZ EARLE COSMETICS

UK locations	London, S.East
UK sites	7
Sector	Consumer Goods
Definition	Skincare Company
How owned	Private
Founded	1995
Turnover	Not disclosed
Profit	Not disclosed
Staff	202
Average age	38
Male : Female	16 : 84
Earnings £35,000+	12%

BEST COMPANIES INDEX

best company 2007

FIRST CLASS

★

2007 BCI = 669.8

WORKPLACE INSIGHTS

Liz Earle has a team dedicated to taking action in many areas to reduce their 'environmental footprint'. They also give a percentage of their profits to selected charities each year.

Liz Earle's leadership style is personal and approachable. This means knowing who people are by name, taking time to 'walk the floor' to get to know them and to involve them and listen to their ideas.

Liz Earle Cosmetics make sure that they really look after their team so that they are motivated to keep delivering great results. Everyone is so committed to giving Liz Earle customers the very best they can and to supporting each other.

MISSION / VISION

Quality, Service and Communication Always.

BEST WORKPLACE FACTORS

GIVING SOMETHING BACK
LEADERSHIP
MY TEAM

GRADUATE VACANCIES

No graduate vacancies have been indicated.

EMPLOYEE COMMENTS

"We make a product of sound ethical and environmental grounding."

"Strong principles and beliefs of the leaders of this organisation make this a great company."

"Everyone works as a team to get things done."

CONTACT DETAILS

Liz Earle Cosmetics, Biskra Beach House, 17 St. Thomas' Street, Ryde, Isle of Wight PO33 2DL
Tel: 01983-618430 www.lizearle.com

KEY

- **Holidays:** Companies offering a minimum of 25 days annual leave
- **Maternity:** Companies offering over Statutory Matternity Pay
- **Childcare:** On-site nursery or vouchers
- **Women:** At least 33% of senior managers are women
- **Long Service:** 40% of employees with more than 5 years' service
- **Pensions:** Companies offering a final salary or non-contributory/ contributory pension scheme
- **Charity Activities:** 10% of staff undertake charitable activities during business hours
- **Gym:** On-site gym or subsidised gym memberships
- **Shares:** Companies where employees are offered share options
- **Health Insurance:** Full family cover

1000 670> 500 0 ones to watch

To find out more about this company visit www.bestcompaniesguide.co.uk

1000

MACDONALD & COMPANY

MACDONALD & COMPANY
The Property Recruitment Professionals

UK locations	National
UK sites	3
Sector	Recruitment
Definition	Property Recruitment Consultants
How owned	Public (i.e. stock market listed)
Founded	1994
Turnover	£15.7m
Profit	£2.1m
Staff	94
Average age	28
Male : Female	49 : 51
Earnings £35,000+	56%

<686

BEST COMPANIES INDEX

best company 2007

FIRST CLASS ★

2007 BCI = 686.0

2006 BCI = 733.1 (★★)

ones to watch

WORKPLACE INSIGHTS

Macdonald & Company use an external consultancy to carry out their annual employee survey. The consultancy also facilitates the development of project teams made up of employees in order to address any issues that arise and propose solutions.

500

Each employee receives a generous personal development budget and they can apply to the MD for the "experience fund" to attend a course they would like, non-work related and Macdonald & Company will pay 50% towards it.

The managers at Macdonald & Company regularly take their teams out for dinner or drinks to interact socially and encourage performance. In addition, the MD holds question and answer sessions for employees to find out more about work, the company or the future.

MISSION / VISION

To be the leading professional recruitment consultancy to the property industries worldwide.

BEST WORKPLACE FACTORS

WELL BEING
FAIR DEAL
MY MANAGER

GRADUATE VACANCIES

Recruitment Consultants.

EMPLOYEE COMMENTS

"The company and directors actually care about the employees."

"The financial incentives are extremely rewarding."

"Constantly moving the business forward and working towards making it a better place to work."

CONTACT DETAILS

Macdonald & Company, 40a Dover Street, Mayfair, London W1S 4NW
Tel: 0207 6297220 www.macdonaldandcompany.com

KEY

- **Holidays:** Companies offering a minimum of 25 days annual leave
- **Pensions:** Companies offering a final salary or non-contributory/contributory pension scheme
- **Maternity:** Companies offering over Statutory Matternity Pay
- **Charity Activities:** 10% of staff undertake charitable activities during business hours
- **Childcare:** On-site nursery or vouchers
- **Gym:** On-site gym or subsidised gym memberships
- **Women:** At least 33% of senior managers are women
- **Shares:** Companies where employees are offered share options
- **Long Service:** 40% of employees with more than 5 years' service
- **Health Insurance:** Full family cover

0

martinwardanderson
a Randstad company

MARTIN WARD ANDERSON

UK locations	National
UK sites	9
Sector	Recruitment
Definition	Professional Recruitment Specialist
How owned	Private
Founded	1988
Turnover	Not disclosed
Profit	Not disclosed
Staff	167
Average age	28
Male : Female	46 : 54
Earnings £35,000+	28%

BEST COMPANIES INDEX

best company 2007

FIRST CLASS

★

2007 BCI = 668.3

WORKPLACE INSIGHTS

Martin Ward Anderson present the Going The Extra Mile Award. Staff can either nominate themselves or be nominated by any Manager/Director. The prize is a weekend break for two to include one extra day's holiday. The value of the prize £1,000.

Managers support all day to day activities of the teams and often attend meetings with clients and candidates to show commitment from the company.

Martin Ward Anderson only hires outstanding people. People with excellent communication skills, a flair for sales and a desire to succeed and make a difference within their sector.

MISSION / VISION

Our mission is to be the financial recruitment consultancy of exclusive choice for employees, employers and jobseekers.

BEST WORKPLACE FACTORS

FAIR DEAL
MY MANAGER
MY TEAM

GRADUATE VACANCIES

Recruitment Consultants within our operational teams.

EMPLOYEE COMMENTS

"Good bonus schemes and incentives."

"Good team relationships supported by experienced managers."

"We feel as though we are working as a team to achieve our common goals."

CONTACT DETAILS

Martin Ward Anderson, 7 Savoy Court, Strand, London WC2R 0EL
Tel: 0207 2402233 www.martinwardanderson.com

KEY

- **Holidays:** Companies offering a minimum of 25 days annual leave
- **Maternity:** Companies offering over Statutory Matternity Pay
- **Childcare:** On-site nursery or vouchers
- **Women:** At least 33% of senior managers are women
- **Long Service:** 40% of employees with more than 5 years' service
- **Pensions:** Companies offering a final salary or non-contributory/ contributory pension scheme
- **Charity Activities:** 10% of staff undertake charitable activities during business hours
- **Gym:** On-site gym or subsidised gym memberships
- **Shares:** Companies where employees are offered share options
- **Health Insurance:** Full family cover

To find out more about this company visit www.bestcompaniesguide.co.uk

1000

MERRILL LYNCH

Merrill Lynch

UK locations	National
UK sites	6
Sector	Financial
Definition	Investment Bank
How owned	Public (i.e. stock market listed)
Founded	1914
Turnover	£2,459.0m
Profit	£695.0m
Staff	5548
Average age	34
Male : Female	67 : 33
Earnings £35,000+	79%

BEST COMPANIES INDEX

best company 2007

FIRST CLASS

★

2007 BCI = 688.5

<689

ones to watch

WORKPLACE INSIGHTS

Development at Merrill Lynch is aligned to the business and the individual. Delivery methods include classroom, online and virtual delivery as well as pod casts on blackberry to enable even those most mobile to take advantage of development opportunities.

Employee forums held regularly get feedback from employees on issues. These are small group sessions with members of senior management. After the event, any outstanding questions are answered and the feedback is circulated to a broader audience.

Merrill Lynch provides a range of benefits via a flexible benefits programme and numerous on site facilities and services. On site facilities range from a state of the art gym to beauty therapy to dry cleaning to our new organic food café.

500

MISSION / VISION

We are a firm with strong forward momentum in our financial performance, our prospects for growth, our client relationships & the communities where we live & work. With the interests of our employees, clients, & shareholders aligned we face the future with a clear sense of purpose & enthusiasm for the opportunities ahead.

BEST WORKPLACE FACTORS

PERSONAL GROWTH
MY COMPANY
FAIR DEAL

GRADUATE VACANCIES

Global Markets, Investment Banking, Technology, Private Clients, Risk, Research.

EMPLOYEE COMMENTS

"Colleagues are supportive, willing to help advise and assist."

"Merrill Lynch is a work place full of intelligent, motivated people."

"Staff benefits are fabulous as is the flexible working policy."

CONTACT DETAILS

Merrill Lynch, 2 King Edward Street, London EC1A 1HQ
Tel: 0207 6281000 www.ml.com

KEY

- **Holidays:** Companies offering a minimum of 25 days annual leave
- **Pensions:** Companies offering a final salary or non-contributory/ contributory pension scheme
- **Maternity:** Companies offering over Statutory Matternity Pay
- **Charity Activities:** 10% of staff undertake charitable activities during business hours
- **Childcare:** On-site nursery or vouchers
- **Gym:** On-site gym or subsidised gym memberships
- **Women:** At least 33% of senior managers are women
- **Shares:** Companies where employees are offered share options
- **Long Service:** 40% of employees with more than 5 years' service
- **Health Insurance:** Full family cover

0

To find out more about this company visit www.bestcompaniesguide.co.uk

MICHAEL PAGE INTERNATIONAL

Michael Page INTERNATIONAL

UK locations	National
UK sites	48
Sector	Recruitment
Definition	Global Recruitment Consultancy
How owned	Public (i.e. stock market listed)
Founded	1976
Turnover	£269.6m
Profit	£31.9m
Staff	1510
Average age	30
Male : Female	47 : 53
Earnings £35,000+	41%

BEST COMPANIES INDEX

best company 2007

FIRST CLASS

★

2007 BCI = 695.4

2006 BCI = 692.6 (★)

WORKPLACE INSIGHTS

Experienced managers who are seeking to be developed into directors undertake a 360 degree exercise covering a number of different competencies, detailed feedback from subordinates, peers and superiors which becomes the basis for the development plan.

Teamwork is the core to the positive culture engendered by Michael Page people which creates long friendships and the combination of striving for success and having fun.

Leaders within Michael Page International are classic 'Player Managers' in that they are all fully operational and responsible for meeting candidates, clients, transacting business and personally generating revenue as a result.

MISSION / VISION

At Michael Page we take pride in what we do, the company we work for and the people we work with. We have a passion to achieve the very best for our clients and candidates. Michael Page turn difficulty into an opportunity to demonstrate ability.

BEST WORKPLACE FACTORS

MY MANAGER
MY TEAM
LEADERSHIP

GRADUATE VACANCIES

Majority of operating disciplines.

EMPLOYEE COMMENTS

"Development is something that is really important to my manager."

"Within my specific office there is a great sense of teamwork."

"Great leadership and clear direction."

CONTACT DETAILS

Michael Page International, Page House, 1 Dashwood Lang Road, The Bourne Business Park, Addlestone, Surrey KT15 2QW
Tel: 01932 264000 www.michaelpage.co.uk

1000

695>

500

0

ones to watch

KEY

Holidays: Companies offering a minimum of 25 days annual leave
Maternity: Companies offering over Statutory Matternity Pay
Childcare: On-site nursery or vouchers
Women: At least 33% of senior managers are women
Long Service: 40% of employees with more than 5 years' service
Pensions: Companies offering a final salary or non-contributory/contributory pension scheme
Charity Activities: 10% of staff undertake charitable activities during business hours
Gym: On-site gym or subsidised gym memberships
Shares: Companies where employees are offered share options
Health Insurance: Full family cover

1000

<664

ones to watch

500

0

MICHELMORES SOLICITORS

Michelmores

UK locations	London, S.West
UK sites	3
Sector	Law
Definition	Professional Legal Services
How owned	Partnership/LLP
Founded	1885
Turnover	Not disclosed
Profit	Not disclosed
Staff	225
Average age	40
Male : Female	Not available
Earnings £35,000+	Not available

BEST COMPANIES INDEX

best company 2007

FIRST CLASS

★

2007 BCI = 663.6

WORKPLACE INSIGHTS

Michelmores provide a fully equipped gym and a qualified fitness instructor to work with all staff on all issues relating to wellness and health. All the members of the Firm are entitled to regular health check ups with dietary advice.

Each department at Michelmores has an away day during business hours, such as surfing in Cornwall, sailing or a Dartmoor adventure/picnic. An extensive social programme includes treasure hunts, family games and departmental teams in our annual charity run.

Michelmores prefer to honour team success over individual recognition. The Company Commercial department were offered a weekend in France if they met a particular target, which they did. They reward long term service, excellent contributions by individuals by way of discretionary bonus.

MISSION / VISION

Michelmores are committed to providing equal opportunity for all. As a business, we place paramount importance on service to clients. We fully recognise the importance of team working and actively encourage and support all our staff.

BEST WORKPLACE FACTORS

WELL BEING
MY TEAM
FAIR DEAL

GRADUATE VACANCIES

No graduate vacancies have been indicated.

EMPLOYEE COMMENTS

"They are caring and flexible employers."

"Everybody is friendly and helpful and there is a warm atmosphere about the place."

"The whole ethos of the firm is that you are greatly valued from junior members of staff to senior level."

CONTACT DETAILS

Michelmores Solicitors, Woodwater House, Pynes Hill, Exeter, Devon EX2 5WR
Tel: 01392 688688 www.michelmores.com

KEY

- **Holidays:** Companies offering a minimum of 25 days annual leave
- **Maternity:** Companies offering over Statutory Matternity Pay
- **Childcare:** On-site nursery or vouchers
- **Women:** At least 33% of senior managers are women
- **Long Service:** 40% of employees with more than 5 years' service
- **Pensions:** Companies offering a final salary or non-contributory/ contributory pension scheme
- **Charity Activities:** 10% of staff undertake charitable activities during business hours
- **Gym:** On-site gym or subsidised gym memberships
- **Shares:** Companies where employees are offered share options
- **Health Insurance:** Full family cover

MILLS & REEVE

MILLS & REEVE

UK locations	National
UK sites	4
Sector	Law
Definition	Legal Firm
How owned	Partnership/LLP
Founded	1880
Turnover	£49.1m
Profit	£8.0m
Staff	717
Average age	37
Male : Female	33 : 67
Earnings £35,000+	43%

BEST COMPANIES INDEX

best company 2007

FIRST CLASS

★

2007 BCI = 689.0

2006 BCI = 687.0 (★)

689>

ones to watch

WORKPLACE INSIGHTS

Employees at Mills & Reeve are supported by a highly professional in-house training & development team that trains, coaches and educates in everything employees need to know, such as business development, personal skills or legal know-how.

Wellbeing benefits available to staff include an employee assistance programme, company doctor, discounts for BUPA and local gyms. Company also looking to promote their occupational health services to provide awareness days for health issues such as smoking and blood pressure.

The leadership promotes a consultative working environment with regular two way communication via business presentations, the executive bulletin board and one-to-one meetings with all new starters or in employee forum meetings.

MISSION / VISION

Our distinctive approach to clients and staff will enable us to continue to generate profitable growth in our chosen sectors.

BEST WORKPLACE FACTORS

FAIR DEAL
WELL BEING
LEADERSHIP

GRADUATE VACANCIES

Trainee Solicitors.

EMPLOYEE COMMENTS

"The benefits package is brilliant."

"Mills & Reeve treat their employees as a valuable commodity, to be looked after and nurtured."

"The leader of this organisation is inspirational."

CONTACT DETAILS

Mills & Reeve, Francis House, 112 Hills Road, Cambridge CB2 1PH
Tel: 01223 364422 www.mills-reeve.com

KEY

- **Holidays:** Companies offering a minimum of 25 days annual leave
- **Maternity:** Companies offering over Statutory Matternity Pay
- **Childcare:** On-site nursery or vouchers
- **Women:** At least 33% of senior managers are women
- **Long Service:** 40% of employees with more than 5 years' service
- **Pensions:** Companies offering a final salary or non-contributory/contributory pension scheme
- **Charity Activities:** 10% of staff undertake charitable activities during business hours
- **Gym:** On-site gym or subsidised gym memberships
- **Shares:** Companies where employees are offered share options
- **Health Insurance:** Full family cover

MODIS INTERNATIONAL

UK locations	National
UK sites	8
Sector	Recruitment
Definition	IT Recruitment Consultancy
How owned	Partnership/LLP
Founded	1998
Turnover	£149.2m
Profit	Not disclosed
Staff	211
Average age	34
Male : Female	64 : 36
Earnings £35,000+	6%

BEST COMPANIES INDEX

best company 2007

FIRST CLASS

★

2007 BCI = 662.5

WORKPLACE INSIGHTS

There is a flexible approach from the management where enjoyment is a key criterion. Employees are expected to fully commit themselves to their roles within Modis. Those who do will flourish with the working environment and generous incentive schemes in place.

Modis have an open door policy so employees are able to input into all recent initiatives and their own personal development. Modis are open to providing any member of staff with the tools that they believe they need to do their job better or more efficiently.

Modis are flexible in working hours for staff with children and personal needs. They show employees how to make the most out of their working day so that they can leave on time.

MISSION / VISION

To be a global IT services provider supporting our clients in achieving their goals by providing superior service and top quality technical solutions.

BEST WORKPLACE FACTORS

MY MANAGER
PERSONAL GROWTH
WELL BEING

GRADUATE VACANCIES

Recruitment Consultants, IT, Engineering.

EMPLOYEE COMMENTS

"I feel I can truly be myself and am supported so much by my Manager."

"I have many opportunities to develop my career and I feel like a valued member of the team."

"We show flexibility to individual needs both with working flexibly and through personal support."

CONTACT DETAILS

Modis International, 33 Queen Street, London EC4R 1BR
Tel: 0207 0386400 www.modisintl.com

KEY

- **Holidays:** Companies offering a minimum of 25 days annual leave
- **Maternity:** Companies offering over Statutory Matternity Pay
- **Childcare:** On-site nursery or vouchers
- **Women:** At least 33% of senior managers are women
- **Long Service:** 40% of employees with more than 5 years' service
- **Pensions:** Companies offering a final salary or non-contributory/ contributory pension scheme
- **Charity Activities:** 10% of staff undertake charitable activities during business hours
- **Gym:** On-site gym or subsidised gym memberships
- **Shares:** Companies where employees are offered share options
- **Health Insurance:** Full family cover

To find out more about this company visit www.bestcompaniesguide.co.uk

MONEYQUEST (UK)

UK locations	Scotland
UK sites	2
Sector	Financial - Credit/Finance/Mortgage
Definition	Finance Intermediary
How owned	Private
Founded	1989
Turnover	£8.5m
Profit	£0.3m
Staff	156
Average age	28
Male : Female	47 : 53
Earnings £35,000+	6%

BEST COMPANIES INDEX

best company 2007

FIRST CLASS ★

2007 BCI = 662.3

2006 BCI = 666.8 (★)

662>

ones to watch

WORKPLACE INSIGHTS

Social interaction is across the board from directors to junior members of staff. moneyQuest harness a culture of equality. An open door policy is in place by their senior managers and their directors.

Team work and decision making are essential ingredients for the delivery of excellent service but personal appetites such as integrity and credibility are also necessary for enhancing the value standards and culture of the company.

Each year moneyQuest host their mQ Staff Awards Ceremony in December. This black tie event recognises employees contributions over the previous 12 months and is seen as the highlight of the company calendar.

MISSION / VISION

Building the No.1 consumer company of choice through the provision of best advice, service and products, "first time every time" without the need to charge a broker fee.

BEST WORKPLACE FACTORS

LEADERSHIP
MY TEAM
MY COMPANY

GRADUATE VACANCIES

No graduate vacancies have been indicated.

EMPLOYEE COMMENTS

"Even though the company is now huge the directors still have their feet firmly on the ground."

"There is a family feel within all teams throughout the company."

"The people and principles the company is based on."

CONTACT DETAILS

moneyQuest (UK), 123 St Vincent Street, Glasgow G2 5EA
Tel: 0141 5659380 www.moneyquest.co.uk

KEY

- **Holidays:** Companies offering a minimum of 25 days annual leave
- **Maternity:** Companies offering over Statutory Matternity Pay
- **Childcare:** On-site nursery or vouchers
- **Women:** At least 33% of senior managers are women
- **Long Service:** 40% of employees with more than 5 years' service
- **Pensions:** Companies offering a final salary or non-contributory/contributory pension scheme
- **Charity Activities:** 10% of staff undertake charitable activities during business hours
- **Gym:** On-site gym or subsidised gym memberships
- **Shares:** Companies where employees are offered share options
- **Health Insurance:** Full family cover

To find out more about this company visit www.bestcompaniesguide.co.uk

NATIONAL CHILDMINDING ASSOCIATION

ncma

UK locations	National
UK sites	19
Sector	Charity
Definition	Registered Childcare Charity
How owned	Charity
Founded	1977
Turnover	£16.6m
Profit	Not disclosed
Staff	405
Average age	43
Male : Female	5 : 95
Earnings £35,000+	10%

BEST COMPANIES INDEX

best company 2007

FIRST CLASS ★

2007 BCI = 685.2

2006 BCI = 747.6 (★★★)

1000

<685

500

0

ones to watch

WORKPLACE INSIGHTS

NCMA provide generous dependants' leave policy (up to 10 days per annum) and unpaid leave, short or long term, which can be used for extended holidays or career break reasons.

Employees are able to participate in national campaigns to raise funds during working hours. For example, Breast Cancer Awareness days.

Staff are supported by line managers who are encouraged to have regular informal staff support meetings to ensure that they are happy in their role and to provide staff with a platform on which to raise any issues they may have during a dedicated time.

MISSION / VISION

NCMA's core purpose is to promote quality home-based childcare for the benefit of children, families and communities.

BEST WORKPLACE FACTORS

FAIR DEAL
GIVING SOMETHING BACK
MY MANAGER

GRADUATE VACANCIES

No graduate vacancies have been indicated.

EMPLOYEE COMMENTS

"Holidays can be booked at short notice and the company is usually accommodating."

"The NCMA is a charity and committed to helping families and is not profit driven."

"The support of my manager and her encouragement has made it possible for me to take on a completely new role."

CONTACT DETAILS

National Childminding Association, Royal Court, 81 Tweedy Road, Bromley, Kent BR1 1TG
Tel: 0845 8800044 www.ncma.org.uk

KEY

- **Holidays:** Companies offering a minimum of 25 days annual leave
- **Maternity:** Companies offering over Statutory Matternity Pay
- **Childcare:** On-site nursery or vouchers
- **Women:** At least 33% of senior managers are women
- **Long Service:** 40% of employees with more than 5 years' service
- **Pensions:** Companies offering a final salary or non-contributory/ contributory pension scheme
- **Charity Activities:** 10% of staff undertake charitable activities during business hours
- **Gym:** On-site gym or subsidised gym memberships
- **Shares:** Companies where employees are offered share options
- **Health Insurance:** Full family cover

To find out more about this company visit www.bestcompaniesguide.co.uk

national savings & investments

NATIONAL SAVINGS & INVESTMENTS

UK locations	National
UK sites	4
Sector	Financial
Definition	Retail Financial Services
How owned	Government
Founded	1861
Turnover	£11,920.0m
Profit	£268.0m
Staff	134
Average age	38
Male : Female	48 : 52
Earnings £35,000+	53%

BEST COMPANIES INDEX

best company 2007

FIRST CLASS

★

2007 BCI = 660.3

2006 BCI = 654.5

WORKPLACE INSIGHTS

NS&I introduced the initiative for employees to have 2 days a year for charitable/voluntary work of their choice. 6 individuals have taken this opportunity up and have included working with our corporate charity and with the local community supporting outreach groups.

NS&I offer a variety of initiatives and have policies in place that support and encourage employees work life balance and wellbeing. Other initiatives include discounts on private healthcare, limited free car parking spaces and courtesy refreshments.

NS&I's culture and most importantly, its people, make it a small organisation that can provide real 'stretch and challenge' and visibly demonstrate how it values the contribution of every individual.

MISSION / VISION

Our overall aim is to help reduce the cost to the taxpayer of government borrowing now and in the future. With this in mind our single strategic objective is to provide the Government with cost-effective retail finance compared with raising funds on the wholesale market.

BEST WORKPLACE FACTORS

GIVING SOMETHING BACK
WELL BEING
MY COMPANY

GRADUATE VACANCIES

No specific graduate vacancies have been indicated.

EMPLOYEE COMMENTS

"Staff can take two days with pay to help the less advantaged or other good causes."

"Good balance between work demands and pressure people are put under."

"The culture – it is friendly, welcoming and non-political."

CONTACT DETAILS

National Savings & Investments, Charles House, 375 Kensington High Street, London W14 8SD
Tel: 0207 3489200 www.nsandi.com

KEY

- **Holidays:** Companies offering a minimum of 25 days annual leave
- **Maternity:** Companies offering over Statutory Matternity Pay
- **Childcare:** On-site nursery or vouchers
- **Women:** At least 33% of senior managers are women
- **Long Service:** 40% of employees with more than 5 years' service
- **Pensions:** Companies offering a final salary or non-contributory/ contributory pension scheme
- **Charity Activities:** 10% of staff undertake charitable activities during business hours
- **Gym:** On-site gym or subsidised gym memberships
- **Shares:** Companies where employees are offered share options
- **Health Insurance:** Full family cover

To find out more about this company visit www.bestcompaniesguide.co.uk

NOMINET

UK locations	S.East
UK sites	1
Sector	Not for Profit
Definition	Domain Name Registry
How owned	Private
Founded	1996
Turnover	Not disclosed
Profit	Not disclosed
Staff	111
Average age	35
Male : Female	47 : 53
Earnings £35,000+	26%

BEST COMPANIES INDEX

FIRST CLASS

★

2007 BCI = 668.8

2006 BCI = 634.6

WORKPLACE INSIGHTS

Nominet continually works towards maintaining a high performance culture. Performance is rewarded. Employees receive a remuneration package that provides security, choice and is also competitive in the market as demonstrated by annual market rate research.

Nominet acts on the belief that work life balance is important to employee wellbeing. The package helps all employees irrespective of their circumstances and extends certain benefits to their families.

At Nominet they are very supportive of their employees getting involved in fundraising for charities of their choice. They match employee fund-raising efforts pound for pound to a set limit and encourage participation at all levels.

MISSION / VISION

Vision: To be the leading supplier of registry services. Mission: To excel in the management of the .uk domain and the provision of registry services in response to the needs of our customers and stakeholders.

BEST WORKPLACE FACTORS

FAIR DEAL
WELL BEING
GIVING SOMETHING BACK

GRADUATE VACANCIES

No graduate vacancies have been indicated.

EMPLOYEE COMMENTS

"Good teamwork and lovely people to work with."

"Nominet cares about its employees and offers good benefits to reflect this."

"Nominet are family friendly and supportive of the individual needs of each employee."

CONTACT DETAILS

Nominet, Sandford Gate, Sandy Lane West, Oxford OX4 6LB
Tel: 01865 332361 www.nominet.org.uk

KEY

Holidays: Companies offering a minimum of 25 days annual leave
Maternity: Companies offering over Statutory Matternity Pay
Childcare: On-site nursery or vouchers
Women: At least 33% of senior managers are women
Long Service: 40% of employees with more than 5 years' service
Pensions: Companies offering a final salary or non-contributory/ contributory pension scheme
Charity Activities: 10% of staff undertake charitable activities during business hours
Gym: On-site gym or subsidised gym memberships
Shares: Companies where employees are offered share options
Health Insurance: Full family cover

To find out more about this company visit www.bestcompaniesguide.co.uk

NORTH EAST COUNCIL ON ADDICTIONS

UK locations	N.East
UK sites	19
Sector	Health
Definition	Voluntary Sector Organisation
How owned	Charity
Founded	1984
Turnover	£5.3m
Profit	£0.3m
Staff	168
Average age	42
Male : Female	27 : 73
Earnings £35,000+	1%

BEST COMPANIES INDEX

best company 2007

FIRST CLASS

★

2007 BCI = 662.6

1000

663>

ones to watch

500

0

WORKPLACE INSIGHTS

Staff attend monthly supervision meetings. This includes matters which relate to personal issues and includes discussing how outside factors are affecting work and enabling people to deal with stress.

Through the expertise & commitment of staff, they contribute to the development of various treatment initiatives & associated activities, aimed at eliminating individuals' addiction and to help them adjust to a normal life style in the community free of addictions.

Due to the wide geographical spread of work locations, NECA recognises the importance to have an appropriate framework to ensure effective communication from Headquarters together with management support to individual workers.

MISSION / VISION

To promote the prevention, recognition and treatment, of problems related to the use of alcohol, drugs related substances and gambling.

BEST WORKPLACE FACTORS

WELL BEING
GIVING SOMETHING BACK
MY MANAGER

GRADUATE VACANCIES

No graduate vacancies have been indicated.

EMPLOYEE COMMENTS

"Excellent support from others when I have felt under pressure or stressed."

"The knowledge that the end product improves the lives of our clients & therefore their neighbourhood ultimately benefits."

"I feel supported by my manager and others in the team."

CONTACT DETAILS

North East Council on Addictions, Thorne House, 88-89 West Road, Newcastle upon Tyne NE15 6PR
Tel: 0191 2983544 www.neca.co.uk

KEY

Holidays: Companies offering a minimum of 25 days annual leave
Maternity: Companies offering over Statutory Matternity Pay
Childcare: On-site nursery or vouchers
Women: At least 33% of senior managers are women
Long Service: 40% of employees with more than 5 years' service
Pensions: Companies offering a final salary or non-contributory/ contributory pension scheme
Charity Activities: 10% of staff undertake charitable activities during business hours
Gym: On-site gym or subsidised gym memberships
Shares: Companies where employees are offered share options
Health Insurance: Full family cover

To find out more about this company visit www.bestcompaniesguide.co.uk

NORTHERN COUNTIES HOUSING ASSOCIATION

UK locations	National
UK sites	16
Sector	Housing Associations
Definition	Registered Social Landlord
How owned	Not for Profit
Founded	1966
Turnover	£76.9m
Profit	£0.4m
Staff	620
Average age	42
Male : Female	34 : 66
Earnings £35,000+	7%

BEST COMPANIES INDEX

best company 2007

FIRST CLASS ★

2007 BCI = 661.0

2006 BCI = 659.0 (★)

WORKPLACE INSIGHTS

NCHA have a Charitable Trust that gives practical help to their tenants who are unable to afford to maintain a modest standard of living. Help is in the form of grants to provide basic items such as cookers, bedding, pots and pans and crockery.

Employees have a say in the range of employment benefits NCHA provide. They have a Staff Council representing employees' interests. Through these initiatives support for staff to stop smoking, free counselling services have been introduced.

NCHA help employees to take responsibility for their own development by making it an integral part of their performance management process and provide a mentoring programme for self & career development.

MISSION / VISION

Really making a difference to customers, to homes & services by achieving excellence.

BEST WORKPLACE FACTORS

GIVING SOMETHING BACK
MY COMPANY
PERSONAL GROWTH

GRADUATE VACANCIES

No graduate vacancies have been indicated.

EMPLOYEE COMMENTS

"There are lots of events organised and charity so we often give back to the community which I like."

"It is pleasing to know that by doing my job I am helping people find homes who really need it."

"The ongoing support and training provided by NCHA is excellent."

CONTACT DETAILS

Northern Counties Housing Association, Bower House, 1 Stable Street, Hollinwood, Oldham OL9 7LH
Tel: 0161 2197000 www.ncha.co.uk

KEY

Holidays: Companies offering a minimum of 25 days annual leave
Maternity: Companies offering over Statutory Matternity Pay
Childcare: On-site nursery or vouchers
Women: At least 33% of senior managers are women
Long Service: 40% of employees with more than 5 years' service
Pensions: Companies offering a final salary or non-contributory/ contributory pension scheme
Charity Activities: 10% of staff undertake charitable activities during business hours
Gym: On-site gym or subsidised gym memberships
Shares: Companies where employees are offered share options
Health Insurance: Full family cover

To find out more about this company visit www.bestcompaniesguide.co.uk

NUTRICIA

NUTRICIA

UK locations	S.West
UK sites	1
Sector	Manufacturing
Definition	Specialist Nutrition Company
How owned	Private
Founded	1997
Turnover	Not disclosed
Profit	Not disclosed
Staff	531
Average age	39.4
Male : Female	24 : 76
Earnings £35,000+	20%

BEST COMPANIES INDEX

best company 2007

FIRST CLASS

★

2007 BCI = 666.7

667>

ones to watch

WORKPLACE INSIGHTS

Nutricia are determined to create and cherish an atmosphere where their people and their businesses thrive. Trust comes first. Nutricia trust their employees to do the right thing for their consumers, their business and their community.

Supporting their community is important to Nutricia and they have strong ties with local children's organisations. They don't shout about it much but their support of local groups has been the backbone of their community involvement for the last 25 years.

Nutricia are quick to recognise and celebrate success. Being spontaneous and having some fun is what makes life worth living.

MISSION / VISION

Baby Division: To revolutionise our baby and toddler offering in order to give the best nutritional start for future generations. Clinical Division: Our purpose is to improve and extend vulnerable peoples' lives through advanced medical nutrition.

BEST WORKPLACE FACTORS

MY COMPANY
GIVING SOMETHING BACK
MY TEAM

GRADUATE VACANCIES

No graduate vacancies have been indicated.

EMPLOYEE COMMENTS

"Nutricia is a very progressive, successful company which respects, motivates and rewards employees."

"The company encourages staff to work with the community on local charity projects."

"Good teamwork and support from both line manager and the team."

CONTACT DETAILS

Nutricia Ltd, Newmarket Avenue, White Horse Business Park, Trowbridge, Wiltshire BA14 0XQ
Tel: 01225 711677

KEY

Holidays: Companies offering a minimum of 25 days annual leave
Maternity: Companies offering over Statutory Matternity Pay
Childcare: On-site nursery or vouchers
Women: At least 33% of senior managers are women
Long Service: 40% of employees with more than 5 years' service
Pensions: Companies offering a final salary or non-contributory/ contributory pension scheme
Charity Activities: 10% of staff undertake charitable activities during business hours
Gym: On-site gym or subsidised gym memberships
Shares: Companies where employees are offered share options
Health Insurance: Full family cover

To find out more about this company visit www.bestcompaniesguide.co.uk

1000

<668

ones to watch

500

0

OGILVY ADVERTISING

Ogilvy Advertising

UK locations	London
UK sites	1
Sector	Media
Definition	Advertising Agency
How owned	Partnership/LLP
Founded	1905
Turnover	Not disclosed
Profit	Not disclosed
Staff	350
Average age	34
Male : Female	51 : 49
Earnings £35,000+	42%

BEST COMPANIES INDEX

best company 2007

FIRST CLASS

★

2007 BCI = 668.4

WORKPLACE INSIGHTS

Ogilvy identify star talent potential within the Company and will invest both time and money in these individuals to enable them to fulfill their potential.

Ogilvy is a communications agency that does advertising but thinks bigger than every other agency. The people are genuinely nice and smart. Working at Ogilvy Advertising means working hard but also having a lot of laughs.

Ogilvy support and supplement departmental team building events and took the Account Management department of 90 people to Barcelona earlier this year.

MISSION / VISION

Our people vision is: To make Ogilvy a place where anyone who's any good wants to work.

BEST WORKPLACE FACTORS

MY MANAGER
MY COMPANY
MY TEAM

GRADUATE VACANCIES

Account Management and Account Planning.

EMPLOYEE COMMENTS

"I feel I can approach my seniors with any issues/problems I may have."

"The organisation has a strong set of principles and a clear vision."

"Team members work hard and support and help each other to get work done."

CONTACT DETAILS

Ogilvy Advertising, 10 Cabot Square, Canary Wharf, London E14 4QB
Tel: 0207 3453000 www.ogilvy.co.uk

KEY

Holidays: Companies offering a minimum of 25 days annual leave

Maternity: Companies offering over Statutory Maternity Pay

Childcare: On-site nursery or vouchers

Women: At least 33% of senior managers are women

Long Service: 40% of employees with more than 5 years' service

Pensions: Companies offering a final salary or non-contributory/contributory pension scheme

Charity Activities: 10% of staff undertake charitable activities during business hours

Gym: On-site gym or subsidised gym memberships

Shares: Companies where employees are offered share options

Health Insurance: Full family cover

To find out more about this company visit www.bestcompaniesguide.co.uk

PARASOL

UK locations	N.West
UK sites	1
Sector	Financial
Definition	Payroll Umbrella Company
How owned	Private
Founded	2000
Turnover	£20.2m
Profit	£0.2m
Staff	83
Average age	33
Male : Female	23 : 77
Earnings £35,000+	13%

BEST COMPANIES INDEX

best company 2007

FIRST CLASS

★

2007 BCI = 693.6

WORKPLACE INSIGHTS

Parasol has an 'Employee of the Month' award, which recognises exceptional contributions. They award an Employee of the Month Certificate, presented by the Managing Director and £50 worth of vouchers is given as a gift.

Parasol has hosted an employee Health Awareness Day, where free information was given on various health issues, such as stress and back pain. In addition, visualisation sessions were conducted, along with free massages for employees.

Managing Director of Parasol, Rob Crossland, is very hands on when required. His leadership style is democratic and he likes to get to know everyone personally. When the going gets tough, senior management become involved in day to day roles.

MISSION / VISION

To provide a totally web based payroll umbrella company facility for consultants along with pioneering web based accountancy facilities to provide competitively priced products with first class customer service.

BEST WORKPLACE FACTORS

MY COMPANY
WELL BEING
LEADERSHIP

GRADUATE VACANCIES

IT, Accounts, HR.

EMPLOYEE COMMENTS

"There is a great sense of a common goal which makes working relationships easy and enjoyable."

"The management really do care about their employees."

"Appreciation, recognition and thanks from Rob Crossland, Managing Director for how hard people work."

CONTACT DETAILS

Parasol Ltd, Parasol House, 840 Ibis Court, Centre Park, Warrington WA1 1RL
Tel: 0870 7443908 www.parasolgroup.co.uk

KEY

- **Holidays:** Companies offering a minimum of 25 days annual leave
- **Pensions:** Companies offering a final salary or non-contributory/ contributory pension scheme
- **Maternity:** Companies offering over Statutory Matternity Pay
- **Charity Activities:** 10% of staff undertake charitable activities during business hours
- **Childcare:** On-site nursery or vouchers
- **Gym:** On-site gym or subsidised gym memberships
- **Women:** At least 33% of senior managers are women
- **Shares:** Companies where employees are offered share options
- **Long Service:** 40% of employees with more than 5 years' service
- **Health Insurance:** Full family cover

To find out more about this company visit www.bestcompaniesguide.co.uk

PENTA CONSULTING

penta consulting

UK locations	S.East
UK sites	1
Sector	Recruitment
Definition	Global staffing solutions
How owned	Private
Founded	1998
Turnover	Not disclosed
Profit	Not disclosed
Staff	92
Average age	28
Male : Female	76 : 24
Earnings £35,000+	40%

BEST COMPANIES INDEX

best company 2007

FIRST CLASS ★

2007 BCI = 681.8

2006 BCI = 664.8 (★)

WORKPLACE INSIGHTS

Penta communicate regularly with all members of staff face to face, through their interactive intranet, via email and in small groups as well as holding more formal meetings, including twice yearly off-site meetings to discuss continuous improvement.

Penta have engaged a business trainer to work with the management team in order to improve leadership skills and qualities. Some of the team are also following a course of Neuro Linguistic Programming in order to improve their communication skills.

The Training and Development Coordinator is responsible for identifying and delivering individual training needs. Each quarter he undertakes an appraisal of training needs with all members of staff and then jointly creates a three month training plan.

MISSION / VISION

We will ensure that you have the right resources at the right time to maximise your business potential.

BEST WORKPLACE FACTORS

MY COMPANY
MY MANAGER
PERSONAL GROWTH

GRADUATE VACANCIES

IT Delivery Consultants, Telecommunication Delivery Consultants, Researchers.

EMPLOYEE COMMENTS

"Penta is a company that truly values its people and the contribution they make to the business."

"The management team work hard to find the right role for you."

"Penta offers great opportunities for personal and professional development."

CONTACT DETAILS

Penta Consulting Ltd, Chervil House, 28 Stafford Road, Wallington, Surrey SM6 9AA
Tel: 0208 6473999 www.pentaconsulting.com

KEY

- **Holidays:** Companies offering a minimum of 25 days annual leave
- **Maternity:** Companies offering over Statutory Matternity Pay
- **Childcare:** On-site nursery or vouchers
- **Women:** At least 33% of senior managers are women
- **Long Service:** 40% of employees with more than 5 years' service
- **Pensions:** Companies offering a final salary or non-contributory/ contributory pension scheme
- **Charity Activities:** 10% of staff undertake charitable activities during business hours
- **Gym:** On-site gym or subsidised gym memberships
- **Shares:** Companies where employees are offered share options
- **Health Insurance:** Full family cover

To find out more about this company visit www.bestcompaniesguide.co.uk

Personnel & Care Bank
Recruitment Consultants

PERSONNEL & CARE BANK

UK locations	National
UK sites	8
Sector	Recruitment
Definition	Recruitment Consultancy
How owned	Private
Founded	1992
Turnover	£15.0m
Profit	£0.4m
Staff	71
Average age	34
Male : Female	14 : 86
Earnings £35,000+	11%

BEST COMPANIES INDEX

b ★ best company 2007

FIRST CLASS

★

2007 BCI = 672.8

1000

673>

500

0

ones to watch

WORKPLACE INSIGHTS

Managers coach by working alongside staff during the course of each week motivating and demonstrating skills so staff skills improve in a practical and positive manner.

Personnel & Care Bank is such an exciting and collaborative Company with passionate people all around wanting to be the best through raising standards and exceeding the normal boundaries of service provision.

PCB invests 25 days a year into each member's personal development programme through a wide range of training, coaching and events. Every new staff member is treated individually and has a specially designed induction programme.

MISSION / VISION

Vision: To exceed expectations not just meet them.
Mission: To offer outstanding service to candidates, clients and internal staff always in every possible way.

BEST WORKPLACE FACTORS

MY MANAGER
MY COMPANY
PERSONAL GROWTH

GRADUATE VACANCIES

Recruitment Consultants, Business Development.

EMPLOYEE COMMENTS

"I find my manager is very approachable and is a great role model for me to learn from."

"It is a fair and caring company."

"Personnel & Care Bank makes every effort to invest in each individual's career progression."

CONTACT DETAILS

Personnel & Care Bank Recruitment Consultants, Wentworth Lodge, Great North Rd, Welwyn Garden City, Herts AL8 7SR
Tel: 01707 387990 www.personnelcarebank.co.uk

KEY

Holidays: Companies offering a minimum of 25 days annual leave
Maternity: Companies offering over Statutory Matternity Pay
Childcare: On-site nursery or vouchers
Women: At least 33% of senior managers are women
Long Service: 40% of employees with more than 5 years' service
Pensions: Companies offering a final salary or non-contributory/ contributory pension scheme
Charity Activities: 10% of staff undertake charitable activities during business hours
Gym: On-site gym or subsidised gym memberships
Shares: Companies where employees are offered share options
Health Insurance: Full family cover

To find out more about this company visit www.bestcompaniesguide.co.uk

1000

<660

ones to watch

500

0

PHOENIX PLC

phoenix

UK locations	S.East
UK sites	1
Sector	Media
Definition	Integrated Marketing/PR agency
How owned	Private
Founded	1989
Turnover	Not disclosed
Profit	Not disclosed
Staff	53
Average age	31
Male : Female	36 : 64
Earnings £35,000+	30%

BEST COMPANIES INDEX

best company 2007

FIRST CLASS

★

2007 BCI = 660.2

2006 BCI = 661.6 (★)

WORKPLACE INSIGHTS

Employees at Phoenix enjoy monthly "phoenix nights" out to restaurants and clubs in the local area as well as charity events and dinners, teambuilding afternoons off site and away weekends to encourage team bonding and socialising.

Every month, Phoenix employees attend a meeting - the "Chill and Fill" – which includes an update on what's happening in the business, new business and work that's been done. New employees and leavers are announced and Phoenix Person of the Month is awarded.

Two of Phoenix's directors are trainers in Stephen Covey's 7 habits of highly effective people, and all employees receive training on this during their first year, as they find this gives everyone common principles to work by and understand each other.

MISSION / VISION

To do work we're really good at (and proud of) that we are really passionate about and at which we can make a profit.

BEST WORKPLACE FACTORS

MY TEAM
MY MANAGER
PERSONAL GROWTH

GRADUATE VACANCIES

Client Services, Creative.

EMPLOYEE COMMENTS

"My team is very supportive and I feel that we all work well together."

"People truly believe in everything they do here."

"I've never experienced such a fun, supportive, beneficial and motivating place to work."

CONTACT DETAILS

Phoenix plc, The Chapel of Ideas, Reigate Road, Leatherhead, Surrey KT22 8RA
Tel: 01372 372372 www.phoenixplc.com

KEY

- **Holidays:** Companies offering a minimum of 25 days annual leave
- **Maternity:** Companies offering over Statutory Maternity Pay
- **Childcare:** On-site nursery or vouchers
- **Women:** At least 33% of senior managers are women
- **Long Service:** 40% of employees with more than 5 years' service
- **Pensions:** Companies offering a final salary or non-contributory/contributory pension scheme
- **Charity Activities:** 10% of staff undertake charitable activities during business hours
- **Gym:** On-site gym or subsidised gym memberships
- **Shares:** Companies where employees are offered share options
- **Health Insurance:** Full family cover

To find out more about this company visit www.bestcompaniesguide.co.uk

POSITIVE STEPS OLDHAM

POSITIVE STEPS OLDHAM

UK locations	N.West
UK sites	3
Sector	Charity
Definition	Public Services
How owned	Private
Founded	1997
Turnover	£8.3m
Profit	Not disclosed
Staff	182
Average age	37
Male : Female	29 : 71
Earnings £35,000+	3%

BEST COMPANIES INDEX

★ best company 2007

FIRST CLASS

★

2007 BCI = 670.9

2006 BCI = 684.5 (★)

WORKPLACE INSIGHTS

Positive Steps Oldham regularly dispose of redundant IT equipment via an organisation which rebuilds and distributes to the developing world with a guarantee of no more than 5% of waste ending up in landfill.

Positive Steps provide a range of family-friendly options and benefits such as flu jab, gym membership, subsidised Christmas party, child care vouchers, IT schemes etc.

Most staff at Positive Steps feel able to mix with people from all parts and levels of the organisation. Managers are not distant from others which makes work more effective and social activities more productive.

MISSION / VISION

To provide an integrated range of advice, information, guidance and support services, which enable all individuals living working or learning in the community of Oldham to realise their full potential in work and life.

BEST WORKPLACE FACTORS

GIVING SOMETHING BACK
WELL BEING
FAIR DEAL

GRADUATE VACANCIES

Connexions, Youth Offending Service, Drugs and Alcohol Action Team, Human Resources.

EMPLOYEE COMMENTS

"An organisation that truly makes a difference to the town."

"Positive Steps is a caring company and look after their employees."

"From senior management down to cleaning staff, everyone is respected and treated equally."

CONTACT DETAILS

Positive Steps Oldham, Medtia Place, 80 Union Street, Oldham, Lancashire OL1 1DT
Tel: 0161 6219400 www.PositiveStepsOldham.org.uk

KEY

Holidays: Companies offering a minimum of 25 days annual leave
Maternity: Companies offering over Statutory Matternity Pay
Childcare: On-site nursery or vouchers
Women: At least 33% of senior managers are women
Long Service: 40% of employees with more than 5 years' service
Pensions: Companies offering a final salary or non-contributory/ contributory pension scheme
Charity Activities: 10% of staff undertake charitable activities during business hours
Gym: On-site gym or subsidised gym memberships
Shares: Companies where employees are offered share options
Health Insurance: Full family cover

Premier Group
We Get People

PREMIER GROUP

UK locations	National
UK sites	14
Sector	Recruitment
Definition	Recruitment Consultancy
How owned	Private
Founded	1990
Turnover	Not disclosed
Profit	Not disclosed
Staff	126
Average age	31
Male : Female	28 : 72
Earnings £35,000+	30%

BEST COMPANIES INDEX

best company 2007

FIRST CLASS

★

2007 BCI = 667.7

WORKPLACE INSIGHTS

The Managing Director and members of the Management team frequently visit each of the 14 branches to engage with employees across the business. As all of Premier Group's offices are open plan, they will log onto a PC at the bank of desks where the team sit.

Premier Group offer an 'Educational Assistance Programme' which provides financial assistance to employees who wish to further their education in fields that are directly related to their current role or future roles within the business.

All new starters at Premier Group have a comprehensive Orientation within their first week which includes information on the Company, HR, Health & Safety, and general office information. Each person also attends a 2 day National Induction.

MISSION / VISION

To be recognised as the absolute market leader in ALL its markets in the core competency of GETTING THE BEST FIT BETWEEN CLIENTS AND CANDIDATES.

BEST WORKPLACE FACTORS

MY MANAGER
FAIR DEAL
PERSONAL GROWTH

GRADUATE VACANCIES

Sales - Trainee Consultants.

EMPLOYEE COMMENTS

"The manager and leaders of the company are very passionate about the organisation."

"This is truly an organisation that recognises that it exists purely because of and for its employees."

"Good opportunities for progression based on individual performance."

CONTACT DETAILS

Premier Group, 30-31 Furnival Street, London EC4A 1JQ
Tel: 0207 2695850 www.premiergroup.com

KEY

- **Holidays:** Companies offering a minimum of 25 days annual leave
- **Pensions:** Companies offering a final salary or non-contributory/contributory pension scheme
- **Maternity:** Companies offering over Statutory Matternity Pay
- **Charity Activities:** 10% of staff undertake charitable activities during business hours
- **Childcare:** On-site nursery or vouchers
- **Gym:** On-site gym or subsidised gym memberships
- **Women:** At least 33% of senior managers are women
- **Shares:** Companies where employees are offered share options
- **Long Service:** 40% of employees with more than 5 years' service
- **Health Insurance:** Full family cover

To find out more about this company visit www.bestcompaniesguide.co.uk

PRICE & MYERS CONSULTING ENGINEERS

PRICE & MYERS
CONSULTING ENGINEERS

UK locations	London, E.Midlands
UK sites	2
Sector	Engineering
Definition	Consulting Structural Engineers
How owned	Partnership/LLP
Founded	1978
Turnover	Not disclosed
Profit	Not disclosed
Staff	119
Average age	30
Male : Female	76 : 24
Earnings £35,000+	53%

BEST COMPANIES INDEX

best company 2007

FIRST CLASS

★

2007 BCI = 692.9

WORKPLACE INSIGHTS

Price & Myers support several construction industry charitable events including Little Britain Sailing Challenge, Windsor Half Marathon and Dragon Boat Race. Staff join in and have fun as well allowing the company to make charitable contributions.

Vouchers are handed out and a champagne reception held for staff for length of service milestones, when achieving further professional qualifications and when they are promoted.

Price & Myers try to do everything they can to accommodate the health and personal needs of their staff, whether this is leaving early to watch their children's school play, waiting at home for deliveries or offering support and time off during personally difficult times.

MISSION / VISION

Price & Myers recognise the importance of employees, recognising employees individuality, nurturing strengths of employees, rewarding effort as well as achievement, desire to contribute in a positive way to our built environment.

BEST WORKPLACE FACTORS

GIVING SOMETHING BACK
FAIR DEAL
WELL BEING

GRADUATE VACANCIES

Structural engineering, Sustainability, IT.

EMPLOYEE COMMENTS

"Strong emphasis on social interaction between staff and with the general industry community."

"Benefits are good and they look after their staff very well."

"The wellbeing of the employees is valued highly."

CONTACT DETAILS

Price & Myers Consulting Engineers, 30 Newman Street, London W1T 1LT
Tel: 0207 6315128 www.pricemyers.com

KEY

- **Holidays:** Companies offering a minimum of 25 days annual leave
- **Maternity:** Companies offering over Statutory Matternity Pay
- **Childcare:** On-site nursery or vouchers
- **Women:** At least 33% of senior managers are women
- **Long Service:** 40% of employees with more than 5 years' service
- **Pensions:** Companies offering a final salary or non-contributory/contributory pension scheme
- **Charity Activities:** 10% of staff undertake charitable activities during business hours
- **Gym:** On-site gym or subsidised gym memberships
- **Shares:** Companies where employees are offered share options
- **Health Insurance:** Full family cover

To find out more about this company visit www.bestcompaniesguide.co.uk

RAGDALE HALL HEALTH HYDRO

UK locations	E.Midlands
UK sites	1
Sector	Leisure
Definition	Destination Spa
How owned	Private
Founded	1990
Turnover	Not disclosed
Profit	Not disclosed
Staff	488
Average age	31
Male : Female	21 : 79
Earnings £35,000+	1%

BEST COMPANIES INDEX

best company 2007

FIRST CLASS

★

2007 BCI = 667.2

2006 BCI = 664.4 (★)

WORKPLACE INSIGHTS

All Ragdale Hall employees can access the gym and exercise classes free of charge and the health & fitness professionals are encouraged to give time and advice to employees. Free beauty and holistic treatments are also made available to employees if necessary.

The Ragdale Team Development Programme ensures everyone is trained in the skills they need to carry out their job and can develop their skills and talents to enable them to progress within Ragdale and to reach their full potential.

Managing Director Michael Isaacs has spent time working within various departments at Ragdale to understand their needs and get to know people better. He has worked as a Room Cleaner, Trainee Chef and Porter and has spent time within the Treatments Department.

MISSION / VISION

We aim to offer our guests a stay of such high quality that it exceeds their expectations.

BEST WORKPLACE FACTORS

WELL BEING
MY TEAM
LEADERSHIP

GRADUATE VACANCIES

No graduate vacancies have been indicated.

EMPLOYEE COMMENTS

"No matter how you feel there is always someone on hand to listen and care and make a difference."

"Friendly, helpful staff that work for each other as part of a team."

"The leaders of the organisation are down to earth and approachable."

CONTACT DETAILS

Ragdale Hall Health Hydro, Ragdale Village, Nr Melton Mowbray, Leicestershire LE14 3PB
Tel: 01664 434831 www.ragdalehall.co.uk

KEY

- **Holidays:** Companies offering a minimum of 25 days annual leave
- **Pensions:** Companies offering a final salary or non-contributory/ contributory pension scheme
- **Maternity:** Companies offering over Statutory Matternity Pay
- **Charity Activities:** 10% of staff undertake charitable activities during business hours
- **Childcare:** On-site nursery or vouchers
- **Gym:** On-site gym or subsidised gym memberships
- **Women:** At least 33% of senior managers are women
- **Shares:** Companies where employees are offered share options
- **Long Service:** 40% of employees with more than 5 years' service
- **Health Insurance:** Full family cover

To find out more about this company visit www.bestcompaniesguide.co.uk

RED COMMERCE

UK locations	London
UK sites	2
Sector	Recruitment
Definition	SAP Recruitment Consultancy
How owned	Private
Founded	2000
Turnover	£21.0m
Profit	Not disclosed
Staff	92
Average age	29
Male : Female	63 : 37
Earnings £35,000+	Not available

BEST COMPANIES INDEX

FIRST CLASS

★

2007 BCI = 689.1

WORKPLACE INSIGHTS

Red Commerce organised a white collar boxing event where they provided professional training for three of their consultants to take on another London-based company. The winner of each fight chose a charity to which the company donated £5,000.

All employees at Red Commerce have monthly reviews with line management to assess performance and determine development points. This ensures any development points are addressed as early and effectively as possible and that it ties in with formal training.

All tiers of management at Red Commerce, up to and including the CEO, actively operate an open door policy; employees are encouraged to seek advice from the best placed person in the organisation. This is indicative of the openness of Red Commerce.

MISSION / VISION

To become the leading niche supplier of SAP resource to our clients across Europe.

BEST WORKPLACE FACTORS

MY COMPANY
PERSONAL GROWTH
MY MANAGER

GRADUATE VACANCIES

Sales, Marketing, Finance, IT.

EMPLOYEE COMMENTS

"The passion and drive that this company embodies runs throughout the organisation."

"Great prospects for career development."

"The management team know what needs to be done to be successful and give full support to people."

CONTACT DETAILS

Red Commerce, 4th Floor Quadrant House, 80 - 82 Regent St, London W1B 5AU
Tel: 0207 9316400 www.redcommerce.com

KEY

Holidays: Companies offering a minimum of 25 days annual leave
Maternity: Companies offering over Statutory Matternity Pay
Childcare: On-site nursery or vouchers
Women: At least 33% of senior managers are women
Long Service: 40% of employees with more than 5 years' service
Pensions: Companies offering a final salary or non-contributory/ contributory pension scheme
Charity Activities: 10% of staff undertake charitable activities during business hours
Gym: On-site gym or subsidised gym memberships
Shares: Companies where employees are offered share options
Health Insurance: Full family cover

To find out more about this company visit www.bestcompaniesguide.co.uk

1000

689>

ones to watch

500

0

1000

RIPPLE GROUP

Ripple GROUP

UK locations	N.West
UK sites	2
Sector	Manufacturing
Definition	Shopfitter/POP Specialists
How owned	Private
Founded	1982
Turnover	£3.7m
Profit	£0.1m
Staff	51
Average age	40
Male : Female	78 : 22
Earnings £35,000+	6%

<687

ones to watch

BEST COMPANIES INDEX

best company 2007

FIRST CLASS

★

2007 BCI = 686.9

2006 BCI = 678.3 (★)

WORKPLACE INSIGHTS

Ripple Group focus on employee engagement which is achieved through a structured, open and supportive appraisal system and effective coaching of its team members.

Through company presentations Ripple have an open approach and share information regarding activity, performance and the vision for the future.

The senior managers, managers and supervisors at Ripple actively interact with other employees on a day to day basis.

500

MISSION / VISION

The company has a "can do" attitude & teamwork ethos providing a high quality end to end service aimed at "challenging the performance of retail space" & enhancing customers' profitability.

BEST WORKPLACE FACTORS

MY TEAM
LEADERSHIP
MY MANAGER

GRADUATE VACANCIES

Sales & Marketing.

EMPLOYEE COMMENTS

"Ripple is a good place to work for great team spirit."

"Give our Operations Director a red cape because he brings the best out of everyone."

"My Manager lets me get on with my work under my own steam."

CONTACT DETAILS

Ripple Group, Greenacres Road, Oldham, Lancs OL4 2AB
Tel: 0161 6248201 www.ripple.co.uk

KEY

Holidays: Companies offering a minimum of 25 days annual leave
Maternity: Companies offering over Statutory Matternity Pay
Childcare: On-site nursery or vouchers
Women: At least 33% of senior managers are women
Long Service: 40% of employees with more than 5 years' service
Pensions: Companies offering a final salary or non-contributory/ contributory pension scheme
Charity Activities: 10% of staff undertake charitable activities during business hours
Gym: On-site gym or subsidised gym memberships
Shares: Companies where employees are offered share options
Health Insurance: Full family cover

0

To find out more about this company visit www.bestcompaniesguide.co.uk

RM

UK locations	National
UK sites	12
Sector	IT/Internet Services
Definition	Educational ICT Solutions
How owned	Private
Founded	1973
Turnover	£262.3m
Profit	£14.6m
Staff	1406
Average age	36
Male : Female	65 : 35
Earnings £35,000+	35%

BEST COMPANIES INDEX

best company 2007

FIRST CLASS

★

2007 BCI = 668.6

2006 BCI = 657.2

669>

ones to watch

WORKPLACE INSIGHTS

RM has pioneered the development of the 'ecoquiet' low-noise, low-heat, low-energy PC that uses up to two-thirds less power than a 'standard' PC, but provides similar levels of power. Seeking to reduce their carbon impact further, by planting trees for each unit sold.

RM appreciate the importance of developing the individual beyond their current work role and continue to practice their 'Learning for Life' scheme, which encourages employees to learn a new skill that is not job related.

CEO Tim Pearson has recently introduced a personal blog, in which he shares insights about the business and seeks feedback. RM Directors hold regular lunches with employees of all grades in order to get feedback on how the employees feel.

MISSION / VISION

RM is about improving the life chances of people "worldwide" by delivering outstanding education products and services that help teachers to teach and learners to learn.

BEST WORKPLACE FACTORS

GIVING SOMETHING BACK
WELL BEING
LEADERSHIP

GRADUATE VACANCIES

Engineers, Programmers, Consultants, Business Analysts, Designers.

EMPLOYEE COMMENTS

"This company feels like a great community with goals I can believe in."

"Individuals are really empowered to make changes and develop."

"The company make you feel that you are truly capable of achieving success and makes you aim high."

CONTACT DETAILS

RM Plc, 183 Milton Park, Abingdon, Oxfordshire OX14 4SE
Tel: 08709 200200 www.rm.com

KEY

- **Holidays:** Companies offering a minimum of 25 days annual leave
- **Maternity:** Companies offering over Statutory Matternity Pay
- **Childcare:** On-site nursery or vouchers
- **Women:** At least 33% of senior managers are women
- **Long Service:** 40% of employees with more than 5 years' service
- **Pensions:** Companies offering a final salary or non-contributory/ contributory pension scheme
- **Charity Activities:** 10% of staff undertake charitable activities during business hours
- **Gym:** On-site gym or subsidised gym memberships
- **Shares:** Companies where employees are offered share options
- **Health Insurance:** Full family cover

To find out more about this company visit www.bestcompaniesguide.co.uk

1000

ones to watch

<694

500

0

roffeypark
developing people and organisations

ROFFEY PARK

UK locations	S.East
UK sites	1
Sector	Education
Definition	Executive Education & Research
How owned	Private
Founded	1967
Turnover	£5.9m
Profit	£0.3m
Staff	87
Average age	43
Male : Female	31 : 69
Earnings £35,000+	29%

BEST COMPANIES INDEX

best company 2007

FIRST CLASS

★

2007 BCI = 693.8

WORKPLACE INSIGHTS

Roffey Park provide facilities free of charge to local community organisations such as the Samaritans and Young Enterprise and they held a Family and Community Day during the Summer to which staff, their families and the local community were invited.

Roffey Park offer staff and their families free use of their leisure facilities, which include a swimming pool, Jacuzzi, sauna, steam room, gym and 40 acres of grounds. Personal gym inductions are offered to all staff to encourage a healthy lifestyle.

Employee involvement in decision-making is encouraged at Roffey Park, through projects such as contributing to corporate identity guidelines, website design, annual staff conference arrangements and redecoration designs.

MISSION / VISION

Our purpose is to work with organisations & their people to create a more enlightened way of working. To shed light on organisational issues & create clarity where there is confusion. To promote creative business enlightened working & build enlightened organisations by awakening the potential of working people.

BEST WORKPLACE FACTORS

GIVING SOMETHING BACK
WELL BEING
MY COMPANY

GRADUATE VACANCIES

No specific graduate vacancies have been indicated.

EMPLOYEE COMMENTS

"It is a values led organisation with a great history and I'm proud to be a part of it."

"People here genuinely care about each other and what we do."

"Roffey Park is an inspirational place to work."

CONTACT DETAILS

Roffey Park Institute, Forest Road, Horsham, West Sussex RH12 4TB
Tel: 01293 851644 www.roffeypark.com

KEY

Holidays: Companies offering a minimum of 25 days annual leave

Maternity: Companies offering over Statutory Matternity Pay

Childcare: On-site nursery or vouchers

Women: At least 33% of senior managers are women

Long Service: 40% of employees with more than 5 years' service

Pensions: Companies offering a final salary or non-contributory/ contributory pension scheme

Charity Activities: 10% of staff undertake charitable activities during business hours

Gym: On-site gym or subsidised gym memberships

Shares: Companies where employees are offered share options

Health Insurance: Full family cover

To find out more about this company visit www.bestcompaniesguide.co.uk

Ryder

RYDERHKS

UK locations	National
UK sites	4
Sector	Architects
Definition	Architectural practice
How owned	Private
Founded	1982
Turnover	£6.2m
Profit	£0.2m
Staff	90
Average age	34
Male : Female	76 : 24
Earnings £35,000+	32%

BEST COMPANIES INDEX

best company 2007

FIRST CLASS

★

2007 BCI = 666.1

666>

ones to watch

WORKPLACE INSIGHTS

The RyderHKS Academy enables staff at all levels of development to engage in appropriate ongoing training to maximise their potential as individuals and to ensure that the company operates at continually improving levels of performance.

RyderHKS have a number of season tickets for Newcastle United and staff are given an option to entertain friends and family at these events.

In order to encourage children to consider architecture and the wider construction industry as a serious career choice they work closely with school children to tackle these issues.

MISSION / VISION

Our aim is to continue to make the practice stronger to the benefit of our staff & clients, to endeavour to stay ahead of our competitors, to create ever better design opportunities, to further enhance our design reputation & to return healthy profits.

BEST WORKPLACE FACTORS

PERSONAL GROWTH
FAIR DEAL
GIVING SOMETHING BACK

GRADUATE VACANCIES

Architecture, Architectural Technologists, Business Support, Interior Design.

EMPLOYEE COMMENTS

"Opportunities to learn and develop my skills."

"The organisation is generally very flexible in allowing things which other companies would not."

"It focuses on one ambition to improve the environment in which we live."

CONTACT DETAILS

RyderHKS, Generator Studios, Trafalgar Street, Newcastle upon Tyne NE1 2LA
Tel: 0191 2695454 www.ryderhks.com

KEY

- **Holidays:** Companies offering a minimum of 25 days annual leave
- **Maternity:** Companies offering over Statutory Matternity Pay
- **Childcare:** On-site nursery or vouchers
- **Women:** At least 33% of senior managers are women
- **Long Service:** 40% of employees with more than 5 years' service
- **Pensions:** Companies offering a final salary or non-contributory/ contributory pension scheme
- **Charity Activities:** 10% of staff undertake charitable activities during business hours
- **Gym:** On-site gym or subsidised gym memberships
- **Shares:** Companies where employees are offered share options
- **Health Insurance:** Full family cover

To find out more about this company visit www.bestcompaniesguide.co.uk

1000

<692

500

0

SCHOOL TRENDS

UK locations	Yorkshire
UK sites	2
Sector	Consumer Goods
Definition	Supply School Services
How owned	Trust/Employee owned/Mutual
Founded	1989
Turnover	Not disclosed
Profit	Not disclosed
Staff	130
Average age	37
Male : Female	21 : 79
Earnings £35,000+	5%

BEST COMPANIES INDEX

best company 2007

FIRST CLASS

★

2007 BCI = 691.5

2006 BCI = 706.5 (★★)

WORKPLACE INSIGHTS

Volunteers from School Trends help out in a local school, to enable teaching staff time to plan and prepare lessons for the following week and to give pupils a morale boost to know that people are interested in them and want to help them to achieve their best.

School Trends employees are shareholders and vote in members of a Governing Council. All policies that impact employees including pay & benefits have to be approved by these employee representatives & they also have responsibility for appointing the MD.

The Jonesy Award, in memory of one of the company's original founders is presented annually to the person who in the view of employees most embodies the spirit of the community company philosophy of School Trends.

MISSION / VISION

It is the vision of School Trends to offer people with shared goals & values the opportunity for continued personal & professional development by cultivating a caring & rewarding environment where people feel inspired, respected & appreciated.

BEST WORKPLACE FACTORS

GIVING SOMETHING BACK
WELL BEING
MY TEAM

GRADUATE VACANCIES

No graduate vacancies have been indicated.

EMPLOYEE COMMENTS

"Our culture in driven by sound values of which everybody has had an opportunity to contribute to."

"Every employee would go that extra mile to help a fellow colleague."

"Helpful, dedicated people who work as a team."

CONTACT DETAILS

School Trends, Westfield Business Area, Carley Drive, Westfield, Sheffield S20 8NQ
Tel: 0870 1650161 www.schooltrends.co.uk

KEY

Holidays: Companies offering a minimum of 25 days annual leave

Pensions: Companies offering a final salary or non-contributory/contributory pension scheme

Maternity: Companies offering over Statutory Matternity Pay

Charity Activities: 10% of staff undertake charitable activities during business hours

Childcare: On-site nursery or vouchers

Gym: On-site gym or subsidised gym memberships

Women: At least 33% of senior managers are women

Shares: Companies where employees are offered share options

Long Service: 40% of employees with more than 5 years' service

Health Insurance: Full family cover

To find out more about this company visit www.bestcompaniesguide.co.uk

SCOTTISH UFI

we can help you fit learning into your life

UK locations	Scotland
UK sites	1
Sector	Education
Definition	NDPB learning broker
How owned	Government
Founded	1999
Turnover	Not disclosed
Profit	Not disclosed
Staff	76
Average age	Not available
Male : Female	45 : 55
Earnings £35,000+	20%

BEST COMPANIES INDEX

best company 2007

FIRST CLASS ★

2007 BCI = 674.1

2006 BCI = 633.7

674>

ones to watch

WORKPLACE INSIGHTS

learndirect Scotland is about providing learning to under-privileged areas and business.

learndirect Scotland offer a free wellbeing programme to all staff, subsidised yoga sessions and money towards eye care.

learndirect Scotland have monthly socials where staff finish work early and free drinks and food is provided by the company.

MISSION / VISION

To help individuals and small businesses across Scotland to realise their potential through learning, at a time, place, pace & style that suits their needs.

BEST WORKPLACE FACTORS

GIVING SOMETHING BACK
WELL BEING
MY TEAM

GRADUATE VACANCIES

No graduate vacancies have been indicated.

EMPLOYEE COMMENTS

"I like working for an organisation which helps people to change their lives."

"People within the company are approachable and helpful when you have a problem, be it work related or personal."

"Never before have I worked with such a dynamic team."

CONTACT DETAILS

Scottish Ufl, Alhambra House, 45 Waterloo Street, Glasgow G2 6HS
Tel: 0141 2856000 www.learndirectscotland.com

KEY

Holidays: Companies offering a minimum of 25 days annual leave

Maternity: Companies offering over Statutory Matternity Pay

Childcare: On-site nursery or vouchers

Women: At least 33% of senior managers are women

Long Service: 40% of employees with more than 5 years' service

Pensions: Companies offering a final salary or non-contributory/ contributory pension scheme

Charity Activities: 10% of staff undertake charitable activities during business hours

Gym: On-site gym or subsidised gym memberships

Shares: Companies where employees are offered share options

Health Insurance: Full family cover

SIMPLYHEALTH GROUP

simplyhealth

UK locations	National
UK sites	11
Sector	Financial - Insurance
Definition	Healthcare solutions provider
How owned	Trust/Employee owned/Mutual
Founded	1922
Turnover	£276.9m
Profit	£25.4m
Staff	1165
Average age	37
Male : Female	31 : 69
Earnings £35,000+	13%

BEST COMPANIES INDEX

best company 2007

FIRST CLASS

★

2007 BCI = 694.5

WORKPLACE INSIGHTS

Simplyheath businesses hold charitable fund and community days, allocated by a staffing committee. Fourteen volunteers helped a local school create two 'outdoor' rooms. The Group also sees its role as one of encouraging good health & fitness in the community.

At Simplyhealth they recognise that healthy, happy and contented employees provide the best service for their customers and help create a positive and enjoyable atmosphere for everyone to work in.

Simplyhealth offer study assistance to fund an individual's course of study i.e. professional qualifications, higher education and diplomas etc.

MISSION / VISION

To be the best healthcare company we can be.

BEST WORKPLACE FACTORS

GIVING SOMETHING BACK
WELL BEING
FAIR DEAL

GRADUATE VACANCIES

No graduate vacancies have been indicated.

EMPLOYEE COMMENTS

"The CSR work and charity work is excellent and does make you proud to work for the group."

"They care about their staff and try to encourage a healthy work environment."

"The fringe benefits like the pension plan and free cash plan help."

CONTACT DETAILS

Simplyhealth Group, Hambleden House, Andover, Hampshire SP10 1LQ
Tel: 01264 353211 www.simplyhealth.co.uk

KEY

- **Holidays:** Companies offering a minimum of 25 days annual leave
- **Maternity:** Companies offering over Statutory Matternity Pay
- **Childcare:** On-site nursery or vouchers
- **Women:** At least 33% of senior managers are women
- **Long Service:** 40% of employees with more than 5 years' service
- **Pensions:** Companies offering a final salary or non-contributory/ contributory pension scheme
- **Charity Activities:** 10% of staff undertake charitable activities during business hours
- **Gym:** On-site gym or subsidised gym memberships
- **Shares:** Companies where employees are offered share options
- **Health Insurance:** Full family cover

1000
<695
ones to watch
500
0

To find out more about this company visit www.bestcompaniesguide.co.uk

housing
south liverpool

SLH GROUP

UK locations	N.West
UK sites	2
Sector	Housing Associations
Definition	Registered Social Landlord
How owned	Private
Founded	1999
Turnover	£14.9m
Profit	£1.8m
Staff	86
Average age	41
Male : Female	37 : 63
Earnings £35,000+	8%

BEST COMPANIES INDEX

best company 2007

FIRST CLASS

★

2007 BCI = 690.0

2006 BCI = 621.2

WORKPLACE INSIGHTS

SLH Group has a Junior Board made up of young people between the ages of 11-18. They have among their responsibilities a Bursary Budget to allocate to deserving applicants and they have recruited people for a youth warden scheme to clean up their environment.

Staff benefit from coaching, mentoring, formal college courses, training sessions, team events, personal development training such as Springboard for Women and Navigator for men, group coaching for teams and job shadowing.

SLH Group seeks to allow staff members some time in the day when they can claw some time back for them to enjoy. This might be quiet time in the wellbeing room, a massage, some life coaching or a stress awareness session teaching relaxation techniques.

MISSION / VISION

Making South Liverpool a better place to live and work.

BEST WORKPLACE FACTORS

GIVING SOMETHING BACK
LEADERSHIP
MY TEAM

GRADUATE VACANCIES

No graduate vacancies have been indicated.

EMPLOYEE COMMENTS

"As an organisation SLH is being productive for the community and striving to do it's very best."

"The chief executive and senior management make staff feel valued."

"There's a buzz about the place & it feels as if everyone is working towards the same objectives."

CONTACT DETAILS

SLH Group, Parklands, Conleach Road, Speke, Liverpool L24 0TY
Tel: 0151 2855600 www.slhgroup.co.uk

KEY

- **Holidays:** Companies offering a minimum of 25 days annual leave
- **Maternity:** Companies offering over Statutory Matternity Pay
- **Childcare:** On-site nursery or vouchers
- **Women:** At least 33% of senior managers are women
- **Long Service:** 40% of employees with more than 5 years' service
- **Pensions:** Companies offering a final salary or non-contributory/ contributory pension scheme
- **Charity Activities:** 10% of staff undertake charitable activities during business hours
- **Gym:** On-site gym or subsidised gym memberships
- **Shares:** Companies where employees are offered share options
- **Health Insurance:** Full family cover

To find out more about this company visit www.bestcompaniesguide.co.uk

SMART GROUP RECRUITMENT SOLUTIONS

UK locations	S.West
UK sites	5
Sector	Recruitment
Definition	Recruitment Agency
How owned	Partnership/LLP
Founded	1999
Turnover	Not disclosed
Profit	Not disclosed
Staff	57
Average age	32
Male : Female	16 : 84
Earnings £35,000+	11%

BEST COMPANIES INDEX

best company 2007

FIRST CLASS

★

2007 BCI = 673.6

WORKPLACE INSIGHTS

Smart have a dedicated training manager and systems administrator and several key training providers who work with the management team to select the best training available for the employees needs.

Smart have a 360 degree approach to staff appraisals so employees and managers appraise each other at the same time. The management team are very approachable, visible and on hand at all times for all staff.

The Christmas party and Summer BBQ are all paid for by Smart Group including taxis and accommodation. In addition employees will take part in team building events and meals out to encourage team bonding.

MISSION / VISION

Delivering recruitment solutions beyond expectations, through our commitment to build long-term Win Win partnerships both with clients and candidates.

BEST WORKPLACE FACTORS

PERSONAL GROWTH
MY MANAGER
MY TEAM

GRADUATE VACANCIES

No graduate vacancies have been indicated.

EMPLOYEE COMMENTS

"Great opportunities to develop within the company."

"Hands on managers who are not afraid to pull their weight and support you."

"Friendly approachable people working towards a common goal."

CONTACT DETAILS

Smart Group Recruitment Solutions, 81a Old Christchurch Road, Bournemouth, Dorset BH1 1EW
Tel: 01202 629000 www.smartgroup.co.uk

KEY

- **Holidays:** Companies offering a minimum of 25 days annual leave
- **Maternity:** Companies offering over Statutory Maternity Pay
- **Childcare:** On-site nursery or vouchers
- **Women:** At least 33% of senior managers are women
- **Long Service:** 40% of employees with more than 5 years' service
- **Pensions:** Companies offering a final salary or non-contributory/contributory pension scheme
- **Charity Activities:** 10% of staff undertake charitable activities during business hours
- **Gym:** On-site gym or subsidised gym memberships
- **Shares:** Companies where employees are offered share options
- **Health Insurance:** Full family cover

To find out more about this company visit www.bestcompaniesguide.co.uk

Specsavers Opticians

SPECSAVERS OPTICAL SUPERSTORES

UK locations	National
UK sites	6
Sector	Retail
Definition	Optical retail support
How owned	Private
Founded	1984
Turnover	Not disclosed
Profit	Not disclosed
Staff	260
Average age	35
Male : Female	61 : 39
Earnings £35,000+	32%

BEST COMPANIES INDEX

best company 2007

FIRST CLASS

★

2007 BCI = 689.2

2006 BCI = 630.3

689>

ones to watch

WORKPLACE INSIGHTS

Specsavers provides a high energy and fun working environment for people of all ages and have a culture in which genuine talent is able to quickly rise to the top. Working for Specsavers is something to be very passionate about.

Specsavers has carried out a survey that has exposed the fact that 1 in 5 occupational drivers have not had an eye test in over 5 years. Specsavers is therefore campaigning to have the legislation tightened to help improve safety on our roads.

The leadership team in Specsavers is very accessible. All Board Directors have an open door policy, whilst the co-founder, Mary Perkins, does not even have an office.

MISSION / VISION

To be the best value opticians satisfying personal eye care needs at affordable prices, simply, clearly, and consistently.

BEST WORKPLACE FACTORS

MY COMPANY
GIVING SOMETHING BACK
LEADERSHIP

GRADUATE VACANCIES

No graduate vacancies have been indicated.

EMPLOYEE COMMENTS

"A progressive company committed to family values."

"Happy to earn money but sharing some of that with charities."

"Good communication and enthusiasm from the leader of organisation."

CONTACT DETAILS

Specsavers Optical Superstores, Melrose House, 42 Dingwall Road, Croydon CR0 2NE
Tel: 0238 0626940 www.specsavers.co.uk

KEY

Holidays: Companies offering a minimum of 25 days annual leave
Maternity: Companies offering over Statutory Matternity Pay
Childcare: On-site nursery or vouchers
Women: At least 33% of senior managers are women
Long Service: 40% of employees with more than 5 years' service
Pensions: Companies offering a final salary or non-contributory/ contributory pension scheme
Charity Activities: 10% of staff undertake charitable activities during business hours
Gym: On-site gym or subsidised gym memberships
Shares: Companies where employees are offered share options
Health Insurance: Full family cover

To find out more about this company visit www.bestcompaniesguide.co.uk

1000

SSTL

SURREY
SATELLITE TECHNOLOGY LTD

UK locations	S.East
UK sites	1
Sector	Engineering
Definition	Small Satellite Manufacturer
How owned	Private
Founded	1985
Turnover	£21.1m
Profit	£0.5m
Staff	191
Average age	34
Male : Female	83 : 17
Earnings £35,000+	52%

BEST COMPANIES INDEX

best company 2007

FIRST CLASS

★

2007 BCI = 659.6

<660

ones to watch

WORKPLACE INSIGHTS

SSTL's business is to design and build satellites used for earth mapping or disaster monitoring. The types of images captured are used for disaster mitigation, such as looking at flooding, earthquakes, deforestation, crop monitoring & other agricultural applications.

500

SSTL is truly a unique company. It is a vibrant, exciting and growing company that has managed to keep an informal family feel despite expanding to over 200 employees.

We have a Thank You scheme whereby managers can recommend employees who have made a significant contribution and are rewarded with Amazon vouchers.

MISSION / VISION

Vision: Changing the economics of space.
Mission: To be the leading supplier of small satellite missions and related services worldwide.

BEST WORKPLACE FACTORS

GIVING SOMETHING BACK
MY COMPANY
FAIR DEAL

GRADUATE VACANCIES

Spacecraft Systems / Aerospace / Satellite Communications / Mechanical Engineering.

EMPLOYEE COMMENTS

"Makes a real difference in the world, played a key part in the Tsunami & Hurricane Katrina disaster relief."

"There is a lovely family feel about the company that I have not experienced in former jobs."

"Since I have worked here I have had pay rises, bonuses & generous perks."

CONTACT DETAILS

SSTL, Tycho House, Surrey Space Centre, 20 Stephenson Road, Surrey Research Park, Guildford GU2 7YE
Tel: 01483 803803 www.sstl.co.uk

KEY

Holidays: Companies offering a minimum of 25 days annual leave

Maternity: Companies offering over Statutory Matternity Pay

Childcare: On-site nursery or vouchers

Women: At least 33% of senior managers are women

Long Service: 40% of employees with more than 5 years' service

Pensions: Companies offering a final salary or non-contributory/ contributory pension scheme

Charity Activities: 10% of staff undertake charitable activities during business hours

Gym: On-site gym or subsidised gym memberships

Shares: Companies where employees are offered share options

Health Insurance: Full family cover

0

To find out more about this company visit www.bestcompaniesguide.co.uk

STRATHCLYDE HOMES GROUP

UK locations	Scotland
UK sites	1
Sector	Property
Definition	New Homes Developers
How owned	Private
Founded	1990
Turnover	£23.7m
Profit	£1.7m
Staff	80
Average age	40
Male : Female	75 : 25
Earnings £35,000+	30%

BEST COMPANIES INDEX

best company 2007

FIRST CLASS

★

2007 BCI = 673.1

WORKPLACE INSIGHTS

The Directors & staff of Strathclyde Homes have implemented and continue to promote initiatives. Some examples of this are perfect attendance bonus, staff suggestion scheme with rewards, events committee for staff social outings, birthday and holidays.

Directors/Senior Management at Strathclyde have the responsibility of monitoring department staff workloads ensuring that no one is working excessive hours.

Strathclyde Homes involve all their staff in every aspect of the business, regularly updating them on their business plan by various lines of communication.

MISSION / VISION

It is the mission of Strathclyde Homes to aim to "exceed the expectations" of our customers, our people, and our industry supply chain. We will achieve this by the continuous evaluation of, our products, our service & the development of our people.

BEST WORKPLACE FACTORS

FAIR DEAL
WELL BEING
MY COMPANY

GRADUATE VACANCIES

No graduate vacancies have been indicated.

EMPLOYEE COMMENTS

"Directors are always looking at ideas that will benefit the staff."

"The company has a caring side that makes you feel supported."

"Strathclyde Homes is a good company as they genuinely believe employees are assets to the company."

CONTACT DETAILS

Strathclyde Homes Group, Castelcary, Glasgow G68 0DT
Tel: 01324 840909 www.strathclydehomes.com

KEY

- **Holidays:** Companies offering a minimum of 25 days annual leave
- **Maternity:** Companies offering over Statutory Matternity Pay
- **Childcare:** On-site nursery or vouchers
- **Women:** At least 33% of senior managers are women
- **Long Service:** 40% of employees with more than 5 years' service
- **Pensions:** Companies offering a final salary or non-contributory/ contributory pension scheme
- **Charity Activities:** 10% of staff undertake charitable activities during business hours
- **Gym:** On-site gym or subsidised gym memberships
- **Shares:** Companies where employees are offered share options
- **Health Insurance:** Full family cover

TAYLOR VINTERS

UK locations	E.England
UK sites	1
Sector	Law
Definition	Law Firm
How owned	Partnership/LLP
Founded	1988
Turnover	Not disclosed
Profit	Not disclosed
Staff	212
Average age	39
Male : Female	25 : 75
Earnings £35,000+	41%

BEST COMPANIES INDEX

FIRST CLASS

★

2007 BCI = 664.7

WORKPLACE INSIGHTS

Managing Partner Christine Berry publishes a weekly Monday morning email setting out news & events for the coming week, highlights of the firm's activities, client events and information about firm-wide projects.

A modular programme (STAR) is available for the support team to help them engage more directly and to increase their understanding of the business. Continuing professional development points are awarded to those who attend this training.

Taylor Vinters has a social committee, arranges regular events & organises the annual Christmas party. Events include horse racing at Newmarket, 10-pin bowling, karaoke evenings and quiz nights & each team has a designated budget from which to organise their own events.

MISSION / VISION

To be recognised as a focused and entrepreneurial business; building relationships which create value for our clients and ourselves.

BEST WORKPLACE FACTORS

LEADERSHIP
FAIR DEAL
WELL BEING

GRADUATE VACANCIES

Trainee solicitors.

EMPLOYEE COMMENTS

"Our managing partner is an inspirational leader who is always available to staff."

"They are always very rewarding, arranging social evenings, bonuses and special lunches."

"Employees' health and wellbeing are very high on the priority scale."

CONTACT DETAILS

Taylor Vinters, Merlin Place, Milton Road, Cambridge CB4 0DP
Tel: 01223 423444 www.taylorvinters.com

KEY

- **Holidays:** Companies offering a minimum of 25 days annual leave
- **Maternity:** Companies offering over Statutory Matternity Pay
- **Childcare:** On-site nursery or vouchers
- **Women:** At least 33% of senior managers are women
- **Long Service:** 40% of employees with more than 5 years' service
- **Pensions:** Companies offering a final salary or non-contributory/ contributory pension scheme
- **Charity Activities:** 10% of staff undertake charitable activities during business hours
- **Gym:** On-site gym or subsidised gym memberships
- **Shares:** Companies where employees are offered share options
- **Health Insurance:** Full family cover

To find out more about this company visit www.bestcompaniesguide.co.uk

THE AUTHENTIC FOOD COMPANY

UK locations	N.West
UK sites	3
Sector	Manufacturing
Definition	Food Manufacturing
How owned	Private
Founded	1985
Turnover	£20.0m
Profit	£1.0m
Staff	180
Average age	37
Male : Female	61 : 39
Earnings £35,000+	13%

BEST COMPANIES INDEX

best company 2007

FIRST CLASS ★

2007 BCI = 666.7

2006 BCI = 666.1 (★)

WORKPLACE INSIGHTS

At least 10% of Authentic Food's employees take part in voluntary work during the year such as cutting back the trees in a local park. In addition, staff can nominate charities to raise funds for including a school building project in India.

Authentic Food's leader, Parminder Basran hosts an annual presentation and question & answer session with all employees. In addition, he runs an employee suggestion scheme via email where employees can earn cash rewards for new and innovative ideas.

They are a family owned company who genuinely care about their employees. They show this by focusing on developing people's strengths and acknowledging their weaknesses and are working with Dr Alex Linley at the Centre for Applied Positive Psychology to improve further.

MISSION / VISION

Our recipe for success is to create international cuisine by: Being a team of caring people in a happy professional & quality conscious environment. Servicing a range of select customers with a menu of tasty meals blended with ingredients from specially chosen suppliers.

BEST WORKPLACE FACTORS

GIVING SOMETHING BACK
LEADERSHIP
WELL BEING

GRADUATE VACANCIES

QA, Marketing, IT, Sales, Production.

EMPLOYEE COMMENTS

"The company give so much back to charities and worthy causes."

"The leaders of the company have a caring and sharing attitude."

"Very flexible with people who have families."

CONTACT DETAILS

The Authentic Food Company, Sharston Green Business Park, Robeson Way, Manchester M22 4SW
Tel: 0161 4954000 www.theauthenticfoodcompany.com

KEY

- **Holidays:** Companies offering a minimum of 25 days annual leave
- **Maternity:** Companies offering over Statutory Matternity Pay
- **Childcare:** On-site nursery or vouchers
- **Women:** At least 33% of senior managers are women
- **Long Service:** 40% of employees with more than 5 years' service
- **Pensions:** Companies offering a final salary or non-contributory/contributory pension scheme
- **Charity Activities:** 10% of staff undertake charitable activities during business hours
- **Gym:** On-site gym or subsidised gym memberships
- **Shares:** Companies where employees are offered share options
- **Health Insurance:** Full family cover

To find out more about this company visit www.bestcompaniesguide.co.uk

THE INSTITUTE OF CANCER RESEARCH

The Institute of Cancer Research

UK locations	London, S.East
UK sites	3
Sector	Health
Definition	Biomedical Research Organisation
How owned	Government
Founded	1909
Turnover	Not disclosed
Profit	Not disclosed
Staff	855
Average age	39
Male : Female	41 : 59
Earnings £35,000+	30%

BEST COMPANIES INDEX

best company 2007

FIRST CLASS

★

2007 BCI = 695.0

WORKPLACE INSIGHTS

Part of the Institute's Mission is to educate and train the cancer researchers of the future. To do this, they run a scheme whereby employees spend time in local schools making science real to primary and secondary school pupils.

The Institute demonstrates its commitment to staff wellbeing by provision of a full Occupational Health Service including smoking cessation treatment, health promotion events and an Employee Assistance Programme covering staff and their families.

With the support of the Learning & Development team, every department at The Institute provides personal development programmes, spreading learning across the organisation. They also use external resources to widen the range available to staff and students.

MISSION / VISION

That people may live their lives free from the fear of cancer as a life threatening disease.

BEST WORKPLACE FACTORS

GIVING SOMETHING BACK
WELL BEING
FAIR DEAL

GRADUATE VACANCIES

Science, IT, PR/Marketing, Fundraising.

EMPLOYEE COMMENTS

"The company is working towards a common goal which is very worthwhile."

"I think that the Institute values its employees and offers us a great environment in which to work."

"Staff benefits such as holiday, sick pay, pension & sports facilities are all brilliant."

CONTACT DETAILS

The Institute of Cancer Research, 123 Old Brompton Rd, London SW7 3RP
Tel: 0207 3528133 www.icr.ac.uk

KEY

Holidays: Companies offering a minimum of 25 days annual leave
Maternity: Companies offering over Statutory Matternity Pay
Childcare: On-site nursery or vouchers
Women: At least 33% of senior managers are women
Long Service: 40% of employees with more than 5 years' service
Pensions: Companies offering a final salary or non-contributory/ contributory pension scheme
Charity Activities: 10% of staff undertake charitable activities during business hours
Gym: On-site gym or subsidised gym memberships
Shares: Companies where employees are offered share options
Health Insurance: Full family cover

To find out more about this company visit www.bestcompaniesguide.co.uk

THE MARKETING STORE

UK locations	National
UK sites	3
Sector	Media
Definition	Marketing Communications Agency
How owned	Private
Founded	1986
Turnover	Not disclosed
Profit	Not disclosed
Staff	193
Average age	34
Male : Female	47 : 53
Earnings £35,000+	51%

BEST COMPANIES INDEX

best company 2007

FIRST CLASS

★

2007 BCI = 681.1

WORKPLACE INSIGHTS

"Thanks for That" are Awards for employees nominated by colleagues who they believe are worthy. Individuals get recognition & a personalised reward up to the value of £25 (e.g. vouchers, wine, or clothes). Each recipient is announced at the bi-weekly company meeting.

Spot bonuses are in place to reward outstanding achievement. Anything up to £10k can be paid out.

The Marketing Store helps their people to be the best by providing coaching and feedback. They make people feel valued and appreciated and celebrate their achievements. Their success is based on the success of their people.

MISSION / VISION

Vision: To be the best ideas company in the world.
Mission: To harness the creativity of all our people to deliver great ideas that bring the spirit of our clients' brands to life.

BEST WORKPLACE FACTORS

MY TEAM
FAIR DEAL
MY MANAGER

GRADUATE VACANCIES

Account management, Creative, Planning.

EMPLOYEE COMMENTS

"The team atmosphere and support is amazing."

"Great perks, important things like private healthcare, bonus scheme at the end of the year."

"I feel valued by my manager."

CONTACT DETAILS

The Marketing Store, Brand Building, 14 James Street, London WC2E 8BU
Tel: 0207 7452100 www.themarketingstore.com

1000

681>

500

0

ones to watch

KEY

Holidays: Companies offering a minimum of 25 days annual leave

Maternity: Companies offering over Statutory Matternity Pay

Childcare: On-site nursery or vouchers

Women: At least 33% of senior managers are women

Long Service: 40% of employees with more than 5 years' service

Pensions: Companies offering a final salary or non-contributory/ contributory pension scheme

Charity Activities: 10% of staff undertake charitable activities during business hours

Gym: On-site gym or subsidised gym memberships

Shares: Companies where employees are offered share options

Health Insurance: Full family cover

THE RHEAD GROUP

Rhead Group
abrhead.com

UK locations	W.Midlands, N.West
UK sites	23
Sector	Construction
Definition	Quantity Surveying & Project Services
How owned	Private
Founded	1985
Turnover	£11.2m
Profit	Not disclosed
Staff	71
Average age	33
Male : Female	75 : 25
Earnings £35,000+	52%

BEST COMPANIES INDEX

best company 2007

FIRST CLASS

★

2007 BCI = 688.7

WORKPLACE INSIGHTS

Each employee at Rhead has an appraisal within which they agree a personal development plan. This may consist of further education, training, personal encouragement and can expand all facets involving their position and future positions with the company.

The leaders of Rhead are very hands on, acting as mentors to all employees. In addition, they have an open door policy whereby any employee can approach a senior member of the team or a director to discuss anything.

Rhead sponsor several charities each year and encourage employees to participate in charity causes and events. They offer sponsorship to individuals participating in charitable events.

MISSION / VISION

We seek to deliver solutions to our clients that are comprehensive, committed, and complementary.

BEST WORKPLACE FACTORS

PERSONAL GROWTH
LEADERSHIP
GIVING SOMETHING BACK

GRADUATE VACANCIES

Quantity Surveying, Risk Management, Trainee Business Manager.

EMPLOYEE COMMENTS

"There are excellent prospects within the company for staff to progress."

"All the directors and associates are approachable and hands on."

"The company's ethical policy is excellent."

CONTACT DETAILS

The Rhead Group, 9 Market Place, Warwick, Warwickshire CV34 4SA
Tel: 01926 491333 www.abrhead.com

KEY

- **Holidays:** Companies offering a minimum of 25 days annual leave
- **Maternity:** Companies offering over Statutory Matternity Pay
- **Childcare:** On-site nursery or vouchers
- **Women:** At least 33% of senior managers are women
- **Long Service:** 40% of employees with more than 5 years' service
- **Pensions:** Companies offering a final salary or non-contributory/ contributory pension scheme
- **Charity Activities:** 10% of staff undertake charitable activities during business hours
- **Gym:** On-site gym or subsidised gym memberships
- **Shares:** Companies where employees are offered share options
- **Health Insurance:** Full family cover

To find out more about this company visit www.bestcompaniesguide.co.uk

The WRIGLEY Company Ltd.

THE WRIGLEY COMPANY

UK locations	S.West
UK sites	3
Sector	Manufacturing
Definition	Confectionery Manufacture/Sales
How owned	Public (i.e. stock market listed)
Founded	1911
Turnover	£214.2m
Profit	£62.9m
Staff	673
Average age	41
Male : Female	63 : 37
Earnings £35,000+	12%

BEST COMPANIES INDEX

best company 2007

FIRST CLASS

★

2007 BCI = 683.9

684>

ones to watch

WORKPLACE INSIGHTS

At the Wrigley Company National Conference, a 'Big Picture' event was used with 38 managers facilitating tables of 8 employees to discover key leadership, business and cultural messages via a Map on their table with fun activities and interaction.

Employees at The Wrigley Company are recognised through Training Day Awards for significant contributions in Safety, Quality, Productivity & Leadership & National Conference Awards such as Company Leadership Behaviours and Flexible Working Champion.

They are committed to tackling the issue of gum litter in an effective and sustainable manner by working in partnership with key stakeholders in government & external organisations to educate people to dispose of their used gum responsibly.

MISSION / VISION

Wrigley brands woven into the fabric of everyday life around the world.

BEST WORKPLACE FACTORS

LEADERSHIP
FAIR DEAL
GIVING SOMETHING BACK

GRADUATE VACANCIES

Management, Sales, Customer Marketing.

EMPLOYEE COMMENTS

"I have great confidence in the leadership team for the long term future with exciting times ahead."

"We receive an excellent benefits package which is improving all the time."

"The company has excellent moral values."

CONTACT DETAILS

The Wrigley Company, Estover, Plymouth, Devon PL6 7PR
Tel: 01752 701107 www.wrigley.com

KEY

Holidays: Companies offering a minimum of 25 days annual leave
Maternity: Companies offering over Statutory Maternity Pay
Childcare: On-site nursery or vouchers
Women: At least 33% of senior managers are women
Long Service: 40% of employees with more than 5 years' service
Pensions: Companies offering a final salary or non-contributory/contributory pension scheme
Charity Activities: 10% of staff undertake charitable activities during business hours
Gym: On-site gym or subsidised gym memberships
Shares: Companies where employees are offered share options
Health Insurance: Full family cover

1000

THOMAS VALE CONSTRUCTION

THOMAS VALE construction

UK locations	National
UK sites	6
Sector	Construction
Definition	Regional Construction Company
How owned	Private
Founded	1992
Turnover	Not disclosed
Profit	Not disclosed
Staff	482
Average age	40.9
Male : Female	82 : 18
Earnings £35,000+	31%

<696

ones to watch

BEST COMPANIES INDEX

best company 2007

FIRST CLASS

★

2007 BCI = 695.9

WORKPLACE INSIGHTS

Employees who join the Health Plan can claim 100% of dental & optical bills and 75% of a range of other medical & complimentary treatments. The scheme covers 100% towards diagnostic appointments allowing staff to see a consultant without long waits.

Thomas Vale has developed a Succession Planning Strategy to identify & develop business leaders for the future, so they have the appropriate training and skills in preparation for their developing roles & responsibilities.

The leaders operate an open door policy, an informal relaxed culture, social events, strong management/ employee CSR Programme.

500

MISSION / VISION

Our aim is to deliver a quality construction service, on time, within budget and that meets our clients aspirations within a culture of openness and trust.

BEST WORKPLACE FACTORS

WELL BEING
PERSONAL GROWTH
LEADERSHIP

GRADUATE VACANCIES

IT, Marketing, Construction.

EMPLOYEE COMMENTS

"Thomas Vale has a great reputation for looking after its staff and personnel."

"The training is second to none and the prospects are endless."

"The leadership by the MD is inspirational for all and I like the direction in which he is taking us."

CONTACT DETAILS

Thomas Vale Construction, Lombard House, Worcester Road, Stourport on Severn, Worcestershire DY13 9BZ
Tel: 01299 827770 www.thomasvale.com

KEY

Holidays: Companies offering a minimum of 25 days annual leave
Maternity: Companies offering over Statutory Matternity Pay
Childcare: On-site nursery or vouchers
Women: At least 33% of senior managers are women
Long Service: 40% of employees with more than 5 years' service
Pensions: Companies offering a final salary or non-contributory/ contributory pension scheme
Charity Activities: 10% of staff undertake charitable activities during business hours
Gym: On-site gym or subsidised gym memberships
Shares: Companies where employees are offered share options
Health Insurance: Full family cover

0

To find out more about this company visit www.bestcompaniesguide.co.uk

THOMSON Directories™

THOMSON DIRECTORIES

UK locations	National
UK sites	14
Sector	Advertising
Definition	Directory Publishers
How owned	Private
Founded	1980
Turnover	£120.0m
Profit	£28.7m
Staff	1012
Average age	34
Male : Female	42 : 58
Earnings £35,000+	17%

BEST COMPANIES INDEX

best company 2007

FIRST CLASS

★

2007 BCI = 669.8

2006 BCI = 713.8 (★★)

WORKPLACE INSIGHTS

Thomson Directories have had wellbeing events where staff received massage treatments free of charge; free fruit and water were distributed. An NHS quit smoking team; representatives of local gyms and a back clinic were invited to speak to employees.

Outstanding Business Awards can be achieved by employees, linked to performance for sales and based on nominations which are submitted to a committee for Head Office. The prize for the 2006 winners is a 3 day luxury holiday to Cape Town.

NVQ accredited management development programmes for team leaders & advanced management skills for experienced managers are available, as well as development programmes for the shining stars of the business and interactive leadership programmes.

MISSION / VISION

Being the best, embracing change, passionate about learning and development, comfortable with risk, rewarding excellence, trying harder than everyone else, and living the values.

BEST WORKPLACE FACTORS

WELL BEING
FAIR DEAL
MY MANAGER

GRADUATE VACANCIES

No graduate vacancies have been indicated.

EMPLOYEE COMMENTS

"I have always felt that the company truly values its employees."

"Everyone has opportunity to be recognised for outstanding performance."

"The management and staff within Thomson are an integral part of the success of this organisation."

CONTACT DETAILS

Thomson Directories, Thomson House, 296 Farnborough Road, Hampshire GU14 7NU
Tel: 01252 516111 www.thomsondirectories.com

KEY

Holidays: Companies offering a minimum of 25 days annual leave

Maternity: Companies offering over Statutory Maternity Pay

Childcare: On-site nursery or vouchers

Women: At least 33% of senior managers are women

Long Service: 40% of employees with more than 5 years' service

Pensions: Companies offering a final salary or non-contributory/ contributory pension scheme

Charity Activities: 10% of staff undertake charitable activities during business hours

Gym: On-site gym or subsidised gym memberships

Shares: Companies where employees are offered share options

Health Insurance: Full family cover

To find out more about this company visit www.bestcompaniesguide.co.uk

1000
670>
ones to watch
500
0

1000

<689

500

0

ones to watch

Trimedia
Harrison Cowley

TRIMEDIA COMMUNICATIONS UK

UK locations	London, Scotland
UK sites	3
Sector	Media
Definition	Public Relations
How owned	Private
Founded	2000
Turnover	£1.6m
Profit	£0.4m
Staff	55
Average age	27
Male : Female	24 : 76
Earnings £35,000+	44%

BEST COMPANIES INDEX

best company 2007

FIRST CLASS

★

2007 BCI = 688.6

2006 BCI = 688.3 (★)

WORKPLACE INSIGHTS

Trimedia ensure they enable staff to bond outside work within their teams / other colleagues. This is done by giving teams an annual budget to spend on socialising together and by more organised events such days at the races and pub quizzes.

Trimedia is a people-driven business and they fully recognise the importance of highly-motivated and well-rewarded staff. Trimedia continuously seek to find better and more innovative ways of keeping their staff happy.

Trimedia have implemented two awards; Lone Star is a monthly individual award for outstanding performance where the winner receives a cash bonus. Dream Team is a monthly team award for outstanding performance where the winning team receives a meal out together.

MISSION / VISION

Our Employees - Support individual career growth through guidance & training. The Business - Act professionally & ethically at all times. Our Clients - Work hard to exceed expectations & deliver compelling campaigns. Work Environment - Provide a stimulating work space that engenders creativity.

BEST WORKPLACE FACTORS

MY TEAM
MY MANAGER
FAIR DEAL

GRADUATE VACANCIES

Marketing, PR.

EMPLOYEE COMMENTS

"Respect for other members of my team, we work hard & enjoy each other's company."

"I have trust in my Manager and team are respectful and inspiring."

"Good holiday package and benefits towards study."

CONTACT DETAILS

Trimedia Communications UK, Trimedia House, 29-35 Lexington Street, London W1F 9AH
Tel: 0207 0257500 www.trimediauk.com

KEY

- **Holidays:** Companies offering a minimum of 25 days annual leave
- **Maternity:** Companies offering over Statutory Maternity Pay
- **Childcare:** On-site nursery or vouchers
- **Women:** At least 33% of senior managers are women
- **Long Service:** 40% of employees with more than 5 years' service
- **Pensions:** Companies offering a final salary or non-contributory/ contributory pension scheme
- **Charity Activities:** 10% of staff undertake charitable activities during business hours
- **Gym:** On-site gym or subsidised gym memberships
- **Shares:** Companies where employees are offered share options
- **Health Insurance:** Full family cover

To find out more about this company visit www.bestcompaniesguide.co.uk

VEALE WASBROUGH

VealeWasbrough Lawyers

UK locations	S.West
UK sites	1
Sector	Law
Definition	Legal Professional Services
How owned	Partnership/LLP
Founded	1988
Turnover	£13.2m
Profit	Not disclosed
Staff	250
Average age	38
Male : Female	30 : 70
Earnings £35,000+	28%

BEST COMPANIES INDEX

best company 2007

FIRST CLASS

★

2007 BCI = 664.5

1000

665>

ones to watch

500

0

WORKPLACE INSIGHTS

Veale Wasbrough encourages employees to introduce new staff to the firm, by providing a staff introduction bonus of up to £1500 if a new solicitor is successfully employed. A new business bonus also rewards staff who bring new clients to the firm.

New employees at Veale Wasbrough receive up to 10 days of off the job training over the course of their first three years, in addition to an induction programme, with tailored training for each role, introducing them to all aspects of the firm.

Seven members of staff at Veale Wasbrough have been elected to a Consultation & Information Group, representing teams from across the firm. The topics for consultation include strategies and policies affecting the development of the firm and its staff.

MISSION / VISION

Our combination of specialist expertise, genuine team work, and client commitment, sets us apart. That's why we're confident we can deliver the best and most effective legal solutions to help people succeed.

BEST WORKPLACE FACTORS

FAIR DEAL
WELL BEING
MY MANAGER

GRADUATE VACANCIES

Law - Training Contracts for solicitors.

EMPLOYEE COMMENTS

"I feel encouraged to succeed and my hard work is continuously rewarded."

"I am made to feel like an individual rather than just another employee."

"Assistance and support is readily available and senior staff provide their time willingly."

CONTACT DETAILS

Veale Wasbrough, Orchard Court, Orchard Lane, Bristol BS1 5WS
Tel: 0117 9252020 www.vwl.co.uk

KEY

Holidays: Companies offering a minimum of 25 days annual leave

Maternity: Companies offering over Statutory Matternity Pay

Childcare: On-site nursery or vouchers

Women: At least 33% of senior managers are women

Long Service: 40% of employees with more than 5 years' service

Pensions: Companies offering a final salary or non-contributory/ contributory pension scheme

Charity Activities: 10% of staff undertake charitable activities during business hours

Gym: On-site gym or subsidised gym memberships

Shares: Companies where employees are offered share options

Health Insurance: Full family cover

1000

★ ★ ★

★ ★

★ <690

ones to watch

500

0

VODAFONE UK

vodafone

UK locations	National
UK sites	357
Sector	Communications/Telecom
Definition	Mobile Network Operator
How owned	Public (i.e. stock market listed)
Founded	1985
Turnover	£5,000.0m
Profit	£698.0m
Staff	10057
Average age	33
Male : Female	55 : 45
Earnings £35,000+	22%

BEST COMPANIES INDEX

best company 2007

FIRST CLASS

★

2007 BCI = 689.8

2006 BCI = 676.2 (★)

vodafone

WORKPLACE INSIGHTS

Line managers are willing to give employees paid time off to volunteer. In one year 3000 employees undertook voluntary charitable activity with over 950 separate fundraising events taking place that were supported by Vodafone.

Vodafone Legends is the huge recognition & reward scheme, recognising people who are making the biggest contribution to the business. Any employee can nominate someone. Nominations are assessed by a team of expert assessors from across the business & the final 100 are taken on an all expenses paid holiday.

Vodafone contributes £10 per person towards Christmas team events. Customer Management teams in Consumer & Enterprise also have annual award ceremonies to recognise excellence in Customer Management.

MISSION / VISION

Vision: We will be the communications leader in an increasingly connected world.
Mission: Helping our customers to make the most of now.

BEST WORKPLACE FACTORS

GIVING SOMETHING BACK
FAIR DEAL
MY TEAM

GRADUATE VACANCIES

No graduate vacancies have been indicated.

EMPLOYEE COMMENTS

"I enjoy working for Vodafone as I have great opportunities to be part of charity work."

"Vodafone values its staff, has excellent benefits financially and rewards us when goals have been met."

"The sense of 'Team' in not only the store but the entire company."

CONTACT DETAILS

Vodafone UK, Vodafone House, The Connection, Newbury, Berkshire RG14 2FN
Tel: 01635 686846 www.vodafone.co.uk

KEY

Holidays: Companies offering a minimum of 25 days annual leave
Maternity: Companies offering over Statutory Matternity Pay
Childcare: On-site nursery or vouchers
Women: At least 33% of senior managers are women
Long Service: 40% of employees with more than 5 years' service
Pensions: Companies offering a final salary or non-contributory/ contributory pension scheme
Charity Activities: 10% of staff undertake charitable activities during business hours
Gym: On-site gym or subsidised gym memberships
Shares: Companies where employees are offered share options
Health Insurance: Full family cover

WEST SUFFOLK COLLEGE

UK locations	E.England
UK sites	7
Sector	Education
Definition	Further Education College
How owned	Government
Founded	1993
Turnover	£21.0m
Profit	£0.8m
Staff	449
Average age	45
Male : Female	38 : 62
Earnings £35,000+	8%

BEST COMPANIES INDEX

best company 2007

FIRST CLASS

★

2007 BCI = 695.1

WORKPLACE INSIGHTS

West Suffolk College believe very firmly in supporting & developing staff and have committed to a healthy staff development budget. They run in house training sessions throughout the year and on specifically designated staff development days.

West Suffolk College support a wide range of charities throughout each academic year. They also work with a number of local community bodies such as district councils and development agencies in partnerships to help better serve the community.

Celebratory lunches are held by the college for all staff and teams of staff are thanked for extra efforts by hosting lunches, taking individuals out to lunch or sharing successes with a champagne toast.

MISSION / VISION

Vision: To be recognised locally and nationally as an outstanding College.
Mission: To provide excellent education & training which develops skills that contribute to the success of the individual & the economy.

BEST WORKPLACE FACTORS

PERSONAL GROWTH
GIVING SOMETHING BACK
MY TEAM

GRADUATE VACANCIES

No graduate vacancies have been indicated.

EMPLOYEE COMMENTS

"People are given the encouragement and the support to thrive in their different roles."

"Fundraising for local and national charities is a big part of college life."

"The people are what make the college a lovely place to work."

CONTACT DETAILS

West Suffolk College, Out Risbygate, Bury St Edmunds, Suffolk IP33 3RL
Tel: 01284 701301 www.westsuffolk.ac.uk

KEY

Holidays: Companies offering a minimum of 25 days annual leave
Maternity: Companies offering over Statutory Matternity Pay
Childcare: On-site nursery or vouchers
Women: At least 33% of senior managers are women
Long Service: 40% of employees with more than 5 years' service
Pensions: Companies offering a final salary or non-contributory/ contributory pension scheme
Charity Activities: 10% of staff undertake charitable activities during business hours
Gym: On-site gym or subsidised gym memberships
Shares: Companies where employees are offered share options
Health Insurance: Full family cover

1000 · 695> · 500 · 0 · ones to watch

WINDRUSH FROZEN FOODS

windrush

UK locations	S.East
UK sites	3
Sector	Logistics/Wholesale/Distribution
Definition	Wholesaler Distributor
How owned	Private
Founded	1995
Turnover	£23.0m
Profit	Not disclosed
Staff	75
Average age	40
Male : Female	81 : 19
Earnings £35,000+	19%

BEST COMPANIES INDEX

best company 2007

FIRST CLASS

★

2007 BCI = 670.9

<671

WORKPLACE INSIGHTS

Windrush take responsibility for their actions when dealing with customers, suppliers or each other.

The company is owned and managed by Robert Arpino and Alan Savage. They bought the company in 1995 and expanded its operations to include importation and re-distribution of frozen, chilled and ambient goods to the food-service market.

Windrush's goal is to reduce the amount of travel by an employee by 20% and thus car emissions by 20% by providing all employees at least 1 day a week as home working.

MISSION / VISION

It is our objective to always embrace the following four key words into all our personal and corporate activities: SERVICE, KNOWLEDGE, RESPONSIBILITY, QUALITY.

BEST WORKPLACE FACTORS

FAIR DEAL
LEADERSHIP
GIVING SOMETHING BACK

GRADUATE VACANCIES

Supply Chain, Finance.

EMPLOYEE COMMENTS

"They pay me an excellent salary plus great benefits."

"There is strong leadership at the top of the company."

"Small team but people really pull together to get the job done."

CONTACT DETAILS

Windrush Frozen Foods, Unit 7c Avenue 2, Station Lane Industrial Estate, Witney, Oxon OX28 4YQ
Tel: 01993 774452 www.windrushfrozen.com

KEY

Holidays: Companies offering a minimum of 25 days annual leave

Maternity: Companies offering over Statutory Matternity Pay

Childcare: On-site nursery or vouchers

Women: At least 33% of senior managers are women

Long Service: 40% of employees with more than 5 years' service

Pensions: Companies offering a final salary or non-contributory/ contributory pension scheme

Charity Activities: 10% of staff undertake charitable activities during business hours

Gym: On-site gym or subsidised gym memberships

Shares: Companies where employees are offered share options

Health Insurance: Full family cover

To find out more about this company visit www.bestcompaniesguide.co.uk

YORKSHIRE FORWARD

UK locations	Yorkshire & Humber
UK sites	5
Sector	Public
Definition	Regional Development Agency
How owned	Government
Founded	1999
Turnover	Not disclosed
Profit	Not disclosed
Staff	402
Average age	38
Male : Female	42 : 58
Earnings £35,000+	25%

BEST COMPANIES INDEX

best company 2007

FIRST CLASS

★

2007 BCI = 689.9

2006 BCI = 693.4 (★)

690>

ones to watch

WORKPLACE INSIGHTS

Yorkshire Forward has made a commitment to implement an Environmental Management System (EMS) based upon the European Eco-Management and Audit Scheme (EMAS). Amongst other things, this system monitors waste and recycling activity.

Each director at Yorkshire Forward, including the Chief Executive, take it in turns to put aside a pre-notified date and time for a Surgery, whereby staff are able to go along to their offices unannounced to discuss any topic of interest or concern to them.

Yorkshire Forward will fund employee participation in keep-fit activities such as gym membership up to an annual total of £700. In addition each member of staff is offered an annual health check including advice on healthier lifestyles.

MISSION / VISION

We want Yorkshire and Humber to be recognised as a World Leader in improving our economy by 2009.

BEST WORKPLACE FACTORS

GIVING SOMETHING BACK
MY MANAGER
WELL BEING

GRADUATE VACANCIES

All areas.

EMPLOYEE COMMENTS

"The work we do does make an enormous difference to the region, which makes me feel proud."

"My line manager takes an active & genuine interest in my personal development."

"The CEO genuinely supports flexible working and work life balance."

CONTACT DETAILS

Yorkshire Forward, Victoria House, 2 Victoria Place, Leeds LS11 5AE
Tel: 0113 3949600 www.yorkshire-forward.com

KEY

- **Holidays:** Companies offering a minimum of 25 days annual leave
- **Maternity:** Companies offering over Statutory Matternity Pay
- **Childcare:** On-site nursery or vouchers
- **Women:** At least 33% of senior managers are women
- **Long Service:** 40% of employees with more than 5 years' service
- **Pensions:** Companies offering a final salary or non-contributory/ contributory pension scheme
- **Charity Activities:** 10% of staff undertake charitable activities during business hours
- **Gym:** On-site gym or subsidised gym memberships
- **Shares:** Companies where employees are offered share options
- **Health Insurance:** Full family cover

A GOAL WITHOUT A PLAN
IS JUST A WISH
Antoine De Saint-Exupery

ONES TO WATCH

STAR GAZING

Some organisations may not have achieved star status.
But what is important is that they are reaching for the stars,
and committed to becoming great employers.
So the Ones to Watch are definitely worth keeping an eye on.

KEY

- **Holidays:** Companies offering a minimum of 25 days annual leave
- **Pensions:** Companies offering a final salary or non-contributory/contributory pension scheme
- **Maternity:** Companies offering over Statutory Maternity Pay
- **Charity Activities:** 10% of staff undertake charitable activities during business hours
- **Childcare:** On-site nursery or vouchers
- **Gym:** On-site gym or subsidised gym memberships
- **Women:** At least 33% of senior managers are women
- **Shares:** Companies where employees are offered share options
- **Long Service:** 40% of employees with more than 5 years' service
- **Health Insurance:** Full family cover

1000

ones to watch

<631

500

ADVANCE

UK locations	National
UK sites	9
Sector	Not for Profit
Definition	Registered Social Landlord
How owned	Member organisation
Founded	1974
Turnover	£19.7m
Profit	Not disclosed
Staff	456
Average age	42
Male : Female	20 : 80
Earnings £35,000+	6%

CONTACT DETAILS

Advance Housing & Support Ltd
2 Witan Way, Witney,
Oxon OX28 6FH
Tel: 01993 772885
www.advanceuk.org

MISSION / VISION

We want to provide the best housing support and employment options available to people with learning disabilities or mental health problems in order to make their lives better.

BEST WORKPLACE FACTORS

GIVING SOMETHING BACK
FAIR DEAL
PERSONAL GROWTH

BEST COMPANIES INDEX

2007 BCI = 630.5
2006 BCI = 667.0

GRADUATE VACANCIES

No graduate vacancies have been indicated.

To find out more about these companies visit www.bestcompaniesguide.co.uk

AMICUSHORIZON GROUP

UK locations	London, S.East
UK sites	82
Sector	Housing Associations
Definition	Social Housing
How owned	Trust/Employee owned/Mutual
Founded	1964
Turnover	£134.2m
Profit	£6.8m
Staff	1025
Average age	44
Male : Female	30 : 70
Earnings £35,000+	12%

CONTACT DETAILS

AmicusHorizon Group
Grosvenor House, 125 High Street,
Croydon CR0 9XP
Tel: 0208 7268600
www.amicushorizon.org.uk

MISSION / VISION

Creating neighbourhoods where people want to live through the provision of excellent homes and services.

BEST WORKPLACE FACTORS

GIVING SOMETHING BACK
FAIR DEAL
MY MANAGER

BEST COMPANIES INDEX

2007 BCI = 609.4

GRADUATE VACANCIES

Asset Management, Surveying, IT, Development.

1000
ones to watch
609>
500

KEY

- **Holidays:** Companies offering a minimum of 25 days annual leave
- **Maternity:** Companies offering over Statutory Maternity Pay
- **Childcare:** On-site nursery or vouchers
- **Women:** At least 33% of senior managers are women
- **Long Service:** 40% of employees with more than 5 years' service
- **Pensions:** Companies offering a final salary or non-contributory/contributory pension scheme
- **Charity Activities:** 10% of staff undertake charitable activities during business hours
- **Gym:** On-site gym or subsidised gym memberships
- **Shares:** Companies where employees are offered share options
- **Health Insurance:** Full family cover

ANGUS COLLEGE

UK locations	Scotland
UK sites	5
Sector	Education
Definition	Education and Training
How owned	Government
Founded	1956
Turnover	£10.2m
Profit	£0.1m
Staff	246
Average age	43
Male : Female	33 : 67
Earnings £35,000+	10%

CONTACT DETAILS

Angus College
Keptie Road, Arbroath,
Angus DD11 3EA
Tel: 01241 432600
www.angus.ac.uk

MISSION / VISION

To provide high quality education and training opportunities which are accessible beneficial relevant and innovative.

BEST WORKPLACE FACTORS

GIVING SOMETHING BACK
FAIR DEAL
PERSONAL GROWTH

BEST COMPANIES INDEX

2007 BCI = 623.4

GRADUATE VACANCIES

No graduate vacancies have been indicated.

1000
ones to watch
623>
500

ARINC

UK locations	S.East
UK sites	3
Sector	Education
Definition	Aviation Communication Solutions
How owned	Private
Founded	1997
Turnover	£25.6m
Profit	£1.7m
Staff	98
Average age	34
Male : Female	68 : 32
Earnings £35,000+	72%

CONTACT DETAILS

ARINC
Pegasus One, Pegasus Place,
Gatwick Road, Crawley West Sussex RH10 9AY
Tel: 01293 641200
www.arinc.com

MISSION / VISION

You won't believe what we can do.

BEST WORKPLACE FACTORS

GIVING SOMETHING BACK
PERSONAL GROWTH
MY MANAGER

BEST COMPANIES INDEX

2007 BCI = 610.3

GRADUATE VACANCIES

No graduate vacancies have been indicated.

1000 <610 500

ones to watch

KEY

Holidays: Companies offering a minimum of 25 days annual leave
Maternity: Companies offering over Statutory Maternity Pay
Childcare: On-site nursery or vouchers
Women: At least 33% of senior managers are women
Long Service: 40% of employees with more than 5 years' service
Pensions: Companies offering a final salary or non-contributory/ contributory pension scheme
Charity Activities: 10% of staff undertake charitable activities during business hours
Gym: On-site gym or subsidised gym memberships
Shares: Companies where employees are offered share options
Health Insurance: Full family cover

ASTER GROUP

UK locations	S.West, S.East
UK sites	5
Sector	Housing Associations
Definition	Housing and Support
How owned	Private
Founded	2005
Turnover	Not disclosed
Profit	Not disclosed
Staff	714
Average age	44
Male : Female	38 : 62
Earnings £35,000+	9%

CONTACT DETAILS

Aster Group
Sarsen Court, Horton Avenue,
Devizes, Wiltshire SN10 2AZ
Tel: 01380 726001
www.aster.org

MISSION / VISION

Vision: Passion for Excellence. Pride in Performance.
Mission: To be a leading provider of high quality affordable homes and services and to help create thriving and successful communities.

BEST WORKPLACE FACTORS

GIVING SOMETHING BACK
PERSONAL GROWTH
FAIR DEAL

BEST COMPANIES INDEX

2007 BCI = 629.5
2006 BCI = 613.1

GRADUATE VACANCIES

No graduate vacancies have been indicated.

1000 <630 500

ones to watch

To find out more about these companies visit www.bestcompaniesguide.co.uk

AVECIA

UK locations	N.West, N.East
UK sites	2
Sector	Manufacturing
Definition	Biopharmaceutical Contract Manufacturer
How owned	Private
Founded	1999
Turnover	Not disclosed
Profit	Not disclosed
Staff	501
Average age	37
Male : Female	62 : 38
Earnings £35,000+	23%

CONTACT DETAILS

Avecia
PO Box 42, Hexagon Tower,
Blackley, Manchester M9 8ZS
Tel: 0161 7211013
www.avecia.com

MISSION / VISION

To be a world-leading biologics contract manufacturing organisation providing outstanding capability and service in process development, manufacturing and related services to companies developing new biotechnology-based medicines.

BEST WORKPLACE FACTORS

GIVING SOMETHING BACK
MY TEAM
PERSONAL GROWTH

BEST COMPANIES INDEX

2007 BCI = 606.2

GRADUATE VACANCIES

R & D, Engineering, Quality, Manufacturing.

1000
606>
ones to watch
500

KEY

- **Holidays:** Companies offering a minimum of 25 days annual leave
- **Pensions:** Companies offering a final salary or non-contributory/ contributory pension scheme
- **Maternity:** Companies offering over Statutory Maternity Pay
- **Charity Activities:** 10% of staff undertake charitable activities during business hours
- **Childcare:** On-site nursery or vouchers
- **Gym:** On-site gym or subsidised gym memberships
- **Women:** At least 33% of senior managers are women
- **Shares:** Companies where employees are offered share options
- **Long Service:** 40% of employees with more than 5 years' service
- **Health Insurance:** Full family cover

AYLESWORTH FLEMING

UK locations	National
UK sites	3
Sector	Advertising
Definition	Advertising Public Relations
How owned	Private
Founded	1985
Turnover	£38.5m
Profit	£0.7m
Staff	170
Average age	30
Male : Female	42 : 58
Earnings £35,000+	28%

CONTACT DETAILS

Aylesworth Fleming Limited
Aardvark House, Poole Hill,
Bournemouth BH2 5PS
Tel: 01202 295723
www.TheAd.biz

MISSION / VISION

Innovate. Inform. Inspire.

BEST WORKPLACE FACTORS

WELL BEING
LEADERSHIP
FAIR DEAL

BEST COMPANIES INDEX

2007 BCI = 647.9

GRADUATE VACANCIES

Press & Public Relations, Graphic Design, Marketing.

1000
648>
ones to watch
500

B BRAUN MEDICAL

1000 · <658 · ones to watch · 500

UK locations	Yorks & Humber
UK sites	4
Sector	Health
Definition	Healthcare Products Distributor
How owned	Private
Founded	1998
Turnover	Not disclosed
Profit	Not disclosed
Staff	390
Average age	38
Male : Female	51 : 49
Earnings £35,000+	18%

CONTACT DETAILS

B Braun Medical
Thorncliffe Park, Sheffield S35 2PW
Tel: 0114 2259000
www.bbraun.co.uk

MISSION / VISION

We will become 1st choice for Healthcare Providers and our own people.

BEST WORKPLACE FACTORS

WELL BEING
GIVING SOMETHING BACK
MY COMPANY

BEST COMPANIES INDEX

2007 BCI = 658.3
2006 BCI = 663.0

GRADUATE VACANCIES

Sales & Marketing, HR, Finance & IT

KEY

- **Holidays:** Companies offering a minimum of 25 days annual leave
- **Pensions:** Companies offering a final salary or non-contributory/ contributory pension scheme
- **Maternity:** Companies offering over Statutory Maternity Pay
- **Charity Activities:** 10% of staff undertake charitable activities during business hours
- **Childcare:** On-site nursery or vouchers
- **Gym:** On-site gym or subsidised gym memberships
- **Women:** At least 33% of senior managers are women
- **Shares:** Companies where employees are offered share options
- **Long Service:** 40% of employees with more than 5 years' service
- **Health Insurance:** Full family cover

BAXTERSTOREY

1000 · <617 · ones to watch · 500

UK locations	National
UK sites	300
Sector	Hospitality
Definition	Business Catering Specialists
How owned	Private
Founded	2004
Turnover	Not disclosed
Profit	Not disclosed
Staff	2638
Average age	36
Male : Female	46 : 54
Earnings £35,000+	3%

CONTACT DETAILS

BaxterStorey
The Waterfront, 300 Thames Valley Park Drive,
Reading, Berkshire RG6 1PT
Tel: 0118 9356700
www.baxterstorey.com

MISSION / VISION

Vision: To be the best contract caterer ever by creating a dynamic environment
Mission: To be the best food service provider ever.

BEST WORKPLACE FACTORS

WELL BEING
LEADERSHIP
MY MANAGER

BEST COMPANIES INDEX

2007 BCI = 617.0

GRADUATE VACANCIES

Catering, Operational, Management.

To find out more about these companies visit www.bestcompaniesguide.co.uk

BCP

UK locations	London, S.East
UK sites	2
Sector	Travel
Definition	Parking Booking Agent
How owned	Private
Founded	1978
Turnover	Not disclosed
Profit	Not disclosed
Staff	105
Average age	30
Male : Female	31 : 69
Earnings £35,000+	5%

CONTACT DETAILS

BCP
Floor 4, Astral Towers,
Betts Way, Crawley RH10 9XA
Tel: 01293 594617
www.parkbcp.co.uk

MISSION / VISION

Delivering results with passion, professionalism, integrity and fun.

BEST WORKPLACE FACTORS

MY MANAGER
LEADERSHIP
WELL BEING

BEST COMPANIES INDEX

2007 BCI = 622.4

GRADUATE VACANCIES

ICT, Marketing, Commercial & HR.

1000
ones to watch
622>
500

KEY

- **Holidays:** Companies offering a minimum of 25 days annual leave
- **Pensions:** Companies offering a final salary or non-contributory/ contributory pension scheme
- **Maternity:** Companies offering over Statutory Maternity Pay
- **Charity Activities:** 10% of staff undertake charitable activities during business hours
- **Childcare:** On-site nursery or vouchers
- **Gym:** On-site gym or subsidised gym memberships
- **Women:** At least 33% of senior managers are women
- **Shares:** Companies where employees are offered share options
- **Long Service:** 40% of employees with more than 5 years' service
- **Health Insurance:** Full family cover

BETFAIR

UK locations	London, E.England
UK sites	2
Sector	Leisure
Definition	Online Betting Exchange
How owned	Private
Founded	2000
Turnover	Not disclosed
Profit	Not disclosed
Staff	937
Average age	32
Male : Female	82 : 18
Earnings £35,000+	43%

CONTACT DETAILS

Betfair
Waterfront, Hammersmith Embankment,
Winslow Road, London W6 9HP
Tel: 0208 8348000
www.betfaircorporate.com

MISSION / VISION

Our aim is simple: we want to be the unassailable choice of the punter by providing the best value, service and protection.

BEST WORKPLACE FACTORS

MY COMPANY
LEADERSHIP
FAIR DEAL

BEST COMPANIES INDEX

2007 BCI = 635.5

GRADUATE VACANCIES

ICT, Marketing, Risk/Fraud, Finance, Communications.

1000
ones to watch
636>
500

BHSF GROUP

1000

UK locations	W.Midlands
UK sites	1
Sector	Financial - Insurance
Definition	Health Insurance
How owned	Private
Founded	1873
Turnover	£27.8m
Profit	£4.2m
Staff	123
Average age	40
Male : Female	41 : 59
Earnings £35,000+	8%

<658

ones to watch

500

CONTACT DETAILS

BHSF Group
Gamgee House, 2 Darnley Road,
Birmingham B16 8TE
Tel: 0121 4543601
www.bhsf.co.uk

MISSION / VISION

Maximise customer satisfaction as to the value and quality of our products and the standard of service we provide. Create an environment that encourages each member of our team to realise their full potential. Grow the business.

BEST WORKPLACE FACTORS

GIVING SOMETHING BACK
WELL BEING
LEADERSHIP

BEST COMPANIES INDEX

2007 BCI = 658.1
2006 BCI = 615.0

GRADUATE VACANCIES

Sales & Marketing, Customer Service, Finance, IT & HR.

KEY

- **Holidays:** Companies offering a minimum of 25 days annual leave
- **Pensions:** Companies offering a final salary or non-contributory/ contributory pension scheme
- **Maternity:** Companies offering over Statutory Maternity Pay
- **Charity Activities:** 10% of staff undertake charitable activities during business hours
- **Childcare:** On-site nursery or vouchers
- **Gym:** On-site gym or subsidised gym memberships
- **Women:** At least 33% of senior managers are women
- **Shares:** Companies where employees are offered share options
- **Long Service:** 40% of employees with more than 5 years' service
- **Health Insurance:** Full family cover

BLUECARE SOCIAL CARE

1000

UK locations	London
UK sites	1
Sector	Recruitment
Definition	Recruiting social care professionals
How owned	Not available
Founded	Not available
Turnover	Not disclosed
Profit	Not disclosed
Staff	73
Average age	Not disclosed
Male : Female	Not disclosed
Earnings £35,000+	Not disclosed

ones to watch

<624

500

CONTACT DETAILS

Bluecare Social Care
61 Southwark Street, London Bridge SE1 0HL
Tel: 0207 8618955
www.social.bluegroupinternational.com

MISSION / VISION

Bluecare places and manages qualified social workers and social care professionals within the public, private, and voluntary care sectors throughout the UK. We aim to partner our candidates from graduation through to senior professional managerial status.

BEST WORKPLACE FACTORS

FAIR DEAL
MY TEAM
MY MANAGER

BEST COMPANIES INDEX

2007 BCI = 623.8

GRADUATE VACANCIES

No graduate vacancies have been indicated.

BUSINESS ENVIRONMENT

UK locations	National
UK sites	10
Sector	Business Services
Definition	Serviced Offices
How owned	Private
Founded	1994
Turnover	Not disclosed
Profit	Not disclosed
Staff	71
Average age	27
Male : Female	39 : 61
Earnings £35,000+	14%

CONTACT DETAILS

Business Environment
Groveland Court, London EC4M 9EH
Tel: 020 79596000
www.beoffices.com

MISSION / VISION

Vision: Together we are building the Business Lifestyle that everyone wants.

BEST WORKPLACE FACTORS

WELL BEING
GIVING SOMETHING BACK
MY MANAGER

BEST COMPANIES INDEX

2007 BCI = 623.6

GRADUATE VACANCIES

Sales & Marketing, Estates Management, Accounting.

1000

ones to watch

624>

500

KEY

- **Holidays:** Companies offering a minimum of 25 days annual leave
- **Pensions:** Companies offering a final salary or non-contributory/ contributory pension scheme
- **Maternity:** Companies offering over Statutory Maternity Pay
- **Charity Activities:** 10% of staff undertake charitable activities during business hours
- **Childcare:** On-site nursery or vouchers
- **Gym:** On-site gym or subsidised gym memberships
- **Women:** At least 33% of senior managers are women
- **Shares:** Companies where employees are offered share options
- **Long Service:** 40% of employees with more than 5 years' service
- **Health Insurance:** Full family cover

CAMPBELL HOOPER SOLICITORS

UK locations	London
UK sites	1
Sector	Law
Definition	Private Practice Solicitors
How owned	Partnership/LLP
Founded	2006
Turnover	Not disclosed
Profit	Not disclosed
Staff	115
Average age	38
Male : Female	39 : 61
Earnings £35,000+	48%

CONTACT DETAILS

Campbell Hooper Solicitors
35 Old Queen Street, London SW1H 9JD
Tel: 0207 2229070
www.campbellhooper.com

MISSION / VISION

Creating solutions is our business. We will achieve our mission through: - Being available and accessible - Listening - Understanding your needs and tailoring the solution for you - Giving clear advice - Being creative - Working with a constructive attitude.

BEST WORKPLACE FACTORS

PERSONAL GROWTH
MY MANAGER
FAIR DEAL

BEST COMPANIES INDEX

2007 BCI = 641.5

GRADUATE VACANCIES

Trainee Solicitors.

1000

ones to watch

642>

500

1000

CDI ANDERSELITE

UK locations	National
UK sites	13
Sector	Recruitment
Definition	Technical Staffing Solutions
How owned	Partnership/LLP
Founded	1983
Turnover	£101.0m
Profit	Not disclosed
Staff	384
Average age	29
Male : Female	53 : 47
Earnings £35,000+	8%

ones to watch

<621

CONTACT DETAILS

CDI AndersElite
Capital House, Houndwell Place,
Southampton SO14 1HU
Tel: 0232 0223511
www.anderselite.com

500

MISSION / VISION

Provide technical, IT and permanent placement professionals to the built environment, rail, public sector, and IT services markets by leveraging empowered professionals and technology.

BEST WORKPLACE FACTORS

WELL BEING
PERSONAL GROWTH
MY TEAM

BEST COMPANIES INDEX

2007 BCI = 620.7

GRADUATE VACANCIES

No graduate vacancies have been indicated.

KEY

- **Holidays:** Companies offering a minimum of 25 days annual leave
- **Pensions:** Companies offering a final salary or non-contributory/ contributory pension scheme
- **Maternity:** Companies offering over Statutory Maternity Pay
- **Charity Activities:** 10% of staff undertake charitable activities during business hours
- **Childcare:** On-site nursery or vouchers
- **Gym:** On-site gym or subsidised gym memberships
- **Women:** At least 33% of senior managers are women
- **Shares:** Companies where employees are offered share options
- **Long Service:** 40% of employees with more than 5 years' service
- **Health Insurance:** Full family cover

1000

CENTRE FOR HIGH PERFORMANCE DEVELOPMENT

UK locations	London
UK sites	1
Sector	Consulting
Definition	Leadership Development Consultancy
How owned	Private
Founded	1996
Turnover	Not disclosed
Profit	Not disclosed
Staff	67
Average age	32
Male : Female	37 : 63
Earnings £35,000+	37%

ones to watch

<644

CONTACT DETAILS

Centre for High Performance Development
Suites 3-5, Swan Court,
9 Tanner Street, London SE3 7UQ
Tel: 0870 7700111
www.chpd.com

500

MISSION / VISION

Vision: For the Top 100 companies to have CHPD leaders.
Mission: Global leaders in developing high performance leaders.

BEST WORKPLACE FACTORS

PERSONAL GROWTH
MY COMPANY
LEADERSHIP

BEST COMPANIES INDEX

2007 BCI = 643.7
2006 BCI = 732.4

GRADUATE VACANCIES

Business Development, Client Sevices, IT and Consultancy

To find out more about these companies visit www.bestcompaniesguide.co.uk

CHEAPFLIGHTS.CO.UK

UK locations	London
UK sites	2
Sector	Media
Definition	Travel Deals Directory
How owned	Private
Founded	1996
Turnover	Not disclosed
Profit	Not disclosed
Staff	54
Average age	33
Male : Female	63 : 37
Earnings £35,000+	70%

CONTACT DETAILS

Cheapflights.co.uk
49 Marylebone High Street,
London W1U 5HJ
Tel: 020 74673552
www.cheapflights.co.uk

MISSION / VISION

To be the best source of flights and travel deals.

BEST WORKPLACE FACTORS

FAIR DEAL
WELL BEING
MY MANAGER

BEST COMPANIES INDEX

2007 BCI = 611.7

GRADUATE VACANCIES

No graduate vacancies have been indicated.

1000 ★ ★ ★ ★ ★ ★ ones to watch 612> 500

KEY

- **Holidays:** Companies offering a minimum of 25 days annual leave
- **Pensions:** Companies offering a final salary or non-contributory/contributory pension scheme
- **Maternity:** Companies offering over Statutory Maternity Pay
- **Charity Activities:** 10% of staff undertake charitable activities during business hours
- **Childcare:** On-site nursery or vouchers
- **Gym:** On-site gym or subsidised gym memberships
- **Women:** At least 33% of senior managers are women
- **Shares:** Companies where employees are offered share options
- **Long Service:** 40% of employees with more than 5 years' service
- **Health Insurance:** Full family cover

CHESS

UK locations	N.West
UK sites	1
Sector	Communications/Telecom
Definition	Business Telecoms Provider
How owned	Private
Founded	1993
Turnover	£17.6m
Profit	£0.3m
Staff	79
Average age	32
Male : Female	49 : 51
Earnings £35,000+	14%

CONTACT DETAILS

Chess Plc
Bridgford House, Heyes Lane,
Alderley Edge, Cheshire SK9 7JP
Tel: 0845 6127000
www.chesstelecom.com

MISSION / VISION

Vision: To be recognised as 'the choice' for business voice and data solutions.
Mission: Not to be known as the best of the best but as the only ones who do what we do.

BEST WORKPLACE FACTORS

LEADERSHIP
MY TEAM
PERSONAL GROWTH

BEST COMPANIES INDEX

2007 BCI = 647.2
2006 BCI = 665.0

GRADUATE VACANCIES

IT & Marketing.

1000 ★ ★ ★ ★ ★ ★ ones to watch 647> 500

CITY & GUILDS

UK locations	National
UK sites	14
Sector	Not for Profit
Definition	Vocational Qualifications Provider
How owned	Trust/Employee owned/Mutual
Founded	1878
Turnover	£92.0m
Profit	£7.5m
Staff	950
Average age	38
Male : Female	40 : 60
Earnings £35,000+	25%

CONTACT DETAILS

City & Guilds
1 Giltspur Street, London EC1A 9AA
Tel: 0207 2943370
www.cityandguilds.com

MISSION / VISION

We will become a world-leading provider of qualifications and learning support for work and adult life.

BEST WORKPLACE FACTORS

GIVING SOMETHING BACK
LEADERSHIP
MY COMPANY

BEST COMPANIES INDEX

2007 BCI = 645.4
2006 BCI = 656.9

GRADUATE VACANCIES

No graduate vacancies have been indicated.

1000 · <645 · ones to watch · 500

KEY

- **Holidays:** Companies offering a minimum of 25 days annual leave
- **Pensions:** Companies offering a final salary or non-contributory/ contributory pension scheme
- **Maternity:** Companies offering over Statutory Maternity Pay
- **Charity Activities:** 10% of staff undertake charitable activities during business hours
- **Childcare:** On-site nursery or vouchers
- **Gym:** On-site gym or subsidised gym memberships
- **Women:** At least 33% of senior managers are women
- **Shares:** Companies where employees are offered share options
- **Long Service:** 40% of employees with more than 5 years' service
- **Health Insurance:** Full family cover

COHN & WOLFE

UK locations	London
UK sites	1
Sector	Business Services
Definition	Public Relations Consultancy
How owned	Public (i.e. stock market listed)
Founded	1989
Turnover	Not disclosed
Profit	Not disclosed
Staff	101
Average age	28
Male : Female	18 : 82
Earnings £35,000+	45%

CONTACT DETAILS

Cohn & Wolfe
30 Orange Street, London WC2H 7LZ
Tel: 020 73315300
www.cohnwolfe.com

MISSION / VISION

To bring a tradition of innovative thinking and a passion for getting results to every client engagement. With the courage to do things differently and an aggressive entrepreneurial spirit our people drive our clients' success.

BEST WORKPLACE FACTORS

FAIR DEAL
MY MANAGER
LEADERSHIP

BEST COMPANIES INDEX

2007 BCI = 639.5
2006 BCI = 651.1

GRADUATE VACANCIES

Account Handlers.

1000 · <640 · ones to watch · 500

To find out more about these companies visit www.bestcompaniesguide.co.uk

CONOCOPHILLIPS LIMITED MARKETING (JET)

UK locations	National
UK sites	2
Sector	Energy
Definition	Fuel Sales Marketing
How owned	Public (i.e. stock market listed)
Founded	2002
Turnover	Not disclosed
Profit	Not disclosed
Staff	118
Average age	39
Male : Female	54 : 46
Earnings £35,000+	38%

MISSION / VISION

We will be a challenging dynamic customer focused organisation delivering industry leading Return on Capital Employed within the full value chain.

BEST WORKPLACE FACTORS

FAIR DEAL
WELL BEING
MY COMPANY

BEST COMPANIES INDEX

2007 BCI = 637.9

CONTACT DETAILS

ConocoPhillips Limited Marketing (Jet)
Centre 2, Kingmaker Court,
Warwick Technology Park, Warwick CV34 6DB
Tel: 01926 404000
www.conocophillips.co.uk

GRADUATE VACANCIES

Marketing.

1000
★ ★ ★
★ ★
★
638>
ones to watch
500

KEY

- **Holidays:** Companies offering a minimum of 25 days annual leave
- **Pensions:** Companies offering a final salary or non-contributory/ contributory pension scheme
- **Maternity:** Companies offering over Statutory Maternity Pay
- **Charity Activities:** 10% of staff undertake charitable activities during business hours
- **Childcare:** On-site nursery or vouchers
- **Gym:** On-site gym or subsidised gym memberships
- **Women:** At least 33% of senior managers are women
- **Shares:** Companies where employees are offered share options
- **Long Service:** 40% of employees with more than 5 years' service
- **Health Insurance:** Full family cover

COVENTRY SOLIHULL WARWICKSHIRE PARTNERSHIP

UK locations	W.Midlands
UK sites	90
Sector	Not for Profit
Definition	Economic Development & Connexions
How owned	Partnership/LLP
Founded	2002
Turnover	Not disclosed
Profit	Not disclosed
Staff	363
Average age	42
Male : Female	19 : 81
Earnings £35,000+	6%

MISSION / VISION

Investment jobs and a better life for everyone in Coventry and Warwickshire.

BEST WORKPLACE FACTORS

GIVING SOMETHING BACK
FAIR DEAL
MY MANAGER

BEST COMPANIES INDEX

2007 BCI = 652.6
2006 BCI = 662.4

CONTACT DETAILS

Coventry Solihull Warwickshire Partnership
First Floor Tower Court, Foleshill Enterprise Park,
Courtaiulds Way, Coventry CV6 5QT
Tel: 02476 707400
www.cswp.org.uk

GRADUATE VACANCIES

No graduate vacancies have been indicated.

1000
★ ★ ★
★ ★
★
653>
ones to watch
500

1000

<615

500

CULFORD SCHOOL

UK locations	E.Anglia
UK sites	1
Sector	Education
Definition	Independent Boarding School
How owned	Trust/Employee owned/Mutual
Founded	1881
Turnover	Not disclosed
Profit	Not disclosed
Staff	265
Average age	47
Male : Female	33 : 67
Earnings £35,000+	12%

CONTACT DETAILS

Culford School
Bury St Edmunds,
Suffolk IP28 6TX
Tel: 01284 728615
www.culford.co.uk

MISSION / VISION

Culford exists to provide an education that is challenging, enriching, and fun, for our pupils and gives us a stimulating and rewarding environment in which to work. We aim to be the independent boarding and day school of choice in the area.

BEST WORKPLACE FACTORS

MY COMPANY
PERSONAL GROWTH
GIVING SOMETHING BACK

BEST COMPANIES INDEX

2007 BCI = 615.0

GRADUATE VACANCIES

Teaching & ICT.

KEY

Holidays: Companies offering a minimum of 25 days annual leave

Pensions: Companies offering a final salary or non-contributory/contributory pension scheme

Maternity: Companies offering over Statutory Maternity Pay

Charity Activities: 10% of staff undertake charitable activities during business hours

Childcare: On-site nursery or vouchers

Gym: On-site gym or subsidised gym memberships

Women: At least 33% of senior managers are women

Shares: Companies where employees are offered share options

Long Service: 40% of employees with more than 5 years' service

Health Insurance: Full family cover

1000

<607

500

CV TRAVEL

UK locations	London
UK sites	1
Sector	Travel
Definition	Specialist Holiday Tour Operator
How owned	Private
Founded	1972
Turnover	Not disclosed
Profit	Not disclosed
Staff	56
Average age	37
Male : Female	21 : 79
Earnings £35,000+	9%

CONTACT DETAILS

CV Travel
Thames Wharf Studios, Rainville Road,
London W6 9HA
Tel: 020 73845850
www.cvtravel.co.uk

MISSION / VISION

Vision: To establish CV Travel as one of the leading specialist independent travel groups in the UK.
Mission: We aim to create memorable holiday experiences for our valued clients leaving them with the desire to return to us in the future and recommend us.

BEST WORKPLACE FACTORS

LEADERSHIP
MY MANAGER
MY COMPANY

BEST COMPANIES INDEX

2007 BCI = 607.0

GRADUATE VACANCIES

No graduate vacancies have been indicated.

To find out more about these companies visit www.bestcompaniesguide.co.uk

DARWIN RHODES

UK locations	National
UK sites	6
Sector	Recruitment
Definition	Financial Services Recruitment
How owned	Private
Founded	1996
Turnover	Not disclosed
Profit	Not disclosed
Staff	73
Average age	28
Male : Female	51 : 49
Earnings £35,000+	37%

CONTACT DETAILS

Darwin Rhodes
No. 1 Threadneedle Street, London EC2R 8AW
Tel: 0207 4488550
www.darwinrhodes.com

MISSION / VISION

Vision: We aspire to be the market leader in all our specialist sectors in every global location.
Mission: To be the Best Professional Services Recruiter in the World.

BEST WORKPLACE FACTORS

WELL BEING
FAIR DEAL
MY TEAM

BEST COMPANIES INDEX

2007 BCI = 631.9

GRADUATE VACANCIES

Sales.

1000
632>
ones to watch
500

KEY

- **Holidays:** Companies offering a minimum of 25 days annual leave
- **Pensions:** Companies offering a final salary or non-contributory/contributory pension scheme
- **Maternity:** Companies offering over Statutory Maternity Pay
- **Charity Activities:** 10% of staff undertake charitable activities during business hours
- **Childcare:** On-site nursery or vouchers
- **Gym:** On-site gym or subsidised gym memberships
- **Women:** At least 33% of senior managers are women
- **Shares:** Companies where employees are offered share options
- **Long Service:** 40% of employees with more than 5 years' service
- **Health Insurance:** Full family cover

DICKINSON DEES

UK locations	Yorks & Humber, N.East
UK sites	3
Sector	Law
Definition	Legal Services
How owned	Partnership/LLP
Founded	1975
Turnover	£46.5m
Profit	£15.8m
Staff	825
Average age	36
Male : Female	32 : 67
Earnings £35,000+	28%

CONTACT DETAILS

Dickinson Dees
St Ann's Wharf, 112 Quayside,
Newcastle upon Tyne NE99 1SB
Tel: 0191 2799000
www.dickinson-dees.com

MISSION / VISION

We value clients, those we work with and relationships based on mutual understanding, respect, openness & integrity. Our focus on results for clients goes hand in hand with enthusiasm and enjoyment of work.

BEST WORKPLACE FACTORS

WELL BEING
PERSONAL GROWTH
MY TEAM

BEST COMPANIES INDEX

2007 BCI = 627.2
2006 BCI = 663.4

GRADUATE VACANCIES

Trainee Solicitors.

1000
627>
ones to watch
500

1000

DLA PIPER UK

UK locations	National
UK sites	8
Sector	Law
Definition	Legal Services Provider
How owned	Partnership/LLP
Founded	1764
Turnover	Not disclosed
Profit	Not disclosed
Staff	2833
Average age	35
Male : Female	39 : 61
Earnings £35,000+	45%

<624

CONTACT DETAILS

DLA Piper UK
Noble Street, London EC2V 7EE
Tel: 08700 111111
www.dlapiper.com

500

MISSION / VISION

To be the leading global business law firm Delivering quality value-added services to our clients globally and locally.

BEST WORKPLACE FACTORS

LEADERSHIP
PERSONAL GROWTH
GIVING SOMETHING BACK

BEST COMPANIES INDEX

2007 BCI = 623.9
2006 BCI = 647.4

GRADUATE VACANCIES

Legal.

KEY

Holidays: Companies offering a minimum of 25 days annual leave

Pensions: Companies offering a final salary or non-contributory/ contributory pension scheme

Maternity: Companies offering over Statutory Maternity Pay

Charity Activities: 10% of staff undertake charitable activities during business hours

Childcare: On-site nursery or vouchers

Gym: On-site gym or subsidised gym memberships

Women: At least 33% of senior managers are women

Shares: Companies where employees are offered share options

Long Service: 40% of employees with more than 5 years' service

Health Insurance: Full family cover

1000

DUPLO INTERNATIONAL

UK locations	S.East
UK sites	2
Sector	Business Services
Definition	Print Finishing Solutions
How owned	Private
Founded	1988
Turnover	£27.4m
Profit	£1.3m
Staff	102
Average age	45
Male : Female	71 : 29
Earnings £35,000+	25%

<638

CONTACT DETAILS

Duplo International
Sandown Industrial Park, Mill Road,
Esher, Surrey KT10 8BL
Tel: 01372 468131
www.duplointernational.com

500

MISSION / VISION

To add value for our customers by supplying profitable innovative and quality solutions in the form of equipment, service and support.

BEST WORKPLACE FACTORS

WELL BEING
MY MANAGER
FAIR DEAL

BEST COMPANIES INDEX

2007 BCI = 637.8
2006 BCI = 651.3

GRADUATE VACANCIES

No graduate vacancies have been indicated.

To find out more about these companies visit www.bestcompaniesguide.co.uk

EAST HOMES

UK locations	London, E.England
UK sites	3
Sector	Housing Associations
Definition	Affordable Housing
How owned	Trust/Employee owned/Mutual
Founded	1979
Turnover	£47.2m
Profit	£0.8m
Staff	178
Average age	37
Male : Female	36 : 64
Earnings £35,000+	13%

CONTACT DETAILS

East Homes
3 Tramway Ave, London E15 4PN
Tel: 0208 5222000
www.east-homes.co.uk

MISSION / VISION

Vision: To be the leading provider of quality affordable homes for rent and sale in east London and Essex.
Mission: To make a positive and lasting contribution to the neighbourhoods in which we work.

BEST WORKPLACE FACTORS

GIVING SOMETHING BACK
MY MANAGER
LEADERSHIP

BEST COMPANIES INDEX

2007 BCI = 649.0

GRADUATE VACANCIES

No graduate vacancies have been indicated.

1000

649>

ones to watch

500

KEY

Holidays: Companies offering a minimum of 25 days annual leave

Pensions: Companies offering a final salary or non-contributory/contributory pension scheme

Maternity: Companies offering over Statutory Maternity Pay

Charity Activities: 10% of staff undertake charitable activities during business hours

Childcare: On-site nursery or vouchers

Gym: On-site gym or subsidised gym memberships

Women: At least 33% of senior managers are women

Shares: Companies where employees are offered share options

Long Service: 40% of employees with more than 5 years' service

Health Insurance: Full family cover

ELITE HOMES GROUP

UK locations	N.West, Yorks & Humber
UK sites	22
Sector	Property
Definition	Housebuilder
How owned	Private
Founded	1985
Turnover	Not disclosed
Profit	Not disclosed
Staff	140
Average age	38
Male : Female	66 : 34
Earnings £35,000+	34%

CONTACT DETAILS

Elite Homes Group
Redwood House, Woodlands Park,
Newton le Willows, Merseyside WA12 OHT
Tel: 0870 3503535
www.elitehomes.co.uk

MISSION / VISION

To produce homes of great design quality and value for money with the best customer choice backed by the best customer service.

BEST WORKPLACE FACTORS

MY MANAGER
MY COMPANY
MY TEAM

BEST COMPANIES INDEX

2007 BCI = 651.3
2006 BCI = 654.2

GRADUATE VACANCIES

No graduate vacancies have been indicated.

1000

651>

ones to watch

500

1000

ELMBRIDGE BOROUGH COUNCIL

UK locations	S.East
UK sites	34
Sector	Public
Definition	Local Authority
How owned	Local Authority
Founded	1974
Turnover	£58.4m
Profit	Not disclosed
Staff	415
Average age	46
Male : Female	40 : 60
Earnings £35,000+	15%

MISSION / VISION

To be recognised as one of the best Borough Councils by 2008.

BEST WORKPLACE FACTORS

GIVING SOMETHING BACK
WELL BEING
FAIR DEAL

BEST COMPANIES INDEX

2007 BCI = 637.5

ones to watch

<638

CONTACT DETAILS

Elmbridge Borough Council
Civic Centre, High Street,
Surrey KT10 9SD
Tel: 01372 474474
www.elmbridge.gov.uk

GRADUATE VACANCIES

No graduate vacancies have been indicated.

500

KEY

- **Holidays:** Companies offering a minimum of 25 days annual leave
- **Pensions:** Companies offering a final salary or non-contributory/ contributory pension scheme
- **Maternity:** Companies offering over Statutory Maternity Pay
- **Charity Activities:** 10% of staff undertake charitable activities during business hours
- **Childcare:** On-site nursery or vouchers
- **Gym:** On-site gym or subsidised gym memberships
- **Women:** At least 33% of senior managers are women
- **Shares:** Companies where employees are offered share options
- **Long Service:** 40% of employees with more than 5 years' service
- **Health Insurance:** Full family cover

1000

EMERALD GROUP PUBLISHING

UK locations	Yorks & Humber
UK sites	1
Sector	Media
Definition	Scholarly Management Publisher
How owned	Private
Founded	1967
Turnover	£21.1m
Profit	£5.9m
Staff	176
Average age	38
Male : Female	45 : 55
Earnings £35,000+	10%

MISSION / VISION

To have a positive impact on the business world through providing valuable services and products for those who educate and develop managers. To be seen as partner of choice in the markets in which we choose to compete.

BEST WORKPLACE FACTORS

WELL BEING
GIVING SOMETHING BACK
MY MANAGER

BEST COMPANIES INDEX

2007 BCI = 645.3

ones to watch

<645

CONTACT DETAILS

Emerald Group Publishing
60-62 Toller Lane, Bradford,
West Yorkshire BD8 9BY
Tel: 01274 777700
www.emeraldinsight.com

GRADUATE VACANCIES

No graduate vacancies have been indicated.

500

To find out more about these companies visit www.bestcompaniesguide.co.uk

ESRI (UK)

UK locations	National
UK sites	7
Sector	IT/Internet Services
Definition	Geographic Information Systems
How owned	Private
Founded	1994
Turnover	£33.0m
Profit	£4.0m
Staff	240
Average age	38
Male : Female	78 : 23
Earnings £35,000+	69%

CONTACT DETAILS

ESRI (UK)
Millennium House, 65 Walton Street,
Aylesbury, Buckinghamshire HP21 7QG
Tel: 01296 745500
www.esriuk.com

MISSION / VISION

To convince our customers and potential customers of the powerful benefits of geographic information systems.

BEST WORKPLACE FACTORS

FAIR DEAL
GIVING SOMETHING BACK
PERSONAL GROWTH

BEST COMPANIES INDEX

2007 BCI = 658.1

GRADUATE VACANCIES

Consultancy Department.

1000

658>

ones to watch

500

KEY

Holidays: Companies offering a minimum of 25 days annual leave
Pensions: Companies offering a final salary or non-contributory/ contributory pension scheme
Maternity: Companies offering over Statutory Maternity Pay
Charity Activities: 10% of staff undertake charitable activities during business hours
Childcare: On-site nursery or vouchers
Gym: On-site gym or subsidised gym memberships
Women: At least 33% of senior managers are women
Shares: Companies where employees are offered share options
Long Service: 40% of employees with more than 5 years' service
Health Insurance: Full family cover

FAIRBANKS ENVIRONMENTAL

UK locations	N.West
UK sites	1
Sector	Business Services
Definition	Wetstock Management Specialists
How owned	Private
Founded	1996
Turnover	Not disclosed
Profit	Not disclosed
Staff	56
Average age	37
Male : Female	54 : 46
Earnings £35,000+	4%

CONTACT DETAILS

Fairbanks Environmental
The Technology Management Centre, Moss Lane View,
Skelmersdale, Lancashire WN8 9TN
Tel: 01695 51775
www.fairbanks.co.uk

MISSION / VISION

To provide the Best Wetstock Monitoring and Management Service in the World.

BEST WORKPLACE FACTORS

GIVING SOMETHING BACK
WELL BEING
LEADERSHIP

BEST COMPANIES INDEX

2007 BCI = 627.4
2006 BCI = 672.2

GRADUATE VACANCIES

Marketing.

1000

627>

ones to watch

500

1000

FISHER GERMAN

UK locations	National
UK sites	7
Sector	Property
Definition	Rural Property Consultancy
How owned	Partnership/LLP
Founded	2000
Turnover	Not disclosed
Profit	Not disclosed
Staff	159
Average age	38
Male : Female	48 : 52
Earnings £35,000+	25%

MISSION / VISION

Our aim is to build and maintain good client relationships founded on the consistent and cost effective delivery of services that satisfy their needs and will be reliable and informative whilst preserving high standards of professional integrity.

BEST WORKPLACE FACTORS

WELL BEING
FAIR DEAL
PERSONAL GROWTH

BEST COMPANIES INDEX

2007 BCI = 638.1

<638

CONTACT DETAILS

Fisher German
40 High Street, Market Harborough,
Leicestershire LE16 7NX
Tel: 01858 410200
www.fishergerman.co.uk

GRADUATE VACANCIES

Rural Practice & Associated Chartered Surveying.

500

KEY

- **Holidays:** Companies offering a minimum of 25 days annual leave
- **Pensions:** Companies offering a final salary or non-contributory/ contributory pension scheme
- **Maternity:** Companies offering over Statutory Maternity Pay
- **Charity Activities:** 10% of staff undertake charitable activities during business hours
- **Childcare:** On-site nursery or vouchers
- **Gym:** On-site gym or subsidised gym memberships
- **Women:** At least 33% of senior managers are women
- **Shares:** Companies where employees are offered share options
- **Long Service:** 40% of employees with more than 5 years' service
- **Health Insurance:** Full family cover

1000

GB GROUP

UK locations	N.West
UK sites	1
Sector	IT/Internet Services
Definition	Data & Identity Specialists
How owned	Public (i.e. stock market listed)
Founded	1999
Turnover	£12.8m
Profit	Not disclosed
Staff	129
Average age	36
Male : Female	62 : 38
Earnings £35,000+	46%

MISSION / VISION

Our future is our ability to innovate. By investing in our specialist knowledge and technical expertise we will reach our goal of doubling our revenue every two years between now and 2012.

BEST WORKPLACE FACTORS

MY COMPANY
MY MANAGER
PERSONAL GROWTH

BEST COMPANIES INDEX

2007 BCI = 641.4

<641

CONTACT DETAILS

GB Group
GB House, Kingsfield Court,
Chester Business Park, Chester CH4 9GB
Tel: 01244 657333
www.gb.co.uk

GRADUATE VACANCIES

Sales, IT and Marketing.

500

To find out more about these companies visit www.bestcompaniesguide.co.uk

GORDON RAMSAY ROYAL HOSPITAL ROAD

UK locations	London
UK sites	1
Sector	Hospitality
Definition	Fine Dining Restaurant
How owned	Partnership/LLP
Founded	1998
Turnover	Not disclosed
Profit	£0.3m
Staff	52
Average age	28
Male : Female	87 : 13
Earnings £35,000+	2%

CONTACT DETAILS

Gordon Ramsay Royal Hospital Road
1 Catherine Place, London SW1E 6DX
Tel: 020 75921360
www.gordonramsay.com

MISSION / VISION

Combining contemporary elegance, an intimate ambience and unparalleled service, Gordon Ramsay Royal Hospital Road has the hallmark of true excellence honoured with three Michelin Stars.

BEST WORKPLACE FACTORS

FAIR DEAL
LEADERSHIP
PERSONAL GROWTH

BEST COMPANIES INDEX

2007 BCI = 614.1

GRADUATE VACANCIES

No graduate vacancies have been indicated.

1000
★ ★ ★ ★ ★ ★
614>
ones to watch
500

KEY

- **Holidays:** Companies offering a minimum of 25 days annual leave
- **Pensions:** Companies offering a final salary or non-contributory/ contributory pension scheme
- **Maternity:** Companies offering over Statutory Maternity Pay
- **Charity Activities:** 10% of staff undertake charitable activities during business hours
- **Childcare:** On-site nursery or vouchers
- **Gym:** On-site gym or subsidised gym memberships
- **Women:** At least 33% of senior managers are women
- **Shares:** Companies where employees are offered share options
- **Long Service:** 40% of employees with more than 5 years' service
- **Health Insurance:** Full family cover

GRAINGER TRUST

UK locations	National
UK sites	8
Sector	Property
Definition	Property Management
How owned	Public (i.e. stock market listed)
Founded	1912
Turnover	£205.7m
Profit	£71.7m
Staff	218
Average age	37
Male : Female	44 : 56
Earnings £35,000+	33%

CONTACT DETAILS

Grainger Trust
Citygate St James Boulevard, Newcastle upon Tyne
NE1 4JE
Tel: 0191 2611819
www.graingertrust.co.uk

MISSION / VISION

We will continue to build our business through astute investment and disposal, innovation, and a group-wide commitment to tenant care, employee development, environmental responsibility and community service.

BEST WORKPLACE FACTORS

FAIR DEAL
WELL BEING
PERSONAL GROWTH

BEST COMPANIES INDEX

2007 BCI = 637.0
2006 BCI = 650.1

GRADUATE VACANCIES

Property Management, Surveying, Sales & Acquisitions.

1000
★ ★ ★ ★ ★ ★
637>
ones to watch
500

1000

GRUNDFOS PUMPS

UK locations	National
UK sites	4
Sector	Manufacturing
Definition	Pump/Pumping Systems Sales
How owned	Trust/Employee owned/Mutual
Founded	1964
Turnover	Not disclosed
Profit	Not disclosed
Staff	160
Average age	Not available
Male : Female	Not available
Earnings £35,000+	Not available

ones to watch <642

CONTACT DETAILS

Grundfos Pumps
Grovebury Road, Leighton Buzzard,
Beds LU7 4TL
Tel: 01525 850000
www.grundfos.com

500

MISSION / VISION

It is our mission - the basis of our existence - to successfully develop, produce and sell high-quality pumps and pumping systems world-wide, contributing to a better quality of life and a healthy environment.

BEST WORKPLACE FACTORS

GIVING SOMETHING BACK
PERSONAL GROWTH
FAIR DEAL

BEST COMPANIES INDEX

2007 BCI = 641.6
2006 BCI = 665.1

GRADUATE VACANCIES

No graduate vacancies have been indicated.

KEY

- **Holidays:** Companies offering a minimum of 25 days annual leave
- **Pensions:** Companies offering a final salary or non-contributory/ contributory pension scheme
- **Maternity:** Companies offering over Statutory Maternity Pay
- **Charity Activities:** 10% of staff undertake charitable activities during business hours
- **Childcare:** On-site nursery or vouchers
- **Gym:** On-site gym or subsidised gym memberships
- **Women:** At least 33% of senior managers are women
- **Shares:** Companies where employees are offered share options
- **Long Service:** 40% of employees with more than 5 years' service
- **Health Insurance:** Full family cover

1000

HAYLEY CONFERENCE CENTRES

UK locations	National
UK sites	8
Sector	Business Services
Definition	Conference/Training Venues
How owned	Private
Founded	1991
Turnover	£41m
Profit	Not disclosed
Staff	835
Average age	23
Male : Female	46 : 54
Earnings £35,000+	3%

ones to watch <631

CONTACT DETAILS

Hayley Conference Centres
Horwood House, Conference Centre,
Mursley Road, Little Horwood, Bucks MK17 0PH
Tel: 01296 722100
www.hayley-conf.co.uk

500

MISSION / VISION

Hayley Conference Centres inspire learning, epitomise quality, and guarantee comfort. To achieve this we provide an exceptional learning and service environment in professional efficient and welcoming venues.

BEST WORKPLACE FACTORS

MY MANAGER
MY TEAM
MY COMPANY

BEST COMPANIES INDEX

2007 BCI = 630.6
2006 BCI = 678.1

GRADUATE VACANCIES

All Areas.

To find out more about these companies visit www.bestcompaniesguide.co.uk

HEANTUN HOUSING ASSOCIATION

UK locations	W.Midlands
UK sites	16
Sector	Housing Associations
Definition	Housing/Care Provider
How owned	Trust/Employee owned/Mutual
Founded	1973
Turnover	£11.3m
Profit	£0.3m
Staff	285
Average age	43
Male : Female	26 : 74
Earnings £35,000+	3%

CONTACT DETAILS

Heantun Housing Association
3 Wellington Road, Bilston,
West Midlands WV14 6AA
Tel: 01902 571100
www.heantun.org

MISSION / VISION

Housing: Helping people in need to meet their housing aspirations. Care: Helping people live with pride and dignity. New Bilston: Local regeneration involving local people.

BEST WORKPLACE FACTORS

GIVING SOMETHING BACK
WELL BEING
MY COMPANY

BEST COMPANIES INDEX

2007 BCI = 632.0

GRADUATE VACANCIES

No graduate vacancies have been indicated.

1000

632>

ones to watch

500

KEY

- **Holidays:** Companies offering a minimum of 25 days annual leave
- **Pensions:** Companies offering a final salary or non-contributory/contributory pension scheme
- **Maternity:** Companies offering over Statutory Maternity Pay
- **Charity Activities:** 10% of staff undertake charitable activities during business hours
- **Childcare:** On-site nursery or vouchers
- **Gym:** On-site gym or subsidised gym memberships
- **Women:** At least 33% of senior managers are women
- **Shares:** Companies where employees are offered share options
- **Long Service:** 40% of employees with more than 5 years' service
- **Health Insurance:** Full family cover

HOUSING SOLUTIONS GROUP

UK locations	S.East
UK sites	13
Sector	Not for Profit
Definition	Affordable Housing Provider
How owned	Trust/Employee owned/A Mutual
Founded	2000
Turnover	£17.2m
Profit	£2.2m
Staff	133
Average age	45
Male : Female	51 : 49
Earnings £35,000+	23%

CONTACT DETAILS

Housing Solutions Group
Crown House, Crown Square,
Waldeck Road, Maidenhead Berkshire SL6 8BY
Tel: 01628 543100
www.housingsolutions.co.uk

MISSION / VISION

An organisation renowned for excellence in all we do and one that people are proud to be a part of. The No.1 provider of affordable housing in Maidenhead.

BEST WORKPLACE FACTORS

WELL BEING
GIVING SOMETHING BACK
MY MANAGER

BEST COMPANIES INDEX

2007 BCI = 659.2

GRADUATE VACANCIES

No graduate vacancies have been indicated.

1000

659>

ones to watch

500

1000

ILVA

UK locations	National
UK sites	4
Sector	Retail
Definition	Home Furnishings Retailer
How owned	Private
Founded	1974
Turnover	Not disclosed
Profit	Not disclosed
Staff	695
Average age	28
Male : Female	51 : 49
Earnings £35,000+	4%

MISSION / VISION

We will strive to create the best place to work for the most committed competent employees in order to create the best furniture stores offering the best place to shop for our customers.

BEST WORKPLACE FACTORS

MY TEAM
WELL BEING
FAIR DEAL

BEST COMPANIES INDEX

2007 BCI = 614.5

ones to watch <615

CONTACT DETAILS

ILVA
1210 Parkview, Arlington Business Park,
Theale, Reading RG7 4TY
Tel: 0845 0837950
www.ilva.co.uk

GRADUATE VACANCIES

No graduate vacancies have been indicated.

500

KEY

- **Holidays:** Companies offering a minimum of 25 days annual leave
- **Pensions:** Companies offering a final salary or non-contributory/contributory pension scheme
- **Maternity:** Companies offering over Statutory Maternity Pay
- **Charity Activities:** 10% of staff undertake charitable activities during business hours
- **Childcare:** On-site nursery or vouchers
- **Gym:** On-site gym or subsidised gym memberships
- **Women:** At least 33% of senior managers are women
- **Shares:** Companies where employees are offered share options
- **Long Service:** 40% of employees with more than 5 years' service
- **Health Insurance:** Full family cover

1000

IMAGE SOURCE

UK locations	London
UK sites	1
Sector	Media
Definition	Photographic Library
How owned	Private
Founded	1999
Turnover	Not disclosed
Profit	Not disclosed
Staff	61
Average age	28
Male : Female	52 : 48
Earnings £35,000+	30%

MISSION / VISION

To be the leading international creator owner and supplier of the world's best-selling stock images for creative professionals.

BEST WORKPLACE FACTORS

MY COMPANY
LEADERSHIP
WELL BEING

BEST COMPANIES INDEX

2007 BCI = 637.7

ones to watch <638

CONTACT DETAILS

Image Source
41 Great Pulteney Street, London W1F 9NZ
Tel: 0207 8515600
www.imagesource.com

GRADUATE VACANCIES

Sales and Marketing.

500

To find out more about these companies visit www.bestcompaniesguide.co.uk

INDIEFIELD

UK locations	London
UK sites	2
Sector	Public
Definition	Market Research Fieldwork
How owned	Private
Founded	1998
Turnover	£3.7m
Profit	£1.1m
Staff	60
Average age	31
Male : Female	35 : 65
Earnings £35,000+	0%

CONTACT DETAILS

Indiefield
47 London Road, Enfield,
Middlesex EN2 6DS
Tel: 0208 2458000
www.indiefield.co.uk

MISSION / VISION

Our mission is to look after all our clients and to supply the highest quality recruitment, interviewing and data, delivered with professionalism friendliness, individual pride and in keeping with our company values.

BEST WORKPLACE FACTORS

MY TEAM
MY MANAGER
FAIR DEAL

BEST COMPANIES INDEX

2007 BCI = 657.6
2006 BCI = 678.4

GRADUATE VACANCIES

Marketing.

1000
658>
ones to watch
500

KEY

Holidays: Companies offering a minimum of 25 days annual leave

Pensions: Companies offering a final salary or non-contributory/contributory pension scheme

Maternity: Companies offering over Statutory Maternity Pay

Charity Activities: 10% of staff undertake charitable activities during business hours

Childcare: On-site nursery or vouchers

Gym: On-site gym or subsidised gym memberships

Women: At least 33% of senior managers are women

Shares: Companies where employees are offered share options

Long Service: 40% of employees with more than 5 years' service

Health Insurance: Full family cover

INNOGISTIC

UK locations	S.West, S.East
UK sites	2
Sector	IT/Internet Services
Definition	Software Developers
How owned	Private
Founded	1997
Turnover	£3m
Profit	Not disclosed
Staff	55
Average age	35
Male : Female	67 : 33
Earnings £35,000+	35%

CONTACT DETAILS

Innogistic
2nd Floor, 25 Marsh Street,
Bristol BS1 4AQ
Tel: 0117 9046622
www.innogistic.co.uk

MISSION / VISION

The expertise, dedication and outstanding service of Innogistic combined with the support of our customers will ensure mutual success.

BEST WORKPLACE FACTORS

GIVING SOMETHING BACK
FAIR DEAL
MY TEAM

BEST COMPANIES INDEX

2007 BCI = 605.4

GRADUATE VACANCIES

Software Developers & Project Managers.

1000
ones to watch
605>
500

1000

INTERPUB

UK locations	National
UK sites	16
Sector	Hospitality
Definition	Beds and Bars
How owned	Private
Founded	1993
Turnover	Not disclosed
Profit	Not disclosed
Staff	223
Average age	28
Male : Female	59 : 41
Earnings £35,000+	3%

ones to watch

<607

500

CONTACT DETAILS

Interpub
The Stag, Hawthorn Lane,
East Burnham, Burnham Beeches, Bucks SL2 3TA
Tel: 01753 647603
www.interpub.co.uk

MISSION / VISION

Fantastic experience for all our team and customers
Unite to get bums in bars and heads on beds.

BEST WORKPLACE FACTORS

MY TEAM
MY MANAGER
WELL BEING

BEST COMPANIES INDEX

2007 BCI = 607.4

GRADUATE VACANCIES

No graduate vacancies have been indicated.

KEY

Holidays: Companies offering a minimum of 25 days annual leave
Pensions: Companies offering a final salary or non-contributory/contributory pension scheme
Maternity: Companies offering over Statutory Maternity Pay
Charity Activities: 10% of staff undertake charitable activities during business hours
Childcare: On-site nursery or vouchers
Gym: On-site gym or subsidised gym memberships
Women: At least 33% of senior managers are women
Shares: Companies where employees are offered share options
Long Service: 40% of employees with more than 5 years' service
Health Insurance: Full family cover

1000

KEOGHS

UK locations	N.West, W.Midlands
UK sites	2
Sector	Law
Definition	Legal Services
How owned	Partnership/LLP
Founded	1968
Turnover	£20m
Profit	Not disclosed
Staff	478
Average age	35
Male : Female	28 : 72
Earnings £35,000+	19%

ones to watch

<621

500

CONTACT DETAILS

Keoghs
2 The Parklands, Bolton BL6 4SE
Tel: 01204 677000
www.keoghs.co.uk

MISSION / VISION

To deliver cost effective legal services in the fields of dispute resolution and business advice on a national basis. To be recognised as approachable, innovative, flexible and dynamic, always putting the clients' and customers' needs before our own.

BEST WORKPLACE FACTORS

FAIR DEAL
GIVING SOMETHING BACK
LEADERSHIP

BEST COMPANIES INDEX

2007 BCI = 621.3
2006 BCI = 634.2

GRADUATE VACANCIES

Trainee Solicitors.

KWIK-FIT FINANCIAL SERVICES

UK locations	Scotland
UK sites	1
Sector	Financial - Insurance
Definition	Insurance Intermediary
How owned	Private
Founded	1995
Turnover	£43.9m
Profit	£4.9m
Staff	810
Average age	29
Male : Female	43 : 57
Earnings £35,000+	2%

CONTACT DETAILS

Kwik-Fit Financial Services
1 Masterton Way, Tannochside Park,
Uddingston G71 5PU
Tel: 01698 817000
www.kwik-fitinsurance.co.uk

MISSION / VISION

To make KFFS a fantastic place to work for our people. To ensure we deliver 100% customer delight to both internal and external customers. To be industry leading in everything we do.

BEST WORKPLACE FACTORS

WELL BEING
FAIR DEAL
MY TEAM

BEST COMPANIES INDEX

2007 BCI = 621.6
2006 BCI = 695.5

GRADUATE VACANCIES

I.S, Marketing & E-Commerce

1000
622>
ones to watch
500

KEY

Holidays: Companies offering a minimum of 25 days annual leave
Pensions: Companies offering a final salary or non-contributory/contributory pension scheme
Maternity: Companies offering over Statutory Maternity Pay
Charity Activities: 10% of staff undertake charitable activities during business hours
Childcare: On-site nursery or vouchers
Gym: On-site gym or subsidised gym memberships
Women: At least 33% of senior managers are women
Shares: Companies where employees are offered share options
Long Service: 40% of employees with more than 5 years' service
Health Insurance: Full family cover

LOOP CUSTOMER MANAGEMENT

UK locations	Yorks & Humber, Wales
UK sites	2
Sector	Business Services
Definition	Managed Customer Services
How owned	Private
Founded	2000
Turnover	£18.4m
Profit	£0.4m
Staff	576
Average age	35
Male : Female	26 : 74
Earnings £35,000+	2%

CONTACT DETAILS

Loop Customer Management
No 1 Midpoint Business Park, Bradford BD3 7AY
Tel: 01274 260000
www.loop.co.uk

MISSION / VISION

Great Customer Experiences through Great People.

BEST WORKPLACE FACTORS

WELL BEING
MY MANAGER
MY TEAM

BEST COMPANIES INDEX

2007 BCI = 656.6
2006 BCI = 688.6

GRADUATE VACANCIES

No graduate vacancies have been indicated.

1000
657>
ones to watch
500

1000

LYRECO UK

UK locations	National
UK sites	25
Sector	Business Services
Definition	Office Supplies
How owned	Private
Founded	1988
Turnover	£255.0m
Profit	£25.0m
Staff	1773
Average age	36
Male : Female	68 : 32
Earnings £35,000+	5%

ones to watch

<648

500

CONTACT DETAILS

Lyreco UK
Deer Park Court, Donnington Wood,
Telford, Shropshire TF2 7NB
Tel: 01952 293000
www.lyreco.co.uk

MISSION / VISION

To delight customers, be proud of what we do and grow like crazy.

BEST WORKPLACE FACTORS

GIVING SOMETHING BACK
LEADERSHIP
MY COMPANY

BEST COMPANIES INDEX

2007 BCI = 647.5
2006 BCI = 643.6

GRADUATE VACANCIES

No graduate vacancies have been indicated.

KEY

- **Holidays:** Companies offering a minimum of 25 days annual leave
- **Pensions:** Companies offering a final salary or non-contributory/contributory pension scheme
- **Maternity:** Companies offering over Statutory Maternity Pay
- **Charity Activities:** 10% of staff undertake charitable activities during business hours
- **Childcare:** On-site nursery or vouchers
- **Gym:** On-site gym or subsidised gym memberships
- **Women:** At least 33% of senior managers are women
- **Shares:** Companies where employees are offered share options
- **Long Service:** 40% of employees with more than 5 years' service
- **Health Insurance:** Full family cover

1000

MAJESTIC WINE

UK locations	National
UK sites	133
Sector	Retail
Definition	Multiple Wine Retailer
How owned	Public (i.e. stock market listed)
Founded	1980
Turnover	£172.2m
Profit	£14.5m
Staff	741
Average age	29
Male : Female	73 : 27
Earnings £35,000+	4%

ones to watch

<633

500

CONTACT DETAILS

Majestic Wine
Majestic House, Otterspool Way,
Herts WD25 8WW
Tel: 01923 298200
www.majestic.co.uk

MISSION / VISION

Majestic differentiates itself by the high diversity of its customer service and advice the diversity and quantity of stock available.

BEST WORKPLACE FACTORS

MY TEAM
MY MANAGER
LEADERSHIP

BEST COMPANIES INDEX

2007 BCI = 632.9
2006 BCI = 632.2

GRADUATE VACANCIES

No graduate vacancies have been indicated.

MARTIN CURRIE INVESTMENT MANAGEMENT

UK locations	London, Scotland
UK sites	2
Sector	Financial
Definition	Specialist Investment Manager
How owned	Trust/Employee owned/A Mutual
Founded	1985
Turnover	Not disclosed
Profit	Not disclosed
Staff	208
Average age	37
Male : Female	57 : 43
Earnings £35,000+	56%

CONTACT DETAILS

Martin Currie Investment Management
Saltire Court, 20 Castle Terrace,
Edinburgh EH1 2ES
Tel: 0131 2295252
www.martincurrie.com

MISSION / VISION

We are working as a team to create an excellent company.

BEST WORKPLACE FACTORS

PERSONAL GROWTH
MY COMPANY
GIVING SOMETHING BACK

BEST COMPANIES INDEX

2007 BCI = 606.6
2006 BCI = 605.0

GRADUATE VACANCIES

Investment.

1000
ones to watch
607>
500

KEY

- **Holidays:** Companies offering a minimum of 25 days annual leave
- **Pensions:** Companies offering a final salary or non-contributory/ contributory pension scheme
- **Maternity:** Companies offering over Statutory Maternity Pay
- **Charity Activities:** 10% of staff undertake charitable activities during business hours
- **Childcare:** On-site nursery or vouchers
- **Gym:** On-site gym or subsidised gym memberships
- **Women:** At least 33% of senior managers are women
- **Shares:** Companies where employees are offered share options
- **Long Service:** 40% of employees with more than 5 years' service
- **Health Insurance:** Full family cover

MAZDA

UK locations	S.East
UK sites	1
Sector	Logistics/Wholesale/Distribution
Definition	Car Manufacturer/Wholesaler
How owned	Private
Founded	2001
Turnover	Not disclosed
Profit	Not disclosed
Staff	103
Average age	35
Male : Female	58 : 42
Earnings £35,000+	50%

CONTACT DETAILS

Mazda
Riverbridge House, Anchor Boulevard,
Dartford, Kent DA2 6QH
Tel: 01322 622600
www.mazda.co.uk

MISSION / VISION

To maximise profitable returns to Mazda Corporation through the sale of vehicles parts and accessories.

BEST WORKPLACE FACTORS

MY COMPANY
MY TEAM
PERSONAL GROWTH

BEST COMPANIES INDEX

2007 BCI = 658.5

GRADUATE VACANCIES

All Areas.

1000
ones to watch
659>
500

1000

MCCANN ERICKSON COMMUNICATIONS HOUSE

UK locations	N.West
UK sites	1
Sector	Advertising
Definition	Integrated Marketing Communications
How owned	Partnership/LLP
Founded	1989
Turnover	Not disclosed
Profit	Not disclosed
Staff	257
Average age	40
Male : Female	47 : 53
Earnings £35,000+	26%

MISSION / VISION

We move People to Act.

BEST WORKPLACE FACTORS

MY TEAM
MY COMPANY
WELL BEING

BEST COMPANIES INDEX

2007 BCI = 634.7

ones to watch

<635

CONTACT DETAILS

McCann Erickson Communications House
Bonis Hall Lane, Prestbury,
Cheshire SK10 4EF
Tel: 01625 822200
www.mecommshouse.co.uk

GRADUATE VACANCIES

Account Handling, Digital Media, Production.

500

KEY

- **Holidays:** Companies offering a minimum of 25 days annual leave
- **Pensions:** Companies offering a final salary or non-contributory/ contributory pension scheme
- **Maternity:** Companies offering over Statutory Maternity Pay
- **Charity Activities:** 10% of staff undertake charitable activities during business hours
- **Childcare:** On-site nursery or vouchers
- **Gym:** On-site gym or subsidised gym memberships
- **Women:** At least 33% of senior managers are women
- **Shares:** Companies where employees are offered share options
- **Long Service:** 40% of employees with more than 5 years' service
- **Health Insurance:** Full family cover

1000

MCDONALD'S RESTAURANTS

UK locations	National
UK sites	660
Sector	Retail
Definition	Quick Service Restaurant
How owned	Public (i.e. stock market listed)
Founded	1974
Turnover	£1,103.4m
Profit	£36.9m
Staff	38751
Average age	24
Male : Female	55 : 45
Earnings £35,000+	1%

MISSION / VISION

To be the best restaurant experience.......by far. To be people focused and customer driven.....passionately. To inspire others with our can-do attitude....always.

BEST WORKPLACE FACTORS

WELL BEING
FAIR DEAL
GIVING SOMETHING BACK

BEST COMPANIES INDEX

2007 BCI = 627.3
2006 BCI = 642.0

ones to watch

<627

CONTACT DETAILS

McDonald's Restaurants
11-59 High Road, East Finchley,
London N2 8AW
Tel: 0870 2413300
www.mcdonalds.co.uk

GRADUATE VACANCIES

Restaurant Management.

500

To find out more about these companies visit www.bestcompaniesguide.co.uk

MESSAGELABS

UK locations	London, S.West
UK sites	2
Sector	IT/Internet Services
Definition	Managed Service Provider
How owned	Private
Founded	2000
Turnover	Not disclosed
Profit	Not disclosed
Staff	260
Average age	33
Male : Female	73 : 27
Earnings £35,000+	50%

MISSION / VISION

To be globally recognised as the defining force in messaging security and management services.

BEST WORKPLACE FACTORS

MY COMPANY
FAIR DEAL
LEADERSHIP

BEST COMPANIES INDEX

2007 BCI = 626.8
2006 BCI = 605.9

1000 / 627> / ones to watch / 500

CONTACT DETAILS

MessageLabs
1240 Lansdowne Court, Gloucester Business Park,
Gloucester GL3 4AB
Tel: 01452 627200
www.messagelabs.com

GRADUATE VACANCIES

Software Development, Infrastructure Support.

KEY

- **Holidays:** Companies offering a minimum of 25 days annual leave
- **Pensions:** Companies offering a final salary or non-contributory/contributory pension scheme
- **Maternity:** Companies offering over Statutory Maternity Pay
- **Charity Activities:** 10% of staff undertake charitable activities during business hours
- **Childcare:** On-site nursery or vouchers
- **Gym:** On-site gym or subsidised gym memberships
- **Women:** At least 33% of senior managers are women
- **Shares:** Companies where employees are offered share options
- **Long Service:** 40% of employees with more than 5 years' service
- **Health Insurance:** Full family cover

MOUCHEL PARKMAN

UK locations	National
UK sites	100
Sector	Engineering
Definition	Professional Services
How owned	Public (i.e. stock market listed)
Founded	1907
Turnover	£365.2m
Profit	£27.4m
Staff	4344
Average age	39
Male : Female	74 : 26
Earnings £35,000+	26%

MISSION / VISION

To make a real and positive difference to the communities we serve, improving quality of life wherever we operate.

BEST WORKPLACE FACTORS

WELL BEING
PERSONAL GROWTH
MY MANAGER

BEST COMPANIES INDEX

2007 BCI = 651.6
2006 BCI = 636.1

1000 / 652> / ones to watch / 500

CONTACT DETAILS

Mouchel Parkman
West Hall, Parvis Road,
West Byfleet, Surrey KT14 6EZ
Tel: 01932 337000
www.mouchelparkman.com

GRADUATE VACANCIES

Engineering, Business, Commercial.

1000

MUIR GROUP HOUSING ASSOCIATION

UK locations	National
UK sites	34
Sector	Housing Associations
Definition	Registered Housing Association
How owned	Private
Founded	1968
Turnover	£15.2m
Profit	£1.1m
Staff	169
Average age	45
Male : Female	30 : 70
Earnings £35,000+	9%

MISSION / VISION

The excellent provision and management of high quality affordable housing for those in need.

BEST WORKPLACE FACTORS

FAIR DEAL
GIVING SOMETHING BACK
WELL BEING

BEST COMPANIES INDEX

2007 BCI = 635.0

ones to watch <635

CONTACT DETAILS

Muir Group Housing Association
Old Government House, Dee Hills Park,
Chester CH3 5AR
Tel: 01244 313613
www.muir.org.uk

500

GRADUATE VACANCIES

No graduate vacancies have been indicated.

KEY

- **Holidays:** Companies offering a minimum of 25 days annual leave
- **Pensions:** Companies offering a final salary or non-contributory/contributory pension scheme
- **Maternity:** Companies offering over Statutory Maternity Pay
- **Charity Activities:** 10% of staff undertake charitable activities during business hours
- **Childcare:** On-site nursery or vouchers
- **Gym:** On-site gym or subsidised gym memberships
- **Women:** At least 33% of senior managers are women
- **Shares:** Companies where employees are offered share options
- **Long Service:** 40% of employees with more than 5 years' service
- **Health Insurance:** Full family cover

1000

NORTHWEST REGIONAL DEVELOPMENT AGENCY

UK locations	N.West
UK sites	11
Sector	Public
Definition	Regional Development Agency
How owned	Government
Founded	1999
Turnover	£408.9m
Profit	Not disclosed
Staff	380
Average age	41
Male : Female	45 : 55
Earnings £35,000+	35%

MISSION / VISION

Our vision is to transform England's Northwest into a dynamic sustainable international economy which competes on the basis of knowledge, advanced technology and an excellent quality of life for all.

BEST WORKPLACE FACTORS

GIVING SOMETHING BACK
FAIR DEAL
PERSONAL GROWTH

BEST COMPANIES INDEX

2007 BCI = 628.5

ones to watch <629

CONTACT DETAILS

Northwest Regional Development Agency
PO Box 37, Renaissance House,
Centre Park, Warrington, Cheshire WA1 1XB
Tel: 01925 400100
www.nwda.co.uk

500

GRADUATE VACANCIES

Policy, Research, Analysis, Finance, Economics, Project Support, Marketing, Procurement, Planning, Business.

OGCBUYING.SOLUTIONS

UK locations	N.West
UK sites	3
Sector	Public
Definition	Procurement Agency
How owned	Government
Founded	2001
Turnover	£0.07m
Profit	Not disclosed
Staff	276
Average age	42
Male : Female	51 : 49
Earnings £35,000+	28%

CONTACT DETAILS

OGCbuying.solutions
5th Floor, Royal Liver Building,
Liverpool L3 1PE
Tel: 0845 4102222
www.ogcbuyingsolutions.gov.uk

MISSION / VISION

Savings for the Nation.

BEST WORKPLACE FACTORS

GIVING SOMETHING BACK
WELL BEING
FAIR DEAL

BEST COMPANIES INDEX

2007 BCI = 657.3
2006 BCI = 638.0

GRADUATE VACANCIES

Procurement, Marketing, Planning, Energy.

1000
657>
ones to watch
500

KEY

- **Holidays:** Companies offering a minimum of 25 days annual leave
- **Pensions:** Companies offering a final salary or non-contributory/ contributory pension scheme
- **Maternity:** Companies offering over Statutory Maternity Pay
- **Charity Activities:** 10% of staff undertake charitable activities during business hours
- **Childcare:** On-site nursery or vouchers
- **Gym:** On-site gym or subsidised gym memberships
- **Women:** At least 33% of senior managers are women
- **Shares:** Companies where employees are offered share options
- **Long Service:** 40% of employees with more than 5 years' service
- **Health Insurance:** Full family cover

P&MM

UK locations	S.East
UK sites	1
Sector	Business Services
Definition	Performance Improvement Specialists
How owned	Public (i.e. stock market listed)
Founded	1989
Turnover	Not disclosed
Profit	Not disclosed
Staff	146
Average age	36
Male : Female	37 : 63
Earnings £35,000+	27%

CONTACT DETAILS

P&MM
Rockingham Drive, Linford Wood,
Milton Keynes, Bucks MK14 6LY
Tel: 01908 608000
www.p-mm.co.uk

MISSION / VISION

To be a top 3 player in any market that we operate in or choose to enter.

BEST WORKPLACE FACTORS

FAIR DEAL
GIVING SOMETHING BACK
MY COMPANY

BEST COMPANIES INDEX

2007 BCI = 658.7
2006 BCI = 714.9

GRADUATE VACANCIES

No graduate vacancies have been indicated.

1000
659>
ones to watch
500

1000

PHILIPS ELECTRONICS UK

UK locations	S.East
UK sites	5
Sector	Consumer Goods
Definition	Healthcare Lifestyle Technology
How owned	Public (i.e. stock market listed)
Founded	1891
Turnover	Not disclosed
Profit	Not disclosed
Staff	1509
Average age	40
Male : Female	58 : 42
Earnings £35,000+	32%

ones to watch

<626

500

CONTACT DETAILS

Philips Electronics UK Ltd
The Philips Centre, Guildford Business Park,
Surrey GU2 8XH
Tel: 01293 815000
www.philips.co.uk

MISSION / VISION

We improve the quality of peoples lives through timely introduction of meaningful technological innovations.

BEST WORKPLACE FACTORS

GIVING SOMETHING BACK
WELL BEING
LEADERSHIP

BEST COMPANIES INDEX

2007 BCI = 626.0

GRADUATE VACANCIES

Sales, Marketing, Finance, Engineering, Research.

KEY

- **Holidays:** Companies offering a minimum of 25 days annual leave
- **Pensions:** Companies offering a final salary or non-contributory/ contributory pension scheme
- **Maternity:** Companies offering over Statutory Maternity Pay
- **Charity Activities:** 10% of staff undertake charitable activities during business hours
- **Childcare:** On-site nursery or vouchers
- **Gym:** On-site gym or subsidised gym memberships
- **Women:** At least 33% of senior managers are women
- **Shares:** Companies where employees are offered share options
- **Long Service:** 40% of employees with more than 5 years' service
- **Health Insurance:** Full family cover

1000

PROTOCOL EDUCATION

UK locations	National
UK sites	15
Sector	Education
Definition	Education Supply Agency
How owned	Private
Founded	2001
Turnover	Not disclosed
Profit	Not disclosed
Staff	167
Average age	28
Male : Female	27 : 73
Earnings £35,000+	8%

ones to watch

<620

500

CONTACT DETAILS

Protocol Education
40 -43 Chancery Lane, London WC2A 1JA
Tel: 0207 4408440
www.protocol-education.com

MISSION / VISION

We aim to be the market leader by being the first choice for staffing needs in the education sector.

BEST WORKPLACE FACTORS

MY TEAM
MY MANAGER
PERSONAL GROWTH

BEST COMPANIES INDEX

2007 BCI = 619.7

GRADUATE VACANCIES

No graduate vacancies have been indicated.

To find out more about these companies visit www.bestcompaniesguide.co.uk

REED LEARNING

UK locations	National
UK sites	10
Sector	Business Services
Definition	Training and Recruitment
How owned	Private
Founded	2000
Turnover	£22.4m
Profit	£0.2m
Staff	165
Average age	30
Male : Female	30 : 70
Earnings £35,000+	10%

CONTACT DETAILS

Reed Learning
6th Floor, Kiln House,
210 New Kings Road, London SW6 4NZ
Tel: 0207 3847332
www.reedlearning.co.uk

MISSION / VISION

To be the leading provider of Education and Training Services in our chosen markets.

BEST WORKPLACE FACTORS

MY MANAGER
PERSONAL GROWTH
GIVING SOMETHING BACK

BEST COMPANIES INDEX

2007 BCI = 658.3
2006 BCI = 642.2

GRADUATE VACANCIES

All Areas.

1000

658>

ones to watch

500

KEY

- **Holidays:** Companies offering a minimum of 25 days annual leave
- **Pensions:** Companies offering a final salary or non-contributory/contributory pension scheme
- **Maternity:** Companies offering over Statutory Maternity Pay
- **Charity Activities:** 10% of staff undertake charitable activities during business hours
- **Childcare:** On-site nursery or vouchers
- **Gym:** On-site gym or subsidised gym memberships
- **Women:** At least 33% of senior managers are women
- **Shares:** Companies where employees are offered share options
- **Long Service:** 40% of employees with more than 5 years' service
- **Health Insurance:** Full family cover

RETAIL HUMAN RESOURCES

UK locations	National
UK sites	10
Sector	Recruitment
Definition	Retail Recruitment Consultancy
How owned	Private
Founded	1999
Turnover	£5.9m
Profit	£0.8m
Staff	80
Average age	29
Male : Female	Not available
Earnings £35,000+	Not available

CONTACT DETAILS

Retail Human Resources
Heathfield House, 430 Archway Road,
Highgate, London N6 4JH
Tel: 0870 8501911
www.rhr.co.uk

MISSION / VISION

To become the most effective supplier of recruitment and selection services to the retail and leisure industries in the UK. To be renowned for being honest and professional.

BEST WORKPLACE FACTORS

FAIR DEAL
MY MANAGER
MY TEAM

BEST COMPANIES INDEX

2007 BCI = 656.6

GRADUATE VACANCIES

No graduate vacancies have been indicated.

1000

657>

ones to watch

500

1000

<605

500

ROADCHEF MOTORWAYS

UK locations	National
UK sites	20
Sector	Retail
Definition	Motorway Service Operator
How owned	
Founded	1972
Turnover	Not disclosed
Profit	Not disclosed
Staff	2535
Average age	Not available
Male : Female	Not available
Earnings £35,000+	Not available

CONTACT DETAILS

RoadChef Motorways
RoadChef House, Norton Canes,
MSA Betty's Lane, Cannock, Staffordshire WS11 9UX
Tel: 01543 272597
www.roadchef.com

MISSION / VISION

To be the best motorway services operator in the UK.

BEST WORKPLACE FACTORS

WELL BEING
FAIR DEAL
MY TEAM

BEST COMPANIES INDEX

2007 BCI = 604.6

GRADUATE VACANCIES

No graduate vacancies have been indicated.

KEY

- **Holidays:** Companies offering a minimum of 25 days annual leave
- **Pensions:** Companies offering a final salary or non-contributory/ contributory pension scheme
- **Maternity:** Companies offering over Statutory Maternity Pay
- **Charity Activities:** 10% of staff undertake charitable activities during business hours
- **Childcare:** On-site nursery or vouchers
- **Gym:** On-site gym or subsidised gym memberships
- **Women:** At least 33% of senior managers are women
- **Shares:** Companies where employees are offered share options
- **Long Service:** 40% of employees with more than 5 years' service
- **Health Insurance:** Full family cover

1000

<647

500

ROBSON TAYLOR

UK locations	National
UK sites	4
Sector	Recruitment
Definition	IT Sales Recruitment
How owned	Private
Founded	1997
Turnover	Not disclosed
Profit	Not disclosed
Staff	54
Average age	30
Male : Female	57 : 43
Earnings £35,000+	44%

CONTACT DETAILS

Robson Taylor
Manchester International Office Centre, Styal Road,
Manchester M22 5WB
Tel: 0161 4933000
www.robsontaylor.com

MISSION / VISION

To be the company of choice for organisations looking to recruit Sales Professionals throughout Europe.

BEST WORKPLACE FACTORS

FAIR DEAL
MY MANAGER
MY TEAM

BEST COMPANIES INDEX

2007 BCI = 646.6

GRADUATE VACANCIES

Account Execs, Consultants.

ROK

UK locations	National
UK sites	50
Sector	Construction
Definition	Development Building Maintenance
How owned	Public (i.e. stock market listed)
Founded	2001
Turnover	£556.0m
Profit	£16.1m
Staff	3278
Average age	34
Male : Female	87 : 13
Earnings £35,000+	21%

CONTACT DETAILS

Rok
Rok Centre, Septre Court,
40 Tower Hill, London EC3N 4DE
Tel: 01392 3540000
www.rokgroup.com

MISSION / VISION

Rok aims to become the nation's local builder by operating from a network of offices in major towns across the UK using dedicated teams who live and work in their communities.

BEST WORKPLACE FACTORS

WELL BEING
MY COMPANY
PERSONAL GROWTH

BEST COMPANIES INDEX

2007 BCI = 655.7
2006 BCI = 686.7

GRADUATE VACANCIES

IT, Quantity Surveying, Construction Management, Bus. Management, Accountancy.

1000
656>
ones to watch
500

KEY

- **Holidays:** Companies offering a minimum of 25 days annual leave
- **Pensions:** Companies offering a final salary or non-contributory/ contributory pension scheme
- **Maternity:** Companies offering over Statutory Maternity Pay
- **Charity Activities:** 10% of staff undertake charitable activities during business hours
- **Childcare:** On-site nursery or vouchers
- **Gym:** On-site gym or subsidised gym memberships
- **Women:** At least 33% of senior managers are women
- **Shares:** Companies where employees are offered share options
- **Long Service:** 40% of employees with more than 5 years' service
- **Health Insurance:** Full family cover

SAFFRON HOUSING TRUST

UK locations	E.England
UK sites	18
Sector	Housing Associations
Definition	Affordable Housing and Services
How owned	Private
Founded	1973
Turnover	£13.7m
Profit	Not disclosed
Staff	164
Average age	43
Male : Female	61 : 39
Earnings £35,000+	7%

CONTACT DETAILS

Saffron Housing Trust
Saffron Barn, Swan Lane,
Long Stratton, Norwich, Norfolk NR15 2XP
Tel: 01508 532000
www.saffronhousing.co.uk

MISSION / VISION

We are determined to deliver the best possible housing service for the people of the area. We now have a real opportunity to work together with the Council and our customers to create a better housing future.

BEST WORKPLACE FACTORS

GIVING SOMETHING BACK
FAIR DEAL
WELL BEING

BEST COMPANIES INDEX

2007 BCI = 606.9

GRADUATE VACANCIES

No graduate vacancies have been indicated.

1000
607>
ones to watch
500

1000

SAPIENT

UK locations	London
UK sites	1
Sector	Consulting
Definition	Business Innovation Consulting
How owned	Public (i.e. stock market listed)
Founded	1990
Turnover	Not disclosed
Profit	Not disclosed
Staff	170
Average age	32
Male : Female	85 : 15
Earnings £35,000+	86%

MISSION / VISION

Being a great company enabling human potential.

BEST WORKPLACE FACTORS

FAIR DEAL
GIVING SOMETHING BACK
MY COMPANY

BEST COMPANIES INDEX

2007 BCI = 618.7
2006 BCI = 728.3

ones to watch

<619

CONTACT DETAILS

Sapient
1 Exchange Tower, Harbour Exchange Square,
Limeharbour, London E14 9GE
Tel: 020 77864500
www.sapient.co.uk

GRADUATE VACANCIES

Technology.

500

KEY

- **Holidays:** Companies offering a minimum of 25 days annual leave
- **Pensions:** Companies offering a final salary or non-contributory/contributory pension scheme
- **Maternity:** Companies offering over Statutory Maternity Pay
- **Charity Activities:** 10% of staff undertake charitable activities during business hours
- **Childcare:** On-site nursery or vouchers
- **Gym:** On-site gym or subsidised gym memberships
- **Women:** At least 33% of senior managers are women
- **Shares:** Companies where employees are offered share options
- **Long Service:** 40% of employees with more than 5 years' service
- **Health Insurance:** Full family cover

1000

SAS

UK locations	National
UK sites	3
Sector	IT/Internet Services
Definition	Software Solutions Provider
How owned	Private
Founded	1980
Turnover	£63.2m
Profit	Not disclosed
Staff	396
Average age	39
Male : Female	63 : 37
Earnings £35,000+	58%

MISSION / VISION

To add value for our customers and be central to their success. Our software & services help you do more with data than you ever thought possible.

BEST WORKPLACE FACTORS

GIVING SOMETHING BACK
MY COMPANY
PERSONAL GROWTH

BEST COMPANIES INDEX

2007 BCI = 629.2
2006 BCI = 612.7

ones to watch

<629

CONTACT DETAILS

SAS
Wittington House, Henley Road,
Medmenham, Marlow, Bucks SL7 2EB
Tel: 01628 486933
www.sas.com/uk

GRADUATE VACANCIES

IT, Consulting.

500

SCOTT BROWNRIGG

UK locations	London, S.East
UK sites	5
Sector	Architects
Definition	Architect Planning & Interior Design
How owned	Private
Founded	1993
Turnover	£13.6m
Profit	£2.2m
Staff	179
Average age	38
Male : Female	72 : 28
Earnings £35,000+	51%

CONTACT DETAILS

Scott Brownrigg
St. Catherine's Court, 46-48 Portsmouth Road,
Guildford, Surrey GU2 4DU
Tel: 01483 568686
www.scottbrownrigg.com

MISSION / VISION

Our mission is to combine vision with action to make a positive difference - creatively, commercially, consistently.

BEST WORKPLACE FACTORS

PERSONAL GROWTH
FAIR DEAL
MY COMPANY

BEST COMPANIES INDEX

2007 BCI = 644.2

GRADUATE VACANCIES

Architecture, Planning.

1000
644>
ones to watch
500

KEY

- **Holidays:** Companies offering a minimum of 25 days annual leave
- **Pensions:** Companies offering a final salary or non-contributory/ contributory pension scheme
- **Maternity:** Companies offering over Statutory Maternity Pay
- **Charity Activities:** 10% of staff undertake charitable activities during business hours
- **Childcare:** On-site nursery or vouchers
- **Gym:** On-site gym or subsidised gym memberships
- **Women:** At least 33% of senior managers are women
- **Shares:** Companies where employees are offered share options
- **Long Service:** 40% of employees with more than 5 years' service
- **Health Insurance:** Full family cover

SOUTH STAFFORDSHIRE WATER

UK locations	W.Midlands
UK sites	5
Sector	Utilities
Definition	Water Supply
How owned	Private
Founded	1991
Turnover	Not disclosed
Profit	Not disclosed
Staff	370
Average age	42
Male : Female	75 : 25
Earnings £35,000+	12%

CONTACT DETAILS

South Staffordshire Water
Green Lane, Walsall,
West Midlands WS2 7PD
Tel: 01922 638282
www.south-staffs-water.co.uk

MISSION / VISION

Going forward together, to provide the best value for money in all we do, of any water supplier in the UK.

BEST WORKPLACE FACTORS

GIVING SOMETHING BACK
WELL BEING
LEADERSHIP

BEST COMPANIES INDEX

2007 BCI = 612.1
2006 BCI = 623.4

GRADUATE VACANCIES

No graduate vacancies have been indicated.

1000
612>
ones to watch
500

To find out more about these companies visit www.bestcompaniesguide.co.uk

1000

SPECSAVERS OPTICAL GROUP

UK locations	Guernsey
UK sites	2
Sector	Retail
Definition	Optical Retail Support
How owned	Private
Founded	1984
Turnover	Not disclosed
Profit	Not disclosed
Staff	502
Average age	36
Male : Female	44 : 56
Earnings £35,000+	24%

ones to watch

<643

CONTACT DETAILS

Specsavers Optical Group Ltd
La Villiaze, St Andrews,
Guernsey GY6 8YP
Tel: 01480 236000
www.specsavers.co.uk

500

MISSION / VISION

To be the best value opticians, satisfying personal eyecare needs at affordable prices, simply, clearly, and consistently.

BEST WORKPLACE FACTORS

LEADERSHIP
GIVING SOMETHING BACK
WELL BEING

BEST COMPANIES INDEX

2007 BCI = 643.2
2006 BCI = 667.4

GRADUATE VACANCIES

No graduate vacancies have been indicated.

KEY

- **Holidays:** Companies offering a minimum of 25 days annual leave
- **Pensions:** Companies offering a final salary or non-contributory/contributory pension scheme
- **Maternity:** Companies offering over Statutory Maternity Pay
- **Charity Activities:** 10% of staff undertake charitable activities during business hours
- **Childcare:** On-site nursery or vouchers
- **Gym:** On-site gym or subsidised gym memberships
- **Women:** At least 33% of senior managers are women
- **Shares:** Companies where employees are offered share options
- **Long Service:** 40% of employees with more than 5 years' service
- **Health Insurance:** Full family cover

1000

SRG

UK locations	National
UK sites	9
Sector	Recruitment
Definition	Science Recruitment Specialists
How owned	Public (i.e. stock market listed)
Founded	1990
Turnover	Not disclosed
Profit	Not disclosed
Staff	85
Average age	28
Male : Female	44 : 56
Earnings £35,000+	21%

ones to watch

<649

CONTACT DETAILS

SRG
Buckland House, Waterside Drive,
Langley Business Park, Slough, Berkshire SL3 6EZ
Tel: 01753 585588
www.srg.co.uk

500

MISSION / VISION

To be recognised as the undisputed market-leading provider of staff and staffing solutions to the broad-based scientific community including clinical and process industries.

BEST WORKPLACE FACTORS

MY MANAGER
MY TEAM
PERSONAL GROWTH

BEST COMPANIES INDEX

2007 BCI = 649.4

GRADUATE VACANCIES

No graduate vacancies have been indicated.

STYLES & WOOD GROUP

UK locations	National
UK sites	4
Sector	Property
Definition	Property Services Company
How owned	Private
Founded	1981
Turnover	£170.7m
Profit	£6.4m
Staff	370
Average age	41
Male : Female	84 : 16
Earnings £35,000+	65%

CONTACT DETAILS

Styles & Wood Group
Aspect House, Manchester Road,
Altrincham, Cheshire WA14 5PG
Tel: 0161 9266000
www.stylesandwood.co.uk

MISSION / VISION

To build excellence into our people and the service we offer the customer, by actively encouraging personal development, teamwork and a progressive quality standard.

BEST WORKPLACE FACTORS

LEADERSHIP
MY COMPANY
PERSONAL GROWTH

BEST COMPANIES INDEX

2007 BCI = 656.7
2006 BCI = 674.1

GRADUATE VACANCIES

No graduate vacancies have been indicated.

1000 ★ ★ ★ ★ ★ ★ 657> ones to watch 500

KEY

- **Holidays:** Companies offering a minimum of 25 days annual leave
- **Pensions:** Companies offering a final salary or non-contributory/ contributory pension scheme
- **Maternity:** Companies offering over Statutory Maternity Pay
- **Charity Activities:** 10% of staff undertake charitable activities during business hours
- **Childcare:** On-site nursery or vouchers
- **Gym:** On-site gym or subsidised gym memberships
- **Women:** At least 33% of senior managers are women
- **Shares:** Companies where employees are offered share options
- **Long Service:** 40% of employees with more than 5 years' service
- **Health Insurance:** Full family cover

SUPERDRUG (HEALTH AND BEAUTY BY AS WATSON)

UK locations	National
UK sites	742
Sector	Retail
Definition	Health and Beauty Retail
How owned	Private
Founded	2002
Turnover	Not disclosed
Profit	Not disclosed
Staff	13488
Average age	31
Male : Female	25 : 75
Earnings £35,000+	3%

CONTACT DETAILS

Superdrug (Health and Beauty by AS Watson)
118 Beddington Lane, Croydon,
Surrey CR0 4TB
Tel: 0208 6847000
www.superdrug.com

MISSION / VISION

'Gotta Have it Products at Gotta Have it Prices'.

BEST WORKPLACE FACTORS

WELL BEING
MY TEAM
MY COMPANY

BEST COMPANIES INDEX

2007 BCI = 610.8

GRADUATE VACANCIES

No graduate vacancies have been indicated.

1000 ★ ★ ★ ★ ★ ★ 611> ones to watch 500

1000

<635

500

THATCHAM

UK locations	S.East
UK sites	1
Sector	Not for Profit
Definition	Automotive Research
How owned	Limited by guarantee
Founded	1969
Turnover	£10.2m
Profit	£0.01m
Staff	132
Average age	42
Male : Female	81:19
Earnings £35,000+	20%

CONTACT DETAILS

Thatcham
Colthrop Way, Thatcham,
Berks RG19 4NR
Tel: 01635 293166
www.thatcham.org

MISSION / VISION

We are committed to creating an inspirational working environment, to being the pre-eminent originator of independent automotive information and standards, and to generating exceptional value for all our stakeholders.

BEST WORKPLACE FACTORS

GIVING SOMETHING BACK
WELL BEING
MY COMPANY

BEST COMPANIES INDEX

2007 BCI = 635.3

GRADUATE VACANCIES

No graduate vacancies have been indicated.

KEY

Holidays: Companies offering a minimum of 25 days annual leave
Pensions: Companies offering a final salary or non-contributory/contributory pension scheme
Maternity: Companies offering over Statutory Maternity Pay
Charity Activities: 10% of staff undertake charitable activities during business hours
Childcare: On-site nursery or vouchers
Gym: On-site gym or subsidised gym memberships
Women: At least 33% of senior managers are women
Shares: Companies where employees are offered share options
Long Service: 40% of employees with more than 5 years' service
Health Insurance: Full family cover

1000

<651

500

THE CHILDREN'S MUTUAL

UK locations	S.East
UK sites	1
Sector	Financial
Definition	Savings for Children
How owned	Private
Founded	1881
Turnover	£140.9m
Profit	£18.8m
Staff	66
Average age	40
Male : Female	56 : 44
Earnings £35,000+	39%

CONTACT DETAILS

The Children's Mutual
Brockbourne House, 77 Mount Ephraim,
Tunbridge Wells, Kent TN4 8GN
Tel: 01892 775465
www.thechildrensmutual.co.uk

MISSION / VISION

Quite simply we're the only UK company that specialises exclusively in savings for children.

BEST WORKPLACE FACTORS

WELL BEING
MY TEAM
GIVING SOMETHING BACK

BEST COMPANIES INDEX

2007 BCI = 651.2
2006 BCI = 669.3

GRADUATE VACANCIES

No graduate vacancies have been indicated.

THE FARM GROUP

UK locations	London
UK sites	6
Sector	Media
Definition	Television Post Production
How owned	Private
Founded	1998
Turnover	£15.1m
Profit	£2.3m
Staff	101
Average age	30
Male : Female	69 : 31
Earnings £35,000+	34%

CONTACT DETAILS

The Farm Group
13 Soho Square, London W1D 3QF
Tel: 0207 4376677
www.farmgroup.tv

MISSION / VISION

To be the best post production company in the world.

BEST WORKPLACE FACTORS

MY TEAM
MY MANAGER
MY COMPANY

BEST COMPANIES INDEX

2007 BCI = 648.1

GRADUATE VACANCIES

Library, IT, AVID (Technical), Accounts, Reception.

1000 648> 500 ones to watch

KEY

- **Holidays:** Companies offering a minimum of 25 days annual leave
- **Pensions:** Companies offering a final salary or non-contributory/contributory pension scheme
- **Maternity:** Companies offering over Statutory Maternity Pay
- **Charity Activities:** 10% of staff undertake charitable activities during business hours
- **Childcare:** On-site nursery or vouchers
- **Gym:** On-site gym or subsidised gym memberships
- **Women:** At least 33% of senior managers are women
- **Shares:** Companies where employees are offered share options
- **Long Service:** 40% of employees with more than 5 years' service
- **Health Insurance:** Full family cover

THE GARDINER CALDWELL GROUP

UK locations	London, N.West
UK sites	5
Sector	Consulting
Definition	Healthcare Communications Agency
How owned	Public (i.e. stock market listed)
Founded	1983
Turnover	Not disclosed
Profit	Not disclosed
Staff	324
Average age	35
Male : Female	30 : 70
Earnings £35,000+	34%

CONTACT DETAILS

The Gardiner Caldwell Group
Victoria Mill, Windmill Street,
Macclesfield SK11 7HQ
Tel: 01626 664000
www.gardiner-caldwell.thomson.com

MISSION / VISION

Continuously improving to be the Best Global Healthcare Communications Organisation.

BEST WORKPLACE FACTORS

PERSONAL GROWTH
FAIR DEAL
MY TEAM

BEST COMPANIES INDEX

2007 BCI = 626.0

GRADUATE VACANCIES

Medical & Scientific Services.

1000 626> 500 ones to watch

1000

THE PENSIONS TRUST

UK locations	National
UK sites	3
Sector	Financial
Definition	Occupational Pension Scheme
How owned	Trust/Employee owned/Mutual
Founded	1956
Turnover	£18.0m
Profit	Not disclosed
Staff	160
Average age	30
Male : Female	42 : 58
Earnings £35,000+	21%

ones to watch

<613

500

CONTACT DETAILS

The Pensions Trust
Verity House, 6 Canal Wharf,
Leeds LS11 5BQ
Tel: 0113 3942520
www.thepensionstrust.org.uk

MISSION / VISION

To be the lowest cost provider of a comprehensive pensions service for our customers.

BEST WORKPLACE FACTORS

GIVING SOMETHING BACK
WELL BEING
FAIR DEAL

BEST COMPANIES INDEX

2007 BCI = 612.7
2006 BCI = 612.0

GRADUATE VACANCIES

No graduate vacancies have been indicated.

KEY

Holidays: Companies offering a minimum of 25 days annual leave

Pensions: Companies offering a final salary or non-contributory/contributory pension scheme

Maternity: Companies offering over Statutory Maternity Pay

Charity Activities: 10% of staff undertake charitable activities during business hours

Childcare: On-site nursery or vouchers

Gym: On-site gym or subsidised gym memberships

Women: At least 33% of senior managers are women

Shares: Companies where employees are offered share options

Long Service: 40% of employees with more than 5 years' service

Health Insurance: Full family cover

1000

THOMAS COOK UK & IRELAND

UK locations	National
UK sites	600
Sector	Travel
Definition	Major Travel Company
How owned	Private
Founded	1841
Turnover	Not disclosed
Profit	£83.3m
Staff	9315
Average age	32
Male : Female	20 : 80
Earnings £35,000+	8%

ones to watch

<629

500

CONTACT DETAILS

Thomas Cook UK & Ireland
Thomas Cook Business Park, Coningsby Road,
Peterborough PE3 8AB
Tel: 01733 417100
www.thomascook.com

MISSION / VISION

To Perfect the Personal Leisure Experience.

BEST WORKPLACE FACTORS

WELL BEING
MY TEAM
MY MANAGER

BEST COMPANIES INDEX

2007 BCI = 629.1
2006 BCI = 640.4

GRADUATE VACANCIES

E-Commerce, Financial Services, Tour Operators.

To find out more about these companies visit www.bestcompaniesguide.co.uk

THORNTONS LAW

UK locations	Scotland
UK sites	5
Sector	Law
Definition	Legal/Investments/Property
How owned	Private
Founded	1990
Turnover	£14.0m
Profit	£3.8m
Staff	331
Average age	37
Male : Female	24 : 76
Earnings £35,000+	18%

CONTACT DETAILS

Thorntons Law
50 Castle Street, Dundee DD1 3RU
Tel: 01382 229111
www.thorntons-law.co.uk

MISSION / VISION

We believe that success breeds success and are proud of what we have achieved. We believe in a progressive approach to our business and to our clients whilst also taking seriously our responsibilities to the local communities across our part of Scotland.

BEST WORKPLACE FACTORS

WELL BEING
FAIR DEAL
LEADERSHIP

BEST COMPANIES INDEX

2007 BCI = 637.3

GRADUATE VACANCIES

Legal.

1000

637>

ones to watch

500

KEY

Holidays: Companies offering a minimum of 25 days annual leave

Pensions: Companies offering a final salary or non-contributory/ contributory pension scheme

Maternity: Companies offering over Statutory Maternity Pay

Charity Activities: 10% of staff undertake charitable activities during business hours

Childcare: On-site nursery or vouchers

Gym: On-site gym or subsidised gym memberships

Women: At least 33% of senior managers are women

Shares: Companies where employees are offered share options

Long Service: 40% of employees with more than 5 years' service

Health Insurance: Full family cover

TITLE RESEARCH GROUP

UK locations	National
UK sites	3
Sector	Professional Services
Definition	Genealogy research services
How owned	Trust/Employee owned/Mutual
Founded	1965
Turnover	Not disclosed
Profit	Not disclosed
Staff	62
Average age	35
Male : Female	48 : 52
Earnings £35,000+	31%

CONTACT DETAILS

Title Research Group
24 Britton Street, London EC1M 5UA
Tel: 0207 5490900
www.titleresearchgroup.com

MISSION / VISION

To be the partner of choice for customers needing to link, people, places, estates, and assets together.

BEST WORKPLACE FACTORS

WELL BEING
FAIR DEAL
GIVING SOMETHING BACK

BEST COMPANIES INDEX

2007 BCI = 643.0
2006 BCI = 662.2

GRADUATE VACANCIES

No graduate vacancies have been indicated.

1000

643>

ones to watch

500

1000

TRADEDOUBLER

UK locations	London
UK sites	1
Sector	Media
Definition	Performance-based Digital Marketing
How owned	Partnership/LLP
Founded	1999
Turnover	£37.3m
Profit	Not disclosed
Staff	71
Average age	28
Male : Female	59 : 41
Earnings £35,000+	34%

<659

ones to watch

CONTACT DETAILS

TradeDoubler
24th Floor, Portland House,
Bressenden Place, London SW1E 5BH
Tel: 0207 7985800
www.tradedoubler.com

500

MISSION / VISION

We change the way you conduct and measure digital marketing through our expertise network and technology.

BEST WORKPLACE FACTORS

MY TEAM
MY MANAGER
PERSONAL GROWTH

BEST COMPANIES INDEX

2007 BCI = 659.0

GRADUATE VACANCIES

Account Management, Technical services & Sales.

KEY

Holidays: Companies offering a minimum of 25 days annual leave
Pensions: Companies offering a final salary or non-contributory/contributory pension scheme
Maternity: Companies offering over Statutory Maternity Pay
Charity Activities: 10% of staff undertake charitable activities during business hours
Childcare: On-site nursery or vouchers
Gym: On-site gym or subsidised gym memberships
Women: At least 33% of senior managers are women
Shares: Companies where employees are offered share options
Long Service: 40% of employees with more than 5 years' service
Health Insurance: Full family cover

1000

TTS GROUP LTD

UK locations	S.East, E.Midlands
UK sites	4
Sector	Logistics/Wholesale/Distribution
Definition	Educational Supplies
How owned	Private
Founded	1985
Turnover	Not disclosed
Profit	Not disclosed
Staff	94
Average age	30
Male : Female	41 : 59
Earnings £35,000+	11%

<653

ones to watch

CONTACT DETAILS

TTS Group Ltd
Nunn Brook Road, Huthwaite,
Nottinghamshire NG17 2HU
Tel: 0800 137525
www.tts-group.co.uk

500

MISSION / VISION

We aim to continuously improve our offering to become the largest supplier of nursery and primary equipment and uphold our dynamic approach to developing all people involved with the TTS story.

BEST WORKPLACE FACTORS

LEADERSHIP
PERSONAL GROWTH
GIVING SOMETHING BACK

BEST COMPANIES INDEX

2007 BCI = 653.4

GRADUATE VACANCIES

No graduate vacancies have been indicated.

To find out more about these companies visit www.bestcompaniesguide.co.uk

VALUECLICK EUROPE

UK locations	London
UK sites	1
Sector	Media
Definition	On-line Marketing Company
How owned	Limited by shares
Founded	1999
Turnover	Not disclosed
Profit	Not disclosed
Staff	89
Average age	30
Male : Female	54 : 46
Earnings £35,000+	39%

MISSION / VISION

We are committed to ensuring that our customers are the number one priority. We have become one of Europe's largest and most comprehensive online marketing companies and remain dedicated to meeting our customers' most challenging needs.

BEST WORKPLACE FACTORS

MY COMPANY
MY TEAM
LEADERSHIP

BEST COMPANIES INDEX

2007 BCI = 649.9

1000

650>

ones to watch

500

CONTACT DETAILS

ValueClick Europe
Cambridge House, 180 Upper Richmond Road,
London SW15 2SH
Tel: 0208 7855800
www.valueclick.co.uk

GRADUATE VACANCIES

Sales/Account Management/Client Service Support.

KEY

- **Holidays:** Companies offering a minimum of 25 days annual leave
- **Pensions:** Companies offering a final salary or non-contributory/contributory pension scheme
- **Maternity:** Companies offering over Statutory Maternity Pay
- **Charity Activities:** 10% of staff undertake charitable activities during business hours
- **Childcare:** On-site nursery or vouchers
- **Gym:** On-site gym or subsidised gym memberships
- **Women:** At least 33% of senior managers are women
- **Shares:** Companies where employees are offered share options
- **Long Service:** 40% of employees with more than 5 years' service
- **Health Insurance:** Full family cover

VIRGIN MOBILE

UK locations	National
UK sites	3
Sector	Communications/Telecom
Definition	Mobile Network Operator
How owned	Private
Founded	1999
Turnover	Not disclosed
Profit	Not disclosed
Staff	1528
Average age	31
Male : Female	50 : 50
Earnings £35,000+	15%

MISSION / VISION

At Virgin Mobile, we do our very best to give people what they want. We concentrate on finding fresh ways to make our service better than everyone else's: more value, more honesty, more help, more fun.

BEST WORKPLACE FACTORS

FAIR DEAL
GIVING SOMETHING BACK
WELL BEING

BEST COMPANIES INDEX

2007 BCI = 647.4

1000

647>

ones to watch

500

CONTACT DETAILS

Virgin Mobile
Willow Grove House, White Horse Business Park,
Trowbridge, Wilts BA14 0TQ
Tel: 01225 895555
www.virgin.com/mobile

GRADUATE VACANCIES

No graduate vacancies have been indicated.

1000

VISITBRITAIN

UK locations	London
UK sites	2
Sector	Public
Definition	Marketing British Tourism
How owned	Government
Founded	2003
Turnover	Not disclosed
Profit	Not disclosed
Staff	246
Average age	35
Male : Female	46 : 54
Earnings £35,000+	38%

ones to watch

<622

500

CONTACT DETAILS

VisitBritain
Thames Tower, Black's Road,
London W6 9EL
Tel: 020 85633000
www.visitbritain.com

MISSION / VISION

To build the value of inbound tourism to Britain England Marketing: To grow the value of the domestic market by encouraging people to spend more on tourism throughout the English regions throughout the year.

BEST WORKPLACE FACTORS

GIVING SOMETHING BACK
WELL BEING
MY MANAGER

BEST COMPANIES INDEX

2007 BCI = 621.9

GRADUATE VACANCIES

All Areas & Disciplines.

KEY

- **Holidays:** Companies offering a minimum of 25 days annual leave
- **Pensions:** Companies offering a final salary or non-contributory/ contributory pension scheme
- **Maternity:** Companies offering over Statutory Maternity Pay
- **Charity Activities:** 10% of staff undertake charitable activities during business hours
- **Childcare:** On-site nursery or vouchers
- **Gym:** On-site gym or subsidised gym memberships
- **Women:** At least 33% of senior managers are women
- **Shares:** Companies where employees are offered share options
- **Long Service:** 40% of employees with more than 5 years' service
- **Health Insurance:** Full family cover

1000

VISUALFILES

UK locations	National
UK sites	3
Sector	IT/Internet Services
Definition	Case Management Solutions
How owned	Private
Founded	1985
Turnover	£11.0m
Profit	£1.5m
Staff	143
Average age	33
Male : Female	73 : 27
Earnings £35,000+	27%

ones to watch

<642

500

CONTACT DETAILS

Visualfiles
6th Floor, Arndale House,
Otley Road, Leeds LS6 2UU
Tel: 0113 2262000
www.visualfiles.com

MISSION / VISION

Visualfiles understands how professionals work & how to release valuable time from their working day, enabling them to concentrate on applying their specialist knowledge, making them more effective and profitable.

BEST WORKPLACE FACTORS

GIVING SOMETHING BACK
MY MANAGER
MY TEAM

BEST COMPANIES INDEX

2007 BCI = 642.0
2006 BCI = 717.0

GRADUATE VACANCIES

All Areas.

WCVA

UK locations	Wales
UK sites	6
Sector	Charity
Definition	Charity Membership Grant-Giver
How owned	Charity
Founded	1934
Turnover	£29.9m
Profit	Not disclosed
Staff	110
Average age	40
Male : Female	35 : 65
Earnings £35,000+	8%

CONTACT DETAILS

WCVA
Baltic House, Mount Stuart Square,
Cardiff CF10 5FH
Tel: 0292 0431700
www.wcva.org.uk

MISSION / VISION

Strengthen voluntary and community action at the heart of a civil society in Wales that is inclusive and offers equality of opportunity. Empowers people to participate and fosters community leadership. Encourages and promotes the independence of voluntary action.

BEST WORKPLACE FACTORS

GIVING SOMETHING BACK
FAIR DEAL
WELL BEING

BEST COMPANIES INDEX

2007 BCI = 638.2

GRADUATE VACANCIES

No graduate vacancies have been indicated.

1000

ones to watch

638>

500

KEY

- **Holidays:** Companies offering a minimum of 25 days annual leave
- **Pensions:** Companies offering a final salary or non-contributory/contributory pension scheme
- **Maternity:** Companies offering over Statutory Maternity Pay
- **Charity Activities:** 10% of staff undertake charitable activities during business hours
- **Childcare:** On-site nursery or vouchers
- **Gym:** On-site gym or subsidised gym memberships
- **Women:** At least 33% of senior managers are women
- **Shares:** Companies where employees are offered share options
- **Long Service:** 40% of employees with more than 5 years' service
- **Health Insurance:** Full family cover

WESTAFF (UK)

UK locations	National
UK sites	25
Sector	Recruitment
Definition	Commercial & Industrial
How owned	Public (i.e. stock market listed)
Founded	1966
Turnover	Not disclosed
Profit	Not disclosed
Staff	121
Average age	27
Male : Female	17 : 83
Earnings £35,000+	4%

CONTACT DETAILS

Westaff (UK)
Friary House, 46-50 Southgate Street,
Gloucester GL1 2DR
Tel: 01452 304090
www.westaff.co.uk

MISSION / VISION

We strive to understand our customers' needs & provide them with the highest quality service. We strive to offer our employees quality, rewarding work opportunities & experiences that deliver job satisfaction & learning opportunities.

BEST WORKPLACE FACTORS

LEADERSHIP
PERSONAL GROWTH
MY MANAGER

BEST COMPANIES INDEX

2007 BCI = 636.1

GRADUATE VACANCIES

No graduate vacancies have been indicated.

1000

ones to watch

636>

500

WESTMINSTER DRUG PROJECT

1000

<653

ones to watch

500

UK locations	London
UK sites	15
Sector	Charity
Definition	Drug Treatment Provider
How owned	Partnership/LLP
Founded	1990
Turnover	£5.0m
Profit	Not disclosed
Staff	191
Average age	Not available
Male : Female	Not available
Earnings £35,000+	Not available

CONTACT DETAILS

Westminster Drug Project Ltd
4th Floor, Kingsway House,
103 Kingsway, London WC2B 6QX
Tel: 0207 4213100
www.wdp-drugs.org.uk

MISSION / VISION

WDP work towards achieving a society which is well informed about drug issues, and where individuals with drug related problems receive the care and support they need.

BEST WORKPLACE FACTORS

GIVING SOMETHING BACK
PERSONAL GROWTH
MY COMPANY

BEST COMPANIES INDEX

2007 BCI = 652.9

GRADUATE VACANCIES

No graduate vacancies have been indicated.

KEY

- **Holidays:** Companies offering a minimum of 25 days annual leave
- **Pensions:** Companies offering a final salary or non-contributory/ contributory pension scheme
- **Maternity:** Companies offering over Statutory Maternity Pay
- **Charity Activities:** 10% of staff undertake charitable activities during business hours
- **Childcare:** On-site nursery or vouchers
- **Gym:** On-site gym or subsidised gym memberships
- **Women:** At least 33% of senior managers are women
- **Shares:** Companies where employees are offered share options
- **Long Service:** 40% of employees with more than 5 years' service
- **Health Insurance:** Full family cover

WESTON GROUP

1000

<650

ones to watch

500

UK locations	E.England
UK sites	12
Sector	Construction
Definition	Property Developer
How owned	Private
Founded	1987
Turnover	£82.8m
Profit	£8.3m
Staff	219
Average age	38
Male : Female	68 : 32
Earnings £35,000+	31%

CONTACT DETAILS

Weston Group
The Weston Group Business Centre, Parsonage Road,
Takeley, Essex CM22 6PU
Tel: 01279 873333
www.weston-group.co.uk

MISSION / VISION

The right product at The right price with The right presentation. This is to help focus all staff on innovation and new concepts to ensure we have the right product and to also focus on quality to ensure our product is of the highest quality.

BEST WORKPLACE FACTORS

FAIR DEAL
GIVING SOMETHING BACK
WELL BEING

BEST COMPANIES INDEX

2007 BCI = 649.6
2006 BCI = 679.8

GRADUATE VACANCIES

Management Trainee.

To find out more about these companies visit www.bestcompaniesguide.co.uk

WILLIAMS MEDICAL SUPPLIES

UK locations	Wales
UK sites	1
Sector	Logistics/Wholesale/Distribution
Definition	Sales Marketing Distribution
How owned	Public (i.e. stock market listed)
Founded	1986
Turnover	Not disclosed
Profit	Not disclosed
Staff	150
Average age	30
Male : Female	50 : 50
Earnings £35,000+	9%

MISSION / VISION

We aim to be the UKs leading service supplier to healthcare professionals, with a reputation for quality own branded products, and a substantial presence in Global Communities.

BEST WORKPLACE FACTORS

GIVING SOMETHING BACK
LEADERSHIP
PERSONAL GROWTH

BEST COMPANIES INDEX

2007 BCI = 631.5

1000

632> ones to watch

500

CONTACT DETAILS

Williams Medical Supplies
Maerdy Industrial Estate, Rhymney,
Gwent NP22 5PY
Tel: 01685 846649
www.wmsplc.co.uk

GRADUATE VACANCIES

No graduate vacancies have been indicated.

KEY

Holidays: Companies offering a minimum of 25 days annual leave

Pensions: Companies offering a final salary or non-contributory/contributory pension scheme

Maternity: Companies offering over Statutory Maternity Pay

Charity Activities: 10% of staff undertake charitable activities during business hours

Childcare: On-site nursery or vouchers

Gym: On-site gym or subsidised gym memberships

Women: At least 33% of senior managers are women

Shares: Companies where employees are offered share options

Long Service: 40% of employees with more than 5 years' service

Health Insurance: Full family cover

WORKMATES & DANIEL OWEN ASSOCIATES

UK locations	National
UK sites	9
Sector	Recruitment
Definition	Construction Recruitment Specialists
How owned	Private
Founded	1986
Turnover	Not disclosed
Profit	Not disclosed
Staff	67
Average age	34
Male : Female	67 : 33
Earnings £35,000+	31%

MISSION / VISION

Our objective is to repeat our successful formula nation-wide and grow into the most successful specialist building agency in the U.K.

BEST WORKPLACE FACTORS

FAIR DEAL
LEADERSHIP
WELL BEING

BEST COMPANIES INDEX

2007 BCI = 608.4

1000

608> ones to watch

500

CONTACT DETAILS

Workmates & Daniel Owen Associates
Hadwyn House, Field Road,
Reading RG1 6AP
Tel: 0118 9508600
www.wingroup.co.uk

GRADUATE VACANCIES

Recruitment Consultants.

1000

WORKSPACE GROUP

UK locations	London
UK sites	43
Sector	Property
Definition	Workspace for SME's
How owned	Public (i.e. stock market listed)
Founded	1987
Turnover	£63.2m
Profit	£15.1m
Staff	167
Average age	40
Male : Female	59 : 41
Earnings £35,000+	20%

CONTACT DETAILS

Workspace Group
Magenta House, 85 Whitechapel Road,
London E1 1DU
Tel: 0207 2477614
www.workspacegroup.co.uk

MISSION / VISION

The Group aims to achieve an acceptable financial return for its shareholders, whilst at the same time providing a service to small business communities, and encouraging urban regeneration and co-operation between the private and public sectors.

BEST WORKPLACE FACTORS

GIVING SOMETHING BACK
LEADERSHIP
MY COMPANY

BEST COMPANIES INDEX

2007 BCI = 631.0

GRADUATE VACANCIES

No graduate vacancies have been indicated.

ones to watch
<631
500

KEY

- **Holidays:** Companies offering a minimum of 25 days annual leave
- **Pensions:** Companies offering a final salary or non-contributory/contributory pension scheme
- **Maternity:** Companies offering over Statutory Maternity Pay
- **Charity Activities:** 10% of staff undertake charitable activities during business hours
- **Childcare:** On-site nursery or vouchers
- **Gym:** On-site gym or subsidised gym memberships
- **Women:** At least 33% of senior managers are women
- **Shares:** Companies where employees are offered share options
- **Long Service:** 40% of employees with more than 5 years' service
- **Health Insurance:** Full family cover

1000

YORKSHIRE WATER

UK locations	Yorks & Humber
UK sites	1
Sector	Utilities
Definition	Water/Waste Water
How owned	Public (i.e. stock market listed)
Founded	1989
Turnover	£698.3m
Profit	£218.0m
Staff	2195
Average age	41
Male : Female	74 : 26
Earnings £35,000+	14%

CONTACT DETAILS

Yorkshire Water
Western House, Halifax Road,
Bradford
Tel: 01274 691111
www.yorkshirewater.com

MISSION / VISION

To be clearly the best water company in the UK.

BEST WORKPLACE FACTORS

GIVING SOMETHING BACK
MY COMPANY
LEADERSHIP

BEST COMPANIES INDEX

2007 BCI = 631.5
2006 BCI = 607.7

GRADUATE VACANCIES

Managerial (water), IT, HR, Regulation & Investment.

ones to watch
<632
500

Qi

QUESTIONS AND INDEX

Interviews are not interrogations.
But it's still a good idea to get
your story straight.

Tell me about yourself.
What are your long-term aims?
What can you bring to this job/company?
What are your strengths/weaknesses?
What's your greatest achievement so far?
What's your favourite colour?
What has been your biggest failure?
What would you like to be better at?
Scon or scone?
Can you act on your own initiative?
How do you run a meeting?
What's the capital of Burkina Faso?
What motivates you?
What management style gets the best results out of you?
How would your colleagues describe you?
Why should we give you this job?

KILLER QUESTIONS

To help you gauge how a company performs within the eight key workplace factors, here are some Killer Questions. Don't worry, no one will actually die if you ask them at your interview. But get the answers and you'll know if the position has any life in it and if the organisation's values fit your own.

LEADERSHIP

- **Are there opportunities for the leader and senior management to listen to staff?**
- **How are the values of the organisation reflected in the actions and style of the senior management?**
- **How do the leadership communicate with the employees?**

MY COMPANY

- **What makes *you* proud to work for this company?**
- **What makes this company unique to work for?**
- **How are employees encouraged to provide ideas for the wider development of the company?**

PERSONAL GROWTH

- **How could I expect to progress within the company in the next three years?**
- **What learning opportunities are available for someone in this role?**
- **How will my performance be reviewed, and how frequently?**

MY MANAGER

- **Who is my line manager? Can I meet them?**
- **What management training do you have in place?**
- **How do managers here support staff?**

MY TEAM

- How does the company promote a team environment?
- What opportunities exist for teams across the organisation to interact together?
- Can I meet the team?

GIVING SOMETHING BACK

- Are there any ways in which the organisation works with the local community?
- What, if any, policies do you have in place concerning environmental issues?
- Are there any ways in which the company supports individuals in their own charitable work, and if so what are they?

FAIR DEAL

- How do pay and benefits compare to sector averages?
- Is there a structured pay review system, if so can you talk me through it?
- Are there any unique ways in which the organisation rewards commitment and effort?

WELLBEING

- How does your staff turnover compare to others in this sector?
- What systems are in place for flexible working?
- What do you do to encourage work/life balance and to ensure staff remain motivated?

ALPHABETICAL INDEX

T

U

V

W

X

Y

ACCREDITATION INDEX

3 STAR

2 STAR

1 STAR

ONE'S TO WATCH

SECTOR INDEX

ADVERTISING

ARCHITECTS

BUSINESS SERVICES

CHARITY

COMMUNICATIONS/TELECOM

CONSTRUCTION

CONSULTING

CONSUMER GOODS

EDUCATION

ENGINEERING

FINANCIAL

FINANCIAL - BANKS/BUILDING SOCIETIES

PROPERTY

PUBLIC

RECRUITMENT

RETAIL

TRAVEL

UTILITIES

REGIONAL INDEX

EAST ANGLIA

EAST ENGLAND

EAST MIDLANDS

GUERNSEY

ISLE OF MAN

JERSEY

LONDON

REGIONAL INDEX

NATIONAL

NORTH EAST

NORTH WEST

FACTOR INDEX

LEADERSHIP

MY COMPANY

PERSONAL GROWTH

MY MANAGER

MY TEAM

GIVING SOMETHING BACK

FACTOR INDEX

FAIR DEAL

WELL BEING